U.S. CARIBBEAN GUIDE

BE A TRAVELER - NOT A TOURIST!

OPEN ROAD TRAVEL GUIDES SHOW YOU HOW TO BE A TRAVELER – NOT A TOURIST!

Whether you're going abroad or planning a trip in the United States, take Open Road along on your journey. Our books have been praised by ***Travel & Leisure, The Los Angeles Times, Newsday, Booklist, US News & World Report, Endless Vacation, American Bookseller, Coast to Coast****, and many other magazines and newspapers!*

Don't just see the world – experience it with Open Road!

ABOUT THE AUTHOR

Janet Groene and her husband Gordon changed directions while in their young 30s, leaving behind Gordon's career as a professional pilot in Illinois. They sold everything, loaded Janet's typewriter and Gordon's cameras aboard a small sloop, and lived happily ever after cruising in the Bahamas and the Caribbean.

Now based in Florida, they travel worldwide and have written more than a dozen books and thousands of newspaper and magazine features. They won the NMMA Director's Award for boating journalism and Janet is a recipient of the Distinguished Achievement in RV Journalism Award. Janet is the author of Open Road's *Caribbean Guide*.

U.S. CARIBBEAN GUIDE

BE A TRAVELER - NOT A TOURIST!

Janet Groene

with Gordon Groene

OPEN ROAD PUBLISHING

1st Edition

To my mother, Ida E. Hawkins, my first proofreader and still the best.

Library of Congress Catalog Card No. 98-66336
ISBN 1-883323-87-8

TABLE OF CONTENTS

1. INTRODUCTION 13

2. EXCITING U.S. CARIBBEAN! - OVERVIEW 15

Puerto Rico 15
U.S. Virgin Islands 16
British Virgin Islands 17

3. SUGGESTED ITINERARIES 19

If You Have Three Days 19
If You Have a Week 20
If You Have Two or More Weeks 21

4. LAND & PEOPLE 22

Land & Sea 22
The People 23
Music of the Caribbean 24

5. A SHORT HISTORY 28

6. PLANNING YOUR TRIP 34

Before You Go 34
- When To Go 34
- Booking Your Trip 35

Getting To The Caribbean 40
- By Air 40
- Travel Insurance 43
- Passports & Visas 44
- Customs 44

Getting Around The Caribbean 44
Cruising The Caribbean 45
About Cruise Prices 46
Booking Your Cruise Or Charter 47
Live-Aboard Yachting 48
Things To Know Before You Go 48
Dive Cruising 50
Eco-Tour Sailing 50
Accommodations 50
Hotel Chains 51
Recommended Reading 53

7. BASIC INFORMATION 55
Banking 55
Business Hours 55
Carnival! 55
Credit Cards 56
Currency 56
Electricity 56
Emergencies 56
Health Concerns 56
Post Service 58
Religious Services 58
Service Charges 59
Taxes 59
Tips 59
Telephones 59
Time Zone 60
Trouble Spots 60
Weddings 61

8. SPORTS & RECREATION 63
Beaches 63
Bicycling 64
Birding 64
Boating 64
Diving & Snorkeling 64
Fitness 64
Golf 65
Hiking 65
Horseback Riding 66

CONTENTS

Kayaking 66
Sailing 66
Tennis 66
Whitewater Rafting 67
Windsurfing 67

9. SHOPPING 68

10. TAKING THE KIDS 72
Keeping Kids Safe 73
Additional Tips 74
Best Resorts for Children 75
The Puerto Rican Advantage 75

11. ECOTOURISM & TRAVEL ALTERNATIVES 77
Ecotourism 77
Spa Vacations 78
Ecotour Sailing 78

12. FOOD & DRINK 79
A Caribbean Food Dictionary 79
Drinks of the Caribbean 84

13. THE U.S. CARIBBEAN'S BEST PLACES TO STAY 86
Puerto Rico 86
U.S. Virgin Islands 89
British Virgin Islands 90
Best Cruises 92

14. PUERTO RICO 95
Arrivals & Departures 98
Orientation 99
Getting Around Puerto Rico 100
Where To Stay 101
  Country Inns – *Paradores* 115
Where To Eat 118
Seeing the Sights 135
  San Juan 135
  Side Trips In & Near San Juan 137

Out on the Island South 138
Northeast of San Juan 139
Northwest 140
The West & Southwest 141
Nightlife & Entertainment 142
Sports & Recreation 144
Shopping 147
Excursions & Day Trips 148
Practical Information 149
Festivals & Special Events 150

15. THE U.S. VIRGIN ISLANDS 155
Arrivals & Departures 156
Orientation 158
Getting Around The U.S. Virgin Islands 159
Where To Stay 162
St. John 162
St. Thomas 167
St. Croix 174
Where To Eat 180
St. Thomas 180
St. Croix 185
St. John 198
Seeing the Sights 200
St. Thomas 200
St. Croix 201
St. John 204
Nightlife & Entertainment 204
Sports & Recreation 207
Shopping 213
Excursions & Day Trips 217
Practical Information 219

16. THE BRITISH VIRGIN ISLANDS 222
Arrivals & Departures 224
Orientation 225
Getting Around The BVI 225
Where To Stay 227
Anegada 227
Guana Island 228
Jost Van Dyke 228
Necker Island 229

Peter Island 230
Tortola 230
Virgin Gorda 235
Where To Eat 239
Tortola 239
Virgin Gorda 242
Seeing the Sights 244
Anegada 244
Jost Van Dyke 244
Salt Island 244
Tortola 244
Virgin Gorda 246
Nightlife & Entertainment 246
Sports & Recreation 247
Shopping 251
Practical Information 253

INDEX 255

MAPS

Puerto Rico 97
U.S. Virgin Islands 157
British Virgin Islands 223

CONTENTS

SIDEBARS

About Currencies 16
Expect A Little Chaos! 18
Don't Call Them Natives 23
The Caribbean's Jewish History 27
Entertainment Guides 36
Home Exchange 38
Travel Checklist 39
Rental Car Alert 45
Cruising Solo 49
Rating The Hotel Rates 52
A Note From The US State Department 54
Health Advisories 58
Phone Home 59
Sour Notes 62
About GPS 65
The Contrarian Shopper 69
About Wood Carvings 70
The Best Islands For Power Shopping 71
Caribbean With Kids 72
How To Handle A Jellyfish Sting 75
Rum Punch Recipe 84
Small Change 99
Foods of Puerto Rico 119
The Dine Around Program 125
Cigar Mania 142
Puerto Rico's Folklore & Flamenco 144
Taken Aback 145
Right Way, Wrong Way 159
Apples To Apples – Comparing Room Amenities 163
A Reminder About Hotel Rates 167
Virgin Islands Hotel Weddings 171
USVI Villa Rentals 177
Hurricane Update 180
Order In On St. John 199
Harbor Night 202
A Blue Ribbon Day 204
Support Your Local Beer 204
Mocko Jumbies 207
Casino Gambling Comes to St. Croix 221
Restaurants for Mariners 243
The BVI's Best Beaches 248
Stamp Of Approval 252

1. INTRODUCTION

Spellbinding is the first word that comes to mind when we remember our first sail into Caribbean waters and the sight of a sandy bottom clearly seen thirty and forty feet under our small sloop. Except for the Dry Tortugas west of Key West, there are no waters like them in the United States mainland because silt, carried to the sea by rivers, clouds even the cleanest seas. It isn't uncommon in the Caribbean for visibility to be 100 feet or more.

In later years we were to see the islands time and again from airplanes large and small. We cruise them in tiny cockleshells and aboard huge ocean liners. We trudge their rain forests and rutted roads. We luxuriate in the best hotels and delight in funky guest houses. We sun on beaches that are alive with families and fun seekers, and we like even better to find a lonely stretch of sand with no footsteps but our own. We salute the islands of the U.S. Caribbean for the sophistication of the dining in even the smallest settlements, yet we can also be happy with a native breakfast of johnnycake and pawpaw and a lunch or rice and beans. Most of all, we love the people of the islands whose bloods have blended to create a unique beauty in many skin colors.

It's with great pride that we add that these folks are Americans. OK, it's not like driving to Ohio or Oklahoma but, compared to traveling to other parts of the Caribbean where you have non-citizen status, this is home with a zip code, American currency, American fast food, telephones and ATMs that work most of the time, plus the stars and stripes fluttering over a courthouse that assures justice under the U.S. Constitution. We have included the British Virgin Islands in this guide because they are so closely combined with the U.S. Virgin Islands that you'd be cheating yourself if you didn't include them in your trip to St. Thomas or St. John.

Say hello to the U.S. Caribbean, where you can combine an exotic island in the sun with all that is familiar and good about Hometown, U.S.A.

2. EXCITING U.S. CARIBBEAN! - OVERVIEW

The **Caribbean Sea** is ringed with a diadem of islands that starts with Cuba, which is only 90 miles off Florida, and spirals southwards through Haiti and the Dominican Republic, the Virgin Islands, the Leewards and Windwards, and Trinidad. Below Cuba are Jamaica and the Caymans; afloat in the Caribbean north of Venezuela are the Dutch Leeward Islands of Aruba, Bonaire, and Curacao as well as some resort islands owned by Venezuela.

If you are confused about what to call them, you're not alone. Even longtime Caribbean visitors have their own favorite ways of calling, categorizing, and collating the islands. All of them are the **West Indies**, called that because Columbus thought he had found India, not a new world. They are also the **Antilles**, called the Lesser Antilles below the U.S. islands and south to Trinidad and the Greater Antilles from Cuba to Puerto Rico including the U.S. Virgin Islands, which are also the start of the string known as the Leewards.

To make things even more confusing, they are also grouped according to political loyalties such as the British Virgin Islands, the British Windwards, the French West Indies, or the Dutch Windwards in the Leewards. You're always safe in referring to any of the islands in this book as the West Indies, the Caribbean, or the Antilles. Briefly, the American Virgins are called the **U.S.V.I.** and the British Virgins are the **B.V.I.**

PUERTO RICO

As colorful as a serape and as warm as a freshly baked tortilla, **Puerto Rico** offers American can-do and convenience, gregarious Latin gaiety, and the kinds of beaches and clear waters for which the Caribbean is richly famed. **San Juan** is a major airline hub that hosts dozens of nonstop flights each day from North America and Europe, so it's a logical choice for a

ABOUT CURRENCIES

Throughout the Caribbean, rates are quoted in U.S. dollars because most Caribbean hotels, restaurants, merchants and even governments think in dollar terms. In the U.S. islands, of course, U.S. currency is the legal tender and it's used almost exclusively, at least for everyday transactions, in the British Virgin Islands too. Even more convenient for the traveler who stays within the U.S. Caribbean is the U.S. postal system. You don't have to worry about finding special stamps. Bring a supply of stamps from home to stick on your letters and post cards, and drop them in any mail box. Your address in the U.S.V.I. or Puerto Rico will have its own, American zip code.

quick, weekend stay in the sunshine. If you can stay longer, vacation in the mountains in a rustic parador or take a suite in a four-star resort patronized by celebrities from around the world. For dining, golf, watersports, a romantic getaway or a family holiday, it's hard to beat America's "shining star," found just east of Cuba and west of the U.S. Virgin Islands.

U.S. VIRGIN ISLANDS

St. Thomas and **St. John** are just east of Puerto Rico and can be seen from there on a clear day. Sister islands, they are polar opposites. St. John is mostly national park land, focusing on eco-tourism and the outdoors. St. Thomas too has picturebook bays and beaches, but its cash registers jingle and its streets stream with cruise ship passengers and day-trippers in search of "duty-free" bargains. Ever since the days when the islands belonged to Denmark, St. Thomas has been a commercial center. To find the "real" St. Thomas means getting out of Charlotte Amalie and into country lodgings that range from charming inns to the plush Ritz-Carlton.

The third of the American islands, **St. Croix**, is in a world of its own well away from the other U.S. and British Virgin Islands. It was here that crops were raised for shipment to St. Thomas; the island is still largely farmland. Its scuba diving and underwater national park are alone worth the trip, but the island also has historic plantations, picturesque settlements at Frederiksted and Christiansted, and great beaches and resorts, all under the U.S. flag.

BRITISH VIRGIN ISLANDS

They're only a brief boat ride from American shores. They're tiny and unspoiled. Yet they are British, lending a sense of "foreign" travel to your vacation in the U.S. Caribbean. So closely tangled with the U.S. Virgin Islands that we couldn't leave them out of this book, they are known as the **B.V.I.** to loyal visitors who come back year after year. **Tortola** is the chief settlement but travelers can also sample the sun-bleached beaches and limpid seas of **Virgin Gorda**, **Jost Van Dyke**, and some thirty other rocks and islets plus the worlds-end island of **Anegada**. It lies north of the B.V.I. in the boundless Atlantic, creating a resting place for seabirds and world-weary humans.

EXPECT A LITTLE CHAOS!

In each section of this book we've described what to expect after you land on the island, but be prepared financially, psychologically, and physically for more hassle, higher heat and humidity, and more expense than you expect. Often, Caribbean hosts dismiss the post-airport part of the trip breezily with, "No problem. Just grab a taxi at the airport and we're only X miles away." The truth is that the cab will probably not be air conditioned, the roads are goat tracks, and what sounds like a short distance is actually a major safari. The day is hot and clammy compared to the climate you just left and, even though you dressed for the tropics, you're still wearing too much. By the time you settle into the broiling cab and drive a mile or two over ruts and potholes with the windows open, you are hot, dusty, thirsty, and thoroughly bummed.

To get to the most remote resorts will require even more: a ride in a rattletrap of a van or small airplane, and perhaps a ferry ride during which you and your luggage get drenched. Even at the most expensive resorts where airport transfers are included, we have fried in nearly-new vehicles whose air conditioners were as dead as their shock absorbers. Vehicles age quickly on small islands. If you rent a car, be prepared for a long squawk list of things that don't work and for bad roads with few aids to navigation. Public transportation is iffy. Where it exists, it's often better suited to the crates of chickens that are your fellow travelers than to tourists in their newest resort duds.

Because of the high costs of buying, operating, and maintaining anything mechanical in the islands, transfers will cost far more than you think they should. Have plenty of change on hand for tips; your bags may grabbed away from you even if they are small and have to be carried only a few feet. As you arrive at the airport in a cab, they'll be whisked out of the trunk and handed to a porter even before you can get out of the car. It's contrived but, in the poorer areas, we never mind handing over the money to men who try so hard to earn it.

Take sturdy, waterproof luggage that can stand up to rough handling, rain, and sea spray. We once stood inside a terminal in Mayagüez during a torrential tropical rain, looking out at our bags sitting in a puddle in the downpour. Covered luggage carts as seen on the mainland are rare at small airports. Even traveling with all carry-ons isn't the answer. You have to carry them up and down stairs because there are no jetways. Carry-ons, except for smallest purses and brief cases, are not allowed aboard small commuter planes. Roll-ons will be taken from you and crammed into the cargo hold with the rest of the luggage. On some commuter flights, the limit is as little as 25 pounds. When the planes are full, luggage is brought on the next flight. We can't say it too often. Travel light.

Be prepared for the worst. Hope for the best. Once you arrive in paradise, you'll know that it was all worthwhile.

3. SUGGESTED ITINERARIES

This is a book about islands, so itineraries will be governed by airlines and ferry schedules, cruise departures and arrivals, tides and winds. Cruise ship ports of call provide only a short look at a small patch of each island, but you'll have enough of a taste of each to help decide which ones you want to return to for longer stays. If your introduction to the Caribbean is aboard a cruise ship, don't make too quick a judgment. Cruisers who hate St. Thomas or San Juan find when they fly in that the "real" island isn't at all the border-town frenzy they saw at the pier.

Aboard a charter boat, you can see strings of islets and cays in a week. In two weeks you can make voyage through a briar patch of islands, stopping at some on the way out and the rest during your return sail. Even if you sail no more than a few miles each day, you'll see dozens of coves, villages, good snorkeling reefs, and shoreside attractions.

IF YOU HAVE THREE TO FOUR DAYS

When all you need is a quick trip to re-charge your batteries in the Caribbean sun, minimize travel time by choosing an island that has the fastest, most direct service from your home city. This will vary according to where you live, the season, and whether charter flights are available in addition to scheduled airlines. Some islands have direct flights only once or twice a week, so careful planning is essential to getting you and out when you want to go.

Islands that have nonstop flights from the United States and Canada include Puerto Rico, which is a major hub for the entire Caribbean, St. Croix, and St. Thomas. Getting to St. John or any of the British Virgins takes a little longer.

We also recommend that, on a visit this brief, you stay in a full-service resort or guest house where you'll get the pampering you long for. Condo living and bareboating are fine for longer stays, and in fact it's part of the fun to provision at local markets. For a power vacation, however, don't waste time shopping, cooking, making beds, and trying to find your way around.

Among our suggested itineraries are:

• Fly into **San Juan** and check into one of the beach hotels within an hour of the airport. This gives you a choice of prices from the regal Hyatt in Dorado and the Westin Rio Mar to smaller hotels and guest houses in metropolitan San Juan itself. In the resorts, spend days reading in a hammock, walking the beach barefoot, sailing a small boat, or playing golf or tennis. If you stay in the city, walk Old San Juan and spend your time in museums and great restaurants.

• Fly to **St. Thomas** or **St. Croix**, where a drive of less than 30 minutes from the airport brings you to a hotel, resort, condo, or guest house. Just as in San Juan, you won't waste time in lines for customs, immigration, and currency exchange. Bring your golf clubs or a suitcase filled with good reading, and let the sun shine in.

IF YOU HAVE A WEEK

• Fly into St. Thomas or San Juan and take a **week-long cruise** aboard one of the ships that starts and ends its itineraries there. They vary seasonally, but a cruise-savvy travel agency such as Cruises, Inc., *Tel. 800/854-0500* or *315/463-9695* can find the right package for you. For example, Carnival offers a seven-day cruise out of San Juan to St. Thomas, St. Maarten, Dominica, Barbados, and Martinique. Princess sails a seven-night itinerary out of San Juan to Barbados, St. Lucia, St. Maarten, St. Kitts, and St. Thomas and another Princess ship goes out of San Juan to Aruba, Caracas, Grenada, Dominica, and St. Thomas. The advantage to cruising is that you're met at the airport and escorted until the cruise is over and you are safely back at the airport, with no time lost in finding your way around. You'll get a taste of the U.S. Caribbean as well as other islands. If you can spare a few days for a pre- or post-cruise stay in St. Thomas or San Juan, so much the better.

• Fly into Beef Island Airport in **Tortola** and enjoy a week-long package at the Bitter End Yacht Club. You can stay on land every night or get a land-sea package that includes some nights aboard a boat. Learn to sail, go snorkeling or scuba diving, hike nature trails, or scoot over to a deserted island in a Boston Whaler and have a picnic.

• Book into **St. Croix** and a stay at the Hotel Caravelle downtown. It's the perfect headquarters for diving, boating, island exploring, shopping and dining around Christiansted, meeting some yachties, and catching rays around the pool. Many of your fellow guests will be from Denmark, lending an international mood to dining and nightlife. On Sunday morning, attend services at the old Danish Lutheran church across the street for a heartwarming welcome from a multi-racial congregation. Never will you feel less like a tourist, more like a traveler.

• Take a week at Bolongo Bay in **St. Thomas**, one of the few all-inclusive resorts in the U.S. Caribbean. There's a full menu of activities all day every day for individuals, couples, families together, kids alone, or parents alone, all included at one price. The children will have lots of adventures in supervised play while parents have time for themselves. When you get together for meals, which are included in the price, you'll have lots to talk about.

• Fly into **San Juan** and transfer to one of the island's elegant golf resorts such as the Hyatt Regency Cerromar Beach Resort & Casino, El Conquistador Resort & Country Club, Westin Rio Mar Beach Resort, or the Wyndham Palmas Del Mar Resort & Villas. Then golf your brains out for a week. Non-golfers in your family will enjoy sunning, beachcombing, sightseeing, shopping, tennis, and horseback riding. The island is known for its fine dining. After dinner, the resorts offer casino gambling.

IF YOU HAVE TWO OR MORE WEEKS

• Book a charter boat with The Moorings out of **Tortola** for a week, starting and ending your vacation with a couple of days ashore at the company's own Mariner Inn. By the time you board the boat you'll be rested and will have provisions rounded up. Under sail you can seek out lonely beaches and seaside bars patronized by yachties from all over the world. Build the ultimate sand castle. Snorkel over pristine reefs. Have a rum swizzle on deck in a quiet anchorage, and hope to see the green flash.

After your cruise when you return to the inn, you'll be grateful for long showers, restaurant meals, and the company of other returning sailors to swap tales with. Explore the rain forest on Mount Sage, drive to beaches you didn't get to by boat, ride horseback on Cane Garden Bay, and shop the quaint boutiques of Road Town. The Moorings also has fleets based in St. Martin, St. Lucia, and Grenada. Try them all later, but start with the user-friendly BVI. .

• Fly into **St. Thomas** and then catch the ferry to **St. John** to camp Virgin Islands National Park. Spend days hiking, snorkeling the underwater trail, cooking on a camp stove, and enrolling in ranger-led nature programs. Then reward yourself with a few days in an air conditioned hotel on St. Thomas before flying home.

• Fly to **Puerto Rico**, rent a car, and stay a night or two at each parador, or government guest house. Built in scenic areas and points of interest such as beaches, mountains, forests or hot springs, these accommodations aren't fancy but they have the basics. All have wholesome, delicious, native food. By the end of two weeks, you will have savored a Puerto Rico that few visitors see.

4. LAND & PEOPLE

LAND & SEA

The lands and seas of the Caribbean make up one of the most geologically interesting places on Earth. Much of the Caribbean Sea is on the continental shelf with great expanses of clear, shallow waters where small boats can cruise for days without losing a view of the bottom 50 or 60 feet below. Yet vast valleys plunge to ocean depths of 29,000 feet and more in the Puerto Rico Trench.

Much of the land is volcanic, rising to peaks that are, in some cases such as Saba, the entire island. The total land area of all the Caribbean islands is only about 90,000 square miles, half the land mass of the United Kingdom, yet only a handful of cities have a population of more than 100,000 people. Among them are San Juan, a major metropolis, and other Puerto Rico cities including Ponce, Bayamon, Mayagüez, Arecibo, and Guaynabo.

The islands of the U. S. Caribbean are a combination of low mountains and plains, rimmed with sandy beaches and surrounded by coral reefs. Around them, waters shoal so gradually that the white sand bottom shines through, creating a neon luminescence in the turquoise waters. St. Croix has a sort of rainforest but only in Puerto Rico do you find the American Caribbean's highest mountains and lush, craggy rainforest.

The U.S. Caribbean's beaches alone are a geology lesson. All of them are formed by nature's grindstone, the sea, which pulverizes volcanic rock to make black sand beaches, or grinds up limestone or chalk to create sands in shades of white, pink, beige and brown. Regularly they are rearranged as storms suck away all the sand from some shores and deposit it somewhere else. New islets are formed, sometimes to be swept away in the next storm. Others grow, rooted with mangroves whose roots capture more sand, and become real islands.

Geology has also played a role in the animal life found in the Caribbean, where species often evolved independently for centuries. A cheerful tree frog called coqui, found only on Puerto Rico, is the island's symbol. Where mongoose were introduced to control rats in the cane fields, they bred in the wild and themselves became a problem. Non-native monkeys brought in by settlers escaped into the wild and formed large populations in some rainforests. Creatures such as whales and turtles, hunted almost to extinction, are making a comeback in Caribbean waters.

The larger islands, including Puerto Rico, offer the largest variety of vegetation, ranging from savannah to tropical scrub. Woodlands include mangrove swamps, dry forests, and jungles euphemistically called rainforests. Crops native to the Americas thrive in the U.S. Caribbean. They include tobacco, ackee, mango, avocado, cacao and sisal. Crops introduced by settlers, some of them still important, include sugar cane, coffee, bananas, coconut, rice, cotton, pineapple, nutmeg, citrus, and many vegetable crops ranging from cabbage to tomatoes.

THE PEOPLE

Except for a few islands down the chain, the people of the Caribbean including the U.S. islands and B.V.I. are predominantly black and tan, with a sprinkling of Amerindian, Asian, and East Indian blood. Puerto Ricans are a blend of proud Spanish blood, Amerindian, and African. Everywhere you'll find beautiful people with skin colors in all hues.

Most islanders are **Christians**, often with an undercurrent of African Voodoo, Obeah, Santeria, or Shango (also spelled Xango). Roman Catholic and major Protestant churches are found on almost every island. Puerto Rico is primarily Roman Catholic; the Danes left a legacy of Lutheranism in the Virgin Islands. Judaism has made an important contribution in the Caribbean since the 16th century and it remains a tiny but vital force in the U.S. Caribbean, especially on St. Thomas.

DON'T CALL THEM NATIVES

You are always safe in saying West Indian or Islander, but the word native is offensive to many people in the Caribbean. We have also encountered situations where locals were offended by the terms "boy" and "guy."

People who live in...	***Are called...***
St. Croix	*Crucians or Cruzans*
St. John	*St. Johnians*
St. Thomas	*St. Thomians*
Puerto Rico	*Puerto Ricans*

Rastafarianism, which hails the late Ethiopian emperor Haile Selassie as its messiah, took root in Jamaica and has some adherents in most other islands. Its members are usually recognized by their beehive "dreadlock" hair, usually covered in a black, red, gold, and green cap indicating traditional Rasta colors.

For all their shades of color and belief, the peoples of the Caribbean have much in common. Except for Puerto Rico, where Spanish or Spanglish is the first language, the West Indian accent has minor variations but it shares a softness, lilt, and range of octaves that is captivating. A question in a man's deep voice can start in a basso profundo and lift at the end to soprano range. A woman's silvery laugh can turn harsh and scolding. A balladeer's voice can turn to gravel or velvet. If you have an ear for language, you'll find yourself falling into its rhythms and convoluted sentence structure.

Culturally, the Caribbean is on a fast track that began with the realization that its own unique cultures need to be cherished and preserved. Dance groups, art galleries, theater and musicals celebrate ancient African, French, English, and Spanish forms. New forms, such as reggae and salsa, have been exported around the world.

Modern arts are welcomed in the islands. San Juan is as sophisticated as any other American city when it comes to symphony, opera, theater, and the internationally famous Casals Festival. Old San Juan has become the Greenwich Village of the tropics. Every island in the U.S. Caribbean has at least one painter, scultor, or photographer who has won international recognition. Maria Henle on St. Croix, daughter of the late photographer Fritz Henle, is a second-generation artist of international renown. Husband and wife team Jan D'Esposo and Manuca Gandia in Old San Juan, Deborah Broad and Mark Austin of Christiansted, and dozens of artists "out on the island" in Puerto Rico make up a who's who of artists.

MUSIC OF THE CARIBBEAN

The sounds pound and punish, puzzling tourists who are trying to sort out such music forms as dubbing, reggae, calypso, salsa, plena, and bomba. They are as familiar in the Caribbean as rockabilly, heavy metal, and leadbelly are to North American ears.

The music and dance of the Caribbean have a language all their own, a patois born in the gavottes and quadrilles of ancient Europe, tempered in torrid Africa, and spun into unique, New World rhythms and harmonies. Early Spanish explorers told of graceful dances performed by Arawak slaves who, with the warlike Caribs, had populated the Caribbean before the first European explorers arrived. Their traditions were added to those of British, Dutch, French, Spanish, and Danish settlers.

Most compelling of all were the contributions of African slaves, who soon outnumbered the combined total of whites and Amerindians, and whose dances and drumbeats were a lifeline of familiarity to captives in a strange land. Even in manacles, they sang and danced. Some say that the languid movements of the merengue are based on the limping gait of a slave wearing a ball and chain.

Pulsing sounds rise from the villages to serenade hilltop hotels. **Calypso** singers stop by diners' tables to improvise outrageous rhymes that are made up on the spot. In Puerto Rico, your table is serenaded by mariachis. When anyone turns on a boom box or brings out a guitar, a spontaneous "**jump-up**" erupts. On Sunday mornings, joyous **Gospel** music rings out from open-air churches in every island hamlet. Every community in Puerto Rico has its patron saint, and the music and feasting go on for more than a week to honor that saint once a year.

As you travel the islands and sort out their great diversity of cultures, the differences in music become clearer. **Reggae**, which evolved from forms called ska and mento, began in Jamaica in the 1920s and '30s when Jamaican cane cutters were sent to Cuba to help with the sugar harvest and Cubans came to Jamaica to return the favor. They sang together, adding a Latin tinge to mento street songs. Radio programs bouncing in from Miami and Memphis added American boogie, blues, and jazz to the mix. Bluesy songs with a mento rhythm formed a short-lived movement called rock steady, which grew into reggae.

Puerto Rico's music has a strong Latin air. Trinidad gave us calypso. In Jamaica, musical instruments called abengs are made from cow horns. **Goombay**, the Bantu word for rhythm, was born in the Bahamas as African tribal rhythms mated with British colonial patterns. The melody is usually played on a piano, guitar or saxophone accompanied by bongos, maracas, or "click sticks." Traditionally performed only by males, it's passed down from father to son.

Goombay in turn has become **Junkanoo** (sometimes spelled Jonkanoo or Jonkunnu), a word used to describe festivals in some islands but now also used to describe the music itself. In Puerto Rico, ballads of 18th and 19th century Spain were performed on native Caribbean instruments used by pre-Columbian Taino Indians. Today part of the Puerto Rican sound are the six-stringed Spanish classical guitar, the 10-string cuatro, tambours made from hollowed-out trees, and guiros made from hollow gourds.

To the trained ear, each form is unique but to newcomers there is a quaint and compelling sameness. Common to almost all Caribbean music is a pattern of call and response and the hypnotic repetition of the same phrase dozens and even hundreds of times. In music, it's called *ostinato,* from a root word meaning obstinate. One of the best examples is cariso, which evolved among slaves on St. Croix. Before newspapers, these newsy ballads were a way of communicating local news. A classic cariso tells the story of the sale of a plantation known as Wheel of Fortune to an unpopular manager named Dunlop. One couplet goes:

Dunlop sell all de potato
He sell all de guinea grass...

Also common to St. Croix is a **storytelling music** known there as **quelbe**. On Nevis the same style is known as string. In the British Virgin Islands it's **fungi** (not to be confused with Puerto Rican fungi, which is a food.) Evolved from a rap-like African storytelling to the beating of a drum, quelbe gradually added European music and whatever instruments were at hand–pots, pans, a sardine can on a stick, dried gourds, plus any available conventional instruments–guitar, ukelele, bongo drums, tambourines. If it's amplified, it's not authentic quelbe. Annual events involving the music include the Fungi Music Fiesta during the Christmas holidays and the Scratch/Fungi Cultural Awards on Emancipation Day in August. Both are held on Tortola.

In addition to their own music, people of the Caribbean embrace the finest music and dance from throughout the world. The annual **Casals Festival** held each June in Puerto Rico and named for immortal cellist Pablo Casals, attracts an international who's who of classical music artists. Traditional Puerto Rican folkloric music is kept alive by groups including the **Compania Musical Perla del Sur**, which performs locally and overseas. Puerto Rico is also home of the annual **Heineken JazzFest**, held in late May. The island's best jazz musicians join international jazz stars for four days and nights of music at the Parque Sixto Escobar.

The Island Center amphitheater on St. Croix and the Reichold Center of the Performing Arts on St. Thomas host programs ranging from ballet to opera, folk dance, to folk rock. The **Caribbean Dance Company** performs at special events on St. Croix. Puerto Rico, with its glittering casinos, has dazzling cabaret shows blaring the brightest new show tunes from New York and London. Monthly musicales at Whim Plantation on St. Croix bring in internationally acclaimed musicians who play unamplified music in an intimate, living room setting.

Most tourist hotels have lounges offering a variety of music from mellow piano bar and easy listening to floor shows and disco as well as combos playing rousing rhumbas and merengues for dancing. Adventurous travelers also like to sample local nightlife, which is often found at its best in tiny, thatch-roofed bars or right on the streets.

The Caribbean has a music all its own born of sunshine and pounding surf, a bonding of many peoples of all colors and backgrounds, and a welcome as wide as the sea itself. Listen. Then let it carry your feet away.

For a list of upcoming music events in the U.S Caribbean islands, write the **Caribbean Tourism Organization**, *20 East 46th Street, New York NY 10017, Tel. 212/682-0435.*

THE CARIBBEAN'S JEWISH HISTORY

Jewish settlers came early to the islands and added yet another golden thread to a tapestry of African, European, and Asian immigrants. Jews, most of them fleeing persecution starting with the Spanish Inquisition and continuing through the Nazi years, began settling in the islands with the earliest Europeans, some directly from Europe and others from other refuges such as Brazil. From here they brought sugar cane, the first to be introduced into the islands. For centuries, other Jews came to the islands from Israel, bringing their expertise in irrigation. Many others were merchants or ship chandlers.

Many of them settled in St. Thomas, where a Jewish congregation was founded in 1796. Tombstones in the island's Jewish cemetery date as early as 1792. The present synagogue was used in recent years by a congregation of Palestinian Arabs until their mosque could be built – one more example of the mellow melting pot that is the Caribbean.

Alexander Hamilton, who was Secretary of the Treasury under George Washington, was born in the West Indies to a Jewish mother. Impressionist painter Camille Pissarro was born to Marrano Jewish parents in St. Thomas. The story is told in Irving Stone's novel Depths of Glory. Victor Borge fled the Holocaust in Europe to settle on St. Croix. Other famous Jews from the islands have included Judah Benjamin, secretary of state for the Confederacy, and U.S. Senator David Yulee.

5. A SHORT HISTORY

For thousands of years before European settlement, the Caribbean islands were roamed by canoes carrying peoples who came to be known as **Caribs** and **Arawaks**. Although other tribal names such as Ciboney, Caiqueto, and Taino crop up, the people who met Christopher Columbus were primarily the warlike, cannibalistic Caribs and the peaceful, agrarian Arawaks.

Tragically, most Amerindian tribes disappeared within a few decades. Many were taken as slaves; others caught European diseases such as measles and pox because they had no natural immunity. Indians died in droves from disease, hunger, oppression, and massacre. Only a few pockets of Caribs remain.

LET'S START WITH COLUMBUS

Modern history is considered to have begun on October 12, 1492, when Christopher Columbus landed on an island that the aborigines knew as Guanahani and the Spanish called San Salvador in what we now call The Bahamas.

Between then and 1504, Columbus made four trans-Atlantic voyages, discovering and claiming island after island for Spain. By 1504 he had found Trinidad, the coast of South America, and the Central American coast, which he still called the **Indies** because he thought he had found a route to Asia.

However, the first maps using the name America began appearing in 1507, taking the name from a Florentine explorer, Amerigo Vespucci, who had discovered the Amazon River. It wasn't until 1513 that Florida, which he thought was yet another island, was sighted by Juan Ponce de Leon. His ornate tomb is now a tourist attraction in San Juan Cathedral.

Almost from the beginning, powerful struggles and intrigues marked Caribbean history. The 38 men left in the Dominican Republic in 1492, supplied only with what they could salvage from the wreckage of the *Santa Maria*, disappeared by the time the next vessels arrived. Spain worked quickly to fortify its holdings, founding settlements in Hispaniola in 1496, Puerto Rico in 1508, and Cuba in 1515.

The Caribbean yielded some gold, which was quickly pounced upon by the conquerors and their queen back in Seville, but by 1521 greater riches were discovered in Mexico and the islands were left to chart their own riches the hard way, by planting sugar and raising cattle.

By 1536, all Europe wanted a piece of the action. The seas were aboil with mighty warships belonging to nations, pirates, and privateers. The Dutch plundered Santiago de Cuba in 1554; Havana fell in 1555; Santo Domingo surrendered in 1586. The British won San Juan in 1595 and the Dutch captured the Spanish silver fleet off Cuba in 1628.

Only part of the battle was fought in the Caribbean. The fortunes of many islands rose and fell according to European treaties resulting from wars thousands of miles from the Caribbean. Some islands changed hands 20 times or more. Meanwhile in the islands, wars were fought on land and sea among Europeans and between Europeans and the few surviving Caribs.

The total land area of all the islands is less than that of England and Scotland, but each harbor was a precious resource and every arable acre of land an economic battleground. Battles roared on, almost always in favor of the British, whose fleet based in Antigua ruled the seas. The plot thickened during the American revolution, when the West Indies were a smuggling crossroads for munitions on their way to the rebels led by General George Washington. A century later, during the American Civil War, the islands would again become havens for smugglers and blockade runners sympathetic to the Confederacy.

In addition to the battles sanctioned by European monarchs, honest settlers throughout the islands had to endure raids by pirates such as Henry Morgan, who operated out of Nassau, and Edward Teach, known as Blackbeard, whose hideaway at Port Royal, Jamaica, was destroyed in an earthquake of Biblical proportions. Two French pirates headquartered in the little Dutch island of Saba. Pirate Piet Heyn, a Netherlander, is said to have taken $5 million in booty back to Holland. The islands were a no-man's land, worked by slaves who were being brought in at the rate of as many as 75,000 persons a year and exploited by anyone who had ships and cannons.

THE END OF SLAVERY

The first major slave rebellion came in 1801, when blacks led by Toussaint Louverture rebelled against the Spanish and set up a free society. Haiti declared itself independent in 1804 under the emperorship of former slave Jean-Jacques Dessalines. By 1834, slaves in all the British islands were free; freedom in the Dutch islands came soon after.

With the introduction of sugar beets into European agriculture, the continent's sweet tooth no longer had to be satisfied by Caribbean plantations. Without slaves to work them, many lands weren't replanted. Experiments in cotton, pineapple, and other crops were tried, often ending in disaster after a blight, a drought, hurricane, or a market collapse.

Suddenly the Caribbean was hardly worth fighting over.

After the Treaty of Paris ended the Spanish-American War, Cuba and Puerto Rico were ceded to the United States, which also bought the Danish Virgin Islands to protect the Americas against the Germans in World War I. Even as late as 1983, when Cuba's building of a major landing field on Grenada was halted by American intervention, the strategic value of the lands and harbors of the Caribbean was realized. Today the same coves that sheltered pirates long ago are transfer points for illegal drugs. The French have a saying: the more things change, the more they stay the same.

STEPPING STONES OF CARIBBEAN HISTORY

3000 BC Settlers begin arriving on the island now known as Puerto Rico.

Circa 1100 BC Taino Indians establish a ceremonial center south of Arecibo.

700 BC Shell heaps grow on St. Croix, discarded by shellfish-eating tribes.

1492-1504 Christopher Columbus makes four voyages to the New World. Within 50 years, most Amerindian inhabitants of Puerto Rico have died of disease, hunger, enslavement, and execution.

1493 The Spanish begin settling Puerto Rico.

1496 Columbus' brother Bartolomé Colon founds Santo Domingo; the first written description of the tobacco plant reaches Europe.

1504 Columbus returns from his last voyage; Isabella of Castille dies.

1518 The first slaves are brought to Puerto Rico three years after sugar cane is introduced.

1521 San Juan is founded; its walls will be completed by 1630; Hernando Cortez destroys the Aztec state and claims Mexico.

1523 The first Christian church in the Americas, San Jose Church, is built in Puerto Rico by the Dominican order; the first marine insurance policies are issued in Florence.

1555 Spanish forces defeat and soon annihilate the native population of the Virgin Islands.

1580 Sir Francis Drake returns from a circumnavigation of the globe; Dutch painter Franz Hals is born; coffee is introduced to Italy. In England, the hit tune of the day is *Greensleeves*.

1593 Bermuda is discovered; Shakespeare debuts *The Taming of the Shrew*; Izaak Walton is born.

1595 Britons Sir Francis Drake and Sir John Hawkins take San Juan; Hawkins dies. The Dutch begin to colonize Indonesia; Sir Walter Raleigh reaches a point 300 miles up the Orinoco River in South America.

1596 Sir Francis Drake dies; the first water closets come into use; tomatoes are introduced to England and soon make their way to the New World.

1650 Holland and England reach an accord about their turf in the New World; Harvard College is founded.

1672 Danes settle the Virgin Islands.

1728 James Cook, who would later introduce breadfruit to the Caribbean, is born; Spain stops its 14-month siege of the English at Gibralter.

1732 A rum factory is built at Gallows Bay, St. Croix. Today it is the Hilty House Inn.

1735 A Lutheran church, now known as the Steeple Building, is built in Christiansted.

1738 Fort Christiansvaern is built on St. Croix.

1779 Captain James Cook dies.

1785 A hillside mansion is built overlooking Charlotte Amalie to become, in modern times, L'Hotel Boynes.

1791 Slaves revolt on Santo Domingo, sending shock waves throughout the Caribbean. The first guillotine is set up in Paris; gaslights appear in England.

1796 Napoleon marries Josephine de Beauharnais, who was born in the West Indies; Spain declares war on England.

1797 Spain captures some bronze cannon from the British and, as a final insult, melts them down to cast a statue of Ponce de Leon. It can now be seen on San Jose Plaza in San Juan.

1808 importation of slaves from Africa is outlawed in the United States but the slave trade continues in the Caribbean and in Florida, which is not yet a state.

1834 Britain frees its Caribbean slaves. Abraham Lincoln wins his first election and becomes an assemblyman in Illinois.

1841 The Grand Hotel opens in Charlotte Amalie; English travel agent Thomas Cook books his first trip.

1843 The slave population of Cuba is estimated at 436,000. The first telegraph line is installed between Washington and Baltimore; Wagner's opera *Flying Dutchman* debuts in Dresden.

1844-1930 The Dominican Republic has 56 revolutions.

1848 France frees its Caribbean slaves; serfdom is outlawed in Austria; Wisconsin becomes a state.

1863 Holland frees its Caribbean slaves; the American Civil War rages; construction of the London subway is begun.

1887 Paul Gauguin lives in the French West Indies, while in England the first Sherlock Holmes story is published.

1898 Spain cedes Puerto Rico, the Philippines and Guam to the United States and agrees to free Cuba.

1909 Victor Borge, who would become a resident of St. Croix, is born in Copenhagen.

1911 The University of Puerto Rico is founded at Mayagüez.

1915 Herman Wouk, whose book *Don't Stop the Carnival* remains one of the best yarns about the Virgin Islands, is born in New York City. In 1998, filming of a pilot film "Walking on Sunshine", based loosely on the book's theme, is shot on St. Croix while a musical version of *Don't Stop the Carnival* takes shape in New York.

1916-1917 Kaiser Wilhelm of Germany has his eyes on the Panama Canal. To protect American interests, the United States buys the Virgin Islands from Denmark for $300 an acre, or $25 million. The United States and Cuba declare war on Germany; John F. Kennedy is born.

1919 400 people die when the Mayagüez Theater burns in San Juan.

1929 World markets collapse, bringing increased suffering to the Caribbean; Kodak introduces 16mm film. In Chicago, a gangland hit becomes known as the St. Valentine's Day Massacre.

1945 Singer José Feliciano is born at Lares, Puerto Rico.

1952 Puerto Ricans vote for Commonwealth status with the United States.

1954 five members of Congress are wounded when supporters of Puerto Rican independence shoot randomly from the spectator gallery in the U.S. House of Representatives.

1955 Hurricane Janet kills 500 in the Caribbean.

1962 The University of the Virgin Islands is founded at Charlotte Amalie.

1965 An uprising in the Dominican Republic brings intervention from the United States.

1967 Antigua, Barbuda, Redonda, Anguilla, St. Kitts, Nevis, St. Lucia, St. Vincent, and Dominica form the West Indies Associated States; in Puerto Rico, voters choose to remain associated with the United States.

1973 The Caribbean Common Market, or Caricom, is formed.

1981 Bob Marley, whose reggae music galvanized Jamaica and spread through the Caribbean and around the world, dies.

1983 American and Caribbean troops land on Grenada to restore order after a coup d'etat that followed four years of leftist rule.

1988 The first St. Croix Triathlon is held. The annual event now attracts top athletes from throughout the world.

1989 Hurricane Hugo devastates St. Croix

1992 Tourism brings $792 million to the U.S. Virgin Islands.

1993 Spanish and English are proclaimed joint official languages in Puerto Rico.

1995 Hurricanes Luis and Marilyn deal a one-two punch to the Virgin Islands and Puerto Rico.

1996 The first Ritz-Carlton opens in the islands at St. Thomas; a second opens in 1997 on Puerto Rico. Puerto Rico produces $31.1 million in portland cement and $15.7 million in commercial fishing.

1997-1998 Recognizing the increasing popularity of the islands for foreigners' weddings, the islands one by one liberalize their marriage rules to allow easier, quicker licensing and documentation. Water Island becomes the fourth U.S. Virgin Island. Improvements begin to its beaches and parks and rumors arise about future development.

6. PLANNING YOUR TRIP

WHEN TO GO

Weather doesn't vary much in the U.S. Caribbean winter and summer but when it does hit the news, it makes headlines. After your first visit to the islands, where you'll see buildings that have stood for hundreds of years, you'll have a better perspective. Yes, hurricanes can cause horrendous destruction, but they are also so infrequent in any given spot that hey are barely worth considering when planning a vacation. Unlike arthquakes, they also give plenty of warning in most cases, giving you the ption of leaving the island or moving to a shelter. With modern weather recasting, most hurricanes take little or no human toll.

We once met the elderly caretaker of a half-ruined mansion on a note island. Hungry to hear the history of this mysterious place, we ssed for dates but she said gently, "I can't read, you know." It was ious that she couldn't relate to the events of the outside world. The she could do for a time reference was "the storm." Births, deaths, and building of the mansion were all before or after The Storm.

Researching it later, we deduced that she was probably talking about urricane of 1936. Obviously, it had been decades since a hurricane ouched her life. Although some islands get the occasional one-two ı, as the Virgin Islands got with Luis and Marilyn, this woman's story e typical. When it's bad, it's bad, but it's so rare in any one family stories are written around it.

nerally, hurricane season starts June 1 and ends on November 1, hat on some islands is celebrated as Hurricane Deliverance Day. orms hit in August and September; the season in general is hotter ier than November through May. Daytime highs at sea level range from the 80s or 90s by day to the low 60s by night, all year. Rarely, a very strong cold front from the United States will reach as far south as the U.S. islands, where the thermometer might plunge as low as 50 degrees for a few hours.

Only in the mountains is there substantial variation, and only in Puerto Rico among the American islands are there any mountains high enough to find substantially cooler air. On an 85-degree day on the beach, it can drop 10 degrees as you climb to 1,800 feet. At 3,000 feet it can be downright chilly. Just in case, take a light jacket when you visit the American Caribbean in winter or are going high into the hills in summer.

Many islands have minor micro-climates that are unique. For example, Puerto Rico's north coast has such an even rainfall that it has no real "wet" season. The west end of St. Croix has enough rain to create green forests filled with vines and ferns while the east end can be dry as a desert.

During hurricane season, June through October, the air is sultrier and breezes less constant in the U.S. Caribbean. September and October can be obscenely still and sticky, and many restaurants and hotels – especially those that are not air conditioned – close at this time. These months are, however, among the best for scuba diving unless, of course, there's a big storm.

According to Stanley Selengut, president of Maho Bay Camps on St. John, annual sunrise temperatures on the island range from 72 to a high of 78. Afternoon temperatures average from a low of 82 in winter to a high of 88 in August and September. Rainhall averages 1.6 inches in dry months and as much as 5.8 inches in the wet season, August through September. Relative humidity averages a 62 in February, the driest month, and 68 July through September, the most humid months.

The Caribbean has become a year-round vacationland. The chief change in summer, aside from quieter winds, is the cost. Rates plunge and resorts add sweeteners such as free greens fees, airport transfers, meals, and much more.

In each life some rain must fall, but I can't remember a day when we didn't see at least some sunshine. In the U.S. Caribbean, even the liquid sunshine is warm and sweet.

BOOKING YOUR TRIP

Travelers With Special Needs

Groups that can help with special travel plans – from nudist resorts to packages for physically-challenged travelers – include:

AMERICAN ASSOCIATION OF RETIRED PERSONS, *601 East Street NW, Washington DC 20049. Tel. 202/434-AARP.* Members and their

ENTERTAINMENT GUIDES

For years we have used the ***Entertainment Guides*** *series of discount books, which entitle book buyers a discount of up to 50% on the hotels, restaurants, and attractions listed. Each volume comes with a credit card-like membership card, which must be used to get the deals mentioned.*

Although the books are costly, they pay for themselves in just a few days at a hotel or resort. ***Entertainment International™ Hotel & Travel Ultimate Savings Directory*** *sells for under $65 and lists lodgings throughout the world including a few islands in the Caribbean. Also available is* ***Entertainment Puerto Rico™****, which includes lodgings and restaurants in Puerto Rico and other islands. For information Tel. 800/445-4137 or write Entertainment Publications, Inc., 2125 Butterfield Road, Troy MI 48084.*

As in most discount deals, some restrictions apply. Hot dates are excluded; reservations may be available only a month or less before the trip; discounts vary. No matter how you slice it however, these books are a budget bonanza.

The company publishes dozens of discount books for cities, countries, and continents worldwide, so choose carefully to get the book that will serve you best at home as well as during your Caribbean travels. Note that they are not guidebooks, but are simply catalogs of discount coupons.

spouses, and sometimes their traveling companions of any age, get discounts at many hotels, car rental agencies, and restaurants.

AMERICAN ASSOCIATION FOR NUDE RECREATION, *1703 North Main Street, Kissimmee FL 34744, Tel. 800/TRY-NUDE, Fax 407/933-7577.*

FLYING WHEELS TRAVEL, *Box 382, Owatonna MN 55060. Tel. 800/525-6790.* This tour operator specializes in clients who are in wheelchairs.

HIDEAWAYS INTERNATIONAL, INC. *767 Islingston Street, Portsmouth NH 03801. Tel. 800/843-4433 or 603/430-4433; fax 430-4444. E-mail info&hideaways.com.* Membership costs $99 a year, which includes a quarterly newsletter about member discounts and travel advice, plus a booklet describing vacation homes that can be rented directly from their owners. Note that the organization is international, with only a handful of listings in the U.S. Caribbean, so membership may be a better value for those travelers who travel worldwide.

BARE NECESSITIES, *1802 West 6th Street, Austin TX 78703, Tel. 512/499-0405, Fax 469-0179.* This travel agency specializes in clothing-optional tours, cruises, and resorts.

SOCIETY FOR THE ADVANCEMENT OF TRAVEL FOR THE HANDICAPPED, *347 Fifth Avenue, Suite 610, New York NY 10016, Tel. 212/447-0027, Fax 725-8253.*

Tour Packagers

Start with your home-town travel agent and local newspaper travel pages, where you'll find news of Caribbean packages that start at your nearest airport. Often, charters are organized once or twice a year from cities that don't usually have non-stop service to the Caribbean.

Countless packagers in North America and Europe offer Caribbean trips, usually focusing on some theme such as diving or adventure travel (see the Eco-Tourism chapter), senior travel, or general travel. They include:

AMERICAN AIRLINES, *Tel. 800/433-7300,* offers complete vacation packages. Ask for the international tour desk.

BACKROADS, 801 Cedar Street, Berkeley CA 94710, *Tel. 510/527-1555, Fax 527-1444; toll-free 800/GO-ACTIVE,* organizes walking, bicycling, hiking, and multi-sport adventure tours in the Caribbean for a few weeks in November and December. Featured are unspoiled islands known for their scenic beauty.

BRITISH WEST INDIAN AIRWAYS VACATIONS, *Tel. 800/780-5501,* offers packages that include airfares. Also included can be stops at more than one island.

GRAND CIRCLE TRAVEL, *347 Congress Street, Boston MA, Tel. 617/350-7500 or 800/248-3737,* is a highly regarded packager of escorted, upscale tours for active senior citizens.

INTERNATIONAL GAY TRAVEL ASSOCIATION, *Tel. 800/448-8550,* in the U.S. and Canada, is a membership organization that offers networking and travel packages for homosexuals and Lesbians.

SAGA INTERNATIONAL HOLIDAYS, *222 Berkeley Street, Boston MA, Tel. 800/343-0273,* specializes in escorted tours for senior citizens aged 50 and older.

TFI TOURS INTERNATIONAL, *34 West 32nd Street, 12th Floor, New York NY 10001, Tel. 212/736-1140 or 800/745-8000,* offers discounted tours and upscale, escorted trips for senior citizens.

TRAVEL PROFESSIONALS LTD., *444 East 52nd Street, Suite 7F, New York NY 10022, Tel. 212/753-1133,* specializes in Caribbean packages including airfare, cruises, condos, villas, hotels, and tours.

HOME EXCHANGE

Your house or vacation home anywhere in the world could be traded with someone who has a house or vacation villa in the Virgin Islands. A two-year membership in the program costs $295. Call ***Home Exchange****, Tel. 404/843-2779 or 800/750-0797.*

Cancellations

Reservation and cancellation policies in most resorts and hotels in the U.S. Caribbean are much tighter than in other parts of the world. To confirm a reservation you may have to make a deposit weeks and even months in advance. The most popular accommodations in the most popular weeks are booked a year or more in advance. To get a refund, advance notice of four to eight weeks may be required and even then you may not get all of your money back.

Before providing a deposit or a credit card number to make confirmed reservations, make sure you understand the hotel's cancellation policies. It's always wise to buy trip cancellation insurance.

The USTOA

When you deal with a tour operator who is an active member of the **United States Tour Operators Association**, you are dealing with a professional who has been in business at least three years under the same ownership and/or management, participates in a Consumer Protection Plan with a $1 million nest egg, has presented at least 16 professional references, and carries $1 million in professional liability insurance. The group has 52 members representing more than 60 companies as well as 223 associated members (such as carriers and suppliers) and 330 allied members (such as public relations firms).

USTOA members who offer packages in the Caribbean include:

CENTRAL HOLIDAYS, *206 Central Avenue, Jersey City NJ 07307, Tel. 201/798-5777*

FRIENDLY HOLIDAYS, INC., *1983 Marcus Avenue, Lake Success NY 11042, Tel. 518/358-1320, Fax 358-1319*

FUNJET VACATIONS, *8907 North Port Washington Road, Milwaukee WI 53217, Tel. 414/351-3553 or 800/558-3050*

GOGO WORLDWIDE VACATIONS, *69 Spring Street, Ramsey NJ 07446, Tel. 201/934-3500, Fax 934-3764*

HOLLAND AMERICA LINE-WESTOURS, *300 Elliott Avenue West, Seattle WA 98119, Tel. 206/281-3535, Fax 281-7110, toll-free 800/637-5029*

KINGDOM TOURS, *22 South River Street, Plains PA 18705, Tel. 717/824-5800, Fax 824-5900*

LAKELAND TOURS, *2000 Holiday Drive, Charlottesville VA 22901, Tel. 804/982-8600, Fax 982-8690*

MLT VACATIONS, *5130 Highway 101, Minnetonka MN 53345, Tel. 612/672-3111, fax 474-9730; toll-free 800/328-0025*

MTU VACATIONS, *2211 Butterfield Road, Downers Grove IL 60515, Tel. 630/271-6000, Fax 271-6011*

NORTHWEST WORLD VACATIONS, *5130 Highway 101, Minnetonka MN 55345, Tel. 612/474-2540, Fax 474-9730*

PREFERRED HOLIDAYS, *1202 Southwest i41st Court, Fort Lauderdale FL 33315, Tel. 954/359-7000, Fax 359-0374*

TNT VACATIONS, *2 Charlesgate West, Boston MA 02215, Tel. 617/262-9200, Fax 638-3418*

For further information write or call **USTOA** at: *342 Madison Avenue, Suite 1522, New York NY 10173, Tel. 212/599-6599, Fax 599-6744.*

TRAVEL CHECKLIST

According to the National Tour Association, the following tips will assure a more carefree vacation:

- *Verify that the travel agent or tour company is a member of a professional association such as the National Tour Association (NTA), United States Tour Operators Association (USTOA), or the American Society of Travel Agents (ASTA).*
- *Make sure the company offers a consumer protection plan.*
- *Carefully read the company's cancellation and refund policies.*
- *Use a credit card. If you pay cash, get a receipt. Get everything in writing.*
- *Verify that the tour company has errors and omissions insurance and protectional liability insurance coverage.*
- *Ask for a reference from a client with whom you are familiar.*
- *Avoid high pressure sales with limited time to evaluate the offer.*
- *Beware of companies sending a courier for a check or requesting a direct bank deposit or certified check.*
- *Decline offers requiring a property sales presentation.*
- *Prior to payment, review written details of the trip.*
- *Request specific hotel and airline names. Terms such as "all major hotels" or "all major airlines" are a warning flag.*
- *If you are given a toll-free number, insist on getting the local number too. This establishes that the tour company has a central office. Never use 900 numbers.*
- *To report travel-related fraud, call the* ***National Fraud Information Center****, Tel. 800/876-7060 or the* ***Federal Trade Commission****, Tel. 202/326-2000 as well as your local and state consumer agencies.*

Going Solo

Single supplements are the bane of solo travelers who see what appears to be an attractive rate and then find it is charged per person, based on two people sharing a room or ship cabin. If you want to have that room to yourself you may have to pay 20-100% more than the per-person fee.

In most cases, that's only reasonable. You think of yourself as using only half the towels and only one of the twin beds, but management sees you as occupying a room that must be cleaned, air conditioned, insured, and maintained pretty much the same whether it's occupied by one, two, or three persons.

Generally, the lowest single supplements are at all-inclusive resorts where meals, sports, and drinks are included. Rates are quoted for two but hosts realize that you're eating and drinking only for one and they give you a price break. A few resorts and ships, and they will be included in individual listings in this book, have single accommodations with one bunk and no extra charges.

Often the single supplement is waived for special seasons or promotions. Still other resorts guarantee to match you with a same-sex roommate. You take your chances that you'll be able to get along with a stranger but, if a roommate can't be found, you get the room or cabin at the "double occupancy" rate. Many travelers think it's worth the gamble. If you prefer to find your own roommate, you can join a club such as **Travel Companion Exchange**, *Box 833, Amityville NY 11701.*

If you're going to share accommodations anyway, think big. The best buys in Caribbean accommodations are not doubles but triples and quads. A typical two-bedroom condo sleeps six, with two in each bedroom and two on a sofabed in the living room. Each twosome pays less than the cost of a double hotel room and you get a full kitchen to boot.

It can be crowded, but some ship cabins also sleep two or more extra people. Or, consider renting an entire villa or chartering a yacht. Per-person costs go down as numbers go up. Just arrange the deal so that others can't back out at the last minute, leaving you with the entire bill for a five-bedroom mansion.

GETTING TO THE CARIBBEAN

BY AIR

The airfare nightmare seems to get worse every year. Our personal rule is to call any airline at least three times. Invariably, we get three different stories so we take the best deal. If we are shopping between two or more airlines, we make several calls to each.

Two big changes are occuring in the travel business. Air lines have reduced their commissions to travel agents, so you may have to pay a fee now for services that used to be free. A travel agent might be more willing to help, fee free, if you book a large packages that include a cruise or resort plus air fare, but the days are past when a travel agent would spend hours on the telephone to find you the lowest air fares. Try calling the air line to find the best package including a hotel.

The second big change is the use of the Internet for self-booking on the air lines either through the line itself or through a discount service such as www.priceline.com, which can also be reached through netsaver.com. The service specializes in rock-bottom fares, especially for last-minute bookings. We find that working the Internet takes a lot of time and doesn't always produce the cheapest fares, but it is worth trying.

A few points:

- Caribbean old-timers travel only with carry-ons if at all possible. Even if you're on the same airline all the way to your destination, there's a chance that your luggage will get lost in Miami or San Juan. If you are on more than one line, which is usually required to reach the more remote islands, chances of loss increase.
- Put new luggage tags on every piece including carry-ons, with the address of your destination in the islands. On the return trip, use tags with your home address.
- Don't buy second-hand tickets or frequent flyer coupons that were issued in someone else's name. Tighter security means a great chance of having your ticket confiscated, leaving you stranded.
- Package tours are almost always a better buy than a la carte travel, but before signing up for air add- on call the airlines and compare. If you have frequent flyer points or are a senior citizen, you can probably do better.

U.S. Numbers for Airlines Operating in the Caribbean

Numbers for large carriers may vary in your city. Check your local phone directory or, to get a different toll-free number that applies in your area, *Tel. 800/555-1212.* Calls to Information are not free. Some of these lines serve the U.S. Caribbean from the United States. Others provide service to the U.S. Caribbean only from other Caribbean islands or from overseas.

- **Aeroflot**, *Tel. 800/995-5555*
- **Aeromexico**, *Tel. 800/237-6639*
- **ALM**, *Tel. 800/327-7230*
- **Air Aruba**, *Tel. 305/551-2400 or 800/882-7822*

- **Air Anguilla**, *Tel. 264/497-2643*
- **Air Canada**, *Tel. 800/776-3000*
- **Air Caribbean** (Trinidad and Tobago), *Tel. 868/623-2500*
- **Air St. Barthélemy**, *Tel.590/87-73-46*
- **Air St. Thomas**, *Tel. 590/27-71-76*
- **Air France**, *Tel. 800/237-2747*
- **Air Jamaica**, *Tel. 800/523-5585* in the U.S. and Canada
- **Air Martinique**, *Tel. 784/458-4528*
- **Air Sunshine**, *Tel. 800/327-8900*
- **Airlines of Carriacou**, *Tel. 483/444-2898*
- **American Airlines**, *Tel. 800/433-7300*; in the USVI *Tel. 800/474- 4884*; in Puerto Rico, *Tel. 800/462-4757*; **American Eagle**, *Tel. 800/433-7300*
- **American Trans Air**, *Tel. 800/225-2995 or 800/382-5892*
- **APR International Air**, *Tel. 305/599-1299*
- **Avia Air**, *Tel.(599/7-30178*
- **British West Indian Airways** (BWIA), *Tel. 800/538-2942*
- **Canadian Airlines**, *Tel. 800/426-7000* in the U.S. and Puerto Rico; in Canada, *Tel. 800/235-9292*
- **Cardinal Airlines**, *Tel. 767/449-0322; in Florida, (305) 238-9040*
- **Carib Aviation**, *Tel. 869/465-3055*
- **Carnival Airlines**, *Tel. 800/437-2110*
- **Cayman Airtours**, *Tel. 800/247-2966*
- **Continental Airlines**, *Tel. 800/231-0856*
- **Delta Airlines**, *Tel. 800/241-4141*
- **Gorda Aero Service**, *Tel. 284/495-2271*
- **Guyana Air**, *Tel. 599/9-613033*
- **Iberia Airlines**, *Tel. 800/772-4642*
- **Island Air** (Caymans), *Tel. 345/949-5152 or 800/922-9606*
- **Leeward Islands Air Transport** (LIAT), *Tel. 246/495-1187*
- **Lufthansa**, *Tel. 800/645-3880*
- **Midway Airlines**, *Tel. 800/446-4392*
- **Northwest Airlines**, *Tel. 800/447-4747*
- **Sunaire Express**, *Tel. 800/595-9501*
- **TWA**, *Tel. 800/221-2000*; in the USVI and Puerto Rico, *Tel. 800/892-8466*
- **Tower Air**, *Tel. 800/452-5531*
- **Mustique Airways**, *Tel. 784/458-4380*
- **St. Vincent Grenadines Air** (SVG Air), *Tel. 784/456-5610*
- **United Air Lines**, *Tel. 800/241-6522*
- **USAirways**, *Tel. 800/428-4322*

TRAVEL INSURANCE

Travel insurance plans are always recommended. What if you get sick and have already paid for an expensive cruise? What if your luggage is lost? What if you are injured and have to be air-lifted home from a tiny cay? It's usually best to get trip cancellation and lost luggage insurance from your travel agency, packager, or cruise line. As with most travel purchases, there is no substitute for doing your homework.

First, know what coverage you already have through existing policies (homeowner, personal liability, and collision damage waiver). Confirm that this coverage applies in Puerto Rico and the U.S. and British Virgin Islands. Second, know what protection is automatically extended to you by the airline, resort, travel agency, or resort. Ask too if they require you to purchase certain coverage such as liability or collision insurance. Lastly, look into several kinds of policies to see what features make sense for you.

Most travel policies are for trips of a few days or weeks. If you travel often, year-round coverage is a better buy. Policies range from a simple coverage that refunds your deposit if your trip is cancelled by a (verifiable) medical emergency, to such premium coverages such as the Love Boat Care Gold policy from Princess Cruises, which allows credit if you cancel even for a non-emergency reason. Available as add-ons to this policy are higher limits for lost baggage and medical coverage.

Medical insurance coverage is available from:

Air-Evac International, *28193 Skywest Drive, Hayward CA 94541, Tel. 510/293-5968. or 800/854-2569*

Health Care Abroad, *107 West Federal Street, Middleburg VA 22118*

International SOS Assistance, *Box 11568, Philadelphia PA 19116, Tel. 215/244-1500 or 800/523-8930*

International Medical Assistance, *Tel. 800/679-2020, Fax 510/293-0458*

Medic Alert, *Tel. 800/825-3785,* provides body-worn identification that reveals to health care workers your allergies or chronic health problem even if you can't speak for yourself. Also offered is a booklet "Hot Weather Survival Guide."

Near Inc., *Box 1339, Calumet City IL 60409, Tel. 708/868-6700 or 800/654-6700*

World Access, Inc., *6600 West Broad Street, Richmond VA 23236, Tel. 804/673-1522 or 800/482-0016*

Travel Protection Plan, *P.O. Box 585627, Orlando FL 32858-5627,* charges a one-time, pre-paid fee of $295 to cover the shipment home of anyone who dies while away from home anywhere in the world. Included are embalming, air freight, and the container any time, anywhere. Once signed on, you're covered for life.

Although it's unlikely that an epidemic will occur in the U.S. islands or B.V.I., travelers can get last-minute information on vaccinations from **The Centers for Disease Control and Prevention** in Atlanta, *Tel. 888/ 232-3228.*

PASSPORTS & VISAS

The U.S. Caribbean and British Virgin Islands do not require U.S. citizens to have a passport, but a passport is one of the most powerful travel documents you can have and we recommend getting one. A voter registration card is no longer accepted as proof of citizenship when you're returning from the U.S. Caribbean or the B.V.I. You need a copy of a birth certificate, green card, naturalization papers, or an expired passport not more than five years old, plus a government-issued photo ID such as a driver's license. A driver's license alone won't do. Rules for Canadians are the same as for U.S. citizens but Britons need passports for the U.S. islands.

CUSTOMS

Things have changed a lot since the days when some islands didn't even permit travelers to bring portable radios with them. You can bring in almost anything except drugs, which are dealt with severely. Leaving the U.S. Caribbean, you pre-clear on that end by going through a brief, easy customs line. You're allowed to bring back purchases worth up to $1,200–twice the allowance in the other Caribbean islands, and up to six bottles of good Virgin Islands or Puerto Rican rum.

GETTING AROUND THE CARIBBEAN

Aviation has replaced the old mail boat as the means of getting around the islands, but ferries are still the most affordable way to go. Hundreds of islands and cays in the U.S. islands and B.V.I. can be reached only by private boat, scheduled ferry, or water taxi. The most economical, reliable way to get to a remote destination by air is to book your ongoing flight with your primary carrier, which will do its best to arrange the most convenient times and connections.

Packages that include airfare, accommodations, and inter-island connections or side trips can be arranged through **American Airlines Vacations**, *Tel. 800/321-2121*; **British West Indian Airways (BWIA) Vacations**, *Tel. 800/247-9297*; **Delta's Dream Vacations**, *Tel. 800/872-7786*; **TWA Getaways**, *Tel. 800/GETAWAY*; and **United Airlines Vaca-**

tions, *Tel. 800/328-6877.* **LIAT**, *Tel. 246/495-1187* offers multi- island tickets. See individual chapters for information on getting between islands by ferry or air.

RENTAL CAR ALERT

If you are younger than 25 or older than age 65, check age limits before counting on renting a car. Some island car rental agencies have minimum or maximum age limits.

CRUISING THE CARIBBEAN

No waters on the planet are more inviting than the clear, cradling seas that surround the islands. Choose among dozens of ways to get out on these waters: liveaboard dive boats, bareboating (you're the driver), crewed charter yachts (with captain only, captain and cook, or captain, cook, and crew), and leviathan "love boats" sailed by almost every major cruise line in the world.

Cruise ships are best booked through travel agents, especially cruise-only agencies. They're found in every major city, so check your Yellow Pages. A time-proven travel agency that books only cruises is **Cruises, Inc.**, *5000 Campuswood Drive, East Syracuse NY 13057, Tel. 800/854-0500 or 315/463-9695.* The company is always abreast of the latest bargains, especially for early or last-minute booking. **Cruise Planners**, *Tel. 888/820-9197,* are also cruise specialists who can offer exciting deals. Good background reading on individual ships is provided by such books as *The World's Most Exciting Cruises* (Hippocrene) and the *Total Traveler by Ship* (Graphic Arts Center Publishing).

Among ships or lines that call at one or more Caribbean islands are:

Carnival Cruise Lines, *Tel. 800/327-7373,* has several ships that sail the Caribbean out of San Juan, Miami, and Fort Lauderdale.

CostaRomantica and **CostaVictoria** offer seven-night luxury Caribbean cruises December through April. Ports of call include San Juan, St. Thomas, Nassau, Key West, Cozumel, Ocho Rios, and Grand Cayman. *Tel. 800/33-COSTA.*

Crystal Cruises, *Tel. 800/446-6620,* is a luxury offering cruises with the finest service.

Cunard's *Sea Goddess 1,* carrying only 116 pampered guests, sails round-trip from St. Thomas to the British Virgin Islands, St. Barts, Antigua, and St. Martin, *Tel. 800/5-CUNARD.* One of the most luxurious ships in the world, *Sea Goddess* offers round-the-clock complimentary caviar and champagne in an atmosphere of an ultra-luxurious resort without canned activities, deck sports, assigned seating nor gratuities. Cunard also sails a variety of other ships in and out of the Caribbean.

Holland America, *Tel. 800/426-0327,* is one of our favorite cruise lines because of its tipping- optional policy. Indonesian crew are so eager to please you may want to tip sometimes, but it's not like other cruise lines where you're told not just to tip but how much is expected. Enroll the children in Club HAL, which has a pod for ages 5-8, another for ages 9-12, and another for teens ages 13 to 17. They'll have their own playmates, supervisors, and play, joining you for lunch and dinner and for family events such as movies and shore excursions.

Norwegian Cruise Line, *Tel. 800/327-7030,* brings out the Viking in you. Handsome Nordic officers bring spit-and-polish to big, comfortable ships that have all the luxuries as well as superb cuisine that cruising is known for.

Princess Cruises, *Tel. 800/LOVE-BOAT*, the line that cruised the original Love Boat, offers seven- and ten-day Caribbean cruises aboard a half dozen luxurious ships. Ports of call include San Juan, St. Thomas, St. Croix, Sint Maarten, Guadeloupe, Dominica, Martinique, St. Lucia, Barbados, Grenada, Caracas, and Aruba.

Royal Olympic Cruises sail out of San Juan, stop at St. Croix and continue down the islands to Venezuela, arriving back in San Juan 10 or 11 days later. The ship carries guest lecturers, and enriches the experience with discussions and seminars on the area's flora, fauna, and culture. Cruise-only fares start at under $1,000 per person, double occuypancy. Air add-ons and airport-ship transfers are available. *Tel. (800) 872-6400.*

Star Clippers (see *Best Places to Stay*) are authentic clipper ships built in modern times, offering the silence of sail and the luxury of a fine yacht or small cruise liner, *Tel. 800/442-0551.*

Windjammer Barefoot Cruises, *Tel. 305/672-6453,* are barebones on the luxuries but laidback and youthful, with a heavy accent on fun and eco-tourism. Five classic sailing ships, the largest fleet of tall ships in the world, sail to more than 60 ports of call in the West Indies and Yucatan,

Windstar Cruises, *Tel. 800/258-7245,* offer the best of sailing and the best of cruise liner luxury in small ships that really sail (see *Best Places to Stay*).

About Cruise Prices

Cruise ships offer a dozen or more cabin categories with hundreds of dollars difference in cost, but that isn't the end of the story. Everything else in the ship is the same for everyone: dining, attentive service, and use of all the ship's facilities. You have to decide if a more spacious cabin is worth the difference in an otherwise-classless society. For many people, it is.

Usually the largest, lightest, airiest cabins are those on top decks, which means the disadvantage of greater motion in rough seas, especially if the cabin is well forward or aft. It's here that you can get a suite with king-size bed and sitting area, big windows, and perhaps a private balcony, mini-bar, personal steward, and other perks.

At the bottom end of the rate scale are windowless, inside cabins deep in the hull. Small and furnished with narrow bunk beds, they aren't for the claustrophobic but in rough seas the lowest cabins amidships have the least motion. A good compromise is an outside cabin two or three decks from the top, as close to amidships as possible for the least movement. Incidentally, the most expensive and cheapest cabins go first. For either, book as early as possible.

In addition to the basic rate, customs and port charges can add up to $200 per week to the cost of a cruise. Most lines also make it crystal clear that tips are not only expected but should amount to $X per passenger per day for the cabin steward, $Y for waiters, and so on. If this sticks in your craw, sail a tips-optional line such as Holland America or Windstar.

Other extras include optional shore excursions plus tips for drivers and guides, bar drinks including soft drinks, and personal needs such as laundry, gambling, babysitting (children's programs are usually free but individual child care is not), beauty salon and spa services, and much more. It's easy to spend twice as much on a cruise as the cost of your initial fare, so be sure to comparison shop for the best total deal. Some of the higher-priced cruises include drinks and shore excursions, making them far more competitive that they seem at first glance. Ask about packages that include airfare and pre- or past-cruise accommodations and tours. They're almost always a better buy than deals you put together by yourself.

Booking a Charter Boat Cruise

Travel agencies, especially those that specialize in cruises, are the best places to shop the vast and confusing Caribbean cruise market. However, travel agents rarely book charters, which are another market entirely. Your best bet is to get copies of *Yachting, Sail,* and *Cruising World* magazines, where crewed and bareboat charters are advertised. You'll see dozens of ads for owner-operated, crewed charters. Also advertising here are charter brokers who match up travelers with the right ship and crew. If you're a qualified sailor and want a boat all to yourself, look for ads run by large fleets, such as **The Moorings**, which can book your entire vacation including the charter, airfare, pre- and post- charter overnights, and provisioning.

Unless you're an experienced charterer, don't deal directly with a boat owner or owner-crewed charter. In a one-on-one deal, you could arrive to find that the boat is dirty or mechanically suspect. Go through a charter broker who can give you a choice of boats and locales, who has personally seen the boat, and can give you the names of some recent clients. If you're going to spend a week or more alone with crew, personality matches are crucial. Generally, owner-crew are the most eager to please but, even here, there are a few weirdos in the business. If the boat is absentee-owned and managed, crew could range from rude to unqualified. Check it out thoroughly.

Two of the best charter outfits in the business, both with long track records, are **The Moorings**, *19345 U.S. 19 North, Clearwater FL 34624, Tel. 800/535-7289*; and **Nicholson Yacht Charters**, *78 Bolton Street, Cambridge MA 02140, Tel. 800/662-6066.* The Moorings has fleets in Tortola, St. Martin, Guadeloupe, Martinique, St. Lucia, and Grenada. Boats are available without crew, with captain only, or with captain and cook. Nicholson's is based in Antigua but has listings throughout the U.S. Caribbean and B.V.I. Either outfit can arrange a pre- or post-charter land stay.

Live-Aboard Yachting

Let's sort out the lingo of **chartering**, a verb that means both to hire the yacht and to allow your yacht to be hired. You can charter a live-aboard boat three ways:

Bareboat means with no crew. If you have sufficient credentials as a sailor to satisfy the fleet owners and their insurance company, you and your family or crew may take command and sail away. Navigation, provisioning and cooking, swabbing the decks, sailing, and all other responsibilities are yours.

Captained charters have a captain aboard to take charge of the boat's sailing, navigation, and maintenance. Cleaning and cooking are still your responsibility.

Crewed charters let you play the guest while others do all the chores and sailing. You can still decide on destinations and schedules, pending the captain's approval depending on safety factors, and the captain will be glad to teach you as much about sailing and piloting as you care to know.

Things to Know Before You Go

- Get recent, firsthand knowledge of the boat and its crew before you book it. Most owner-crews are liveaboards who take great pride in their boats and their hospitality. They charter part of the year to support their own sailing the rest of the year. Corporation-owned boats may or may not have this personal touch.
- If you're bareboating, take the provisioning package, at least for the first day or two. It's far easier than running all over the island to round up a grocery list of staples.

CRUISING SOLO

The best way for a solo traveler to see the Caribbean is aboard ship, but most cruise and charter lines charge a hefty single supplement. You'll save by finding a roommate to share a cabin, each paying half the double occupancy fee. The larger the ship, the more there is to keep you mingling with other passengers. During open seating on most ships, waiters steer you to a table as you enter, filling tables rather than allowing people to sit alone. (It saves work for them if they don't have people scattered all over the dining room.) You'll soon make friends and, if your roommie isn't as companionable as you had hoped, it hardly matters.

One of the best ways to find a fellow traveler is through Jens Jurgen's **Travel Companion Exchange**, *Box 833, Amityville NY 11701, Tel. 516/454-0880, Fax 454-0170. Your travel agent can also match you up with the occasional singles cruise (make sure it's in the age bracket you want). Senior citizens can also travel solo on singles excursions organized by* **Grand Circle Travel**, *347 Congress Street, Boston MA 02210, Tel. 800/221-2610 or 617/350-7500.*

- Most crewed yachts provide all food and drink, and some provide airport transfers, but others do not provide alcohol. On a captained cruise, you will probably be asked to pay for the captain's food as well as your own. Know exactly what is provided for the price you are paying.
- Not all yachts are suitable for very young children, and some skippers do not accept them. Check ahead. Among our friends are many charter couples who tell horror stories about guests who were warned against bringing pets or very small children, but showed up with them anyway knowing that it was too late for the skipper to turn them away. In most cases–including one instance where a poodle fell overboard and was grabbed by a shark – they wished they had heeded the hosts' advice.
- If possible, get a pre-charter package including a night or two in a hotel before you move aboard, especially if you're bareboating. It's just too much to reach the island, move aboard, stow provisions, get checked out, and set sail all in the same day.

For further information:

BVI Charter Yacht Society, *P.O. Box 8309, Cruz Bay USVI 00831.* Fully crewed, luxury sailing craft sleep four to 20 for cruising the British and U.S. Virgin Islands.

The Moorings, *Tel. 800/437-7880* is a worldwide charter powerhouse, offering 15 crewed yachts and 165 bareboats out of Tortola alone.

Nicholson Yacht Charters, *78 Bolton Street, Cambridge MA 02140, Tel. 800/662-6066,* has been in Antigua since Horatio Nelson's day and knows the charter business well. They have a large choice of crewed yachts in the U.S.V.I. and B.V.I.

Yacht Promenade, *Tel. 800/526-5503,* offers six-night cruises for up to 12 passengers. It's based in the B.V.I.

Dive Cruising

Princess Cruises in cooperation with the **Professional Association of Diving Instructors** (PADI) offers a cruise add-on scuba course in which a passenger can become fully certified for $299 plus the cost of a luxury cruise. The program includes an open water dive manual, workbook, dive log book with carrying case, class and video instruction, four supervised dives in the ship's pool, four supervised open water dives in port, and a written exam. Most of the cruise lines listed above offer scuba diving as an extra. **Windstar**, for one, has a divemaster on board. You might also find a liveaboard dive charter through a charter broker.

Eco-tour Sailing

A 12-passenger luxury schooner that winters in the Caribbean, often with experts on board to conduct seminars on the environment is **Kathryn B.**, *Tel. 800/500-6077.* Rates are about $2,800 per person, double occupancy, per week. Itineraries vary each year.

Accommodations in the islands range from some of the world's most palatial hotels to seedy inns, but we've found that even the most humble hostels are usually clean and are furnished with at least the basics. In fact it's rather heartwarming when we see a small inn, struggling to accommodate its guests in the aftermath of a hurricane, doing the best they can with futons and plastic lawn chairs until full refurbishing can be done.

Hosts battle bugs constantly, and the sighting of the occasional cockroach shouldn't be taken as poor housekeeping. Indoors, we have rarely found bugs to be a problem even in open-air lodgings that have no glass nor screens in the windows. Many areas are surprisingly mosquito-free. The smart traveler always brings bug repellent just in case.

Unfortunately for travelers who are on tight budgets, Hostelling International has not yet come to the Caribbean and tent camping/backpacking is limited, if it's allowed at all. However, low-budget travelers can usually find a guest house, usually with breakfast laid on. It probably won't have a private bath, or even hot water at all, let alone a telephone, radio, or television.

No matter how much you pay for a room, however, don't take it for granted that it will be air conditioned. Many travelers dislike AC even on the hottest days, but it's our opinion that you can always turn if off if you don't want it. Except for high altitudes, the islands are hot and humid winter and summer. Countless innkeepers have looked us straight in the eye and said that "we really don't need air conditioning here" even though we were all sweating like stokers. A good fan is a must; air conditioning is a plus even if only during the mid-day heat.

After hotels, the most common accommodations are privately-owned homes, condos, apartments, or villas. Many are built by overseas investors - usually American, Canadian, or British - as a tax shelter. They are booked through word of mouth, with happy customers returning year after year, but don't book blindly. Unless the place is professionally managed, you could arrive to find things broken or uncleaned. It's best to get one that has full-time, on-site management. Many of the best ones are part of a large resort with a restaurant, swimming pool, and other hotel-like features. You may not even know that you're staying in a time share or in a privately-owned villa.

Wheelchair access isn't always good in the Caribbean, but thanks to the Americans With Disabilities Act it is making excellent progress in the U.S. islands. Even in places where there aren't ramps and other aids, however, we have seen young paraplegics in agile chairs go everywhere if they're willing to accept a little help. It's willingly given everywhere - in and out of little airplanes, off and on dive boats, up and down steps, and in and out of hotels that cling to steep hillsides. The same problems faced by persons in wheelchairs also apply to strollers and luggage carts. They just don't work on sand, so don't count on wheels to help with your luggage or to carry the kids..

As you read these pages, you may be surprised at what constitutes Expensive, Moderate, and Budget in various islands. Among the highest priced are the U.S. and British Virgin Islands. Among the least expensive is Puerto Rico. However, we've given the widest possible choice of accommodations in all price ranges. Live like a prince or a pauper. The sunshine, sand and surf are free.

RATING THE RATES

Even though we have listed hotels under Expensive, Moderate, and Budget, it isn't always easy to make the call because all-inclusive resorts are just that. When comparing rates, you must consider what you're getting for the price. Full American Plan (FAP) means three meals daily; MAP, which means Modified American Plan, provides breakfast and dinner. Many resorts offer FAP or MAP for an extra $50 or so per person per day. European Plan, or EP, means accommodations only.

The trend at all-inclusives has been to go well beyond FAP and MAP and to also include all meals, sports, and entertainment. Many such resorts throw in unlimited bar drinks and wine with meals; others serve wine or beer with meals but charge for bar drinks.

To get to the bottom line, add up the cost of eating, drinking, tennis or golf, watersports rentals, scuba tank refills, spa services, airport transfers, tips or service charges, and hotel taxes. Look especially for two terms: ***all-inclusive*** *and* ***package****. Either could mean a big difference in the final cost of a Caribbean holiday.*

In an effort to leave happy surprises on the down side, ***this book quotes winter rates****. In spring and fall, you might save 20-30% and in summer as much as 50% off high season rates. However, there's a trend in the Caribbean to offer more features in summer rather than to chop rates. The word "package" is solid gold in any season, but especially during the dog days. You may be able to get a week's vacation with all the bells and whistles for the cost of accommodations alone at the height of the season.*

Note that the definition of "low-season" can vary widely among islands, and among resorts on the same island. The only way to know for sure is to contact each resort individually. By delaying or advancing your trip just a few days, you can save hundreds of dollars.

HOTEL CHAINS

Chains, alliances and groups that have Caribbean properties that can be booked through toll- free numbers in the U.S. and Canada include:

- **Best Western International**, *Tel. 800/528-1234*
- **Club Med** (ask about memberships), *Tel. 800/259-2633*
- **Crowne Plaza**, *Tel. 800/327-3286*
- **Days Inn**, *Tel. 800/325-2525*
- **Econo Lodge**, *Tel. 800/446-6900*
- **Embassy Suites**, *Tel. 800/362-2779*
- **Golden Tulip Hotels**, *Tel. 800/344-1212*

- **Hilton Hotels**, *800/HILTONS*
- **Hyatt Hotels**, *Tel. 800/228-9000*
- **Holiday Inn**, *Tel. 800/HOLIDAY*
- **Leading Hotels of the World**, *Tel. 800/223-6800*
- **Marriott Hotels**, *Tel. 800/228-9290*
- **Meridien/Forte Hotels & Resorts**, *Tel. 800/543-4300*
- **Mondotels, Inc.** , *Tel. 800/847-4249*
- **Novotel**, *Tel. 800/NOVOTEL*
- **Quality Inn**, *Tel. 800/228-5151*
- **Radisson Hotels**, *800/333-3333*
- **Ramada Inns**, *Tel. 800/2-RAMADA*
- **Ritz-Carlton**, *Tel. 800/241-3333*
- **Rosewood Hotels & Resorts**, *Tel. 800/854-2252*
- **Small Luxury Hotels of the World**, *Tel. 800/525-4800*
- **Sofitel**, *Tel. 800/221-4542*
- **Sonesta Hotels**, *Tel. 800/766-3782*
- **Westin Resorts**, *Tel. 800/WESTINS*
- **Wyndham Hotels**, *Tel. 800/822-4200*

RECOMMENDED READING

Magazines

Caribbean Travel & Life and *Spa Finder* are on newsstands, and *Affordable Caribbean*, P.O. Box 3000, Denville NJ 07834, is available by mail.

Books

Books that are set in the Caribbean or have Caribbean flavor:

- *A Cruising Guide to the Caribbean* by William T. Stone and Anne M. Hays is published by Sheridan House, *145 Palisade Street, Dobbs Ferry NY 10522, Tel. 888/743-7425*. The book is invaluable as a guide to cruising the islands by boat, but it also makes fascinating armchair reading before and after any Caribbean visit whether by land, air, or sea. The book covers many of the islands in this guidebook as well as ports along the Latin American coast of the Caribbean. The authors' personal anecdotes call for reading and re-reading over the years.
- *A Small Place* by Jamaica Kincaid
- *Caribbean* by James Michener
- *Caribbean Guide* by Janet Groene, with Gordon Groene
- *Caribbean with Kids* by Paris Permenter and John Bigley.
- *Caribbean Mystery* by Agatha Christie

- *The Comedians* by Graham Greene
- *Church and Des*, a book of short stories by Philip Wylie
- *The Deep* by Peter Benchley
- *Don't Stop the Carnival* by Herman Wouk
- *Far Tortuga* by Peter Matthiessen
- *Golden Rendezvous* by Alistair MacLean
- *Islands in the Stream* by Ernest Hemingway
- *Mosquito Coast* by Paul Theroux
- *Murder on the Atlantic* by Steve Allen.
- *Wide Sargasso Sea* by Jean Rhys Specialized guides:
- *Caribbean Hideaways* by Ian McKeown (Prentice Hall Travel) covers 100 romantic places for couples.
- *Caribbean Afoot* by M. Timothy O'Keefe (Menasha Ridge Press) is a walking and hiking guide to 29 islands.
- *World Guide to Nude Beaches and Resorts* by Lee Baxandall
- *Out and About, Resorts and Warm-Weather Vacations*, a travel guide for homosexuals. (Hyperion)
- *Cruising Guide to the Leeward Islands* and *Cruising Guide to the Windward Islands* by Chris Doyle (Cruising Guide Publications, Box 1017, Dunedin FL 34697; available through yachting book stores or *Tel. 800/749-8151.)*
- *St. John Feet, Fins, and Four-Wheel Drive* by Pam Griffin (American Paradise Publishing, ISBN 0-9631060-7-4).
- *Yachtsman's Guide to the Virgin Islands and Puerto Rico* (Yachtsman's Guides Publications, Box 281, Atlantic Highlands NJ 07716, *Tel. 800/ 849-8151).*

A NOTE FROM THE U.S. STATE DEPARTMENT

*Request **Tips for Travelers to the Caribbean**, a booklet available for $1 from the Superintendent of Documents, U.S. Government Printing Office, Washington DC 20402. It was last revised in 1993, so can be taken only as a general advisory.*

7. BASIC INFORMATION

BANKING

Banks throughout the Caribbean keep abbreviated hours and, on the smallest islands, may be open only one or two days a week. On the plus side, currency exchanges, and sometimes full-service banks, are often open when flights arrive, even at odd hours. Most have Automatic Teller Machines, which are found throughout the region, but, as with anything else in the islands, it's best not to bet the farm on finding a machine where it's supposed to be, and in working order.

Before leaving on your trip, check with your home bank to see if you need a different PIN in the islands. Your home bank may also be able to give you a list of ATM addresses in the island you'll be visiting.

BUSINESS HOURS

The **siesta** is a time-honored tradition, especially in Puerto Rico, where "only mad dogs and Englishmen go out in the noonday sun." Stores may be closed through the lunch hour and many museums and other attractions will be closed for one or two hours in the middle of the day. Shops' hours are also influenced by cruise ship arrivals and departures.

CARNIVAL!

Carnival (spelled Carnaval on some islands) in the Caribbean can take place any time of year.

Puerto Rico celebrates most of its carnivals just before Lent, but regional dates could vary. Each community celebrates its saint's days for a week or more.

Virgin Islands: Carnival is two days before Ash Wednesday, when it's celebrated with bambooshay, kill t'ing pappy and roas-a-time, all meaning "live it up". There's a carnival queen, prince and princess, calypso singers, street vendors, high hats, horse racing, food fairs, masquerades, parades and enough excess and insanity to last through Lent.

CREDIT CARDS

MasterCard and Visa cards are accepted in almost every tourist shop, hotel, and restaurant in the U.S. Caribbean and B.V.I. Discover has some acceptance, with American Express and Diners Club in a distant fourth place.

CURRENCY

U.S. currency is in use in the British Virgin Islands as well as in the American territories, so there is no worry about currency exchange. However, we recommend carrying a good supply of ones and fives for tips and small purchases at roadside stands and backwoods shops. Travelers' checks and credit cards can take care of the big bills in resorts and high-ticket restaurants.

ELECTRICITY

Electrical service in the U.S. islands the British Virgin Islands is American-style 110-volt, 60-cycle. Many hotels have built-in hair dryers.

EMERGENCIES

When you arrive in your hotel, review emergency procedures. They will include the usual things about what to do in case of fire, and may also include hurricane instructions. Power outages are a fact of life, so locate the candle(s) and matches that are usually provided. On some islands it's also wise to draw a half gallon or so of water to provide a rinse in case the water fails when you're soapy. The 911 system is in use throughout most of the U.S. Caribbean, but check with your hotelier.

HEALTH CONCERNS

People from northern climes often picture the islands as hurricane-lashed sandspits inhabited mostly by boa constrictors, clouds of mosquitoes, and spiders the size of Siamese cats. The good news is that the U.S. Caribbean and most of the other islands are highly advanced in terms of safe drinking water, the availability of emergency medical care, and food sanitation. See individual chapters for specific warnings.

The Caribbean does have its pests, but its chief danger by far is Ol' Sol, the faithful sunshine that brings most of us here in the first place. Sunglasses are crucial, according to Dr. Wayne J. Riley of Baylor College of Medicine in Houston, "especially in...equatorial sand beaches."

Bring with you a supply of high-SPF sunscreen, preferably a waterproof brand that won't come off with perspiration or swimming. Some of the worst sunburns are suffered by swimmers and snorkelers who don't realize they're getting burned right through the water. If you're especially sensitive to sunburn, bring a lightweight, long-sleeve, long-leg outfit such as pajamas to wear while snorkeling, and wear waterproof sunscreen too. There's also a special sunscreen for bald heads. Headsmart, which screens rays but is not greasy, is a spray-on made by Coppertone. "Remember," say the Coppertone folks, "that if your shadow is shorter than you are, you are more likely to sunburn. No shadow? Seek shade!"

Mosquitoes can always be a problem in the tropics, and the World Health Organization now admits that they can't be eradicated. Travelers must bring their own spray-on protection; if you're staying in primitive surroundings, bring your own mosquito netting too. Various designs of drapings for beds or sleeping bags are available from **Magellan's**, *Box 5485, Santa Barbara CA 93150, Tel. 800/962-4943*. Request a free catalog.

Many people find "no-see-ums" to be far peskier than mosquitoes. They can fly through screens and are not deterred by all mosquito sprays. They can cause a watery blister that itches for weeks and can leave scars that last for months. Some tourists, especially heavy drinkers, have had such severe reactions they had to be hospitalized.

Since different repellents work on different body chemistries, take two types in hopes that one of them will work on your skin against no-see-ums. Many people swear by Avon's Skin-So-Soft bath oil, but it doesn't work for everyone.

The same precautions that apply anywhere are also wise in the Caribbean. When in doubt about water, ask. Don't drink water in remote streams and waterfalls; giardia are found throughout the world. Wash or peel fruit before eating it just as you would at home.

Fish poisoning isn't unique to the islands, but one toxin that occurs here is not destroyed by cooking. It's **cigatuera**, sometimes found in fish that feed on reefs. It's rarely a problem in hotels and restaurants but could be a threat if you cook your own catch. Ask locals for guidance before eating barracuda, amberjack, or colorful reef fish.

Cigatuera is a neurotoxin that causes tingling in the mouth, fingers, and toes. Often an initial dose produces only mild symptoms, which get worse with each exposure. So locals, who could be made sicker than a newcomer who is getting cigatuera for the first time, are usually very savvy about what fish to catch and where to catch them.

In years of traipsing through the bush, we've never had an allergic reaction to vegetation. Fortunately we never tangled with the **manchineel tree**, found throughout the Caribbean, which is so poisonous that people have gone temporarily blind just by breathing smoke from a manchineel fire. The trees are not uncommon; ask a local to point one out so you'll always recognize them. Don't touch. Don't even stand under one in the rain. Drips could give you a nasty rash.

As long as you don't taste strange plants or tangle with thorns or cactus, it's likely you won't have severe reactions to plants. You also won't see many snakes in the U.S. Caribbean, thanks to a creature that is even scarier and more slithery. The mongoose was introduced eon ago to kill rats in the sugarcane fields and proved to be a natural control for snakes. Now they've multiplied in the wild until the mongoose is more a pest than snakes ever were. Looking like a cross between a dachshund and an alley cat, it's startling more than harmful. Once you've seen one and realized it's not an oversize rat, you'll know what to expect.

HEALTH ADVISORIES

Get the latest information from the ***Centers for Disease Control****, Tel. 888/232-3228, Fax 232-3229. It's a 24-hour automated line that can provide recorded information, brochures by mail, or information via fax if you have the patience to work your way through all the steps. The Website is www.cdc.gov. AIDS and hepatitis are a threat anywhere, but sunburn is the most common health problem in the U.S. Caribbean. Use sunscreen and wear a long-sleeve shirt, even while snorkeling in shallow water.*

An invaluable guide for frequent travelers is Open Road's "CDC's Complete Guide to Healthy Travel," which presents the Centers for Disease Control's authoritative summaries for all international travel.

POST SERVICE

Mail to the U.S. Caribbean travels with a U.S. zip code and at U.S. rates. If you'll be there for a long time, mail can be forwarded free.

RELIGIOUS SERVICES

The most "insider" thing you can do as a visitor in the Caribbean is to attend local worship services. Dress in your best and act responsibly even if you don't know what is going on. We'd suggest sticking to mainstream denominations, which are found on every island, rather than unusual cults and sects that might consider you to be a snoopy intruder. In fact, some of the darker rites (voodoo, obeah, some Mormon sacraments) are not open to outsiders and it would be a gaffe to try to attend.

We can promise you a warm welcome in church, and a new dimension to the friendships you make on the island. Attending a tiny, open air Baptist church on one cay, we found ourselves the subject of a lengthy sermon, the gist of which was a prayerful request for our safety at sea. We've never felt so loved and honored.

SERVICE CHARGES

Instead of tipping, most hotels and restaurants automatically add 10-20 per cent to bills. Check your bill before leaving additional money under the plate. There's no point in tipping twice.

TAXES

Hotel taxes seem to be soaring in recent years at a pace that is hard for an annual guidebook to keep up with. When asking for rate information, always ask whether taxes and tips are included. If not, be sure you know how much they add because it's not uncommon for tax and service to add another 20-25 per cent to the room rate.

TIPS

Tips are always welcome, so tip the same as you would at home. Tips for the taking of photographs hasn't caught on widely here and we're hoping you won't start a trend. Locals either allow you to take their picture or they don't.

TELEPHONES

Hotel phone charges for overseas calls are excessively high in most cases so, even though you can dial anywhere in the world from most hotel rooms, ask the cost first. Pre-paid cards are used almost exclusively in the Caribbean; many pay phones accept nothing else. Before leaving home, check with your long distance carrier to get the access code you'll use.

PHONE HOME

Through the ***Cable & Wireless Caribbean Cellular*** *you can place or answer calls from almost anywhere on your own cell telephone. In many areas, voice and fax mail can also be arranged. Before leaving home, make arrangements by calling 800/262-8366 in the U.S., 800/567-8366 in Canada, and Tel. 268/480-2628 elsewhere. If you pre-register with the company you can be given a local number in the islands to give to family and business associates before you leave home. You can also begin making calls immediately on your arrival on the island.*

There is no charge for pre-registering. You pay only a $5 daily activation charged on days when the phone is used. Calls made to emergency numbers are free. On any island served by Cable & Wireless, dial O and SND.

Note that hotels and pay phones probably will charge you for connection to an 800 number. Each time you dial your credit card's 800 access code, you incur a charge *even if your party doesn't answer*. As far as the hotel or phone company is concerned, your call was completed with the 800 number answered. At press time, pay phones in Puerto Rico still charge only a dime.

TIME ZONE

Most of the Caribbean covered in this book is on **Atlantic Time**, which is the same as **Eastern Daylight Savings Time**. When the East is on Standard Time, the island time is one hour later than New York time.

TROUBLE SPOTS

Crime varies among islands but it is an increasing problem. Don't bring unnecessary credit cards or expensive jewelry. Keep close tabs on electronics, laptops, cameras, and other items that are easily lifted and sold. Don't take valuables to the beach, not even to be locked in the trunk of the car.

Firearms are generally verboten in the islands, even if you arrive in your own airplane or boat. Penalties are swift and severe.

Driving in the U.S. and British Virgin Islands is on the left. Unlike in the United Kingdom, where steering wheels are also on the left and serve as a constant reminder to drive on the left, the most common cars in the Caribbean were built for the North American market and have right-hand steering. Add to this the poor roads on most islands, and the absence of good maps and road signs, and you have a heads-up situation. Log some time as a passenger before attempting to solo.

Drowning is one of the leading causes of accidental death for Americans visiting the Caribbean. Unwary tourists get in over their heads, literally, with watersports equipment or on surf-pounded beaches that have no warnings nor lifeguards. Sea conditions can change suddenly. Respect local advice.

Drug laws are strict in the islands, but they catch North American visitors unawares because of the lazy, laidback pace of life. If you carry prescription medications, keep them in the original container labeled with the doctor's name, pharmacy, and contents. In the British Virgin Islands, British law applies.

Shopping can be a waste of money if you buy products that will be confiscated on your return. Don't rely on locals to tell you, or even to know, what items cannot be brought into the United States. They include any products made from sea turtles including cosmetics and turtle shell jewelry, fur from spotted cats, feathers and feather products, birds stuffed or alive, crocodile and cayman leather, and black coral. In fact, it's best to avoid buying any coral either in jewelry and au naturel, according to the U.S. Department of State.

WEDDINGS

Most islands welcome the increasingly popular trend among visitors to get married in paradise, so they have streamlined the procedure as much as possible. Nevertheless, it's essential to allow plenty of time because all the paper work must be done during government business hours. Each island has its own holidays; government offices usually close earlier than other businesses. Start by rounding up all the paper work that will be required, including copies of any applicable divorce or death papers and parental consent for underage applicants.

Choose a hotel that has a full-time wedding planner, who can work miracles with the paper work as well as arranging flowers, a photographer, music, and the reception. Usually, residence in the islands of two or more business days is required before application can be made. If the wedding is to be performed by a clergyman, it will be helpful if your home clergyman coordinates with the island-based clergyman who will preside. This is especially important in Catholic rites.

Bring your wedding clothes in carry-on baggage. Murphy's Law requires that if luggage is to be lost, it will be the bags with the wedding gown, veil, tux, and all the matching shoes.

SOUR NOTES

Every vacation has its grace notes but also its clams, those sour notes that can detract from an otherwise perfect vacation. Under individual chapters we've listed warnings but some generalities apply.

In most of the Caribbean be prepared for such things as:

Arrogant airlines *– American Air Lines and its subsidiary, American Eagle, "own" the Caribbean through its hub at Puerto Rico and they know it. Flight personnel are hard working and professional, but most ground support personnel that we've encountered have a don't-give-a-damn attitude towards passengers and baggage. Food service is scanty if at all. Things have improved in recent months but, if you have a choice of air lines explore them all. If you can avoid connections through Miami, especially on American Eagle, do so. Don't travel with a pet unless you can take it as carry-on luggage. Baggage handlers in the Caribbean are the roughest in the world.*

Bold birds *can turn outdoor dining into a swatting war. It's common for greckles or bananaquits to perch at your elbow, waiting for a chance to steal a morsel. And, as soon as you leave the table, they're on your plate. The more they're fed by tourists, the worse things become. At first, you think it's cute but the constant pestering, not to mention the goopy messes, can cure you forever of sharing your table with poultry.*

Bloody sports *such as cockfights are part of the Latin culture.*

Food attitudes *are different in the islands, where family loyalty and sharing are a way of life. Taking food is not a crime, so a cook may maneuver cleverly to minimize what you are fed and to maximize the leftovers that she, by common practice, takes home. If you are paying for food that is prepared by someone else in your lodgings or charter boat, take a close look at where your money goes.*

Island time *is a way of life in which nothing ever happens at the appointed hour. Except for official schedules such as closing time for government bureaus (which may close early, but never late) most things start many minutes later than the announced time. Nothing steams North Americans more than the feeling that locals are doing this just to get your dander up. It isn't you. It's the culture. Relax and enjoy it.*

8. SPORTS & RECREATION

The Caribbean has been one of the most sports-mad areas on earth since before European settlement. Ball courts used by the Arawaks and Caribs have been excavated and it's now known that games similar to those played by the Mayans were played here. The progress of South American Indians up the Caribbean chain could be traced by the ball fields because the game was played with a rubber-like ball made from chicle that could be harvested only on the South American mainland.

Puerto Ricans are passionate baseball players, so North American ball fans will have no shortage of teams to cheer. Golf and tennis came to the islands with Scottish and British settlers. Today's sophisticated golf courses were designed by the biggest names such as Robert Trent Jones, Sr., Robert Trent Jones, Jr., and Pete Dye. Locals have their own favorite sports, and it's always fun for a visitor to see a spirited local game of soccer, rugby, or cricket. Most islands have large gyms, teams, and coaches for all the Olympic sports. See individual chapters for more coverage of the local sports scene.

BEACHES

The best beaches in the U.S. Caribbean and, many of us believe, in the world include **Cane Garden Bay** on Tortola, **Trunk Bay** on St. John, and **Luquillo Beach** in Puerto Rico. When photographers what to shoot the quintessential beach, they often choose **Magens Bay** on St. Thomas. It's a perfect seascape of sand and cerulean waters. **The Baths** on Virgin Gorda are a spectacular spread of sand and cathedral-size boulders. Most of the north shore of St. Croix is a picture postcard beach; so are the beaches at **Hibiscus Beach** Hotel on St. Croix, **Caneel Bay** on St. John, the **Ritz-Carlton** on St. Thomas, and hundreds more too numberous to name.

Find your own favorite beach, and keep it secret. We did.

BICYCLING

Try **BACKROADS**, *Tel. 800/GO-ACTIVE,* for bicycle and mountain biking tours. See individual island listings for names of local bicycle rentals.

BIRDING

Birding tours worldwide are offered by **Field Guides Incorporated**, *Box 60723, Austin TX, Tel. 512/327-4953, Fax 327-9231; toll-free 800/728-4953*. Their Caribbean tours focus is on Trinidad and Tobago but ask about trips to the U.S. Caribbean.

BOATING

There are more ways to get out on the Caribbean waters than can be mentioned here, but of special interest is **Club Nautico** *at Villa Marina Yacht Harbor near Fajardo, Puerto Rico, Tel. 800/BOAT-RENT*. A worldwide membership organization, the Club rents powerboats to its members at a highly discounted price. Many travelers join by the year because it means a big savings on boat rentals at home and anywhere travels take them.

DIVING & SNORKELING

Even though there is a big difference between the training and equipment needed by scuba divers and mere snorkelers, both require the clearest waters with the furthest visibility. Some of the best dive and snorkel spots include:

Buck Island on **St. Croix** is a national park completely surrounded by waters filled with dive and snorkel sites. **Cane Bay** on St. Croix has spectacular drop-offs favored for wall diving.

The **Wreck of the Rhone** off **Salt Island** in the **Virgin Islands** is one of the most famous, most photographed dives in the Caribbean. Off **Dead Chest Island** in the B.V.I. where Blackbeard is said to have marooned 15 men, a coral reef is electric with color and motion. The Caves on **Norman Island** are an exciting place to snorkel or make a night dive. Only 10 miles from Virgin Gorda, the **wreck of the Chikuzen** lies in 75 feet of water. She was scuttled in 1981 to attract reef fish. Today the wreck is home to giant octopus and rays against the ghostly backdrop of the old ship's rigging. **Trunk Bay**, St. John, has a marked, underwater snorkel trail.

FITNESS

For muscle building, slimming, toning, and other specialized work-out vacations, try **Spa Finders**, *Tel. 212/924-6800 or 800/ALL-SPAS.*

ABOUT GPS

More and more tourists are relying on ***Global Positioning Satellites,*** *long known to sailors and pilots as a navigation aid and now coming into land use in trucking fleets, auto travel, and even for hiking. GPS receivers, now available for about $200, fit in a shirt pocket. Taking their reading from three or more satellites, they can tell you exactly where you are in relation to a known destination, such as your hotel or the place you parked your car at the airport.*

Until all maps and guidebooks are geo-coded to give the exact longitude and latitude of every hotel and point of interest, GPS won't replace street addresses. However, once you reach a spot, note your location, and program it into your receiver, you can always ask it how to get back there. It will point in the right direction and tell you how far it is as the crow flies. And it's accurate to a matter of meters! If you'll be doing a lot of hiking and exploring on larger islands, you're ready for GPS.

GOLF

Favorite golf resorts in the U.S. Caribbean include:

Carambola Golf Club, *St. Croix. Tel. 340/778-5638* is not part of but is adjacent to the Sunterra Resort, Carambola Beach, *Tel. 340/778-3800* or *888/503-8760.*

El Conquistador, *San Juan, Puerto Rico, Tel. 787/863-1000 or 800/468-5228,* has an 18-hole championship golf course for the use of its guests.

Hyatt Dorado Beach, *Puerto Rico, Tel. 787/796-1234* or *800/233-1234,* is one of two resorts (the other is the **Hyatt Cerromar Beach**) that offer memorable golf to guests. Between the two resorts, which are side by side, you can play four courses.

Palmas del Mar, *near Humacao in Puerto Rico,* offers outstanding golf in an outstanding resort setting, *Tel. 787/852-6000 or 800/468-3331.*

Westin Rio Mar, *Puerto Rico, Tel. 800/WESTINS,* has two 18-hole championship golf courses in the shadow of El Yunque rainforest.

HIKING

According to outdoor writer M. Timothy O'Keefe, author of *Caribbean Afoot* (Menasha Ridge Press), the ten top hikes in the Caribbean include **St. John**, *U.S. Virgin Islands,* the entire island. In the national park, ranger-led hikes for bird watching, exploring historic ruins, and other explorations are offered almost daily. In the B.V.I., eleven areas are managed by the National Parks Trust. They include the 92-acre **Sage Mountain National Park** with its 1,780-foot peak, the highest point in all the Virgin. **The Baths**, *Virgin Gorda*. It's a tourist attraction, but hikers can walk the entire area beyond the crowds. **El Yunque**, *Puerto Rico*. Again it's touristy, but once you get away from the bus stops there are miles of rainforest trails to explore.

HORSEBACK RIDING

Puerto Rico is especially well known for its paso fino horses. Many other islands also offer riding on mountain trails or beaches. Try **Excursions Extraordinaires**, *Tel. 800/678-2252.*

KAYAKING

Sea kayaking is catching on throughout the islands, so it's likely that your hotel has kayaks for rent or can arrange a kayak expedition for you. A company that can book your trip with major emphasis on kayaking is **Island Trails**, *Tel. 800/233-4366.*

SAILING

Most beach resorts have Sunfish and other small, non-motorized sailboats for guest use, often at no added cost. Fleets are also available at almost all of the all- inclusive resorts.

The two best places to get a bareboat are **The Moorings**, *Tel. 800/353-7289,* and **Nicholson Yacht Charters**, *Tel. 800/662-6066.* **Steve Colgate's Offshore Sailing School** in Tortola offers sailing instruction for future racers and cruisers, *Tel. 941/454-1700 or 800/221-4326.*

For crewed charters, contact the **Virgin Islands Charterboat League**, *Tel. 340/774-3944 or 800/524-2061.*

TENNIS

Virtually every large resort offers tennis. See individual chapters for many more choices.

Biras Creek Estate *on Virgin Gorda* is the perfect hideaway for people who love tennis, sailing, the beach, and nature walks, *Tel. 340/494-3555 or 800/608-9661.*

Sunterra Resort *on St. Croix* offers tennis on Laykold courts and a pro shop to non-guests as well as to guests. *Tel. 340/778-3800* or*888/503-8760.*

El Conquistador *in Puerto Rico* has a full-service tennis facility with a tennis pro, pro shop, clubhouse, and Har-Tru courts, *Tel. 787/863-1000 or 800/468-5228.*

Hyatt Dorado Beach, *Puerto Rico, Tel. 787/796-1234 or 800/233-1234* is one of two resorts (the other is the Hyatt Cerromar Beach) that have plenty of tennis courts for day or night play.

Wyndham Sugar Bay Resort *on St. Thomas* has a dozen Laykold courts, a stadium tennis court, a tennis pro, and plush resort facilities, *Tel. 340/777-7100 or 800/927-7100.*

WHITEWATER RAFTING

Book a rafting vacation with **Excursions Extraordinaires**, *Tel. 800/678-2252.*

WINDSURFING

Most beach resorts offer board sailers for guest use and, on good surfing beaches, concessions often offer board rentals. One company that specializes in vacation packages that center around windsurfing is **Sailboard Vacations**, *Tel. 800/252-1070.*

9. SHOPPING

Thanks to a growing network of international alliances such as NAFTA and the European Union, the words "duty free" are fast losing their magic around the world. Where once the traveler could save smartly in the Caribbean by buying duty-free French perfumes, English China, Irish crystal, and Scottish cashmeres, today's bargains lie only in the fact that you are not paying whatever sales tax or VAT might have applied in your hometown.

For the canny shopper who buys on sale or at discounts, which are rarely seen in Caribbean duty-free shops, the savings can be unimpressive. Add to this the expense of shipping or the hassle of packing and carrying things home and the luster of old-fashioned Caribbean shopping fades.

It's still possible to buy everything from porcelain to silver and expensive watches, and American visitors to the U.S. islands can bring back twice as much tax-free merchandise as from the other islands. Take a closer look at the works of a growing network of local artists, crafters, writers, chefs, sculptors, wood carvers, potters, ironmongers, goldsmiths, basket makers, photographers, publishers, ceramists, weavers, fabric designers, batik artists, knitters, lace makers and seamstresses. You can still shop the U.S. Caribbean for South American amethysts and South African diamonds, but you can also get unique keepsakes that are found only here.

We prefer to pass up Chinese textiles and Italian leather goods in a search for products made by local hands from local raw materials – many of them collectibles that will grow in value. Every island has its artisans and artists, many of them gaining international attention.

Locals have learned that it is more profitable to work with locally available products. Tropical flowers are turned into floral perfumes more compelling than any found in Paris. Locally-grown hot peppers end up in fiery sauces that travelers love to take home to their friends. Exotic fruits end up in jams and preserves, allowing visitors to introduce seagrape or guava or nutmeg jelly to their friends at home. Local sugar cane ends up not only in time-proven rums but in other alcoholic drinks enhanced by such tropic flavors as coconut, guavaberry, coffee, and spices. Hand-picked mountain coffees in Jamaica and Puerto Rico are world famous.

If you're shopping for specific items, such as your Waterford pattern or a Kosta Boda vase, make note of hometown prices and compare them with what you find in the islands. According to travel shopping expert Suzy Gershman in *Travel Holiday* magazine, big savings in the Caribbean are rare. "In my experience, 10 to 20% discounts are the norm," she says. Often you can do better than that at home during a sale.

Island-grown spices turn up in liqueurs, cosmetics and soaps, preserves, jerk mixtures, and spice blends for everything from cakes to pot roast. Whole spices and native seashells are strung into necklaces. Local earths are turned into museum-quality pottery pieces. Shards of broken glass are fished from the sea after being tumbled into smooth-edged jewels, and are mounted to make brooches and earrings.

On almost every island, local palm fronds, straws, grasses and barks are made into basketry unique to that culture. Each island has its own laces too made from ages-old patterns passed from mother to daughter. Plantation-era antiques are sold in many island shops, and it's also possible to shop for new furniture made form native hardwoods.

The more you know about Caribbean cultures, the more fun it is to bring home souvenirs that capture some element of it: carnival masks, dolls in native costume, and santos, the carved saints so loved by Puerto Ricans. Great varieties of music come out of the Caribbean and now it has its own recording studios producing tapes and CDs. You can bring home the best in reggae, salsa, quelbe, calypso, and steel drum, performed and recorded in the islands. And, if you want tee shirts, they are being printed in the Caribbean now too.

THE CONTRARIAN SHOPPER

Sorry, but we just can't rhapsodize as other guidebook writers do about the countless, look-alike, "duty-free" stores found throughout the Caribbean. When we travel, we look for the essence and heart of each destination. When we choose souvenirs, we hope to bring back only something that has meaning and lasting value, a souvenir that will always bring a destination alive for us again. We may buy a recording of local music, a bottle of perfume distilled from local flowers, a painting of a scene we loved, or a craft made by hands we personally grasped. It is this sort of shopping, tied to the land and its people, that we hope to bring you in these pages.

ABOUT WOOD CARVINGS

Throughout the Caribbean, woodcarvers ply their craft and offer it at prices that are, for the most part, hard to resist. Whether you're a serious collector or a novice, the biggest misstep is in buying a piece that is perfect in context but looks simply silly in your living room back in Manchester or Minneapolis. Most carvings are large, crude, and almost impossible to get into your luggage. They may also be (1) made in China or Africa, (2) made from green wood that will split when you get it back to the dry heat of your home, (3) full of worms – look for tiny holes – or (4) all of the above.

Another thing to check for is balance. If the piece is to be hung up or displayed on a flat surface, try it that way. It may sit or hang quite differently from the way it looks in the carver's hands in the village bazaar. To get a serious sculpture as a serious investment, it's better to pay a little more at a trusted gallery.

The Caribbean now has North American-style malls, some of them in special shopping centers built at quays where cruise ship passengers debark. By contrast you can also shop in scores of tiny shops sardined into centuries-old downtown buildings. Throughout the islands, entire new merchant classes have taken root, from the Indians and Pakistanis who operate so many of the shops, to ex-patriot painters and sculptors who came to the islands and never left.

Write the **Superintendent of Documents**, *Mail Stop SSOP, Washington DC 20402-9328*, for information on the booklets *Tips for Travelers to the Caribbean* and *Know Before You Go*. Ask too about booklets covering other of your interests and concerns such as relocating to the islands, working abroad, travel health, and so on.

THE BEST ISLANDS FOR POWER SHOPPING

For Megabucks Shopping: *if you're shopping for a really costly jewel, set of china, or watch, keep in mind that you can bring home more than twice as much in duty-free merchandise from the U.S. Virgin Islands than from other islands. From Puerto Rico, you can bring in unlimited merchandise tax free.*

For Convenient Malls: *the concentration of shops in downtown Charlotte Amalie, St. Thomas, makes for some of the Caribbean's most interesting browsing in old warehouses that have been selling goods for 400 years. Puerto Rico and the Caymans have well-stocked, modern, American-style malls. Quayside shopping in convenient centers is especially good at St. Thomas and San Juan. St. Croix also has a concentration of good downtown shopping at Christiansted.*

For Native Goods: *shop Puerto Rico for art with a Latin flavor and St. Croix for unique Cruzan bracelets. Almost all the islands have local rums and liqueurs, and a number offer excellent coffee too.*

For Imported Goods: *St. Thomas, St. Croix, and San Juan have excellent selections of luxury goods from around the world.*

10. TAKING THE KIDS

West Indians love their children, and family is a strong and loving force here. Resorts that don't have children's programs can always find a capable babysitter for you. Those resorts that do cater to families with kids do it with a capital C. At family-friendly places you can expect all the usual features such as a crib, children's pool, children's program, high chairs, and kiddy menu plus oodles of things for kids to do with other kids and with parents.

If your children are old enough to be tempted by drugs, drill into them how thoroughly a vacation can be ruined by one misstep. The islands seem so easygoing and laidback, visitors can be lulled into thinking that anything goes. At best you could all be thrown off the island after payment of a big fine. At worst, a young person could be jailed. We saw a teenager pulled out of line for drug possession just as he was re-boarding a cruise ship. You can bet that his family's vacation was ruined and his immediate future a nightmare. Remember too that in the B.V.I., British laws apply, and laws in the U. S. territories may be different from those in your hometown.

It takes some planning to find the right resort for all children. Even those resorts that cater to children may not have programs for toddlers under the age of three or four, for children who are not potty trained, or for teenagers. Some resorts welcome children only in summer; some have separate sections for families, away from couples and senior citizens who

CARIBBEAN WITH KIDS

If you're looking for a guide book catering to families, pick up a copy of Open Road's ***Caribbean With Kids*** *by Paris Permenter and John Bigley. The authors guide you to the best of the family-friendly resorts that are growing throughout the Caribbean.*

don't want to be disturbed by the patter of little feet. Exclusive **Caneel Bay**, for example, added a children's program after years of childlessness. Families are housed well away from cottages designed for couples, but many long-time Caneel Bay visitors still grouse about the policy.

Some children's programs operate all year; others are in session only during school holidays. Some resorts welcome children but don't want them in the dining room after 6:30 or 7pm. Do your homework and you'll have the time of your life.

KEEPING KIDS SAFE

The tropics hold few unique hazards for children. However, if your toddler is at the age when everything goes into its mouth, don't let it get hold of any plants, beads, seeds, sticks, or flowers. Even the beautiful oleander, a common landscaping shrub, can be poisonous when eaten. The manchineel tree, found on many tropical beaches, is so poisonous that rain dripping from its leaves can raise skin blisters.

As long as your child's shots are up to date, the Caribbean holds no special fears. Malaria and other tropical diseases are found only in the more remote areas of the most undeveloped island nations, not in the U.S. Caribbean. Thankfully, rabies is virtually nonexistent here, which is one reason why pet restrictions in the islands are so tight. Small dogs and cats in carry-on containers make wonderful travel mates on a trip to the U.S. islands (providing they are allowed at your hotel or resort) but you'll need papers and up-to-date shots.

Mosquito and sandfly bites are a nuisance, easily avoided through the use of bug repellents. Teach children not to touch coral, sea urchins, or pretty jellyfish. They can sting. Wasps, scorpions, and spiders may be seen in the West Indies, just as they are almost everywhere, but aren't worth worrying about unless your child is subject to anaphylactic reactions. In years of tropic travel we have rarely seen them and have never been stung.

The tropics' chief threat is its greatest blessing: the sun. In fact, a tropical tree with red, peeling bark is known by natives as the Tourist Tree. Bring a good supply of a strong waterproof or water resistant sun block as well as light, coverup clothing and a hat with a brim. If the child is old enough to wear sun glasses, bring them too.

A bad burn can occur even on cloudy days. In a white boat on bright sea on a clear day, a burn takes only minutes. Apply the sun block before leaving your lodgings, and re-apply it according to manufacturer directions, especially if you're in and out of the water. According to *Travel Holiday* magazine, a sun block with the SPF of 15 blocks 96 per cent of the sun's burning rays and a 30SPF blocks 98.5 per cent. While a 45 SPF blocks less than three percent more than a 15, it lasts about three times as long.

Seasoned island visitors bring light cotton pajamas with long sleeves and trousers for snorkeling. In clear, shallow water, you may not feel the sun's heat but it can give a bad burn even underwater. Bring a big umbrella to shade tender young skin from sun and rain. Socks help protect bare feet from sun when swimming, and they cushion the fit of rented snorkel fins. Adopt the siesta habit, staying out of the sun at mid-day.

Take beach shoes (jellies, reef runners) for the whole family to protect feet against sharp coral, stones, and broken glass on the beach. Most resort beaches are sandy and clean, but even some of the best beaches have rocky patches.

Drink lots of water, avoid sugary drinks, and make sure that babies who can't talk also get frequent drinks. In the Indies' cooling breezes, perspiration is blown away and children can become dehydrated before you realize it.

ADDITIONAL TIPS

- Don't board the airplane first even though people with children are invited to do so. Why confine restless kids any longer than necessary? Delta, for one, has stopped allowing parents with children to board first.
- Ask cabin attendants if any of the bathrooms have changing tables. Usually at least one does.
- Until the children are older, avoid islands that are reached by multiple transfers involving small airplanes, ferries, and other delays. For now, the big bird and direct flights are best. Remember that after your arrival you have to get to the hotel, often on bad roads and in torrid heat.
- In the Caribbean, you can't count on wheels as you do at home. Strollers and wheeled luggage are no help where you must negotiate stairs, deep sand, and unpaved roads. Even in the U.S. islands where the Americans with Disabilities Act applies, wheelchair/stroller access is usually poor or unavailable. Consider getting a backpack to carry a small child. You'll need your own child safety seat for the airplane(s) and rental cars. Few rental agencies have them.
- Disposable hand wipes are lifesavers, but they're quickly gone. Instead, seal wet wash cloths in zippered plastic bags and use them to clean up sticky hands and faces. Each time you can get to a bathroom, soap and rinse them for the next use.
- Disposable diapers are available in all but the smallest island stores. Pack extra zip-top plastic bags for sealing up nasty diapers until they can be disposed up properly.

- A 36-inch inflatable swimming pool packs in less space than a rain coat, yet it blows up to provide hours of splashy fun for a toddler. If your lodgings have no baby pool, take your own.
- Take plenty of medicated baby powder for heat rash and, if the baby is susceptible, a good salve for diaper rash.
- Don't forget a plastic pail and shovel for building sand castles. The pail can serve as a catch-all for carrying small toys.
- Don't bring home seashells unless you know them to be empty and dry. Even an old shell may contain a hermit crab. Sealed in your luggage, the smell is indescribable.

HOW TO HANDLE A JELLYFISH STING

For jellyfish stings, "Do not rub the wound," says Dr. Wayne J. Riley, director of the Travel Medicine Service at Baylor College of Medicine in Houston. Soak it in salt water, apply baking soda, and remove the animal's tentacles. For a man-o-war, use the same procedure but substitute vinegar for the baking soda. "In treating (these) wounds, do not use fresh water," says Dr. Riley. "The change in salt concentration will increase the toxin release."

Discomfort usually lasts only a few hours but if you have any reason to think a severe reaction is occurring, such as nausea or weakness, get professional help, urges Dr. Riley.

BEST RESORTS FOR CHILDREN

Resorts that are especially recommended for children include the **Hyatts** that have Camp Hyatt, **El Conquistador** or the **Westin Rio Mar** in Puerto Rico, The **Caribe Hilton** in San Juan, **Chenay Bay Beach Resort** on St. Croix, **Sapphire Beach Resort & Marina** on St. Thomas.

When you're choosing a resort, ask questions about the children's program. Is there supervised play in a variety of places, or are the kids just plunked down in front of a video screen to watch old animated movies? Is the children's program included in the price or does it cost extra? A program for two or three children at $30 or more a day adds substantially to your bottom line. Ask too about children's dining including hours and special menus.

THE PUERTO RICAN ADVANTAGE

In Puerto Rico, teenagers can learn Latin dances and conversational Spanish. Youngsters can learn to snorkel. Children of all ages can discover nature on their own level. Parents, grandparents, and children romp on beaches and in swimming pools. Children can stay happy in a supervised "camp" where they make crafts, play games, and hear stories. At most hotels, children under age 18 stay free in a room with two paying adults.

CARIBE HILTON, *Tel. (800) HILTONS, U.S. and Canada.* Camp Coco operates only during school holiday periods, when it is open every day 8am-4pm at a cost of $30 per child daily or $125 weekly. Included are lunch and two snacks. Ages 4-12 have a wide choice of play, contests, field trips, lessons and fun. One activity each day is for the entire family.

CONDADO PLAZA HOTEL & CASINO, *Tel. 800/468-8588,* has Camp Taino for children ages five to 12. The $25 fee includes lunch and camp fun from 10 a.m. to 4 p.m. The hotel also offers teenagers a video room, tennis courts, putting greens, and organized activities.

EL CONQUISTADOR RESORT & COUNTRY CLUB, *Tel. 800/468-5228* offers Camp Coqui for $38 per day including lunch. Age groups of three to nine and nine to 13 go on adventures to the resort's own Palomino Island, take nature hikes, learn crafts, and much more.

EL SAN JUAN HOTEL & CASINO, *Tel. 800/231-3320,* has a daily camp for ages five to 12 at a cost of $28 including lunch and gifts such as a disposable camera, tee shirt, and "sand dollars" for use in the game room.

HYATT RESORTS, *Tel. 800/233-1234* at Dorado Beach have bilingual, certified counselors who direct children's activities 9am to 4pm. The daily fee of $40 includes lunch and gifts such as a hat and, after the fourth visit, a Camp Hyatt backpack. Night camp is $28 per child.

WESTIN RIO MAR RESORT & COUNTRY CLUB, *Tel. 800/WESTIN-1,* has Camp Iguana where "kids are kings." The three-room camp center has an arts and crafts room, playroom, and a TV room that converts to a sleeping room for late night campers. For older children, the Westin offers sailing, tennis, and golf clinics for beginners through advanced. The price is $35 per day for 9am to 3pm including lunch and snacks. A half-day program from 9am to noon without lunch is $20.

WYNDHAM PALMAS DEL MAR RESORT, *Tel. 800/WYNDHAM,* provides a long list of children's groups, activities and discounts depending on the time of year. The Adventure Club plays daily 8:30am to 4:30pm with groupings for children ages four to 13. The rate of $95 weekly, $25 daily, and $15 per half day gets your child lunch, snacks, and a tee shirt.

11. ECOTOURISM & TRAVEL ALTERNATIVES

Environmental tourism is hot worldwide and the U.S. Caribbean has caught the fever for good reason. The islands have some of the world's most pristine beaches, the most unspoiled waters, the most virgin reefs, and ruins and rainforests that have yet to be fully explored. In few other regions of the earth can you find more a sense of ground-floor discovery and wise leaders want to keep it that way.

Most islands have climbed aboard the eco-tourism bandwagon early, and often with such zeal that old-timers are surprised. Where lone travelers could once hike into the bush and set up camp, or cruising boats could drop anchor in remote coves where dinner could be speared, all sorts of new laws, permits, and prohibitions apply. Welcome to the new, environmentally-sensitive Caribbean. See individual chapters for the names of hiking guides, dive operators, and nature tours.

ECOTOURISM

Agencies that can book your trip include:

BACKROADS, *801 Cedar Street, Berkeley CA 94710, Tel. 510/527-1555, Fax 527-1444; toll-free 800/GO-ACTIVE* is a group that organizes walking, bicycling, hiking, and multi-sport adventure tours in the Caribbean for a few weeks in November and December. Featured are unspoiled islands known for their scenic beauty.

ECANTOS TOURS, *Tel. 800/272-7241,* offers trips to Puerto Rico's Mona Island where only 100 visitors are permitted at a time. A camping permit must be obtained, and all food, water and camping gear brought with you. All waste must be packed out. If you want to camp Mona Island on your own, a permit must be obtained from the Puerto Rico Department of Natural resources, *Tel. 809/724-3724.* Camp fees are $4 nightly for adults and $2 for children.

TEXAS RIVER EXPEDITIONS, INC., *Box 583, Terlingua TX 79852, Tel. 800/839-7238 or 915/371-2633, Fax 915/371-2644; Website www.texasriver.com.* Ask about family eco-tours in U.S. Virgin Islands National Park. Specialties include 4-wheel drive, birding, sea kayaking, and photo workshops.

SPA VACATIONS

With the explosion of interest in spas, healthful living, weight loss, muscle building, and other lifestyle-enhancing vacations has come a mushrooming of spa choices in the Caribbean. Some focus on total pampering with massage and therapy; others specialize in a lifestyle change such as heart attack rehabilitation or weight loss; still others accent a skill such as muscle building or toning.

Your key to finding the right package is **Spa Finders**, *91 Fifth Avenue, New York NY 10003, Tel. 212/924-6800, Fax 924-7420, toll-free 800/ALL-SPAS.*

ECOTOUR SAILING

A 12-passenger luxury schooner that winters in the Caribbean, often with experts on board to conduct seminars on the environment is **Kathryn B.**, *Tel. 800/500-6077.* Rates are about $2,800 per person, double occupancy, per week. Itineraries vary each year.

12. FOOD & DRINK

Lucky the Caribbean traveler who gets into the neighborhoods to seek out small restaurants that are frequented by the islanders themselves. Foods here are made by cooks who learned island ways from their parents.

Stop at roadside stands, where sanitation standards are god-knows-what, to buy fresh fruit, homemade drinks such as mavi, an icy jelly nut, sizzling jerk fresh from the fire, fish tea, or goat water. An entirely new language is to be learned here for every island group.

A CARIBBEAN FOOD DICTIONARY

Love 'em or hate 'em, the key to discovering different cultures is to try their foods, the more traditional the better. Take every opportunity to try them in restaurants, where they have been prepared by expert hands, and stop in the outback at roadside stands where a local person can tell you how to eat or prepare strange fruits and vegetables.

Here are some words that will help you in your search:

Accra: a fritter known in Jamaica as **stamp and go**, in Puerto Rico as **bacalaito**, in the French islands as **acrat de morue**, and in the Dutch islands as **cala**. The batter is made from ground beans and a meat or fish, usually salt cod.

Annato: a seed used as flavoring and coloring in Latin dishes.

Asopao: a Puerto Rican soupy stew usually made with rice plus chicken, pork or fish.

Bacalao is the Spanish word for salt cod, which persists as an island favorite centuries after refrigeration made it unnecessary to smother fish in salt as a preservative. It's found on many menus under its English or Spanish name.

Bakes: in Trinidad, baking powder biscuits that are fried. They may be served in the U.S. islands as a starch course, usually with fish.

Bananas, which are known as figs on some islands, come in so many shapes, colors, and sizes in the Caribbean that it's fun to try them all. Don't confuse them with plantains, which never soften and sweeten. They are cooked as a starch.

Blaff is named for the sound made when live fish are thrown into a big pot of spiced boiling water.

Boterkoek are Dutch butter cookies.

Boucan: another word for barbecue and the source for the word buccaneer.

Breadfruit: literally a staff of life in some islands, it's a starchy fruit that shows up on almost every dinner plate fried, baked, or boiled. It has little taste of its own.

Calabaza: any of several varieties of squash, usually called pumpkin.

Calas are bean fritters.

Callaloo: the word refers to the green, which could be compared to spinach, and also to a soup made with the greens plus crabmeat. It spelled many different ways, sometimes with a k.

Capsicum: another name for peppers, which are found in huge variety and abundance, from sweet to fiery, in Caribbean kitchens.

Carambola: a very tart citrus often called star fruit because of its shape. It's sliced thinly and used as a garnish, usually in drinks.

Cashew apple: the part of the cashew that produces the nut, this apple-size red fruit may be stewed or made into jelly.

Cassareep is a flavoring ingredient made by reducing grated cassava root.

Cassava, also called manioc, yuca, or mandioca. More familiar to us as tapioca, this starchy root can be poisonous if eaten raw. It's said that many of the native Arawaks and Caribs committed suicide by eating it to avoid being taken and enslaved by the Spanish.

Chayote is a pear-like vegetable that has little taste but adds a nice crispness to a salad. It can also be cooked and buttered like squash. In French restaurants it's called christophene and may be served stuffed. In other islands it's called chocho.

Cherimoya is a sweet, juicy fruit.

Cocido: stew in Spanish speaking areas.

Coconut is a basic staple, served in countless main dishes, drinks, and desserts. If you buy from a roadside stand, let the seller remove the husk and either crack it for eating or hole it for drinking. Coconut water is cool and refreshing but if the nut is too green its water can cause diarrhea in some people. Cold "jelly" nuts are sold along roadsides.

Conch: pronounced conk. Picture the seashell that sounds like the sea when you hold it to your ear. The delicate white meat from this shell is served in fritters, chowder, or "cracked," which means pounded, dipped in cracker crumbs, and fried. In conch salad, it's served raw and marinated in lime juice. It can be compared to breast of chicken. In French restaurants it may be called lambi.

Coo-coo: a buttery cornbread or polenta studded with okra.

Crapaud: a large frog that tastes like chicken.

Dolphin does not refer to Flipper, the bottle-nose dolphin, but to a meaty, iridescent fish known in the Pacific as mahi-mahi and in the Spanish Caribbean as dorado.

Djon djon: small Haitian mushrooms.

Duckanoo, spelled many ways, is a steamed cornmeal pudding served as a sweet.

Dumb Bread: a dense, crusty, non-yeast bread popular in the Virgin Islands. It derives its name from Dum, which refers to an Indian way of baking bread.

Dumplings are a common starch accompaniment for a Caribbean meal. They can be made with flour or cornmeal, with or without leavening, and are cooked in boiling water, broth, or stew. In Jamaica, they're also called **fufu** or **spinners**.

Escabeche: Fish and sometimes poultry that is cooked, then pickled. In Jamaica it's called **escovitch**. Not to be confused with seviche, which is marinated raw fish.

Festival is a fritter made with flour and cornmeal, deep fried, and sold to go with fried fish. It is flavored with vanilla and allspice.

Frio-frio: means cold-cold and refers to a snow cone, a paper cone filled with crushed ice and dosed with a fruit-flavored syrup.

Fungi, also spelled **funchi** or **fungee**, is a creamy cornmeal pudding usually served as a starch course..

Genep, spelled many ways but pronounced gah-NIP, is a common dooryard fruit rarely served in restaurants or sold at road stands, but you may be offered some. It has a large seed and a sweet, gluey flesh. Pop it into your mouth and smoosh it around for a while, then spit out the seed.

Goat is as familiar to island tables as lamb is to North American menus. It looks and tastes much the same too. It may be called mutton or goat mutton. In Spanish islands it is called **cabrito**. **Goat Water** is actually a hearty soup.

Grizzadas are coconut tarts, sold at almost every market and served at every church bazaar.

Groundnuts is the old African name for peanuts, which are used here in main dish recipes.

Guava is a tartly astringent fruit, lumpy in appearance and loaded with Vitamin C. It appears in ice cream, tarts, and other sweets but especially in firm, sweet guava jelly that is served with cheese and crackers as a dessert. Guavaberry is a cranberry-size red or yellow fruit that grows on trees and is used to flavor liqueurs.

Jack fruit: also called **jaca** or **jaquier**, it looks like a huge breadfruit and has a terrible smell. Its flesh, however, is sweet and its seeds, like breadfruit seeds, can be roasted like chesnuts.

Johnny cake: a cornbread in the United States, Johnny cake in the islands is made with white flour and may be baked or deep fried. Its name derives from "journey" cake because it's a good travel staple.

Kachoiri is a fritter made with garbanzo flour and green onions.

Land crab: anyone who has encountered one of these sci-fi nightmares on a dark beach immediately discards any romantic notions about making love on moonlit sands. The idea of eating these scavengers is even more repulsive, but in skilled hands they're a succulent sensation. The crabs are captured and put on a diet of clean corn for several days until they lose their gamey taste. Only then are they served in the shell, in chowders, and in other traditional crab recipes.

Langouste: also called **langosta** or **lobster**, the spiny lobster provides a chunk of sweet, rich meat in its tail, which is the only part that is eaten.

Loquat: also called Japanese plum in the United States, it's a small, sweet fruit the size of an apricot.

Mamey apple: a colorful favorite on fruit plates, this juicy red fruit is similar to mango.

Mango: a peachy, juicy, very sweet fruit that comes in many shapes, colors, and sizes. Press it with the thumb. When it yields gently, it's ready to peel and eat. Some people are allergic to the skin, so peel it with caution.

Mofongo: a Puerto Rican favorite made from boiled, mashed plantains. They have little taste of their own and are seasoned to the chef's whim.

Old sour: the juice of sour orange trees (you haven't tasted sour until you've tried wild oranges) is salted and allowed to age. It's a popular sauce, shaken over foods much as you'd use vinegar.

Papaya is a sweet, melon-like fruit ranging from deep orange to delicate yellow, often served for breakfast. Papaya, also called **pawpaw**, **lachosa**, or **fruta bomba**, can be peeled, boiled, buttered, and served as a vegetable when it is unripe.

Pasteles: also called **ayucas**, it's a mixture of meat and some starch such as cornmeal plus raisins, almonds, and other flavorings and then steamed in a plantain leaf.

Patty: pronounced pahtty in Jamaica, and called **pastelitis, pastelillos**, or **pastechi**, these are meat pies, perfect for lunch on the go. **Rotis** are somewhat the same. Think of a Cornish pasty, an inexpensive and filling dish.

Peas: could refer to any number of beans, usually dried, such as kidney beans, habichuelas (red kidney beans), gandules (also called pigeon peas, goongoo, or gunga peas) or frijoles negros (black beans). Some form of peas/beans and rice is a staple dish in most islands. When referring to green peas, islanders usually say English peas.

Pepper Pot or pepperpot is one dish in Trinidad and another in Jamaica because of the different seasonings favored. In the U.S. islands it is usually a spicy, thick soup.

Picadillo is a Cuban classic that is a favorite in Miami and Key West as well as in Cuba itself. Made with ground beef, it's somewhat like sloppy joe with raisins and sliced, stuffed olives.

Pilau is also called **pilaf** or **pelau**, a rice dish that often includes meat, poultry, or fish. It may also be just rice and peas.

Plaintains look like bananas, but don't try to eat them raw. They're cooked as a starch or are thinly sliced, fried in oil, salted, and served as a snack. Boiled in a stew, they have only the faintest banana taste and tend to take on the flavor of whatever they are cooked with.

Rotis are dough wrapped around a mixture of meat and potatoes, often spiced with curry.

Rundown is pickled or salt fish cooked with coconut milk, usually served with boiled bananas.

Sanchoco is a Spanish stew, made differently in each stewpot but basically a blend of meat and vegetables.

Sapodilla have a short season, so be sure to try them if you have a chance. Furry green or brown skin peels away to reveal a sweet pulp that tastes like a very juicy pear. Also called **naseberry**.

Scotch bonnet is one of the hottest peppers under the sun.

Sea urchin: the spiny menace that you try to avoid when swimming or diving produces delicious, caviar-like eggs. Also called **sea eggs** or, in the French islands, **oursin**.

Shaddock: also called **pomelo**, is a pungent, grapefruit-like fruit named for the Captain Shaddock who first brought seeds to the islands from Polynesia.

Sofrito: a sauce that is central to many Latin dishes. It's made with onions, garlics, spices, tomatoes, peppers, and a little ham.

Sopito: a rich chowder made with fish and coconut milk.

Soursop: a horrible looking fruit with a heavenly taste somewhat like kiwi.

Stamp and go refers to codfish fritters, a Jamaican favorite.

Star apple has a short season and is tricky to harvest, so count yourself lucky if you get a chance to try one. Under its purple flesh is a jelly-like sweetness.

Sweet potato or **boniato** comes in many colors and may not look at all like the familiar sweet potato eaten in North America. One type of sweet potato is called **tannia**.

Taro is also called **dasheen**, **tannia**, **malanga**, or **elephant's ear**. It looks like a baking potato, has a bland taste, and is used as a starch or filler.

Taro leaves are also called callaloo or elephant's ears. Fritters made from taro leaves and split-pea flour are known as **sahina**.

Ugli fruit: sometimes seen now in North American supermarkets, this cross-bred fruit was developed in Jamaica by joining orange, grapefruit, and tangerine. It's ugly to look at, sweet and citrusy to eat. Jamaicans, whose language borrows from Cockney and Irish, pronounce it *whoogly*.

Yam: different botanically from what we call the sweet potato, this enormous tuber has a furry skin and starchy meat that may be white, orange, or red.

DRINKS OF THE CARIBBEAN

A wise mother once cautioned her children never to drink anything with an umbrella in it. Caribbean drinks tend to be sickly sweet and fruity, laced with rum, and capable of delivering a delayed knockout that catches newcomers unaware. At one all-inclusive resort where all drinks are on the house, we asked how they could afford to serve unlimited bar drinks. "It only takes one day," chuckled the manager. "Drinking drops off dramatically after that. If fact, some guests never drink again."

Rum punch, called *planteur* in the French islands, is every bartender's pride, and each has his or her own secret recipe. Most are largely a blend of sugary fruit juices. The more subtle, untouristy punches combine light and dark rum with a little lime juice and ice.

Every islander has a favorite rum, often tied in with loyalty to a local distillery or bottling plant, and they love it when tourists ask for their recommendations. Reputable bottlers put the country of origin on their labels, so you'll soon be able to make a wise choice. **Cruzan** comes from St. Croix, **Westerhall** from Grenada, **Gosling's** from Bermuda, **Bacardi** mostly from Puerto Rico. **Pusser's Rum**, sold in its own bar in Tortola, was the official rum of the Royal Navy. Although some of the cheaper, no-

RUM PUNCH RECIPE

The time-honored recipe for the perfect punch is easy to remember: One of sour, Two of sweet, Three of strong, Four of weak.

The sour can be lemon or lime juice, the sweet is simple syrup (two cups sugar boiled with one cup water, then cooled), the strong is the rum, and the weak is water or fruit juice. Measured by the shot, cupful, or hogshead, the proportions are the same: one part lemon or lime, two parts simple syrup, three parts rum and four parts water or fruit juice. Depending on the type of rum and juices you choose, you can create an exotic new punch with each try. Traditionally, it's served with a few specks of grated nutmeg.

name rums taste like kerosene, it's possible to get a superb rum for less than the cost of the Coke you mix it with.

Light rums are recommended for use in drinks where gin or vodka might be used, such as martinis. Medium dark rums are the color of bourbon or scotch and are good in almost any drink. Myers dark rum is in a class by itself' – inky, acrid, and the finishing touch in most good rum punches.

Caribbean Drinks

Carib beer comes from St. Kitts and Trinidad

CSR is a clear, sugar cane-based liquor from St. Kitts and Nevis. Often mistaken for rum, it is really more like vodka with a faint hint of white rum. It's usually mixed with a grapefruit-flavored Caribbean soft drink called Ting.

Guavaberries are harvested in the islands and made into a liqueur best known in St. Maarten.

Mauby or Mavi: made from tree bark, spices, and sugar, this drink is non-alcoholic or may be lightly fermented. It's sold along Puerto Rican roadsides.

Mistress Bliden: a specialty of Little Dix Bay on Virgin Gorda and served only during winter holidays, this potent liqueur is made from prickly pear cactus.

Purple Rain is a blend of vodka, blue Curacao, and fruit juices.

Shrob: more likely to be called shrub in English islands, this is a French island liqueur made from rum and bitter oranges.

Coffees of the Caribbean

The world's new love affair with coffee brings new awareness of the variety, quality, and subtle shadings of the coffees to be tasted in the Caribbean. The best known Caribbean coffee is Jamaica's Blue Mountain coffee but even more rare is the small harvest of Puerto Rican coffee. It is so cherished that it is sent to the Vatican.

Legend says that the first coffee plants, which are native to Yemen and had been introduced into Europe, were sent to Martinique by France's Louis XV in 1723. Of the three plants, two died and the survivor ended up in Jamaica. Whatever the true story, Jamaica's governor brought seedlings in from Martinique in 1728 and encouraged coffee planting as an alternative to sugar, on which the island economy was totally dependent. It takes at least five years to get the first cash crop from trees that produce the intensely fragrant arabica bean, which has not only a compelling flavor but only a third the caffeine of the more common *robusta* coffee harvested in South America. Then the beans must be hand picked one at a time, like delicate cherries.

13. THE U.S. CARIBBEAN'S BEST PLACES TO STAY

These are my picks for the best places to stay in the U.S. Caribbean. Rates are for a double room in high season. Check with individual chapters for further information about these hotels in their island context.

PUERTO RICO

RITZ-CARLTON SAN JUAN HOTEL AND CASINO, *6961 State Road 187, Isla Verde, Carolina PR 00979. Tel. 800/241-3333 or locally (787) 253-1700, Fax 253-0700. Rates at this 419-room, 45-suite hotel start at $505; one-bedroom suites start at $1045. The hotel also has a club floor with rooms and suites. It's five minutes from the international airport and 15 minutes from Old San Juan. Through the hotel, get airport transfers for $8 each way.*

A bustling business hotel with a ballroom, meeting rooms and a business center, the Ritz is also ideal for the leisure traveler who wants unabashed luxury in rooms lavished with works by local artists. Each guest room has a stocked honor bar, personal safe, marble bath with hair dryer, scale, and telephone, individual heat and air conditioning control, plush terry robes, three telephoneswith dual lines and data port, and AM/FM radio with digital clock/alarm. Enjoy the 450-foot beach, a full-service spa, and a city location handy to the airport, financial district, Old San Juan, and shopping at Plaza Las Americas. Nightlife and dining at Condado are ten minutes away. Dine in the Vineyard Room, the hotel's signature restaurant serving California and continental cuisine or in more informal restaurants indoors and out. Room service answers 24 hours a day.

Swim in the supersize, 7,200-square foot pool, soak in the whirlpools, play tennis on the hotel's courts, and gamble late and luxuriously in the 17,000 square foot Monte Carlo by the Sea Casino. The hotel's 12,000 square foot spa is created by the Sonoma Mission Inn and Spa, featuring life-enhancing Sonomotherapy treatments. Hotel guests have golf privileges at nearby courses. The Fitness Center offers aerobics, exercise equipment and free weights. Three fishing clubs are nearby; horse racing is 20 minutes away. View are of the sea or of El Yunque rainforest.

On the Club floor with its private lounge and personal concierge staff, guests get complimentary continental breakfast, light lunch, afternoon tea, hors e'oeucres, and a variety of beverages throughout the day and evening. New in 1998, the hotel is surely destinated for five-star status with its twice daily maid service, 24-hour room service and valet parking, child care, and much more.

WESTIN RIO MAR BEACH RESORT & COUNTRY CLUB, *6000 Rio Mar Boulevard, Rio Grande PR 00745. Tel. 787/888-6200; U.S. and Canada 800/4-RIO-MAR OR 800/WESTIN-1. Rates start at this 600-room start at $325 double for a luxury room in winter. Suites are $550 to $2500. The hotel is 19 miles (one hour in most traffic conditions) east of Luis Munoz Marin International Airport, or about $65 by cab. Take Route 3 east to Rio Grande, then left on PR 968.*

This exclusive golf resort is built around an earlier country club development anchored by a Fazio- designed golf course. A Greg Norman-designed, 7,004-yard course was added in 1997. Sprawling across 481 acres framed by miles of beach on one side and El Yunque National Forest on the other, the property has largely been left au naturel with manicured lawns surrounded by swampy lagoons and tangled woodlands bangled with birdlife. Rooms are more cozy than cavernous, filled with comfortable furnishings in Mediterranean moods and colors accented with classic and modern pieces. Balconies look out over the beach or gardens. Even the tiniest balconies have a table and two chairs, just perfect for a breakfast serenaded by coquis.

Rooms have key-lock safe, hair dryer, lighted magnifying mirror, remote control cable television, clock radio, two telephones with voice mail, 24-hour room service, mini-bar with refrigerator, triple sheeting, and other appointments of an outstanding, deluxe hotel.

Dine in two signature restaurants, Palio for gourmet northern Italian and the Club Grille & Chop House for steaks overlooking the golf course. Cafe Carnaval and La Estancia feature Puerto Rican foods and Marbella has menu service and buffet. There's also a poolside restaurant with light meals and frosty drinks, and appetizers and drinks at the Players Bay in the casino. For tapas before dinner or cigars and brandy after, visit Bolero with its sensuous basketweave leather furniture. The Lobby Bar is the resort's nerve center, serving continental breakfast each morning, drinks all day, and entertainment nightly.

The casino opens at noon and buzzes until 2am on week nights, 4am on Friday and Saturday. Le Spa is one of the island's most sophisticated, offering a long menu of services and products. Workout facilities feature the latest machines; a daily activities schedule provides group aerobics as well as games and outings.

Put the children into the Kid's Club; let the teens play the video room; shop the 6,000 square feet of retail space; make an appointment in the beauty salon; use the guest laundry if you like. Car rental, a complete tour desk, and savvy concierge services are all in the front lobby.

All the features of a fine resort are here, but it's staff attitude that provides the final flourish in a winning combination of Puerto Rican warmth and Yanqui can-do.

PALMAS DEL MAR, *Kilometer 84.6 on Road #3, Route 906, Humacao; mailing address: Box 2020, Humacoa, Puerto Rico 00792-2020. Tel. 787/852-6000 or U.S. 800/725-6273. A 45-minute drive from the San Juan airport, the resort has 250 rooms and suites. Rates start at $138 nightly for a double room in low season and range to $710 nightly for a three-bedroom villa in high season. Ask about packages. Included in the resort are the Candelero Hotel and Palmas Inn, which are reserved through the telephone numbers above and the Wyndham Hotel & Villas Tel. 787/852-6000 or 800/468-3331.*

Developed in the 1960s by Charles Fraser, known for his ecologically-sensitive developments, the resort is a complete city with branch banks, churches, school, shops, casino, beauty services, restaurants, lounges, and permanent residents living in homes costing $225,000 to $1 million. Once registered, you can charge everything in "town" to your account.

Your domain includes a Gary Player-designed, 18-hole golf course said to have more scenic holes than any other course in the world, and a tennis center managed by Peter Burwash International. Snorkel right off the beach; take a horse from the Equestrian Center and cantor off through the surf. Scuba dive with the resort's own dive masters, the only on-site dive operation on the island.

Choose a spacious hotel room with a private balcony or a villa to house the entire family. Furnishings are tropical and bright; accessories are drawn from Puerto Rican folk art. The Adventure Club gives children, ages 3 to 13, the time of their lives while adults sun, read, or play golf or tennis. Every day finds a new list of planned activities.

Dine in your choice of a dozen restaurants. Use the workout facilities, scuba, go deep-sea fishing, sail, swim in pools galore, bicycle, and enjoy the camaraderie or keep to yourself. The grounds, graced with 3,000 coconut palms, cover 2,750 acres. If you like a big resort with all the bells and whistles and enough to do for weeks without having to traipse all over the island, this is the place.

U.S. VIRGIN ISLANDS

St. Thomas

RITZ-CARLTON, *699 Great Bay, St. Thomas 00802. Tel. 340/241-3333, Fax 340/775-4444; toll-free 800/241-3333. U.S. and Canada 800/241-3333. High season rates start at $400 per room. Ask about packages. The 148-room, four-suite hotel is 30 minutes from the airport or about $10 per person by taxi. Airport transfer by limousine can be arranged by the hotel, which is found on the island's eastern tip.*

Surely the *ne plus ultra* of St. Thomas resorts and the first Ritz-Carlton in the Caribbean, this one has all the five-star features of other Ritz-Carltons around the globe. From the moment you're welcomed at the portico and ushered across gleaming marble floors to the check-in desk, the coddling from perkily-uniformed staff is complete. Built in the fashion of a grand palazzo, the property rims a fine beach and overlooks a brimming pool with an "infinity" edge that makes you think you're swimming on the horizon.

The main building houses some guest rooms, the lobby, meeting rooms, and The Cafe for fine dining. Out-buildings cluster around a salt pond nature preserve filled with waterfowl. Even from the farthest building, it's only a brief walk to the main building through meticulously groomed grounds and gardens. If you prefer to ride, a driver is only a phone call away. If you'd rather dine in your room, order room service around the clock. It's brought in wicker hampers and set up with starched linens, fresh flowers, shining silver, and Villeroy and Boch tableware.

Everything about the hotel spells quality, from upscale amenities to the waffle weave robes and slippers provided for guest use. Spacious rooms are done in bold royal blue and gold, accented with plaids and colorful prints on the walls. Rooms have hair dryer, iron, mini-bar with refrigerator, telephones in the bath, at bedside, and on the desk, and a private balcony or terrace. Some are roofed and others have a lattice covering, so specify sun or shade when you book the room.

Plan your days around swimming, the beach, sailing excursions aboard the resort's own catamaran, or the tennis courts. The fitness center offers cardio-vascular and advanced strength equipment, private trainers, and aerobics classes. Scuba, deep sea fishing, golf, picnic sails, and in-room massage can be arranged. The hotel has its own beauty salon, and shops selling designer clothing and accessories. We didn't see neckties, and jackets are not required, but this resort calls for your very best resort wear.

St. John

HARMONY RESORT *at Maho Bay, mailing address 17 East 73rd Street, New York NY 10021. Tel. 800/392-9004 or 212/472-9453, Fax 861-6210. Locally, tel. (340) 693-5855. Doubles are $95-$150 nightly plus $15 each additional person. A shuttle from the ferry costs about $5 per person.*

This is the place to rough it next to nature, without air conditioning, room service, or any other luxuries. In 1997 this resort was chosen the World's Most Environmentally Friendly Hotel by 18,000 travel agents. In second place was a hotel in Bali; St. John's Caneel Bay got the bronze. A step up from the same management's Maho Bay Campground, these tent-cottages are made from recycled materials and are sparsely but adequately furnished. Solar panels provide energy to heat bath water and operate the microwave. The design scoops in any trade winds, but on a calm day we wished for some high-voltage air conditioning. Furnished are kitchen gear and all linens. Your camp will have its own bathroom and deck. Use the same transportation, restaurant, cultural events and water sports as Maho Bay Campground.

St. Croix

HOTEL CARAVELLE, *44a Queen Cross Street, Christiansted, 00820. Tel. 800/524-0410. Rates at this AAA Three-Diamond Hotel are from $110. It's in the heart of downtown on the water, a $10 ride from the airport for one or two persons.*

A European-style boutique hotel has been transplanted in the tropics, blending the sunny airiness of a Cruzan resort with modern amenities. It has been generations since the Virgin Islands were Danish, but Danes continue to come to this user-friendly hotel. Rooms, many of them overlooking the harbor, are air conditioned and have mini-refrigerator and cable television. There's a freshwater pool, gift shop, and free parking– a plus if you want to spend a lot of time in parking-deprived Christiansted. The staff love innkeeping, and it shows. This hotel has one of the highest rate of repeat guests in the islands. The restaurant, Wahoo Willy's, is a St. Croix favorite for locals and visitors alike. Ask about dive packages. In summer, a Family Degree package includes an environmental study program.

BRITISH VIRGIN ISLANDS

BITTER END YACHT CLUB & RESORT, *Box 46, Virgin Gorda. Tel. 284/494-2746, U.S. 312/944-5855 or 800/872-2392. Rates start at $450 including all meals. Airport transfers, which are included, involve a taxi ride then a 10-minute boat ride.*

Many of the resorts in the Caribbean are as yachty as they are landlubberly, but this one is especially salty because you can sleep on a boat or in one of the rooms for about the same price. You'll still get maid service, meals in the Yacht Club and, if you want to anchor off for a night, provisions to tide you over. Sea and sails are part of the scene everywhere, whether you're overlooking them from your hilltop villa, trading tall tales with sailors in the bar, or actually sailing one of the big fleet of Sunfish, Lasers, JY15s, Rhodes 19s and J-24s. Introduction to Sailing is a popular course for resort guests.

Zone out on your private veranda overlooking the verdant grounds, or plug into a carnival of good times: island excursions to The Baths and Anegada, snorkeling in reef-sheltered coves, swimming at the pool or one of the resort's three beaches, or joining a group to study marine science. Killbrides Underwater Tours is based at the Club and can do a complete dive package from beginner to advanced, Ginger Island to the wreck of the R*hone.* Dine in the Clubhouse Steak and Seafood Grille or the English Carvery, then dance under the stars at Almond Walk. Not all units here are air conditioned, so specify AC if it's important to you. Provision at The Emporium, which has staples as well as baked goods and takeout dishes.

LITTLE DIX BAY, *P.O. Box 70, Virgin Gorda, British Virgin Islands. U.S. mailing address, P.O. Box 720, Cruz Bay, St. John, VI 00831. Tel. 284/495-5555, Fax 495-5661, U.S. and Canada 800/928-3000. Rates in the 102 units start at $450 double in season. For $95 daily you can add three meals daily; add $75 for breakfast and lunch. Children's meal plans for ages five to twelve are $47.50 and $37.50. Children aged four and under eat free. Escorted transfers from Tortola International Airport are $50 adults, $25 children.*

Lying serenely behind a barrier reef, Little Dix Bay has a half-mile crescent of beach surrounded by 500 acres of forest, seagrape, tamarind, and palms. Founded in 1964 by Laurance Rockefeller, it is now a grand Rosewood resort far different from the somewhat shabby resort that met us on our first visit 20 years ago. With three employees for every guest, it assures a level of pampering that's impressive even in the service-savvy Caribbean.

From the moment you are met at the airport or ferry dock, you're in a world of seabreeze, sun, and luxury. Airy, spacious rooms are furnished with wicker and bamboo, soft pastels and brightly contrasting tropic bouquets. Most rooms are air conditioned but not all are, so specify air if you want it. All have telephones, balconies or terraces. Hike nearby **Gorda National Park** or the resort's own nature trails. Walking sticks are provided in each room, and they come in handy on Cow Hill, the Savannah Trail, or the Pond Bay Trail.

Sightsee by boat or Jeep, play tennis, or enjoy a full menu of watersports. The resort has its own 120-slip marina where boats are waiting to take you sailing, deep sea fishing, or sunset cruising. Ferries run regularly to a sister resort, Caneel Bay on St. John, where you can eat if you're on the Little Dix meal plan. Dining here is in the Pavilion, in the Sugar Mill with its tropical bistro look and wood oven-baked pizzas, or the nautically themed Beach Grill featuring seafood and sandwiches. After dinner, dance to live music on the Pavilion Terrace and walk home along paths lit by tiki torches and scented with frangipani. There's a children's program in season.

BEST CRUISES

The two cruises below deserve to be placed in this chapter, since this is the Caribbean and the best places include these magnificent vessels! Rates are about $500 per person per day, but many special events, discounts, and promotions mean that you can usually pay less.

STAR CLIPPER, *4101 Salzedo Avenue, Coral Gables FL 33146, Tel. 305/442-1611, Fax 305/443-0666; toll-free 800/422-0551.*

"The noblest of all sailing vessels...these were our Gothic cathedrals," wrote historian Samuel Eliot Morison in describing the great clipper ships that once danced around the globe at speeds never before seen at sea. It was thought that their kind would never be seen again. Now clipper ships have entered a luxurious new era with two four-masted barkentines, *Star Clipper* and *Star Flyer.* Classic clippers in the tradition of the majestic clippers of old, the ships are designed from the keel up to house pampered passengers in enormous hulls once destined to hold cargoes of tea and crates of Chinese porcelain.

World trade was transformed with the introduction of spritely, seakindly clipper ships. Their names made history: *Cutty Sark, Flying Cloud, Sea Witch*. Then suddenly, it was over. In 1869, the Suez Canal opened. Steamships replaced sail. A railroad crossed the United States. The splendor of sail was silenced. Until now.

The two new clippers bring all the romance of sail into a twentieth century cruise scene where haute cuisine, air conditioning, spacious cabins, and private baths are expected by even the saltiest of sailors. These ships have it all. Don't confuse them with the many old, wooden windjammers that offer no-frills cabins and shared baths. Swedish yachtsman Mikael Krafft has built authentic, all new clipper ships in a gamble that affluent travelers will pay "love boat" prices to live in luxury while tacking, heeling, luffing, and furling.

Don't worry about jargon. You don't have to know a spanker from a mizzen staysail to bask in all the breezy good fun of a Star Clipper cruise. However, the more you know about sailing, the more you'll be surprised and pleased. All the traditional touches abound: wooden belaying pins, bronze winches, teak decks, miles of brightwork, shrouds surrounded by baggywrinkle, and neat coils of line. The ships also sport high-tech touches: roller furling, self-tailing winches, sparkling white sails in tough new synthetic sailcloths, satellite navigation, and a television in every cabin. Star Clipper has a modest diesel engine, but make no mistake. This sister sails.

Itineraries vary with each trip, but generally sail from St. Thomas to Montserrat through the U.S. and British Virgin Islands, Anguilla, St. Maarten, Saba, St. Barts, Statia, St. Kitts, Antigua, Nevis and Iles Des Saintes. Another itinerary sails between Tobago and Dominica, calling at Martinique, St. Lucia, St. Vincent and the Grenadines, and Barbados. In summer, at least one of the clippers sails a Mediterranean route. Passengers can also sail the transatlantic positioning cruise.

An international staff serves an international passenger list. Half the 200-odd guests aboard a typical clipper cruise are from Europe; many others are yachtsmen; a few are landlubbers in search of an offbeat vacation. Like cruise ships, *Star Clipper* and *Star Flyer* have a couple of swimming pools and plenty of deck chairs. Like charter boats, they carry a full watersports inventory of board sailers, SCUBA and snorkel gear, and inflatable runabouts. Sports operations are directed by professional, multilingual staff. Unlike the ocean-going leviathans, the clippers are able to nose into shallow bays and tie up at smaller docks.

There's a cozy library with fireplace, but that's about the end of the entertainment menu. Passengers are invited to heave halyards, spin the big mahogany wheel, or check charts if they like. There is a versatile singer-instrumentalist aboard to play for nightly Happy Hour, and an Amateur Night in which talented crew members and willing passengers put on a show. There's even gambling aboard, if you don't mind betting on crab races. This old pirate ship tradition has been revived aboard the clippers. Aside from that, nightlife consists of stargazing on deck before retiring to a bunk that jostles gently with the seas, heeled to port or starboard as the winds decree.

WINDSTAR CRUISES, *300 Elliott Avenue West, Seattle WA 98119. Tel. 206/281-3535. Book through your travel agent. Week-long Caribbean cruises start at about $2,000 per person per week including port charges.*

No cruising grounds in the world can compete with the Caribbean's clear waters, faithful trade winds, and a United Nations of islands only a few hours sail from each other. Aboard a Windstar ship, passengers have the best of all worlds: a ship that really sails, cabins as plush as a small hotel room, a different island each morning, and knockout cuisine that's included in one price. A Holland America Line company, Windstar is a slick, savvy operation that offers the best airfares, shore tours, entertainers, and special events thanks to its international network of hospitality professionals.

You'll join your ship in Barbados or St. Thomas depending on the itinerary. Ports of call include the Tobago Cays, Bequia, Barbados, Martinique, Grenada, St. Barts, Iles des Saintes, St. John in the U.S. Virgin Islands, and Tortola, Jost Van Dyke, and Virgin Gorda in the British Virgin Islands. Aruba, Curacao, and Bonaire are included in a 15-day Panama Canal itinerary.

A typical cabin has a queen-size bed that can be converted to two twins, a full-length hanging locker, big portholes, twin vanities, and a private bathroom with shower. Your cabin attendant makes the bed, tidies up, and fills your ice bucket while you're at breakfast. While you're a dinner, your attendant leaves fresh towels, turns down the bed and puts a treat on your pillow. Most activities and watersports, endless meals including beach barbecues, and entertainment are included. The only extras are shore excursions and drinks. These ships cruise the world, sailing the Caribbean only in winter. Plan your cruise as far in advance as possible, both to get the week you want and to take advantage of early booking discounts.

14. PUERTO RICO

Puerto Rico - America's "Shining Star of the Caribbean" - lies between St. Thomas and the Dominican Republic, its north shore on the Atlantic Ocean and its south on the Caribbean Sea. The island is 110 miles long and 35 miles wide. Among its many treasures is El Yunque, the only tropical rainforest in the eastern United States. Only 3 1/2 jet hours from New York and two from Miami, Puerto Rico offers all the spicy Latin flavor of a foreign country, yet you're still at home where U.S. dollars and postage stamps are in use.

Christopher Columbus carried the Spanish flag to island after island but eventually Spain lost most of her Caribbean holdings to the English, French, Dutch, and Danes. Puerto Rico is the only Caribbean island under the U.S. flag where you can still capture the Latino legacy left by the original Conquistadores. For adventurous vacationers, it means a chance to taste mofongo, mavi, juicy tropical fruits, dizzying rum drinks, and lush seafood harvests fresh from the sea. Yet for those who like a touch of home, it also means McDonald's, Pizza Hut, Kentucky Fried Chicken, Sears, Radio Shack, Ma Bell coin telephones that take only a dime, and driving on the right side of the road.

Let's start with the beaches because they rim the island like a necklace of sugar cookies - sandy, sweet, fragrant and warm. The beach resort areas nearest **San Juan** include **Condado**, **Miramar**, **Ocean Park**, and **Isla Verde**. Drive the coast roads around the big island, stopping at every pretty beach you see. For a real getaway, take a ferry to the islands of **Culebra** or **Vieques**, which lie east of Puerto Rico.

Puerto Rico's spine of mountains is a magnet for hikers and nature lovers. It is here in lofty coffee plantations that a special harvest is made each year of rare coffees to be presented to the Vatican. Plan at least three days if you want to explore inland Puerto Rico along the mountain road. You'll probably get lost a few times, meet a lot of friendly natives, stop at a pineapple stand, and eat wonderful food at rundown shacks.

No matter when you go, there's likely to be a fiesta somewhere on the island. It may be a religious or folk festival, a tournament in any sport from auto racing to baseball, or a seasonal harvest celebration. Other festivals such as the Casals Festival each June and the Puerto Rico Heineken Jazz Fest at the end of May, are cultural events that attract world class artists and musicians. Most of the smaller towns are a fiesta in themselves on Friday nights when people dress up and take to the streets. The best blowout in each town is the feast day of its patron saint, when parties go on for a week or more. The largest are those in San Juan (June 23-24), Loiza (June 25), and Ponce (December 6-15).

Waves of settlers arrived on Puerto Rico starting around 3,000 B.C. including Arawaks, followed by the Tainos, whose culture was one of the most advanced in the Americas. Within 50 years of Columbus' first call here in 1493, they had almost disappeared, victims of enslavement and disease.

A Spanish stronghold almost from the beginning of Spanish exploration in the Americas, San Juan was fortified in the early 1500s by **Juan Ponce de León**, who is buried in the San Juan Cathedral. By the 1630s it was a walled city sprawled under the imposing **El Morro**, a 200-acre fort that repelled the most savage English attacks. Only in 1598 was it taken by the English, and then only briefly. Its stones seemingly indestructible through the ages, it's still one of the Caribbean's most majestic forts.

The Spanish quest for gold had some success in Puerto Rico, with meager findings along the rivers, but soon the cash crop became sugar cane harvested on fields tended by slaves brought in from Africa. Their language and lore, and to some extent the color of their skin, melted seamlessly into local culture.

When the world sugar market collapsed, Puerto Rico slumbered through the ages, eking out an income from exporting coffee and tobacco. Running for office in 1929, Luis Muñoz Marin described it as a "land of beggars and millionaires." In 1940, per capita income was only $120. Then came the end of World War II, the building of a Hilton hotel, and the island was transformed forever. The natural hospitality of the people, sunny winters, clear waters, and a continuing building boom in hotels has turned Puerto Rico into a world-class player in leisure and business travel.

When you first hear the ear-piercing cry of the coqui tree frog, which is found only on Puerto Rico, it's a shock. Then this nightly chorus gets into your blood until it's a lullaby. Soon, you can't imagine nights without the coqui's chirp echoing through flower-scented breezes. *"Soy tan puertoriqueño como el coqui"* means "I'm as Puerto Rican as a coqui." The little fellow is pictured everywhere as a symbol of the island.

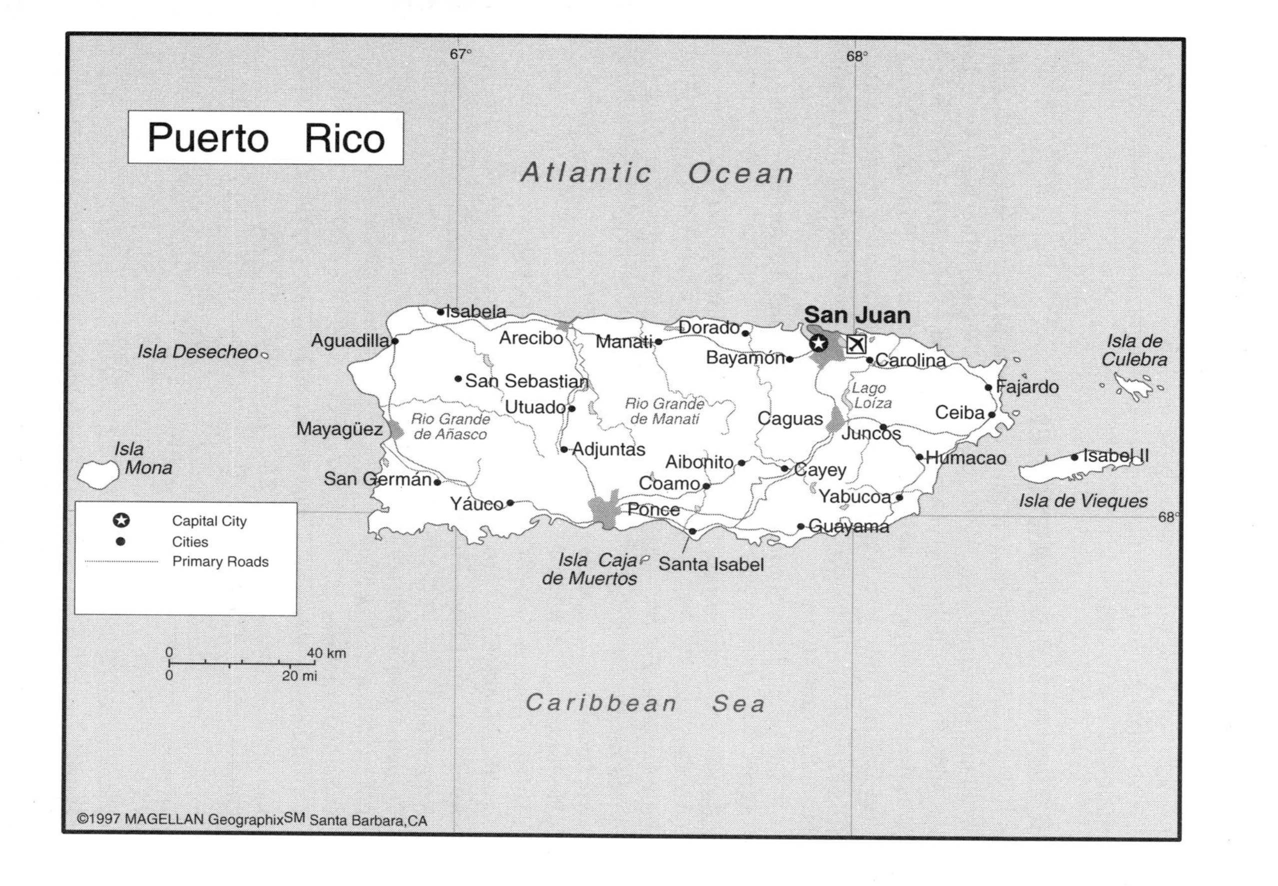
Puerto Rico
67°
68°
Atlantic Ocean
Isabela
Aguadilla
Arecibo
Manatí
Dorado
San Juan
Bayamón
Carolina
Isla Desecheo
Isla de Culebra
San Sebastian
Utuado
Rio Grande de Manatí
Rio Grande de Añasco
Lago Loíza
Fajardo
Ceiba
Caguas
Juncos
Mayagüez
Adjuntas
Isla Mona
Aibonito
Cayey
Humacao
Isabel II
San Germán
Coamo
Yabucoa
Yáuco
Ponce
Guayama
Isla de Vieques
Isla Caja de Muertos
Santa Isabel
Capital City
Cities
Primary Roads
0 40 km
0 20 mi
Caribbean Sea
©1997 MAGELLAN GeographixSM Santa Barbara,CA

Climate

The northern coast of Puerto Rico, exposed to the northeast trade winds, is wetter than the south coast. There is no dry season, just a pleasant spread of sunshine and showers throughout the year. Daytime temperatures in San Juan rarely reach above the low 90s; nighttime lows get no cooler than the low 60s. Be prepared for light, cooling showers in the mountains.

ARRIVALS & DEPARTURES

The Caribbean's main airline hub, San Juan is a beehive of flights from more than a dozen North American cities including New York, Los Angeles, Boston, Baltimore, Detroit, Hartford, Miami, Dallas-Fort Worth, Washington Dulles, Orlando, Philadelphia, Tampa, Toronto, Chicago, and Dallas. From here American Eagle flies to another 40 destinations throughout the Caribbean. San Juan also has direct flights from London, Frankfurt and Madrid.

San Juan's **Luis Munoz Marin International Airport** is served by:

- **ACES**, *Tel. 800/846-2237 or 787/791-5840*
- **Aerolineas Argentinas**, *Tel. 787/791-8181 or 800/333-0276*
- **Air Calypso**, *Tel. 787/253-0020*
- **Air Canada**, *Tel. 800/776-3000*
- **Air France**, *Tel. 800/237-2747*
- **Air Guadeloupe**, *Tel. 787/253-0933*
- **Air Jamaica**, *Tel. 800/523-5585*
- **Air St. Thomas**, *Tel. 800/522-3084 or 787/791-4898*
- **ALM**, *Tel. 800/327-7230*
- **American Air Lines**, *Tel. 787/749-1747*
- **American Eagle**, *787/749-1747*
- **British Airways**, *800/247-9297*
- **BWIA**, *Tel. 800/538-2942*
- **Canadian Airlines**, *Tel. 787/791-0404*
- **Caribbean Air Express**, *Tel. 800/981-9045 or 787/721-5345*
- **Carnival Airlines**, *Tel. 800/274-6140 or 800/824-7386*
- **Continental**, *Tel. 800/525-0280*
- **COPA**, *Tel. 800/9981-8284 or 787/722-6969*
- **Condor**, *Tel. 800/645-3880*
- **Delta**, *Tel. 800/221-1212*
- **Flamenco**, *Tel. 787/723-8110 or 725-7707*
- **Iberia**, *Tel. 800/772-4642 or 787/721-5630*
- **Isla Nena**, *Tel. 741-6362 or 741-1577*
- **KLM**, *Tel. 800/826-7976*
- **LACSA**, *Tel. 800/225-2272 or 787/724-3330*

- **LIAT**, *Tel. 787/791-3838*
- **Martin Air**, *Tel. 800/627-8462*
- **Northwest Airlines**, *Tel. 800/225-2525 or 800/447-4747*
- **Towers Air**, *Tel. 800/221-2500*
- **TWA**, *Tel. 800/221-2000 or 800/892-8466*
- **United**, *Tel. 800/241-6522 or 800/538-2929*
- **US Airways**, *Tel. 800/842-5374*
- **Vieques Air Link**, *Tel. 787/722-3736*

Frequent air service is also available from San Juan to Vieques, from Vieques to Fajardo, from Fajardo to Culebra, and from Vieques to St. Croix. Among the island's private airports is one at the **Hyatt Dorado Beach Hotel**. Mayagüez has an airport served by **American Eagle**. **Carnival Air** flies from New York to Aguadilla and Ponce.

Ferries depart every half hour from **Pier Two** in Old San Juan for Cataño and Hato Rey, *Tel. 788-1155*. For schedules, rate information, and reservations for passenger ferry service among Fajardo, Vieques, and Culebra, call *863-0852*. Transportation for cars is available on the cargo ferry, *Tel. 863-0852*. Allow at least a week for planning and reservations. San Juan is the second largest cruise ship port in the Western Hemisphere, hosting 28 ships that make 748 home port sailings each year. If you are cruising out of San Juan, take as much time as you can afford for pre- and post-cruise stays on the island.

SMALL CHANGE

If you have a lot of luggage, have a good supply of quarters on hand for the rental luggage cart machines. If you're changing planes here from other, non-U.S. islands in the Caribbean, you have to handle your own bags in and out of customs. It can be a long haul without the rental cart. For the telephones, you'll need dimes.

ORIENTATION

Metropolitan San Juan has spread like a giant amoeba that has gobbled up Toa Baja, Cataño, Bayamon, Trujillo Alto, Carolina, and Guayanabo almost as far as Caguas, which will probably soon be part of the megalopolis. **Old San Juan**, an island that forms half the rim of San Juan Bay, is a time machine frozen in the 16th century. It's a place to roam and sightsee, and rest in shaded plazas paved with centuries-old stones. East of Old (or Viejo) San Juan are the high-rise tourist hotels of Condado and Miramar. Hato Rey is the city's financial and commercial hub. In

Guynabo and Hato Rey, you're in the 'burbs with their real estate developments and American-style shopping malls and supermarkets.

From San Juan, Route 3 goes east past **Luquillo** with its famous beach to **Fajardo**, where ferries leave for offshore islands. South of Route 3 spreads **El Yunque,** the magnificent rainforest covering the **Sierra Luquillo**.

Driving south from San Juan takes you through **Caguas** and on to the colonial city of **Ponce**. Or you can head east from Caguas to the resort area of **Humacao**.

It's possible to drive around almost the entire perimeter of the island, going west from Ponce, skirting inland through **San Germán**, and back to the coast at busy **Mayagüez**. Then north to **Aguadilla** and east along the coast to the attractions of **Arecibo** with its radio telescope and the caves of **Rio Camuy**, through the resorts of **Dorado** and back to San Juan. An alternative route, if you have plenty of time, is to drive the spine of the **Cordillera**, the mountain range through the middle of the island.

GETTING AROUND PUERTO RICO

White-painted taxis participating in the **Tourism Taxi Program** operate on a zone system. Fare from the airport to nearby districts including Isla Verde and Puntas las Marias is $8. In Zone 2, from the airport to Condado, Ocean Park, and Miramar, the fare is $12. Zone 3 from the airport to Old San Juan, tourism piers, and Puerta de Tierra is a $16 fare. A Zone 5 fare of $6 applies from the piers to Puerta de Tierra. Fare for the Zone 6 ride from the piers to Condado, Ocean Park and Miramar is $10. Zone 7 is from the piers to Isla Verde, costing $16.

Metered cabs have a $1 initial charge, then charge 10 cents for each additional 1/13 mile plus additional fees for baggage, waiting time, reserved rides, and night travel. Charter taxis charge $20 per hour. If you have complaints about taxis, call the Public Service Commission, *Tel. 756-1919,* or the airport police, *Tel. 791-4155.*

Free trolleys shuttle every 15 minutes from 6am to 2am around the Isla Verde district so it's easy to enjoy all the hotels, clubs and shops of this upscale tourist area without having a car. City buses in the San Juan area are frequent and good. Bus stops are marked by orange, white and magenta signs reading Parada, with yellow and white lines marking bus stops on main highways. Bus terminals are in the Covadonga parking lot in Old San Juan (long-distance buses) and on Plaza de Colon for short routes. For information, Tel. *763-4141.*

Public transportation by *publicos* (vans) covers the island at rates ranging from, for example, $10 to $25 for the trip from San Juan to Mayagüez, depending on the route taken and how many stops are made.

Catch a publico at the airport, Rio Piedras Plaza, or in the town plaza in any community. For information about routes to Mayagüez, call **Lineas Sultana**, *Tel. 765-9377. For* information about publicos to Ponce, *Tel. 764-0540.*

Parking space is at a premium almost everywhere, so consider carefully whether you really need a rental car. Hotels may charge $12 a day or more for parking if it's available at all. Restaurants, if they have parking at all, may require you to valet park. If you do rent a car, avoid cut-rate rental agencies that don't have satellite offices island-wide because you could be stranded if you break down out on the island. Major car rental companies also offer transportation from hotels or the airport to their lots, and their cars are equipped with anti-theft devices.

Rental car agencies include:

- **Avis**, *Tel. 800/874-3556*
- **Budget**, *Tel. 787/791-3685* or *800/468-5822*
- **Hertz**, *Tel. 787/791-0840* or *800/654-3131*
- **National**, *Tel. 787/791-1805 or 800/568-3019*
- **Thrifty**, *Tel. 787/253-2525 or 800/367-2277*

Kemwel Rental Cars can be reserved in the U.S. at *800/678-0678.* For **Wheelchair Getaways Rent-a-Car**, *Tel. 787/726-4023* or *800/868-8028.* In Mayagüez or Ponce, try **Popular Leasing**, *Tel. 787/265-4848 or 800/981-9282.*

WHERE TO STAY

The room tax in hotels that do not have a casino is nine percent; in hotels that have a casino it is 11 percent. Some hotels often charge of 15 percent or more in lieu of tipping. Rates given are for a double room in high season. Unless stated otherwise, major credit cards are accepted.

Old San Juan

GRAN HOTEL EL CONVENTO, *100 Cristo. Tel. 787/723-9020. Rates at this 59-room hotel start at $220. It's a $16 taxi ride from the airport and $6 by cab from the pier.*

You're not just in the heart of history, you are part of history when you stay in a building that is almost 400 years old. Built as a convent and lavishly restored in 1996, this is one of the old city's most talked-about showplaces. Two levels are stores, restaurants and cafes. The hotel covers three floors. Its facilities include a plunge pool, fitness center, small casino, and a full-service business center. The hotel has a restaurant, swimming pool and gaming, and it is wheelchair accessible.

GALLERY INN AT GALERÍA SAN JUAN, *Calle Norzagaray #204-206, Old San Juan PR 00901. Tel. 787/722-1808, Fax 787/724-7360. Rates at this 22-room inn start at $95, suites at $200, Rates include continental breakfast. Cab fare from the airport is $16 and from the pier $6.*

Everything you've ever dreamed of in a bed and breakfast inn is found here in a romantic, 300-year-old building that rambles from the north wall of the old city through a warren of stony courtyards, balconies filled with flowers, and hidden rooms. It's so private, there isn't even a sign outside, so don't arrive without a reservation and directions. Most rooms have private bath and some have air conditioning, but each is so different, so eclectic, that most guests choose a favorite and book it year after year.

Built for a Spanish artillery captain, the home is now the studio of talented artists Jan D'Esopo and Manuco Gandia whose works are part of the decor and are also for sale in the gallery. Visitors can look on as a frenzy of creative activity produces paintings, sculptures, silkscreening, mold making, and bronze castings. In her spare time, Jan plays her Steinway concert grand or brings in talented conservatory students to play for her guests. This is the ideal *pied-a-terre* for exploring the old city on foot. Parking is very limited, so skip the rental car until you're ready to leave for the countryside.

WYNDHAM OLD SAN JUAN, *101 Marina, Old San Juan. Tel. 787/289-7070 or 800/822-4200 U.S. and 800/631-4200 Canada. Rates at this 240-room hotel start at $240; stay on the Concierge level and pay a rate of $275, which includes continental breakfast. It's a $16 taxi ride from the airport.*

Stay in the old city in style and comfort worthy of the fussiest business traveler or vacationer. The hotel has a swimming pool, casual or formal dining, a casino, and is wheelchair accessible.

Greater San Juan – Expensive

CARIBE HILTON, *Fort San Geronimo, Puerto de Tierra, San Juan. Tel. 787/721-0303 or 800/HILTONS in the U.S. and Canada. Rates at this 733-room hotel start at $330, suites at $660. Valet parking is $14 daily, self parking is $5 a day. On the concierge level, breakfast is included. Taxi fare from the airport is $12; from the pier, $6. The hotel can also be reached by the A7 bus.*

The beach is a tiny jewel rarely found in the heart of the city, and the hotel offers classy accommodations for business or pleasure plus a 400-year-old fort to explore and photograph. Oceanview rooms gaze out over crashing surf and the ramparts of Fort San Jeronimo. Work out in the health club or book one of the rooms or suites that has its own Action Stepper fitness machine. There's a full spa, two freshwater pools, six tennis courts lit for night play, a playground for the children, a massive casino, and four excellent restaurants as well as lounges and bars. Accommodations are spacious and posh, offering luxury touches for the leisure traveler plus the desk, telephones, and business center that a working visitor requires.

Camp Coco for children ages 4-12 operates during school vacations and holiday periods at a cost of $3- per child per day or $125 a week. Included are supplies, lunch, and two snacks daily. Kids tennis lessons can be added at special rates. Each day the camp also offers a family activity such as rafting, a limbo contest, dance lessons, bingo, hula hoops, or fish feeding. The resort has an on-site bird sanctuary. Staff are bi-lingual.

CONDADO PLAZA HOTEL & CASINO, *999 Ashford Avenue, Condado PR 00907. Tel. 787/721-1000 or 800/468-8588. Rates at this 587-room hotel start at $220, suites at $320. The hotel is a $12 cab ride from the airport.*

First-class service and accommodations mean a private balcony for every room, a choice of three swimming pools, a sandy beach, black tie gaming and dancing, and a spectrum of restaurants including Mandalay Oriental, Las Palmas poolside grill, elegant Capriccio's, the award-winning La Posada for Puerto Rican food, or Tony Roma's for its famous ribs. Room service and La Posada operate around the clock. It is managed by the same company as El San Juan Hotel & Casino, so guests in either, and at Cobia's Restaurant (tapas) can charge meals to one account.

CROWNE PLAZA BEACH RESORT & CASINO, *Highway 187, Kilometer 1.5, Isla Verde, San Juan PR 00979. Tel. 787/253-2929 or 800/2 CROWNE. Room rates start at $169 plus $6 for parking or $10 for valet parking. From the airport, exit right on Route 26 towards San Juan, then exit right on Highway 187. Just past the traffic light, the hotel is on your left. Drive time is five minutes; cab fare is $8.*

Play blackjack, Baccarat, roulette, craps and the slots by night and bake the days away on renowned Isla Verde Beach. The 254-room, high-rise hotel brings the tropics indoors in its airy rooms and suites. For special perks including nightly turn-down, continental breakfast, newspaper, and nightly hors d'oeuvres and honor bar, stay on the Crowne Plaza Club Floor. Dining is in Windows on the Sea, known for its traditional Puerto Rican dishes. Old San Juan is 15 minutes away, and the concierge can arrange a golf game for you 30 minutes from the hotel.

Although Crowne Plaza Hotels and Resorts can be reserved through Holiday Inn, they have dropped the Holiday Inn name and are distancing themselves from the price-appeal chain.

EL SAN JUAN HOTEL & CASINO, *Avenue Isla Verde, Isla Verde PR 00979. Tel. 787/791-0390; in the U.S., Canada, and U.S. Virgin Islands, call 800/223-6800. Rates in this 389-room, 20-suite hotel start at $320 double. The hotel is a five-minute taxi ride from the airport.*

For luxury leisure travelers and business travelers too, this hotel offers the best of both: 15 acres on the beach, grounds landscaped with palms and flowering shrubs, as well as meeting rooms and a business center. Rooms are air conditioned; some have a Jacuzzi or sunken tub; many have a private terrace or balcony. Lose yourself in the gardens, or savor all the bustle of a big hotel: six restaurants, 24-hour room service, tennis courts that are lit for night play, a state-of-the-art fitness center, and an extensive watersports center with board sailing, deep sea fishing, and parasailing. Ask about the optional meal plan.

RADISSON AMBASSADOR PLAZA HOTEL & CASINO, *1369 Ashford Avenue, Condado, San Juan PR 00907. Tel. 721-7300, U.S. 800/333-3333 . Rates at this 233-room hotel start at $169. It's a $12 taxi ride, or 15 minutes, from the airport.*

You're in Condado's action-packed tourist strip, only ten minutes from Old San Juan, half a block from the beach, and surrounded by shops, restaurants, and bars. The hotel rises in two towers, one of 146 rooms and the other with two-room suites. Stay on the Ambassador Club floor with its own lounge, concierge, and prestige perks. Swim in the rooftop pool, which has its own whirlpool, work on in the fitness center, shop the boutique, choose from three restaurants, and stay late in the Cabaret Lounge to listen to live music. The hotel has its own beauty shop, game room, and travel desk and the casino is said to be one of the island's most user-friendly.

RITZ-CARLTON SAN JUAN HOTEL AND CASINO, *6961 State Road 187, Isla Verde, Carolina PR 00979. Tel. 800/241-3333 or locally (787) 253-1700, Fax 253-0700. Rates at this 419-room, 45-suite hotel start at $505; one-bedroom suites start at $1045. The hotel also has a club floor with rooms and suites. It's five minutes from the international airport and 15 minutes from Old San Juan. Through the hotel, get airport transfers for $8 each way.*

A bustling business hotel with a ballroom, meeting rooms and a business center, the Ritz is also ideal for the leisure traveler who wants unabashed luxury in rooms lavished with works by local artists. Each guest room has a stocked honor bar, personal safe, marble bath with hair dryer, scale, and telephone, individual heat and air conditioning control, plush terry robes, three telephones with dual lines and data port, and AM/FM radio with digital clock/alarm. Enjoy the 450-foot beach, a full-service spa, and a city location handy to the airport, financial district, Old San Juan, and shopping at Plaza Las Americas. Nightlife and dining at Condado are ten minutes away. Dine in the Vineyard Room, the hotel's signature restaurant serving California and continental cuisine or in more informal restaurants indoors and out. Room service answers 24 hours a day.

Swim in the supersize, 7,200-square foot pool, soak in the whirlpools, play tennis on the hotel's courts, and gamble late and luxuriously in the 17,000 square foot Monte Carlo by the Sea Casino. The hotel's 12,000 square foot spa is created by the Sonoma Mission Inn and Spa, featuring life-enhancing Sonomotherapy treatments. Hotel guests have golf privileges at nearby courses. The Fitness Center offers aerobics, exercise equipment and free weights. Three fishing clubs are nearby; horse racing is 20 minutes away. View are of the sea or of El Yunque rainforest.

On the Club floor with its private lounge and personal concierge staff, guests get complimentary continental breakfast, light lunch, afternoon tea, hors d'oeuvres, and a variety of beverages throughout the day and evening. New in 1998, the hotel is surely destined for five-star status with its twice daily maid service, 24-hour room service and valet parking, child care, and much more.

SAN JUAN GRAND BEACH HOTEL & CASINO, *187 Avenida Isla Verde, Isla Verde PR 00913. Tel. 787/791-6100, Fax 791-8525; U.S. 800/443-2009. Rates at this 417-unit hotel start at $220; suites at $270. It's an $8 cab ride from the airport. Parking is $5 per day; valet parking, $10.*

The gambling glitter of the Sands Hotel in Atlantic City is cloned here. On the beach and surrounded by lush, flowery tropical plants, the hotel does a brisk tour and group business. Dine in Ruth's Chris Steak House, Giuseppe for northern Italian cuisine, or the informal cafe.. For the ultimate luxury, stay in the Plaza Club, the resort's five-star prestige section.

Greater San Juan – Moderate

COLONY SAN JUAN BEACH HOTEL, *José M. Tartak #2, Isla Verde PR 00979. Tel. 787/253-0100, extension 2007, Fax 787/253-0220. Rates at the 71-room, 11-suite hotel start at $100. It's an $8 cab ride from the airport.*

When a beachfront hotel is built this close to the airport it is tailor-made for today's shorter vacations. Swim off the beach or in the roof-top pool with its swim-up bar and outdoor whirlpool. The European-style boutique hotel has gourmet dining as well as a terrace bar and grill, a children's center, business center, and valet parking. San Juan's business district and nightlife are all nearby.

EMBASSY SUITES, *8000 Tartak, Isla Verde PR 00902. Tel. 787/791-0505; U.S. 800/362-2779. Rates at this 300-suite hotel start at $175 including breakfast cooked to order and evening cocktails. The hotel is an $8 cab ride, five minutes from the airport.*

Any time we can get a homey, one-bedroom suite with two televisions, microwave, refrigerator, and coffee maker for this price, with a full breakfast on the house, we are sold. The hotel has an Outback Steakhouse, casual dining in the Atrium Cafe, a swimming pool with pool bar, and a casino. It's handy to Old San Juan, the beach, shopping, restaurants, and expressways, and it's wheelchair accessible. Don't confuse this address with the Embassy guest house in Condado.

RADISSON NORMANDIE, *Avenida Muñoz Rivera, Puerto de Tierra, San Juan PR 00902. Tel. 787/729-2929, Fax 787/729-3083; U.S. 800/333-*

3333. Rates at this 177-room hotel start at $117, suites at $205. Rates include breakfast.

A nostalgic favorite, this ship-shaped hotel was built before World War II and named for the French cruise liner *Normandie*. Long a choice for honeymoons in the sunshine and still a great location for vacationing and business, the hotel is refurbished time and again to its original, art deco splendor. The hotel has an excellent restaurant, a lounge, a swimming pool with pool bar, a casino, room service and a beauty salon.

SAN JUAN MARRIOTT RESORT, *1309 Ashford Avenue, San Juan 00907. Tel. 787/722-7000 or 800/981-8546. Rates at this 525-room resort start at $180, suites at $210. Located on the beach in Condado it's a $12 taxi ride from the airport.*

High-rise hotels along San Juan's hotel "strip" can be seen from miles out to sea, and this 21-story beauty tops them all. Entering the lobby, you immediately grasp the sense of luxury and ease that marks a first class, modern hotel with advanced voice mail systems, 24-hour room service, in-room VCRs, and a full range of services including concierge, car rental, tour desk, a shopping arcade, and beauty shop. Live music plays in the lobby during cocktail hour, so it's a good place to meet friends. Dine in Ristorante Tuscany for northern Italian cuisine, the poolside grill, or La Vista which features a theme buffet every evening and, at breakfast and lunch, menu or buffet service. Calypso music plays on Saturday and Sunday afternoons poolside and there's merengue dancing in the lounge Thursday through Sunday from 9pm until almost dawn. The massive pool is a stunner.

Greater San Juan – Budget

CASA CARIBE, *57 Calle Caribe, Condado, San Juan PR 00907. Tel. 787/722-7139. Rates at this 7-room guest house start at $55 including continental breakfast. Cab fare from the airport is $12.*

You're near the beach in a delightful little inn favored by Puerto Ricans and savvy visitors who like the garden setting, breezy porch, and comfortable, clean rooms that have air conditioning and a ceiling fan.

CASA DE PLAYA, *86 Isla Verde, Isla Verde PR 00979. Tel. 787/728-9779. Rates at this 22-room hotel start at $75. From the airport it's an $8 taxi ride.*

Handy to town, the airport, and near the beach is this unassuming hotel with its own restaurant.

DAYS INN CONDADO LAGOON, *6 Clemenceau Avenue, Condado PR 00907. Tel. 787/721-0170 or 800/325-2525. Rates at this 44-room hotel start at $89. Cab fare from the airport is $12.*

The location is ideal for business travel or as a home port while you're exploring Old San Juan, the shopping and dining of "hotel row" and the attractions of the north side of the island. The hotel is a typical, price-appeal Days Inn with a restaurant and a swimming pool.

EL CANARIO BY THE LAGOON, *4 Clemenceau Street, Condado, San Juan PR 00907. Tel. 787/722-8640. Rates at this 40-room hotel start at $65 including breakfast.*

Back from the beach one block and on a quiet street, this small hotel has the homey look and feel of a European inn. Most of the rooms have a balcony and there is a laundry for guest use. The hosts will be glad to arrange tours and to steer you to nearby restaurants and entertainment.

GREEN ISLE INN, *6 Calle Uno, Isla Verde PR 00979. Tel. 787/726-4330 or 787/726-8662, Fax 787/268-2415. Rates start at $42 to $74. The hotel is an $8 taxi ride from the airport and $16 from the pier.*

It's in the heart of the luxury hotels yet it's pittance priced. Walk to beaches, casinos, dining, and shopping. The hotel offers courtesy coffee, furnished kitchenettes, and two big swimming pools.

OLIMPO COURT HOTEL, *603 Avenida Miramar, Miramar. Tel. 787/724-0600. Rates at this 45-room hotel start at $57. Cab fare from the airport is $8.*

Don't expect mints on your pillow at this price, but it's hard to beat the location for the traveler who wants to sleep near the airport. The hotel has its own restaurant, Chayote, Tel. 722-9385.

TRAVEL LODGE, *Route 37, Isla Verde, mail address Box 6007, Loiza, PR 00914; Tel. 787/728-1300 or 800/468-2028. Rates at this 88-room hotel start at $93. From the airport it's an $8 cab ride.*

Just like its sister hotels in the U.S., this chain hotel is a good, solid value without frills and it is handily located on the busy main street. You'll have a comfortable room with bath. The beach is just a short walk away. The hotel has a swimming pool, restaurant, and bar, and it's within walking distance of dozens more good eateries.

WIND CHIMES INN, *53 Taft Street, Condado PR 00911. Tel. 787/727-4153. Rates at this 10-room guest house start at $55 including continental breakfast. Taxi fare from the airport is $12 and it's on the A7 bus route.*

The price is right for a room near the beach and handy to Condado's dazzling convention center, restaurants, hotels, and boutiques. Rooms are air conditioned and have a ceiling fan. Kitchens are available. Walk a block to the beach or just relax on the patio in the shade of palms and flowering vines, listening to the wind chimes. Yes, credit cards are accepted.

Southeast Puerto Rico

PALMAS DEL MAR, *mail address: Box 2020, Humacao, Puerto Rico 00792-2020. Tel. 787/852-6000 or U.S. 800/725-6273. Found at Kilometer 84.6 on Road #3, Route 906, Humacao. A 45-minute drive from the San Juan* *airport, the resort has 250 rooms and suites. Rates start at $138 nightly for a double room in low season and range to $710 nightly for a three-bedroom villa in high season. Ask about packages. Included in the resort are the* ***Candelero Hotel*** *and* ***Palmas Inn****, which are reserved through the telephone numbers above, and the* ***Wyndham Hotel & Villas****, Tel. 787/852-6000 or 800/468-3331.*

Your domain includes a Gary Player-designed, 18-hole golf course said to have more scenic holes than any other course in the world, and a tennis center managed by Peter Burwash International. Snorkel right off the beach; take a horse from the Equestrian Center and cantor off through the surf. Scuba dive with the resort's own dive masters, the only on-site dive operation on the island.

Put yourself in a spacious hotel room with a private balcony or in a villa to house the entire family. Furnishings are tropical and bright; accessories are drawn from Puerto Rican folk art. The Adventure Club gives children, ages 3 to 13, the time of their lives while adults sun, read, or play golf or tennis.

Developed in the 1960s by Charles Fraser, known for his ecologically-sensitive developments, the resort is a complete community with branch banks, churches, school, shops, casino, beauty services, restaurants, lounges, and permanent residents living in homes costing $225,000 to $1 million. Once registered, you can charge everything in "town" to your account.

Choose from an ever-changing list of planned activities, a dozen restaurants, workout facilities, scuba, deep sea fishing, sailing, swimming pools galore, bicycling, and camaraderie without crowding. The grounds, graced with 3,000 coconut palms, cover 2,750 acres.

The **Candelero Resort** reopened in 1998 as a Wyndham after a $4.5 million renovation. Rooms are done in tropical greens and blues. Each has a mini-refrigerator, electronic door lock, in-room safe, and a private balcony or patio. The hotel, which now faces the golf course, has 6,000 square feet of retail shopping.

If you like a big resort with all the bells and whistles and enough to do for weeks without having to traipse all over the island, this is the place.

Selected as one of my Best Places to Stay; see Chapter 13.

East of San Juan – Expensive

EL CONQUISTADOR RESORT & COUNTRY CLUB, *Carretera 987, kilometer 3.4, Las Croabas; Tel. 787/863-1000, Fax 787/863-3280; in the U.S., Canada, and U.S. Virgin Islands, call 800/223-6800 or 800/468-5228. Website www.williamshosp.com. Room rates start at $345; suites at $770. From the San Juan airport, it is 31 miles east to the hotel, which is northeast of Fajardo.*

Splayed around and carved into an imposing bluff overlooking the ocean, this dazzling resort sprawls on for 500 lush acres in the colorful fishing hamlet of Las Croabas. In addition to the hotel there are clusters of accommodations, each a village itself with its own style. Stay in the AAA Five Diamond Las Casitas Village for away-from-it-all privacy in a two- or three-bedroom suite. You'll have a personal butler, 24-hour concierge, private check-in, around-the-clock room service, and nightly turndown with an orchid left on your bed. Stay in Las Olas for panoramic views of the Caribbean; La Marina is harborside and has a salty ambience. The Grand Hotel is the heart of the resort, for guests who prefer a hotel setting. You're surrounded by shops, swimming pools, Jacuzzis, tennis courts and restaurants. Watersports center around private Palomino Island. There's also a marina, 18-hole championship golf course, and fitness center. For the children, Camp Coqui promises all-day, supervised fun.

For added luxury and service, stay on the hotel's Club Conquistador VIP floor, which has its own lounge serving complimentary breakfast, cocktails and afternoon coffee.

HOSTAL BAHIA MAR, *Fulladosa Cove, Culebra, mailing address P.O. Box 41292, Minillas Station, Santurce PR. Tel. 787/717-1855 or 763-5289, Fax 787/754-8409. Rates are $325 nightly for two and $550 nightly for four including meals and taxes.*

The opening of this 16-unit, European style inn on the island of Culebra is exciting news for locals as well as for visitors in search of a fantasy island. High above the cove overlooking Great Harbor, you can see St. Thomas on most days. Fully-equipped units have air conditioning and kitchen with microwave oven. Watersports equipment is available in the cove; swimming and snorkeling are behind the barrier reef in Dakity Cove. The hostel operates a high-speed catamaran to Culebrita Island and whale watching outings. A minimum three-night booking is required.

WESTIN RIO MAR BEACH & COUNTRY CLUB, *6000 Rio Mar Boulevard, Rio Grande PR 00745. Tel. 787/888-6000, Fax 787/888-6600. U.S. and Canada call 800/WESTIN-1 or 800/4 RIO-MAR. Rates start at $325 double; MAP and FAP are available. Children under age 18 sleep free in their parents' room. It's between Rio Grande and Fajardo off Route 3 on Highway 968, Kilometer 1.4, 19 miles east of San Juan and about $65 by taxi from the airport. Parking is $12 daily.*

This 481-acre playground is bordered by the Atlantic, the Mamayes River, and El Yunque Caribbean National Forest. The tennis complex boasts 13 courts and there are two championship golf courses, one a 6,800-yard course designed by George and Tom Fazio and the other a 7,000-yard course created by Greg Norman. The hotel has a complete dive shop offering dives, gear, certification, snorkel trips, and scuba "discovery" courses.

The hotel is done in Mediterranean modern, with classic pieces accented by whimsical shapes and colors. Rooms have balconies overlooking the garden or beach, plus hair dryer, telephones at desk and bedside, signature toiletries, and a safe with key.

Work out in the fitness center and health studio, then choose from a long menu of spa services and treatments including body toning, anti-stress treatment, body wraps, salt glo, deep tissue massage, and jet-leg massage. If you like gambling, seek out the Las Vegas-style casino. It has its own concierge, a player's lounge with drinks and appetizers (under Puerto Rican Law, drinks cannot be served at the gaming tables) five ATM machines including three in the pit area, and free limousine pick-up at the airport for high rollers. Play Caribbean Stud Poker, Let It Ride, Pai Gaw Poker and a Big Six wheel. In addition you can play blackjack (classes for resort guests are free) and 224 slot machines.

Choose among ten places to drink and dine, including the outstanding Palio, the hotel's signature restaurant and a clone of the original in the Swan at Walt Disney World. Nightly theme buffets at Marbella (mar BAY ya) are a buy; for Puerto Rican food try Cafe Carnival or La Estancia. The Grille at the golf club is known for its steaks; Bolero in the hotel is for tapas before dinner and cigars and brandy after.

The children's center is staffed all year; day care costs $35 including lunch, craft supplies and a tee shirt. Babysitting is available at $5 an hour. The hotel has three pools: a quiet pool for adults, a wading pool with sandy play area for tots, and a busier pool with waterfall and water slide for all ages. The hotel has shops and a beauty salon, valet parking, and a free shuttle serving the hotel, tennis center, and golf club.

Selected as one of my Best Places to Stay; see Chapter 13.

East of San Juan – Budget

ANCHOR'S INN, *Route 987, Kilometer 2.7, Fajardo. Tel. 787/863-7200. Rates at this seven-room guest house start at $55 including breakfast.*

Share the same dazzling cape as the exclusive El Conquistador at less than half the price. This inn is near the beach, it is wheelchair accessible, and credit cards are accepted. The inn's restaurant is popular for its local seafood and prime meats. Try its coffee pub too.

CEIBA COUNTRY INN, *Route 977, Kilometer 1.2, Ceiba. Tel. 787/885-0471. Rooms at this nine-room guest house start at $70.*

Wheelchair accessible and handy to the U.S. Naval Station, this is an affordable address for travelers who have a car for sightseeing and restaurants.

Northwest Puerto Rico – Expensive

HYATT DORADO BEACH HOTEL, *Dorado PR 00646. Tel. 787/796-1234 or 800/233-1234. Rates start at $450 for a deluxe double room; casitas at $750. For MAP add $70 daily. The hotel is 22 miles west of San Juan; airport shuttles for the 45-minute ride charge $15.*

The two Hyatts in Dorado are hard to choose between except that this is the one with the two 18-hole golf courses. And what courses they are! Designed by Robert Trent Jones and kept in bandbox condition, they're among the best in the world. Add in a shining crescent of toasty beaches, plenty of tennis courts (some lit for night play), and 1,000 acres of gardened grounds.

Rooms, which have marble baths and terra cotta tile floors, are furnished South Seas style in wicker, rattan and bamboo, accented in ice cream pastels. Your room will have a mini-safe, patio or balcony, air conditioning and ceiling fan, hair dryer, direct dial telephone, mini-bar refrigerator, and cable television. Casita rooms, which are the premium, split-level suites, have skylights. Bathrobes are provided for guest use. Su Casa, the original estate house, serves as the signature restaurant offering gourmet dining in a candlelit, open-air room shrouded in fragrant foliage. Meals are also available in the equally dressy Surf Room and in the more informal Ocean Terrace.

Shuttle buses run between the two Hyatts, giving guests twice the choice of beaches, dining, shops, and other facilities. Camp Hyatt for the kids is one of the best children's programs on the island and it operates year 'round. Miles of pathways make the resort perfect for bicycling.

HYATT REGENCY CERROMAR, *Highway 693 Dorado PR 00646. Tel. 787/796-8903; U.S. 800/233-1234. Rates at this 506-room resort start at $310; suites at $750. Add $65 daily for breakfast and dinner (MAP). The hotel is 22 miles west of San Juan; airport shuttles for the 45-minute ride charge $15.*

One of a Hyatt double play that offers all the restaurants and facilities of two luxury landmark Hyatt Regency resorts, the venerable Cerromar has one of the most eye-popping swimming pools in the world. A 1,776-foot river flows on past waterfalls and grottos from one pool to another. Going with the flow, it takes a delicious half hour just to float the course. The hotel has a full spa, workout facilities, a year-round children's program, 24-hour room service, and 21 tennis courts. Dine indoors or out in a choice of restaurants here and at the neighboring Hyatt.

Room features include a mini-bar, air conditioning, hair dryer, private safe, and tropical decor rich in sea and earth tones. Most have a private balcony.

Northwest Puerto Rico – Moderate

COSTA DORADA BEACH, *Route 466, Kilometer 0.1, Isabella. Tel. 787/872-7255. Rates at this 53-room hotel start at $95. It's a two-hour drive from San Juan, between Arecibo and Aguadilla.*

Don't confuse this with the Hyatt Dorado Beach, which is a far grander, most expensive resort an hour east of here. There is a beach, though, and the hotel has a restaurant, swimming pool, and tennis courts. It's wheelchair accessible, and is a good stopping point on the Atlantic north of the main highway from Arecibo to Aguadilla.

West & Southwest Puerto Rico – Moderate

BEST WESTERN MAYAGÜEZ RESORT & CASINO, *Route 104, Kilometer 0.3, Mayagüez PR 00680. Tel. 787/832-3030, Fax 787/265-3020. Rates at this 141-room hotel start at $125. Ask about packages.*

A booming business hotel as well as a family resort, this affordable chain hotel has a restaurant, lounge, swimming pool, a casino, and tennis courts and it is wheelchair accessible. Expect good, no-frills value.

HOLIDAY INN AND TROPICAL CASINO MAYAGÜEZ, *Route 2, Kilometer 149.9. Tel. 787/833-1100 or 800/HOLIDAY. Rates at this 154-room hotel start at $121. The hotel is two miles north of the city, ten minutes south of the airport.*

Although it's not on the beach, this impressively modern hotel is set on steeply dramatic grounds filled with forestry and flowers. There's a big swimming pool, a casino, a restaurant and a lounge.

West & Southwest Puerto Rico – Budget

GUTIERREZ GUEST HOUSE, *Route 229, Kilometer 16.1, Las Marias. Tel. 827-2087 or 827-3453. Rates at this 13-room guest house start at $47. Credit cards aren't accepted. It's an hour east of Mayagüez in the mountains.*

If all you want is a humble mountain getaway in a pleasant inn with a swimming pool, this is the overnight for you.

Rincón

HORNED DORSET PRIMAVERA HOTEL, *Route 429, Kilometer 3.0, Rincón. Tel. 787/823-4030. Rates at this 30-room hotel start at $280. The hotel is 15 minutes north of the airport at Mayagüez or 2 1/2 hours from San Juan via the northern route through Arecibo then south through Aguadilla.*

Rincón, known as a world capital of surfing, is on a windswept cape overlooking the Mona Passage on Puerto Rico's west coat. Known familiarly as the Primavera, the hotel is a sprawling collection of dashing suites and villas obviously designed for discerning travelers who shun the beaten path. Of all the U.S. Inns and B&Bs nationwide cited in one Zagat Survey, this one was rated 13th. Handmade mahogany furniture, including the stately four-poster beds, was made on the island. Marble and red clay tiles are set off by louvered wood doors that open to balconies overlooking the sea, and rich tapestry-type draperies and upholstery. Bathrooms are lavishly furnished with bidet, footed bathtub, and glowing brass trim.

The main building houses the restaurants. The hotel has a freshwater pool, library, and bar. Rooms have ceiling fan but no radio or television, room service (except breakfast) and no accommodations for children under age 12. Dining is in the open air for breakfast and lunch; dinner in the main dining room offers a choice of open air or air conditioning.

South Coast

PONCE HILTON, *Avenida Santiago Caballeros 14, Ponce. Tel. 787/259-7676, Fax 787/259-7674, or 800/HILTONS. Rates at this 156-room hotel start at $190 plus $10 daily for valet parking and $4.50 daily for self parking. Ask about packages. The hotel is seven minutes from the city.*

Ponce is coming into the spotlight as a tourism center and this exclusive Hilton meets the challenge by offering luxury surroundings, three restaurants, and a casino that jingles from noon to 4am. The cove-shaped swimming pool with its splashy waterfalls is surrounded by tropical landscaping that sets off the striking turquoise and white of the hotel. For children there's a playground and a kids' camp in summer; for working travelers there's a well-equipped business center. Rent a boat or watersports equipment, ride a bicycle, swim off the beach, and let the concierge arrange sightseeing excursions to nearby attractions. The hotel is wheelchair accessible.

DAYS INN PONCE, *Route 1 at Exit 52. Tel. 787/841-1000 or 800/325-2525. Rates at this 121-room hotel start at $90.*

Located in the heart of the city's commercial area, this is a budget-wise choice for the traveler who wants a basic room and bath with a moderately priced restaurant, children's pool, swimming pool, and whirlpool. The hotel is wheelchair accessible and has free cable television with movie channels.

Culebra

Stay for a couple of weeks and you'll be part of the family on this tiny island. Be sure to meet Bostonian Chris Coyle who owns Dewey's Dinghy Dock. He knows the watersports scene, and serves a superb breakfast.

CLUB SEABOURNE, *Culebra PR 00775. Tel. 787/742-3169, Fax 787/742-3176. Villas are priced from $115; rooms from $95.*

This is an out-island hotel built for bare necessities but it's fresh and airy, with air conditioning. Kick back and enjoy the end-of-the-world ambience.

Vieques

Even the Puerto Rico Tourism Company can't always keep up with the lodging and dining situation on this remote island, but you can get the latest skinny from the local town hall, *Tel. 787/741-5000.* Private home rentals can be arranged through Sabin Real Estate, *Tel. 787/741-0023; Fax 787/741-2022.*

CASA DES FRANCÈS, *Box 458, Esperanza, Vieques PR 00765. Tel. 787/741-3751; Fax 787/ 741-2330. Rates at this 18-room guesthouse start at $75.*

A turn-of-the-century plantation mansion and designated historic landmark is your home. Swim in the pool, explore the palm-fringed beach nearby, walk the verdant grounds, and dine each evening on fresh fish or lobster.

CROW'S NEST, *Box 1521, Road 201, Kilometer 1.6, Vieques PR 00765. Tel. 787/741-0033; Fax 787/741-1294. Rates at this 14-room hotel start at $55. Town and the beach are six minutes away.*

The name describes the setting, high atop a hill overlooking rolling green hills in the middle of the island. It's not in town nor on the beach, but the breezes and lofty loneliness of the hills have an appeal all their own. Rooms have a living area and facilities for light cooking. Make your own breakfast and lunch; dine in the oceanview restaurant, one of the best on the island for both food and caring service. Don't miss the weekly Tuesday Happy Hour for bargain drinks and great camaraderie. Hang out in the poolside gazebo or sign up for diving, snorkeling, riding, or an excursion to Phosphorescent Bay.

HACIENDA TAMARINDO, *Box 1569, Route 996, Kilometer 4.5, Vieques PR 00765. Tel. 787/741-8525; Fax 787/741-3215. Rates at this 16-room guesthouse are from $115 including full, American breakfast.*

Owner Linda Vail decorated each room with a special touch of art, antiques or some of her collectibles. The central atrium, split by a three-story-high tamarind tree, is stunning. Half the rooms have an ocean view; others look out over the green countryside. Swim in the pool or walk to the nearby beach. The hotel has no restaurant except for breakfast.

INN ON THE BLUE HORIZON, *Vieques PR 00765. Tel. 787/741-3318; Fax 787/741-3318. Rates at this 15-unit inn are from $150 for a room and from $185 for a bungalow, including breakfast. When booking arrange for pick-up at the airport or ferry dock.*

This hotel offers not only the best digs on the island but also the finest dining. Have breakfast in the terrace restaurant and return for dinner of blackened fish, a hearty creole soup, or an exotic game dish. Go fishing or sailing, or just lounge by the magnificent pool overlooking the sea and outlying cays.

COUNTRY INNS (PARADORES) THROUGHOUT PUERTO RICO

The *parador* network of country inns is sponsored by the Puerto Rican Tourism Company to provide budget lodgings in less-traveled parts of the island. Most sites are chosen for their outstanding natural beauty. Unless stated otherwise, all paradores listed below offer double rooms for less than $76 nightly. All are booked in the U.S. through *Tel. 800/981-7575* or, outside San Juan in Puerto Rico, *Tel. 800/443-0266*. Note that some paradores also have their own toll-free numbers. Accommodations are basic and not all have room telephones, but all take credit cards.

PARADOR BAÑOS DE COAMO, *end of Route 546, mailing address Box 540, Coamo PR 00769. Tel. 787/825-2239, Fax 787/825-2186.*

Bathe in two swimming pools fed by natural hot springs. All 48 rooms have private balconies, are air conditioned, and have a telephone and cable television. The dining room offers local and international dishes and there's a bar.

PARADOR BOQUEMAR, *Box 133, Boquerón PR 00622. Tel. 787/851-2158, Fax 787/851-7600. Overlook Boquerón Bay near Cabo Rojo.*

A nature refuge and other attractions of southwestern Puerto Rico are nearby. The 63 rooms have refrigerators and air conditioning and some overlook the bay. The hotel has a bar, restaurant, and swimming pool.

PARADOR BORINQUEN, *Route 467, Kilometer 2, Borinquen, Aguadilla. Tel. 787/891-0451, Fax 787/882-8008.*

A good home base for exploring northwest Puerto Rico, this 32-room parador has parking food service and a bar, a swimming pool, air conditioning and television. It is wheelchair accessible.

PARADOR EL BUEN CAFÉ, *381 Route 2, Kilometer 84, Hatillo, Tel. 787/898-1000, Fax 787/898-7738.*

Close to beaches, modern shopping malls, and sightseeing including Rio Camuy is this 20-room parador with parking, air conditioning, television, and a nearby beach. It is wheelchair accessible.

HOTEL PARADOR EL FARO, *Route 107, Kilometer 2.1, mailing address Box 5148, Aguadilla PR 00605. Tel. 787/882-8000, Fax 787/882-1030.*

This 32-room parador has air conditioning, telephone, television, a restaurant and bar, tennis courts, and water sports and it's wheelchair accessible.

PARADOR EL SOL, *Calle Santiano Riera Palmer #9, Mayagüez. Tel. 787/834-0303 or 888/765-0303, Fax 787/265-7567.*

This 52-room parador in the heart of the city has a magnificent swimming pool, restaurant and bar, telephones, television, and wheelchair access. Ask about parking when you call for reservations. The parador has air conditioning, food and bar service with live music, tennis courts, a volleyball court, and a playground.

HOTEL PARADOR HACIENDA GRIPIÑAS, *Route 527, Kilometer 2.5, mailing address Box 387, Jayuya PR 00664. Tel. 787/828-1717, Fax 787/828-1719.*

Near the village of Jayuya, known for its crafts and Taino Indian history, this 19-room parador is near one of the island's highest peaks. The old estate house once anchored a coffee plantation and it's surrounded by flowers and shrubbery. Its restaurant specializes in traditional foods.

PARADOR J.B. HIDDEN VILLAGE, *Box 937, Aguada PR 00602. Tel. 787/868-8686, Fax 787/868-3442.*

On a country road near the historic hamlet of Aguada, this 24-room parador has a restaurant that has been named a Méson Gastronomico, indicating exceptional value in good, local cuisine. Your balcony will overlook the swimming pool; nearby are ocean sports, bowling, and roller skating. Rooms are air conditioned, wheelchair accessible, and have cable television and telephone.

PARADOR EL GUAJATACA, *Route 2, Kilometer 103.8, mailing address Box 1538, Quebradillas PR 00678. Tel. 787/895-3070, Fax 787/895-3589; toll-free 800/964-3065.*

A dramatic seashore where the Guajataca River pours into the sea is the setting for this 38-room parador. Rates here are in the $76-$125 category, more than the other paradores, but you'll have a souvenir shop, tennis and volleyball courts, swimming pool, restaurant and bar, air conditioning, telephone, cable television, and a million dollar location.

HOTEL Y PARADOR EL SOL, *9 East Santiago R. Palmer, mailing address Box 1194, Mayaguez PR 00680. Tel. 787/834-0303, Fax 787/265-7567.*

Lower floors of this 52-room parador, which is in downtown Mayagüez, wrap around a tiled swimming pool. Rates include a continental breakfast and the staff are glad to help you find your way around the attractions of the west coast. Rooms have refrigerator, hair dryer, air conditioning, telephone and cable television. The parador has a restaurant and bar.

HOTEL PARADOR JOYUDA BEACH, *Route 102, Kilometer 11.7, mailing address Box 1660, Cabo Rojo PR 00681. Tel. 787/851-5650, Fax 787/265-6940.*

This 43-room hotel is on a beach famous for its seafood restaurants, sunsets, and fishing charters. Play volleyball on the beach and swim in the sea. Rooms have air conditioning, television, and telephone, and there's a restaurant and bar.

HOTEL PARADOR LA FAMILIA, *Route 987, Kilometer 4.1, mailing address Box 21399, Fajardo PR 00738. Tel. 787/863-1193, Fax 787/860-5345.*

Close to El Faro lighthouse, the beaches, and waters of a beautiful resort area, and handy to the ferry terminal where boats leave for Culebra and Vieques, this 28-room parador has air conditioning, a restaurant and bar, and cable television but no room phones.

PARADOR LA HACIENDA JUANITA, *Route 105, Kilometer 23,5, mailing address Box 777, Maricao PR 00606. Tel. 787/838-2550, Fax 787/838-2551, toll-free 800/443-0266.*

Once the greathouse of a 19th century coffee plantation, this 21-room parador is family operated and has a restaurant and bar. Swim or play tennis, then explore the surrounding mountains and rainforest. Rooms have four-poster beds; the lobby is decorated with antique coffee-making equipment.

PARADOR MARTORELL, *6A Ocean Drive, mailing address Box 384, Luquillo PR 00773. Tel. 787/889-2710, Fax 787/889-4520.*

This 10-room, family-run parador is next to famous Luquillo Beach with its colorful vendors, shapely palm trees, and acres of pristine sand. Rooms are air conditioned and have cable television; restaurants are nearby. Rates include a full breakfast.

HOTEL PARADOR OASIS, *64 Luna Street, mailing address Box 144, San Germán PR 00683. Tel. 787/892-1175.*

A historic building makes up part of this 50-room parador in a charming old, inland town. Rooms have air conditioning, telephone, and cable television. The courtyard has a small pool and poolside dining. The parador is wheelchair accessible and it has a small gym.

PARADOR PERICHI'S, *Route 102, Kilometer 14.3, Cabo Rojo, Tel. 787/851-3131, Fax 787/851-0560.*

Facing Rones Island is this 25-room hotel. It's near the beach and has parking, restaurant and bar, volleyball, air conditioning, telephones, and television.

PARADO PICHI'S, *Route 132, Kilometer 204.6, Guayanilla, Tel. 787/835-3335, Fax 787/835-3272.*

This 58-room resort has a swimming pool, parking, a nearby beach, restaurant and bar with live music, television, air conditioning, a playground, and telephones. It is wheelchair accessible.

PARADOR POSADA PORLAMAR, *Box 405 La Parguera, Lajas PR 00667. Tel. 787/899-4015.*

Right on the water in a resort village, this 18-room parador is wheelchair accessible and air conditioned. All around are places to dine and have fun. Boats leave from its dock for the area's outstanding dive sites.

PARADOR VILLA ANTONIO, *Route 115, Kilometer 12.3, Rincón PR. Tel. 787/823-2645, Fax 787/823-3380.*

Cottages and apartments on the beachfront are handy to Rincon and west coast attractions. Enjoy the swimming pool, playground, and tennis courts and use the barbecue. Rates at this 55-room parador are in the $76-$125 range. Rooms are air conditioned and have color television.

PARADOR VILLA PARGUERA, *La Parguera, mailing address Box 273, Lajas PR 00667. Tel. 787/899-7777, Fax 787/899-4435, toll-free 800/288-3975. Rates at this 62-room parador are in the $76 to $125 range.*

Rooms have two double beds, a balcony, air conditioning and telephone and there's a restaurant and bar. Take a night cruise to Phosphorescent Bay, swim in the saltwater pool, and enjoy the Saturday night dancing and show.

PARADOR VISTAMAR, *6205 Route 113, Kilometer 7.9, Quebradillas PR 00678. Tel. 787/895-2065, Fax 787/895-2294.*

When you stay in this 55-room parador you're in the heart of one of Puerto Ricans' favorite vacation regions on a hilltop overlooking the rugged Guajataca coast. There are swimming pools, a basketball court, tennis courts, a laundry, garden pathways, dancing and live music on weekends, and a gift shop. Nearby are the Rio Camuy caves and other points of interest. Rooms have air conditioning, telephone, and cable television and are wheelchair accessible.

PARADOR PERICHI'S, *Route 102, Kilometer 14.3, Cabo Rojo PR 00623. Tel. 787/851-3131, Fax 787/851-0560.*

Many people know this 30-room parador for its steak-and-seafood restaurant but it's also an ideal place to stay while you're exploring southwest Puerto Rico. The design is modern Mediterranean with an open air terrace and landscaped grounds surrounding the basketball and tennis courts and the big swimming pool. Rooms, many of them overlooking Joyuda Beach, have air conditioning, telephone, and cable television and are wheelchair accessible.

WHERE TO EAT

Here is great news for less-than-adventurous foodies! Throughout Puerto Rico, you'll see familiar mainland fast food outlets – not just McDonald's, Subway, Taco Bell, Pizza Hut, and KFC, but more upscale chains such as Chili's and Pizzeria Uno and specialty chains such as Baskin Robbins and Orange Julius. Even Condado's landmark Chart House is one of the California chain, and Palio at the Westin Rio Mar is a clone of the one at the Swan in Walt Disney World.

FOODS OF PUERTO RICO

Puerto Rico's version of bon appetit is ***buon provecho****, a lip-smacking way of starting meals featuring the island's unique blend of old and new, Spanish and Caribbean. "Cocina criolla", or creole cuisine, started with the Tainos, Amerindians who grew cassava, corn, yams, and taro that are still island staples. Yuca flour is the basis for a flat bread that is still an everyday favorite. Introduced by the Spanish were wheat flour, garbanzo beans, cilantro, coconut, garlic, rum, and a cornucopia of vegetables including tomatoes, eggplant, and onions. With African slaves came gandules (pigeon peas), plantains, and okra.*

Island favorites include fried green plantains, or tostones, which are seen commonly on a plate that includes meat, rice , and beans. Fast-food stands offer alcapurrias, a dough of grated taro root and green bananas stuffed with meat, crab, or chicken. Empanadillas are deep-fried turnovers filled with cheese, meat or chicken. Try bacalaitos, fritters made from salt cod, or surrullitos, which are cigar-shaped cornmeal fritters dipped in a sauce made from mayonnaise and ketchup. Rellenos de papa are deep-fried mashed potato balls with a filling of meat, chicken, or cheese. Amarillos are yellow plaintains cooked in butter or oil.

Your criollo meal will probably consist of meat, fish or chicken plus a side dish of arroz blanco, or white rice, and habichuelas, or beans cooked in a pungent sofrito sauce. Try mofongo, a popular side dish of mashed fried green plaintains seasoned with garlic and pork. The national celebration dish is roast suckling pig but Puerto Ricans also love their seafood, often served escabeche style, which means marinated.

For dessert, flan is a favorite that is usually a vanilla custard but is sometimes flavored with coconut, mashed pumpkin, or breadfruit. The local bread pudding, tembleque, will be familiar to mainland taste buds. So will rice pudding, called arroz con dulce. Try one of the tropical versions flavored with tamarind, coconut or soursop. Guava shells served with crackers and cream cheese are a typical dessert. The meal ends with Puerto Rican coffee, drunk black or with whipped, boiled milk.

The locally popular **Pollo Tropical** chain features fruity roast chicken, rice, beans, and plantains. Fast food or gourmet fare, Puerto Rico offers the widest range of Caribbean, Latin, and American foods in the islands. Unless stated otherwise, these restaurants accept credit cards.

Old San Juan – Expensive

CHEF MARISOLL CONTEMPORARY CUISINE, *202 Cristo Street. Tel. 725-7454. Park free for two hours at La Cochera. Hours are Tuesday to*

Friday noon to 2:30pm and Tuesday to Sunday, 7-10pm. Main dishes are priced $20 and higher. Reservations are essential.

Dine in a romantic courtyard on the creations of Marisoll Hernandez who learned her art at Hilton hotels abroad. Only eight tables are available, so make reservations well ahead and prepare yourself for an unusual feast according to the best of today's marketplace. There will be a couple of wonderful soups and perhaps pheasant, a curry, a roast, and always the catch of the day.

LA CHAUMIÈRE, *367 Tetuan Street, Old San Juan behind the Tapia Theater. Tel. 722-3330. Reservations are urged. Main dishes are priced $20 to $40. Hours are 6pm to midnight nightly except Sunday.*

Dine on classic French cuisine in a rustic, heavily beamed room that takes you to the French countryside. Start with one of the patés, oysters Rockefeller, or a soup followed by roast lamb, the chateaubriand with vegetables served for two, veal Oscar, bouillabaisse, or *coq au vin.*

IL PERUGINO, *105 Cristo Street. Tel. 722-5481. Open for dinner nightly 6:30 to 11pm, the restaurant requires reservations after 4pm. Main dishes are priced $20 to $30.*

It calls itself San Juan's best Italian restaurant and displays the awards that seem to prove it. Owner-chef Franco Seccarelli is on hand nightly to make sure guests receive the kindest welcome, superb dining, and one of the most comprehensive wine lists in the city. Try the pastas, polenta with shrimp, carpaccios, rack of lamb, or marinated salmon. The building, a restored, 200-year-old townhouse, is named for Perugia, Franco's home town.

RESTAURANT GALERIA, *205 San Justo, Old San Juan. Tel. 725-0478. Reservations are urged. Open daily except Monday noon to 10pm, the restaurant offers main dishes for $12.95 to $21.95.*

Choose from Cuban and Puerto Rican dishes with international style. Start with the cream soup of the day, escargot in garlic butter, or octopus salad, then try the seafood risotto or the halibut. Live piano music plays Wednesday through Saturday. An area is set aside for smokers.

YUKIYU, *311 Recinto Sur, Old San Juan. Tel. 721-0653. Main courses are priced $10 to $20. Hours are noon to 2:30pm and 5-11pm. Reservations are suggested; parking is by valet.*

You may not get beyond the sushi bar, a rare find in Puerto Rico. Choose from a long list of sushis then move on to the grilled lamb with polenta, fresh salmon with udon noodles, lobster tail in a creamy sauce, fresh cod in basil butter, or hibachi chicken. If you prefer, your favorite stir-fry combinations will be made for you tableside in a frenzy of fiery theatrics.

Old San Juan – Moderate

AL DENTE, *309 Recinto Sur, Old San Juan. Tel. 723-7303. Reservations are recommended. The restaurant is open Monday through Saturday 11:30am to 10:30pm. Main dishes are in the $15-$20 range.*

The style is casual Italian and the food a fusion of continental flavors and fresh Puerto Rican harvests. Start with the spinach stuffed with rice and cheese, then try the specialty of the house, fettuccine with shrimp and red and green sweet peppers. Veal is served in a variety of ways including a delectable, veal-stuffed tortellini; chicken comes in a sassy sauce of white wine, black olives, mushrooms, capers and tomatoes.

AMADEUS, *Calle San Sebastian 4601, Plaza San Jose. Tel. 722-8635 for reservations. Hours are Tuesday through Sunday noon to 2am but last orders are taken at midnight. Entrees are $14-$20.*

Set in an old stone building built for a wealthy trader in the 1700s, Amadeus features a refreshingly different combination of nouvelle cuisine (try the caviar pizza with smoked salmon) and Caribbean flair, such as the christophene salad with crabmeat. Have a vegetable tart before choosing a meat or seafood main dish.

EL PATIO DE SAM, *Calle San Sebastian 102, Plaza San Jose, Old San Juan Tel. 723-1149 or 723-8802. The kitchen is open Sunday through Thursday 11am to midnight and Friday and Saturday until 1am. Main dishes are $10 to $35. Reservations aren't required. Park at Ballaja and your ticket will be validated.*

Lavish use of plants and potted trees turns this air conditioned indoor restaurant into an outdoor patio known among Americans for its juicy burgers. For something different try the seafood-stuffed sole, breaded cheese stuffed shrimp, or rabbit in garlic sauce. Standards such as homemade lasagna, barbecued ribs, and beef *en brochette* are popular with homesick Americans. For dessert there's flan or Hungarian chocolate torte.

LA MALLORQUINA, *207 San Justo Street, Old San Juan. Tel. 722-3261. Hours are Monday through Saturday, 11:30am to 10pm. Main dishes are priced $14 to $30. Reservations are recommended for dinner but are not accepted for lunch.*

Opened in 1848 and set among the arches and courtyards of a colonial-era building filled with antiques, this is a local icon packed at lunch time with visitors. If you want to try traditional Puerto Rican dishes in an old-island setting, this is the place to order asopao (gumbo), arroz con pollo (chicken with rice), garlic soup, corn sticks, and homemade flan.

ROYAL THAI, *Recinto Sur #135, Old San Juan. Tel. 725-8424. Reservations are accepted. Main dishes are priced $16 to $22.*

The only Thai restaurant in town welcomes diners to bright surroundings surrounded by "swimming" fish on the walls and pink and white linen cloths topped with glass. Start with a spring roll or satay, then choose shrimp sautéed in red curry with coconut milk or half a Long Island duckling boned and served flambé in a sauce of choo chee curry paste and coconut milk. Put out the fire with a fruity dessert.

Old San Juan – Budget

BUTTERFLY PEOPLE CAFE, *Calle Fortaleza 152, Old San Juan. Tel. 723-2432. Light dishes are priced $5 to $10 but steaks are also available.*

This is a witty, whimsical operation that we were delighted to find still thriving under the care of thc "butterfly people" we met a few years back. They're a real family who love butterflies and have a real sense of what has lasting appeal to travelers and locals alike. Shop the gallery for butterflies in a variety of art forms. Then lunch on a cold soup, a creamy fruit drink, a steak, or quiche.

HARD ROCK CAFE, *253 Recinto Sur, Old San Juan. Tel. 724-7625. Prices are $4.50 to $17. Reservations aren't required but call for news of special events involving live music or happy hours. Hours are 11am to 2am daily; merchandise is sold 9am to midnight.*

If you "collect" Hard Rock Cafes, this busy, din-filled cafe is one to add to your list. Chicken or beef is served with pico de gallo, guacamole and sour cream. Eat inexpensively on red-hot chili or a sandwich, or splurge on a steak. The sizzling fajitas are a favorite and the classic H.R.C. hamburger is a juicy treat. Rock memorabilia on display includes items that belonged to John Lennon, Pink Floyd, and Phil Collins.

Greater San Juan – Expensive

CASA ITALIA, *275 Avenida Domenech, Hato Rey. Tel. 250-7388. Reservations are recommended; valet parking is available. Owner-chef Massimo Manscuso welcomes dinner guests daily except Mondays. Main dishes are from $20.*

Antipasto, pasta, risotto, meat dishes and seafood come from the kitchen freshly made to order. This warmly elegant living room setting is the place to dine unhurriedly on a traditional succession of appetizers such as the carpaccio of beef, pastas or gnocchi, a porcini risotto, then a main dish of saltimbocca or tournedos Rossini.

CAPRICCIO, *in the Condado Plaza Hotel & Casino, 999 Ashford Avenida, Condado. Tel. 725-9236. Entrees are priced $17 to $25. Diners are offered two hours free parking at the hotel. Reservations are recommended.*

Gaze out over the Atlantic from a relaxed, romantic setting while dining on northern Italian specialties such as chicken Scarpariello or scallopini in marsala sauce with porcini mushrooms.

COMPOSTELA, *106 Avenida Condado, Santurce. Tel. 724-6088. Dinner for two without wine costs about $80. Reservations are suggested. The restaurant is open for dinner daily except Sunday.*

Owner-chef José Manuel Rey prizes himself on adapting peasant dishes for modern tastes. He sprinkles fresh halibut with the juice of freshly roasted pepper and olive oil infused with coriander. His scallops are done with caramelized sweet onions and sautéed foie gras; his duck is roasted with an exotic coffee glaze. The wine cellar boasts 300 labels. White-clothed tables sit among chrome columns and lots of greenery, creating an ambience popular with up-market locals as well as visitors.

EL ZIPPERLE, *352 Roosevelt Avenue, Hato Rey. Tel. 763-1636 or 751-4335. Call for hours and reservations. Main dishes start at $20.*

Dine in a darkly splendid room surrounded by wine vaults filled with one of the finest wine lists in Puerto Rico. The paella Valenciana is a specialty. The family who have operated the restaurant since 1953 also offer such continental choices as wiener schnitzel, roasts, and fresh seafood in delicate sauces. Save room for a Viennese dessert.

GIUSEPPE RISTORANTE, *in the Sands Hotel & Casino, Isla Verde. Tel. 791-1111. Reservations are recommended by owner-chef Giuseppe Acosa. Pastas start at $15; entrees at $20.*

Tables are clustered around a banquette that forms a gazebo for a mountain of flowers. A pink and white decor is anchored by a garnet carpet; paintings ring the room. Giuseppe recommends his trio of three pastas in different sauces. Italian classics on the menu include veal scaloppini in white wine, a meltingly tender osso bucco, steaks, filet, jumbo shrimp in garlic butter and a memorable linguine fruita d'mare.

MIRO MARISQUERIA CATALANA, *76 Condado Avenue, Condado. Tel. 723-9593. Main courses are priced $10 to $25. Use the valet parking. Hours are Tuesday through Sunday, lunch and dinner from 11:30am.*

Pungent Catalonian dishes prepared with the freshest seafood make for a special evening hosted by owner-chef José Lavilla. Start with marinated salt cod with onions and peppers or the calamari, then the superb paella cooked for two or more. Other choices include cod in cream sauce, grilled tuna with peppercorns and roast peppers, baked halibut with fresh herbs or, for parties of six or more, roast suckling pig. If you love to make a meal out of tapas alone, this is the place to choose from a long list that includes salads, fried cheese with tomato marmalade, and homemade Catalan style tomato bread.

NORMANDIE RESTAURANT *in the Radisson Normandie, Avenida Munoz Rivera, Puerto de Tierra, corner of Calle Los Rosales. Tel. 729-2929. Hours are 6-10pm daily. Plan to spend $80 for dinner for two. Parking is $3.*

Located in a showy atrium in a distinctive art deco-era hotel, this restaurant is worth the trip just to see the architecture. Order from the menu of specialties that are cooked tableside, or let the waiter suggest something from tonight's specials. Ask to see the extensive wine list.

PIKAYO, *in the Tanama Princess Hotel, 1 Calle Joffre, Condado. Tel. 721-6194. Dinner for two costs about $80 without wine. Reservations are suggested. It's open Monday through Friday for lunch and dinner and Saturday for dinner only.*

Cajun has come to Puerto Rico with owner-chef Wilo Benet and his wife Lorraine. Order blackened fish or popcorn shrimp, or wonderfully doctored Puerto Rican dishes such as plantain fritters stuffed with bleu cheese or bacalao. He serves his escargot with wild mushrooms and balsamic vinegar and his Louisiana crab cakes with tostones and a buerre blanc made with chipotle peppers.

PORTOBELLO RISTORANTE, *Avenida F.D. Roosevelt 1144, Puerto Nuevo. Tel. 277-0911. Reservations are recommended; valet parking is available. Closed Monday. Entrees start at $17.95; pastas at $12.95.*

The gnocchi in pesto is superb, but for something meatier try the filet mignon, pork chops, salmon, or veal scallops.

RAMIRO'S RESTAURANT, *1106 Magdalena Avenue, Condado. Tel. 721-9056. Main dishes are priced $10 to $35; a multi-course, fixed price dinner is about $60. Reservations and valet parking are essential. Hours are daily noon to 3pm and 6:30 to 11pm.*

You'll remember an evening at Luis Ramiro's as a culinary highlight of a lifetime. Original, deftly created dishes include steamed cuttlefish with herbs, smoked lobster in light lemon sauce, cold avocado cream with smoked salmon, lamb pie with port wine and raisins, lentil and chickpea soup, and artichoke hearts foie gras – and that's just the starters. Main courses include a succulent roast duckling with guava and an unforgettable venison with pear in a sauce of wine, blackberries, and Armagnac or fish mousse served in sweet peppers shaped like flowers. The wine cellar boasts 25,000 bottles bearing 400 labels from wineries around the world. Dress for an upscale neighborhood.

RUTH'S CHRIS STEAK HOUSE, *in the Sands Hotel, 187 Isla Verde Road, Isla Verde. Tel. 253-1717. It's open nightly for dinner; valet parking is complimentary. Plan to spend $80 for dinner for two.*

Revered for its butter-tender, corn-fed prime beef, Ruth's blasts its steaks to seared perfection in an 1800-degree broiler designed by Ruth Fortel herself. After dinner, take in a show at the hotel's own night club.

SWEENEY'S ORIGINAL SCOTCH 'N SIRLOIN, *in the Ambassador Plaza Hotel, 1369 Ashford Avenue, Condado. Tel. 721-9315. Reservations are requested. Plan to spend $80-$100 for dinner for two.*

Make an evening of it at the Ambassador, where you can have a drink at the Sports Bar before dinner at Sweeney's. Then dance after dinner in the Cabaret Lounge or try your luck in the casino. This is a time-honored

THE DINE AROUND PROGRAM

One of the most exciting dining options in the Caribbean is Puerto Rico's ***Dine Around Program****. Pay one set price of $49 per day, which buys breakfast at your hotel and dinner at any of 12 other restaurants in the San Juan area. Ask your travel agent, or inquire when you arrive at your hotel whether it's available. The program does not apply in peak seasons.*

meat and potatoes place, so order a dry-aged steak, prime rib, or rack of lamb. There's also lobster, fresh fish, a salad bar, and an impressive wine list.

Greater San Juan – Moderate

AJILI MOJILI, *Ashford Avenue, Condado. Tel. 725-9195. Make reservations and use the valet parking. Hours are Monday through Thursday, 6 to 10pm Friday and Saturday to 11pm. Main courses are priced $9.95 to $24.95.*

Pronounce it "ah-HILL-ee moh-HILL-ee." Dining here is like going home to Mom, if your mother happens to be Puerto Rican. The air conditioning adds to the comfort of an unpretentious room where the focus is on good food and fellowship. Regional dishes from around the island are featured on a menu that changes twice a month, but there's always arroz con pollo plus pumpkin fritters, a guinea hen of the day, and a selection of mofongos and inexpensive rice dishes. Most of the meats, seafood and produce come from local farms. Desserts come on a trolley. Take your pick.

BACK STREET HONG KONG, *in the El San Juan Hotel & Casino, Route 187, Isla Verde. Tel. 791-1224. Reservations are recommended. Hours are 6pm to midnight nightly except Sunday, when hours are 1pm to midnight. Entrees are priced $18 to about $30.*

The illusion is that of a gracious private home owned by people who have traveled and collected in the Far East. Built for the 1964 World's Fair, the restaurant was shipped here and re-assembled. Entering, it's easy to forget you're in a hotel as you are transported to a Hong Kong street. With attentive service and crisp pink table linens, the restaurant features its orange sauce served with your choice of sautéed lobster, jumbo scallops, diced chicken sliced beef, or jumbo shrimp. Live Maine lobster is almost always on the menu at today's market price. The menu has an impressive selection of Chinese poultry, seafood, and beef specialties, all expertly sauced and presented.

CASA DANTE, *Avenida Isla Verde 39, Isla Verde. Tel. 726-7310. Open every day. Main dishes are $7.95 to $28.95 for a 12-24-ounce lobster tail.*

Dante and Milly personally welcome guests to this relaxed, family,

Puerto Rican restaurant. The house specialty is crushed plantain with your choice of pork, steak, shrimp, lobster, chicken, veal, or fish in a variety of presentations.

CHART HOUSE, *1214 Avenida Ashford. Tel. 724-0110. Reservations are suggested and are a must on weekends; valet parking is available. Hours are daily, 5pm to midnight. Main dishes start at $16.95.*

For those who like a classic steak and seafood house with pasta in place of the ubiquitous French fries, this is the place to start with shrimp cocktail and then launch into a New York strip, extra-thick prime rib, or a charbroiled teriyaki tuna. Try the native dorado (mahi-mahi) in Creole sauce. Vegetarians will like the fettuccine with portobello "steak." House specialties include artichokes in season, served with aioli, and "mud" pie for dessert.

The dress code is resort casual to go with the yachty elegance. The building alone is worth the trip. Once the home of the German consul, the grand villa was built a decade before World War I began.

EL CAIRO RESTAURANT, *Avenida Roosevelt (Route 23) Ensenada #352, Caparra Heights Tel. 273-7140. Valet parking is available; it's open daily for dinner. Main dishes start at $11.75.*

It's fun and different to try this Arabian-Lebanese restaurant and to shop its gift counter for Arabian items and take-out pastries. Belly dancers perform Friday and Saturdays, yet it's all G-rated and families are invited. Start with hummus or falafel, then choose from a host of Middle Eastern classics: shish kebob, steak tartare, curried chicken with Arabian rice, curried lamb, or a plentiful sampler platter filled with all the above and then some.

EL CHOTIS, *Calle O'Neill #187, Hato Rey, about six miles south of Condado off Route 1. Tel. 758-3086. A valet will park your car. Plan to spend about $20-$40 per person for dinner. Call for hours and reservations.*

Relax in what looks like an old Spanish tavern to enjoy paella, a good red wine, and a rousing flamenco (Friday and Saturday). Lobster is served grilled or in Spanish sauce; the tuna and potato salad makes a delicious appetizer or light meal. Many people come here to make a meal out of tapas alone.

EL TAPATIO RESTAURANTES MEXICANOS, *Avenida Jesus T. Piñero 1025, Puerto Nuevo. Tel. 781-2006 or 781-3126. Main dishes start at $11; tacos at $8.95. Reservations are recommended; valet parking is available.*

Show up on a Friday, Saturday, or Sunday for live mariachi music while you dine on traditional Mexican favorites prepared with or without hot, hot peppers. The chicken with mole pablano is a classic – chicken prepared with a hint of chocolate and served with green rice, refried beans, and guacamole. The fajitas platter for two is a feast.

GREENHOUSE RESTAURANT & LOUNGE, *1200 Ashford Avenue, Condado. Tel. 725-4036. It's open for breakfast, lunch and dinner; call ahead for hours and reservations. A wide range of prices allows you to dine on beans and rice, a drink and bread for under $10, or splurge on the lobster for $39.95 plus appetizer, drinks, and dessert.*

We are reminded of a big, bustling, Broadway restaurant where menu choices range from the very modest to the most spendthrift. It's all hearty, no-nonsense, American cuisine with a Puerto Rican touch. The char-broiled steaks and chops, for example, can be ordered *a caballo* (with two eggs) for $2 extra. For breakfast, have a platter-size omelet or eggs Benedict. Later, the chicken crepe at $12.95 is a creamy, luscious lunch or dinner. The black bean soup topped with rice, chopped onion and egg, is a great buy at $4.95. (Bread and butter cost $2 extra except with full meals.) Appetizers include escargot or hearts of palm. Have the Greenhouse Salad, or make a meal of the mammoth chef salad. Main dishes include shrimp, lobster, chicken, pork chops, and steaks. For lighter dining, have a gourmet burger, cold platter, or a sandwich. Homemade cakes are offered for dessert. Like the menu, the wine list starts in the bargain basement with sangria by the pitcher, and escalates to top-floor vintages by the bottle.

HAVANA'S CAFE, *409 Calle del Parque, Stop 23, Santurce. Tel. 725-0888. Main dishes are priced $5 to $20. Hours are 7am to 10pm Monday through Friday and 11:30am to 10pm Saturday and Sunday.*

Enjoy authentic Cuban dishes in a casually elegant room reminiscent of Havana in the 1950s. Try mofongo stuffed with shredded beef or shrimp, fresh codfish, or lobster timbales. Tuesday is cigar night.

HUNAN HOUSE, *141 Avenida F.D. Roosevelt, Hato Rey. Tel. 250-8039. Reservations are accepted. Main dishes range from $10.50 for rice or noodle dishes to $36 for the Peking Duck.*

Comfortably family-oriented, this Chinese restaurant has the usual favorites such as butterfly shrimp and vegetarian dishes plus such inventions as chicken with mango, pearl shrimp, Singapore curried chicken, and beef Mongolian style.

IL CAPO, *Calle Loisa 2478, Puenta Las Marias. Tel. 268-5319. Closed Mondays, the restaurant accepts major credit cards and offers live music on Fridays. Main dishes start at $12.95; pastas at $9.*

Good Italian flavors accompanied by wines from a well-stocked cellar, plus a cozy and comforting ambience for all the family add up to a pleasant evening. Start with melon and prosciutto or carpaccio of beef topped with Parmesan cheese and olive oil dressing. On the pasta list are a memorable ravioli with lobster in champagne cream and a simple, classic lasagnes, or penne with vodka sauce. Main dishes, which include veal Marsala, boneless breast of chicken, sirloin steak, shrimp and salmon, are all served with homemade fettucini marinara.

ICHE'S INTERNATIONAL CUISINE, *Calle Parkside 4, C-2, Guyanabo. Tel. (7887) 782-6910. Main dishes are in the $18-$22 range. Reservations are recommended. Valet parking is available; the restaurant is open daily except Monday for lunch and dinner. On Monday, only lunch is served.*

Richard Kleiman hopes you'll stop by to sample the relaxed elegance of his eclectic restaurant where risotto and tempura share the same page on the menu. Main dishes range from New Zealand lamb to fresh cod.

KIMPO GARDEN, *Avenida Jesus T. Pinero 264, Hato Rey. Tel. 767-0810. Credit cards are accepted; main dishes start at $11.*

David Chang is your host as you relax in a casual restaurant where Szechuan is featured but the lobster is served Cantonese style. Start with the cold noodles in sesame sauce or the crab lau-lau. The chef's specialties include shrimp or lobster in black bean sauce, and a sizzling steak platter with fresh vegetables. Typical Chinese chicken dishes are made with orange sauce, broccoli or scallion, and ginger.

LA FONDA DE CERVANTES, *in the Hotel Iberia, 1464 Wilson Avenue, Condado. Tel. 722-6433. Main dishes are $10 to $20. Call for hours and reservations.*

Dine indoors or out in a Mediterranean ambience with music drifting in from the piano bar. Start with grilled shrimp or an octopus appetizer, then sample a seafood zarzuela, the planked fish, or the paella a la Valenciana for two.

LOS CHAVALES RESTAURANT, *Avenida F.D. Roosevelt #253, Hato Rey. Tel. 767-5017. Valet parking is available; major credit cards are honored noon to midnight, Monday through Saturday. Main dishes start at $20; chateaubriand for two is just under $50.*

Relaxed enough for family dining, but elegant enough for business or romance, this white tablecloth restaurant with its scenic, trompe l'oiel murals has a fine selection of California, French, Spanish and Portuguese wines to complement Spanish and international dishes. Among five menu offerings that serve two or more is a grilled seafood platter, rack of lamb, double sirloin, and a paella like mamacita used to make. Desserts for two include crepes Suzette at $13.95 and baked Alaska at $12.95.

LUPI'S MEXICAN GRILL & SPORTS CANTINA, *Isla Verde Road, Kilometer 1.3, Isla Verde. Tel. 253-2198 or 253-1664. Open daily 11am to 5am. Lupi's doesn't require reservations. Main dishes are $10 to $20.*

A rollicking sports bar with live music nightly after 11pm, this is the place to tank up on zesty Tex-Mex dishes such as fajitas and nachos before an evening of cheering the team and line dancing into a wee hours. Lupi's is also found at 313 Recinto Sur in Old San Juan, *Tel. 722-1874,* with the same hours and live jazz.

MEDITERRANEO RISTORANTE ITALIANO, *Avenida Ashford 1021, Condado. Tel. 723-7006. Parking is in back of the restaurant, which is open daily except Monday. Reservations are recommended. Main dishes are priced $10 to $22.*

Giancarlo and Anna Bonegatti are on hand with a personal invitation to try their homemade pastas, which include ravioli with fresh asparagus, vermicelli served country style with bacon, mushrooms, Italian sausage and green peas, and spaghetti smothered in a succulent seafood mixture. There's also gnocchi and osso bucco, then tiramisu for dessert.

MIRO, *Avenida Condado 76 next to the Hotel El Portal. Tel. 723-9593. Valet parking is available; the restaurant is closed Mondays. Paella for two is $14.95. Other dishes start at $13.25.*

Owner-chef José Lavilla will welcome you to his warmly Catalonian marisqueria and may suggest one of his many inspired specialties such as cod with roasted peppers, tomatoes, garlic, and cinnamon, or the cod with garlic cream. The menu also offers lobster, tuna, chicken, pork medallions and a classic New York strip with onions and mushrooms. For a truly special event, call ahead and arrange to have the suckling pig, a feast that is prepared for six or more.

RESTAURANTE FELIX, *Carretera #1, Kilometer 25, Caguas, 20 miles south of San Juan. Tel. 720-1625. Closed Mondays, the restaurant is open for lunch and dinner. Call for reservations. Plan to spend $50 per couple for dinner.*

Celebrate with lobster or the chateaubriand for two, and don't miss the cream of yautia soup and the Caesar salad.

ST. MORITZ, *Avenida Ashford 1005 in the Hotel Regency, Condado. Tel. 721-0999. Reservations are recommended; all major credit cards are honored. Main dishes start at under $16; the lamb provençale for two is $49.*

The name promises a Swiss touch in this ocean-view dining room. Start with Swiss cheese croquettes and, if you're still in a yodeling mood, have the minced veal with roesti potatoes, or the veal schnitzel cordon bleu. The rack of lamb provençale for two is served with English mustard, a feast of vegetables, and baked potatoes. The dessert cart is laden with choices from flan to fruit tarts.

ZABO, *14 Candina Street, Condado. Tel. 725-9494. The parking entrance is on Ashford across from Citibank. It's open for lunch and dinner, Tuesday through Saturday. Main dishes are $18 to $25.*

Have a drink in the cozy bar, then relax in this restored, 1910 country house while dining on conch fritters in mango and sesame sauce, rack of lamb in tamarind and ginger sauce, or salmon in parchment with black bean sauce. Eat indoors in air conditioning or on the balcony outdoors. This is a popular grazing bar. Many guests come only for tapas or only for dessert.

Greater San Juan – Budget

BIG APPLE, *1407 Ashford Avenue, Condado. Tel. 725-6345. Hours are 7am to 10pm. Prices are $5 to $10.*

Dine in or take out the best in New York deli treats, from mile-high corned beef on rye and bagels with cream cheese to Hebrew National hot dogs and cold meats.

CARUSO ITALIAN RISTORANTE, *1104 Ashford Avenida, Condado. Tel. 723-6876 for hours. Main dishes start at $6.75.*

Like the best little neighborhood Italian restaurant in your home town, Caruso serves up classic southern Italian cuisine in an unpretentious room filled with good smells. The spaghetti in meat sauce is a budget favorite, but there are also veal and chicken dishes, and lobster Fra Diablo at splurge prices depending on size. Flaming desserts and homemade tiramisu are house dessert specialties.

DENNY'S, *in the Isla Verde Mall, Isla Verde. Tel. 253-3080, is open 24 hours. Most main dishes are $10 or less.*

Although this is a member of the popular chain known for its inexpensive meals and Grand Slam breakfasts, it also offers local foods through its Sabroso Criollo menu. Other Denny's are around the city and in major cities island-wide.

FRIDAYS, *Calle Ortegon, in the San Patricio Shopping Center, Guayanabo. From Old San Juan, take Route 18 south, then southwest on Route 1. Tel. 781-4310. Open daily for lunch and dinner and for Sunday brunch 11am to 3pm, the restaurant serves meals for $10 to $20.*

Build your own burger from a choice of a dozen toppings, or splurge on the New York strip steak. This is a big-screen sports bar where you can watch the main event while scarfing down fajitas or loaded potato skins. Or, have a real meal featuring lemon chicken topped with fettucine and spinach. Sunday brunch is a special event.

JERUSALEM RESTAURANT, *Calle O'Neill G-1, Hato Rey. Tel. 764-3265. Nothing on the menu is more than $15; valet parking is available.*

Light eaters can make a feast from one or two appetizers, all of them under $5. They include Middle Eastern musts: baba ganoush, hummus, falafel, or taboulleh. Main dishes focus on fish or lamb, cooked and served in the Arabic manner. The sampler platter is the best buy; for dessert there's baklava. When you call for reservations, ask the best time to arrive for the belly dancer show. It's family oriented, exotic, and straight out of a 1950s movie.

RESTAURANT EL MUELLE 13 RESTAURANT, *Calle O'Neill 177, tel 787/767-7825. Main dishes start at $12. It's open daily; offering valet parking.*

A friendly, family restaurant specializing in seafood offers such local staples as rice with bacalao (cod) or paella Valenciana for two, a superb buy at $25.90. Steaks and chicken are served in a variety of cuts. Try the mofongo with lobster or the lobster salad.

East of San Juan to Fajardo – Expensive

PALIO, *in the Westin Rio Mar Beach Resort, 6000 Rio Mar Boulevard, Rio Grande, 19 miles west of San Juan. Tel. 888-6200. Reservations are essential. The restaurant is open nightly for dinner; take a taxi ($20 from Fajardo) or drive in and valet park for $6. No self-parking is available. Plan to spend $50-$60 for a three-course dinner without wine.*

A woody, Mediterranean room welcomes diners who are first served a tiny pitcher of red wine in a 2,000-year-old tradition of Roman welcome. The food here is northern Italian in a grand sweep of choices. Start with the grilled vegetable terrine, roasted portobello mushrooms with sun-dried tomato dressing, or fried calamari rings served with spicy tomato sauce and roasted pepper aioli. Tuscan white bean soup or Caesar salad precede a meal of inspired pastas or meltingly tender meats such as the 12- ounce filet of Black Angus beef with flamed morels or the rosemary chicken with braised savoy cabbage. Many dishes are accompanied by satiny risottos, which aren't to be missed. Let the sommelier suggest a wine from more than 200 selections; let the server suggest a dessert from tonight's list of sweets.

East of San Juan to Fajardo – Moderate

MARBELLA, *in the Westin Rio Mar Beach Resort, 6000 Rio Mar Boulevard, Rio Grande, 19 miles west of San Juan. Tel. 888-6200. Reservations are recommended. Buffet breakfast is $13.50; lunch $15.95 and dinner $23.95. Only valet parking is available.*

The dramatic decor in a bright, three-story-high room overlooking the sea sets the mood for a riot of great eating from buffets laden with fresh fruits, hot and cold dishes, bushels of breadrolls, and some of the best pastries on the island. Each night celebrates a different theme such as Italian, Caribbean, Puerto Rican, Asian, or Greek, so call ahead to see what's on for tonight. Menu service is also available for those who can resist the buffet.

The hotel's other moderately priced restaurant, **La Estancia**, is in the tennis club and is open for lunch and dinner. Valet park, then take the free shuttle. Pan-seared red snapper is served in orange ginger sauce, Cornish game hem is stuffed with yuca and topped with Spanish sofrito sauce, and there's a mofongo of the day.

East of San Juan to Fajardo – Budget

LOLITA'S, *Carretera 65 de Infanteria, Kilometer 41.8 between Fajardo and Luquillo. Tel. 889-5770. Prices are $2.25 to $12.95. Credit cards and reservations aren't accepted.*

With 24 hours notice you can have mole pablano, but mostly this is an impulse place when you have a yen for Mexican food. A big selection of burritos, tacos, and nachos is budget priced; combination platters are a hearty meal for little *dinero*. Round out the meal with beer, fresh juices, or a cocktail with or without alcohol, ending with the flan.

South Coast

RESTAURANT EL ANCLA, *Avenida Hostos Final 9, Playa Ponce, Ponce. Tel. 840-2450. Reservations are accepted but not required. Main dishes are priced $15 to $35. It's open for lunch and dinner daily.*

You'll be at sea, literally, in a family-run restaurant built on a pier over the water. Start with a half dozen crispy tostones, followed by a paella prepared for two, filet mignon with French fries, or the red snapper in lobster and shrimp sauce.

LA CAVA DE LA HACIENDA, *in the Ponce Hilton, Avenida Santiago Caballeros 14, Ponce. Tel. 787/259-7676. Reservations are urged. Hours are 7am to 10:30pm daily. Plan to spend $35 per person for dinner.*

As the name suggests, La Cava looks like a wine cellar, intimate and darkly cool. It's part of a brighter restaurant, La Hacienda. The two, rambling from one room to the next, offer elegant dining on an inspired menu that changes often. Always excellent are the fish and lobster dishes, fresh vegetables, toothsome breads and rolls, and luscious desserts.

LA TERRAZA, *in the Ponce Hilton, Avenida Santiago Caballeros 14, Ponce. Tel. 787/259-7676. Call ahead for hours and reservations. Plan to spend $25 for dinner.*

Dine outdoors for breakfast, lunch, and dinner, especially at dinner time when such themes as Steak Night or Lobster Night are held. Before dinner, have a margarita at Los Balcones in the hotel and have an after-dinner drink while listening to live Latin sounds in La Bohemia lounge.

PITO'S SEA FOOD CAFE, *Route 2, Kilometer 252, Las Cucharas, a mile southwest of Ponce. Tel. 841-4977. Main courses are $10 to $20. Hours are 11am to midnight daily. Reservations aren't required.*

Sit outdoors overlooking Cucharas Point or indoors in the air conditioning while you dine on chicken steak or fresh fish from the seas off Ponce.

TANAMA RESTAURANT, *in the Holiday Inn & Tropical Casino, Route 2, El Tuque, Ponce. Tel. 844-1200. Two can dine for about $50. Hours are 6am to 10pm Sunday through Thursday, and Friday and Saturday until midnight. Reservations aren't required.*

It's always a nice surprise to find fine local cuisine in a chain hotel. We also like the family-friendly ambience and the sea views. After dinner, there's gaming in the casino or listening in the lounge.

West & Southwest Puerto Rico – Expensive

HORNED DORSET PRIMAVERA, *Route 429, Kilometer 3, south of Rincón Tel. 823-4030. Reservations are essential for dinner and recommended for lunch. Hours are noon to 2:30 daily and dinner seatings at 7pm, 8pm, and 9pm. Main dishes are priced $25 to $30 and a fixed price meal is available for $50 without wine.*

Worth a special trip, this devotedly French restaurant keeps its standards to that of its parent, the Horned Dorset in upstate New York. Accustomed to a sophisticated, international clientele, the chef always has fresh seafood ready for the broiler to serve with an inspired sauce. Also on the menu are Long Island duckling, the finest meats, and delicately steamed vegetables.

West & Southwest Puerto Rico – Moderate

BLACK EAGLE RESTAURANT, *Route 413, Kilometer 1.0, Ensenada, Rincón, tel.823-3510. Main courses are $10 to $20. Hours are 11am to 11pm daily. Reservations aren't required.*

Enjoy the laid back, seaside ambience of this pleasantly touristy restaurant west of Rincón on a breezy point of land. Seafood is caught just offshore and is served flopping-fresh; steaks are flown in the from the United States.

GALLOWAY'S, *Poblado Boquerón, Cabo Rojo (south of Mayaguez). Tel. 254-3302. Main dishes are priced $8.95 to $17.95. Call for hours and reservations.*

Known for its sea views and sunsets, this restaurant specializes in mofongos in a variety of flavors including chicken, lobster, or shrimp and in asopaos, or gumbos. For openers, try the crusty cheese balls.

HOLLY'S RESTAURANT, *in the Holiday Inn, Highway 2, Kilometer 149.9, Mayaguez. Tel. 833-1100. Plan to spend $50 for dinner for two.*

Sample Puerto Rican food, fresh fish, an abundance of island vegetables, and a nice choice of sweets in this quietly elegant spot before an evening of gaming in the casino or listening to salsa sounds in Holly's Lounge.

Puerto Rico's Mesones Gastronómicos

Sponsored by the Puerto Rico Tourism Company, the **Mesones Gastronómicos** program is to restaurants what the parador system is to hotels. The designation simply means that these government-approved restaurants provide authentic Puerto Rican food that meets certain quality standards. Plan to spend $10-$15 per person for dinner, more for fresh lobster or steak. All take major credit cards unless otherwise specified.

- Aguada (north of Mayagüez): **LAS COLINAS**, *in the Parador J.B. Hidden Village, Tel. 868-8686*
- Aguadilla (Northwest Puerto Rico): **DARIO'S GOURMET**, *Route 110, Kilometer 8, Tel. 882-8000;* **DOS AMIGOS**, *Route 107, Kilometer 2.1, Tel. 890-2016*
- Aguas Buenas (South of San Juan): **SIRIMAR**, *Route 156, Kilometer 45.2, Tel. 732-6012*
- Aibonito (west of Cayey): **LA PIEDRA**, *Route 7718, Kilometer 0.8, Tel. 735-1034*
- Cabo Rojo (southwest Puerto Rico): **CASCADA**, *in the Parador Boquemar, Tel. 851-2158;* **PERICHI'S**, *Route 102, Kilometer 14.3, Tel. 851-3131;* **TINO'S**, *Route 102, Kilometer 13.5, Tel. 851-2976*
- Caguas (south of San Juan): **EL PARAISO**, *Route 1, Kilometer 29.1, Tel. 747-2012*
- Cayey: **JARDIN CHIQUITIN**, *Route 1, Tel. 263-2800*
- Coamo (southwest of Cayey): **BAÑOS DE COAMO**, *Route 546, Tel. 825-2239 or 825-2186*
- Dorado (west of San Juan): **LADRILLO**, *334 Méndez Vigo, Tel. 796-2120;* **TERRAZA**, *Marginal C1 and 693, Tel. 796-1242*
- Fajardo (northeast Puerto Rico): **ANCHOR'S INN**, *Route 987, Kilometer 2.7, Tel. 863-7200;* **ROSA'S SEAFOOD**, *536 Tablazo, Puerto Real, Tel. 863-0213*
- Guánica (southeast coast): **LA CONCHA**, *C-4 Principal, Playa Santa, Tel. 821-5522*
- Guayanilla (southwest coast): **PICHI'S**, *Route 132, Tel. 835-4140 or 835-3335*
- Gurabo (south of San Juan): **PAPA JUAN'S**, *Route 942, Tel. 737-2227*
- Hatillo (west of Arecibo): **BUEN CAFÈ**, *Route 2, Kilometer 8.4, Tel. 898-3495. No credit cards.*
- Humacao (southeast of San Juan): **DANIEL SEAFOOD**, *7 Marina, Tel. 852-1784;* **MARIE'S**, *Route 3, Kilometer 70.3, Tel. 852-5471;* **TULIO'S SEAFOOD**, *1 Aduana, Tel. 850-1840*
- Jayuya (halfway between Arecibo and Ponce): **DUJO**,*Route 140, Kilometer 8.2, Tel. 828-1143;* **HACIENDA GRIPIÑAS**, *Route 527, Kilometer 2.5, Tel. 828-1717*
- Juncos (southeast of San Juan): **El TENEDOR**, *1 Emilia Principe, Tel. 734-6673*
- Lajas (southwest coast): **VILLA PARGUERA PARADOR**, *Route 304, Tel. 899-3975*

- Lares (southeast of Arecibo): **LAS CAVERNAS**, *Route 129, Kilometer 19.6, Tel. 897-6463*
- Manatí (between San Juan and Arecibo): **SU CASA**, *Route 670, Kilometer 1.0, Tel. 884-0047*
- Maricao (east of Mayagüez): **CASONA DE JUANITA** *in the Parador Jacienda Juanita, Tel. 838-2550*
- Ponce: **ANCIA**, *9 Hostos, Tel. 840-2450;* **COCHE**, *122 Villa, Tel. 840-1521;* **PITO'S**, *Route 2, Cucharas, Tel. 841-4977*
- Quebradillas (west of Arecibo): **CASABI**, *in the Parador Guajataca, Tel. 895-3070 or 895-2204;* **PARADOR VISTAMAR**, *Route 113, Kilometer 7.9, Tel. 895-2065*
- Rio Grande (east of San Juan): **LAS VEGAS**, *Route 191, Kilometer 1.3, Tel. 887-2526*
- Utuado (between Arecibo and Ponce): **CASA GRANDE**, *in the Parador Casa Grande, Tel.894-3939;* **MESÓN DON ALONSO**, *Route 996, Tel. 894-0516*

SEEING THE SIGHTS

SAN JUAN

If you love old stones, it's a thrill just to stroll the slit-sized lanes of **Old San Juan** to soak up the delicious oldness of it all. Many streets have changed so little that you can imagine yourself in the days of swaggering Conquistadores, shy señoritas batting eyelashes behind their fans, and good friars gliding through the crowds. Then suddenly you see a Sony sign or a carelessly dropped gum wrapper and the 20th century comes rushing back.

Don't drive into the old city, where on-street parking is next to impossible. Instead, ride the two **free trolley tours** that cover two routes in the heart of Old San Juan. They operate every day, 16 hours a day plus evenings during **Gallery Nights** (Noches de Galerias) and they are all wheelchair accessible. If you have a car, park it at the Covadonga lot, where trolley service begins and ends. It's one of a handful of parking areas in the old city. Others are below El Morro, at La Puntilla near El Arsenal, and Felisa Rincón near the Marina.

Get off and on as you please, spending a few minutes here and a few hours there. To "do" the city right, with enough time at museums and the forts plus time out for the many shops and fine restaurants, will take several days of trolleying. For more information about Gallery Nights, *Tel. 723-7080.*

El Morro Castle, *Tel. 729-6960,* is a must, the oldest fortress still extant in the Americas. It was begun early in the 1500s and fell only once, and that briefly, to the English enemy. It saw service as late as World War II. Now managed by the U.S. Park Service, it has a souvenir shop, museums, bookstores, and miles of dungeons and ramparts to explore. Guided tours are given in English at 10am and 2pm and in Spanish at 11am and 3pm.

Also managed by the U.S. Park Service is **San Cristobál** on Norzagaray Street, *Tel. 729-6960*. Connected by moats and tunnels, this fort defended the city against attacks from the land side while El Morro stood sentinel against sea raiders.

Early Spanish planners built the city around grand plazas. A new one is **Quincentennial Plaza** on the city's highest point. It adjoins San José Plaza where you'll find **San José Church**, *Tel. 725-7501*, the second oldest in the Americas, and the ancient Dominican Convent. The church is open daily from 7am to 3pm and offers services on Sundays at noon and 1pm. The convent is the home of a bookshop that sells Puerto Rican literature, posters, and folk art.

The trolley guide will explain that **Casa Blanca**, *Tel. 724-4102,* was the home of **Juan Ponce de León**. See its fountain-filled gardens and its superb museum of artifacts from the 1500s and 1600s. It's open Tuesday through Saturday, 9am to noon and 1pm to 4:30pm. At the end of Cristo Street, **Casa del Libro**, *Tel. 723-0354,* is a printing museum housing one of the most important collections of pre-1500s volumes in the New World. It's open Thursday through Saturday, 11am to 4:30pm. Next door, the **National Crafts Center** displays local arts and crafts and nearby, the Banco Popular has a gallery featuring local arts.

In the **Plaza de la Rogativa**, see a sculpture of women bearing torches, commemorating an event during a British siege in which the women, who were merely staging a religious procession, fooled the English into thinking that reinforcements had arrived.

San Juan Cathedral is a Gothic masterpiece built in 1540 on the ruins of an early cathedral that was destroyed in a hurricane. It's here that the body of Ponce de León, seeker of the Fountain of Youth and Puerto Rico's first governor, lies in a marble vault. Next comes the **Capilla del Cristo** with its silver altar. It was built in gratitude to the Christ of Miracles by a man who had lost control of his horse and would have plunged over the edge of the cliff if a miracle hadn't brought the horse to a stop. The tiny chapel can be seen through the gate but if you want to go inside, it's open Tuesdays 10am to 3:30pm. A **Children's Museum** at 150 Cristo is entered through the legs of a wood giant. Inside, children can frolic through a village of playhouses, play dentist, and learn about cars and airplanes. Hours are Tuesday to Thursday, 9:30am to 3:30pm and weekends 11am to 4pm.

La Fortaleza, *Tel. 721-7000, extension 2211,* a grand ramble of archways and courtyards, is the oldest executive mansion in continuous use in the New World, dating to 1533. Guided tours are offered Monday through Friday, 9am to 4pm.

Seen from the trolley at Fortaleza and San Jose streets is the **Plaza de Armas**, surrounded by Spanish Colonial buildings as ornate as wedding cakes. On the Plaza Colon is the **Tapia Theater**, which is being renovated, and the 18th century Government Reception Center. Walk the Paseo de la Princessa, a boulevard that surrounds the old city walls, to San Juan Gate, the last survivor of the gates that were once the only passages through the mighty city wall.

South of the Plaza de Hostos is the **Arsenal de la Marina**, built in 1800 as a marina for small boats that patrolled the shallow waters around the city. At **La Casita**, home of a tourism information office, stop for information on the following museums, a cold drink and a rest on a park bench.

The **San Juan Museum of Art and History** was once the city's marketplace. Now it's filled with fine arts and changing displays. **The Museum of the Americas**, which opened in 1992, displays folk art of the region. It's open Wednesday through Sunday, 9am to 4:30pm. On the Plaza San Jose, small museums include one devoted to Pablo Casals, the renowned cellist who moved from Spain to Puerto Rico in 1956 to protest the Franco government. The **Casa de los Contrafuentes**, an 18th century home, now houses a **Pharmacy Museum** and the **Latin American Graphic Arts Museum and Gallery**.

The new (1998) **Puerto Rico Museum of Art** in Santurce, *Tel. 787/724-1875,* has permanent collections of Puerto Rican works from the earliest artists to 20th century masters. It's open weekdays 8:30am-noon and 1-3:45pm; Saturday 10am-5pm. It is closed Sunday.

Walk or take a cab to the top of the hill east of the city wall to see the **Carnegie Library**, which dates to 1916 and was restored after a hurricane in 1989.

SIDE TRIPS IN & NEAR SAN JUAN

At the **University of Puerto Rico** on the Avenida Ponce de León in Rio Piedras, *Tel. 764-0000,* browse the museum with its collection of artifacts from the pre-Columbian Taino Indians, and botanical gardens filled with tropical trees, flowering shrubs, bamboo, ponds, palms, and shaded pathways. Hours vary, so call for information.

El Yunque, whose official name is the **Caribbean National Forest**, is found 16 miles east of San Juan. The only tropical rainforest in the U.S. National Forest System, it is laced with roads and hiking paths that take you through sun-dappled trees and flowers deep into gullies wet with waterfalls. It's the home of the rare Puerto Rican parrot, which one ranger who has been here 20 years says he has heard but never seen.

It is a chilly climb to its fog-shrouded peaks and a long, hot walk to depths where waterfalls dash into clear, cold pools. The walk to **El Yunque Peak**, with its awesome view, takes about 45 minutes from the Mount Britton Lookout Tower and two hours each way on the path that leads from the Palo Colorado Visitor Information Center.

The 30-minute hike to **La Mina Falls** takes you through a fern gully filled with shy wildflowers and towering trees, ending at a wispy waterfall. Climb **Yokahu Tower** for panoramic view and stop at the many observation points, visitor information points, and picnic areas for a closer look. The visitor center at **El Portal** has a gift shop with a good selection of nature guides, maps for camping and hiking the 28,000-acre forest, cold drinks, and rest rooms. Whatever your route, it's either hot and wet or cold and wet, so it's wise to take a sun hat and poncho. There are no predatory animals, we were told, and we saw few mosquitoes.

Free tours of the **Bacardi Rum Plant**, *Tel. 788-1500,* with its small museum and pleasant grounds, are offered Monday through Saturday. It's in Cantaño (the point of land on the opposite side from the bay from the airport) at Kilometer 2.6 on Route 888.

Take half a day to seek put the colorful marketplaces in **Rio Piedras** near the plaza and off Canal Street in **Santurce**. Open daily, the outdoor vendors display fresh island produce by locals for locals.

OUT ON THE ISLAND SOUTH

Heading south from San Juan across the mountains, you'll pass the **Carite Forest Reserve** north of Guayama along Route 184. Stop at **Lake Carite**, stopping for snacks at a long line of folksy food stands selling pit-roasted pork, blood sausage, tripe, tropical fruits, and queso blanco (white cheese). In Guayama, the **Casa Cautino Museum** is housed in an 1887 mansion furnished with the belongings of the original family that lived here a century ago. Take the trolley tour of historic **Arroyo**, *Tel. 866-1609.*

Ponce is Puerto Rico's second city, known as the Pearl of the South. Its gas-lit streets are a movie set of neo-colonial buildings in the style known as Ponce Creole, built with riches gained from sugar and shipping. Stop at the tourist office in the Citibank on the Plaza de las Delicias, or *Tel. 841-8160* for information on any Ponce sightseeing. **La Perla Theater** has been a cultural center since 1864, when it opened with a dramatic Catalonian production.

Other must-see sites in Ponce include the **Ponce History Museum**, housed in two buildings dating to 1911 and the Plaza Las Delicias with its **Cathedral of Our Lady of Guadeloupe**. She's the city's patron saint and her feast day in February prompts one of the island's most colorful fiestas.

The plaza is a place for musing and people watching, and its side streets lead past more restored 19th century treasures.

The **Parque de Bombas** (firehouse) was built in 1883 as an exhibition hall and now it is a general museum with Fire Brigade memorabilia. Two restored historic homes are the **Castillo Serralles**, the mansion built by the Don Q rum fortune, and **Casa Paoli**, now a folk center, built as a home for opera star Antonio Paoli at the turn of the century. North of town on the Canas River, **Hacienda Buena Vista** was built in 1883 as the greathouse for a coffee plantation. Tour the house, slave quarters, and the still-functional coffee machinery including the only surviving coffee husker known to exist. Reservations are essential, *Tel. 722-5882.*

Crown jewel of Ponce's sightseeing is the **Ponce Museum of Art**, *Tel. 848-7309,* housing more than 1,000 paintings and 400 sculptures. Its contemporary collections, Italian Baroque pieces, and 19th century pre-Raphaelite paintings are outstanding.

Tibes Indian Ceremonial Center is built on the site of the oldest burial site yet found in the Antilles. A Taino village has been re-created complete with ceremonial ball court, homes, and dance ground. The complex has a museum, exhibits, an orientation movie, and a cafeteria. It's on Route 503, Kilometer 2.7. *Tel. 840-2255.* Hours are 9am to noon and 1 to 4pm daily except Wednesdays and holidays.

If you continue west from Ponce along a route known for its fine seafood restaurants, you'll reach Guanica and the **Dry Forest Reserve** off Route 333. One of the finest examples of tropical dry forest in the world, it's the home of more than 700 varieties of plants, 1,000 types of insects, and more than 100 bird species both migratory and resident. Walk its trails under lignum vitae trees, stopping at picnic areas and Spanish ruins. Between Guanica and La Parquera is the famous **Phosphorescent Bay** (Bahia de Fosforescente). Cruises in the area sail at night to view the natural luminescence in the water. Offshore, dive the continental shelf.

If you follow an inland route west from Ponce towards Mayagüez, it rewards you with a visit to **San Germán**, the second city founded by the Spanish. Its **Porta Coeli Church** dates to 1606 and it streets and plazas still retain the sleepy, sun-baked look of a 17th century colonial village. Leaving on the road to Lajas, you'll pass the **Alfred Ramirez de Arellano y Rosell Art Museum**, *Tel. 892-8870.* Shown are 19th century furniture and a small art collection. It's open Wednesday through Sunday, 10am to noon and 1 to 3pm.

NORTHEAST OF SAN JUAN

Route 3 leading east from San Juan is filled with commuters and commerce as well as tourists rushing to **El Yunque** and the famous beach at **Luquillo**. Almost anywhere along the highway you'll find simple restaurants serving authentic local food at modest prices, as well as roadside stands selling fried foods, fresh produce, and a native drink called mavi. Made from tree bark, it's mildly fermented.

Fajardo and the surrounding area are one of the island's seagoing centers, with massive marinas offering watersports of all kinds. At the island's eastern corner, **Las Cabezas de San Juan Nature Reserve**, locally called El Faro after its 1882 lighthouse, has hiking trails and boardwalks ending at the lighthouse with a spectacular view. From Puerto Real, catch a ferry to **Vieques** where the tiny fishing village of Esperanza has end-of-the-world restaurants and inns. **Mosquito Bay** here is phosphorescent (another bioluminous cove is on the southeast coast). The island offers three museums including a lighthouse, a fort and an old sugar mill. Farther out to sea lies **Culebra**, largely a wildlife refuge, with some first class beaches.

Continuing south from **Fajardo** brings you to Palmas de Mar Resort, a city in itself. In downtown Humacao, see **Casa Roig**, *Tel. 852-8380,* a home built in the 1920s by architect Antonin Nechodoma and now a museum devoted to contemporary art and architecture.

NORTHWEST

Beaches along the Atlantic coast can be rough, but for surfers that means great waves at such places as **Jobos Beach** near Quebradillas. For calmer waters try the area near Isabela known as **The Shacks**. South of Quebradillas, **Lake Guajataca Wildlife Refuge** has miles of hiking paths through lush forests filled with sinkholes.

One of the island's blockbuster attractions is the **Arecibo Observatory**, *Tel. 878-2612,* which holds endless fascination for space groupies. Cornell University has erected mammoth equipment over a giant sinkhole to listen for radio signals from distance galaxies. The visitor center is open to the public Wednesday through Friday noon to 4pm and on Saturday, Sunday and holidays, 9am to 4pm Admission is charged. Bilingual interactive exhibits and video presentations introduce visitors to the world of astronomy.

South of Arecibo on Route 111 west of Utuado, **Caguana Indian Ceremonial Park**, *Tel. 894-7325,* was built 800 years ago by the Taino Indians as a ceremonial and religious site. Its stone walkways and ball courts have been unearthed, and a small museum built. The park is open Wednesday through Sunday 9am to 4:30pm.

East of Arecibo on Punta Morillo, a 19th century **lighthouse** has been restored and outfitted as a museum. It is open Wednesday through Sunday 8am to 5pm, Tel. 8*79-1625*. Just south of Arecibo on Route 10, **Rio Abajo Forest**, *Tel. 724-3724,* offers boat rides on a verdant valley lake. Just as in many national forests, camping is allowed by permit.

Rio Camuy Cave Park, *Tel. 898-3100,* with its caverns and underwater rivers is as ancient and wildly natural as Arecibo is modern and manmade. Near the town of Lares, the Camuy River disappears into a giant labyrinth of caves carved out by the water. Trams carry passengers deep into a sinkhole and cave where impatiens bloom in tiny patches of light admitted by holes in the limestone high above. Truly one of the National Park Service's most exciting rides, the tram can accommodate only limited crowds. Arrive early. The park has picnic areas, rest rooms, a gift shop, and food service.

THE WEST & SOUTHWEST

Cabo Rojo and the picture-postcard fishing village of **Boquerón** surround a long bay that probes three miles inland, spreading one of the island's largest and finest balnearios, or public beaches. **Buyé Beach** north of Boquerón is another beaut; so is **Joyuda Beach** with its long string of seafood restaurants. **Cabo Rojo Wildlife Refuge**, Route 301, Kilometer 5.1, *Tel. 851-7258*, has information displays and nature trails. The bird watching is particularly good.

Although it's a commercial city known for its tuna processing plants, Mayagüez has some appealing attractions. At the city center, the plaza has an imposing statute of **Christopher Columbus** and is surrounded by historic buildings including the **Yaguez Theater**, a National Historic Monument that has been caringly restored. It is used to stage Spanish language plays and concerts. There's a small zoo with a children's playground, and the U.S. Department of Agriculture's Tropical Agricultural Research Station has rambling gardens that invite self-guided tours through acres of exotic plants.

Mona Island, *Tel. 723-1616*, which lies 50 miles off Mayagüez, is managed by the Puerto Rico Department of Natural Resources and can be reached only by chartered boats. The passage can be a frisky one, so consult your doctor about seasick medication. The island is the perfect place for primitive camping at the edge of the world. The best place to find a boat and skipper is in Puerto Real, Cabo Rojo.

Driving north from Mayagüez brings you to **Rincón**, a surf-washed shore in the foothills of La Cadena Mountains. A favorite of eco-tourists, it's a place to catch a whale watching cruise or to hole up in a small country hotel. The **Rincón Maritime Museum** is on Route 413, Kilometer 2.5 and it's open weekdays noon to 4pm.

It's thought that Columbus' exploration of Puerto Rico began somewhere along the northwest coast in 1493. The **Aguadilla** area is locally renowned for its crafts shops and for its coconut palm-fringed beaches. One of the best and calmest is **Crash Boat Beach** north of Aguadilla. **Ramey Air Force Base** is now a civilian area gradually turning to tourism.

NIGHTLIFE & ENTERTAINMENT

Puerto Rico is sufficiently Americanized that most shops stay open through the siesta hours, but also Latin enough to love music, dancing, and socializing long after midnight. Casinos, which usually have adjacent bars, often have live music and dancing and are always a good bet for night owls because they stay open until as late as 4am.

CIGAR MANIA

Smoke stogies with fellow smokers at the Cigar Bar at the El San Juan Hotel & Casino in Isla Verde, Bolero's in Westin Rio Mar Beach in Palmer, Ruth's Chris Steak House in the Sands Hotel, Tuscany Restaurant in the Marriott Hotel, the smoking balcony at the Hard Rock Cafe, Havana's Cafe, the cigar bar at Egipto, the cigar room at Red, and Cafe Europe. It's important to call ahead for hours of cigar evenings because not all cigar-friendly places allow smoking all the time.

Dancing

BABYLON CLUB, *El San Juan Hotel & Casino, Tel. 791-0390.*

MILLENIUM CLUB, *Condado Plaza Hotel & Casino, Tel. 721-1000.*

RED, *at the San Juan Convention Center. Tel. 722-5430.*

Dancing, a cigar room, and a sports bar for ages 21 and over. On Fridays, admission is for ages 23 and over.

LAZER, *on Calle Cruz, Old San Juan. Tel. 725-7581.*

Open every night, offering different themes and age limits.

EGIPTO, *Robert H. Todd Avenue #1, Santurce. Tel. 725-4664.*

Different themes including a sports night, and elegant Friday and Saturday affairs for ages 23 and over.

Dance the merengue at the **COPA ROOM**, *Tel. 791-6100*, or the **PLAYERS LOUNGE** until 3am in the Sands Hotel. Admission is for ages 25 and older. Orchestra music at the **TERRACE BAR** in the Caribe Hilton starts at 8pm on Thursday, 10pm Friday and Saturday, and 2pm Sunday afternoon for dancers of all ages. For a very dressy night out, dance at the **CHICO BAR** in the El San Juan Hotel & Casino, *Tel. 791-1000,* until 1am week nights and 3am Friday and Saturday.

Dance music plays live in the **LOBBY LOUNGE** at the Marriott Hotel, *Tel. 722-7000,* from 7pm to 1am Sunday through Wednesday and 6pm to 3:30am Thursday through Sunday. If you need dance lessons, ask the concierge or front desk. If you're over 40 and love Latin dancing, try **LA FIESTA LOUNGE** in the Condado Plaza, *Tel. 721-1000*. Dancing is

5pm to 2am Monday through Thursday, until 3am Friday and Saturday, and until 1am Sunday.

In the Palmas Del Mar resort at Humacao, drink and dance at the **PALM TERRACE RESTAURANT & LOUNGE**, *Tel. 852-6000*, until 2am.

Good Listening

Listen to live jazz at **CAFE MATISSE** in Condado, *Tel. 723-7910*, on Wednesdays and blues on Fridays, both until 1am In Punta las Marias, jazz starts Fridays at 10pm at **MANGO'S CAFE**, *Tel. 268-4629*. Jazz and Latin rhythms play Friday and Saturday nights from 9:30pm at **VIVAS** in the Condado Beach Hotel & Casino, *Tel. 721-6090*. At the junction of Roosevelt and De Diego Avenues, jazz plays nightly. Order dinner before 10:30 to enjoy the music, which begins after the kitchen closes.

Live Jam Sessions

Live Caribbean music such as salsa is usually (but call ahead to be sure) played at the **CHICO LOUNGE** in the El San Juan Hotel & Casino, San Juan, *Tel. 791-1000*; **EGIPTO**, Robert H. Todd Avenue #1, Santurce, *Tel. 725-4664*; **EL ESCAMBRON BEACH CLUB**, Puerta y Tierra, *Tel. 722-4785*; **PALADIUM**, 65 Infanteria Avenue, Trujillo Alto, *Tel. 760-9069*; and **VICTORIA'S**, 57 Delcafe Street, Condado, *Tel. 724-0975*.

Casinos

Casinos, which are open to hotel guests and non-guests alike, open at noon and close as late as 4am. Dress is casual. Puerto Rican law doesn't permit the serving of drinks at gaming tables, so casinos have lively bars where drinks and snacks are served. If gaming is an important ingredient in your vacation, it's more convenient to stay at a casino hotel.

Hotels with casinos include:

- **Condado Plaza Hotel & Casino**, *Tel. 787/721-1000*
- **El Convento**, *Tel. 787/723-9020*
- **El San Juan Hotel & Casino**, *Tel. 787/791-1000*
- **El Conquistador**, *Tel. 787/863-1000*
- **Crowne Plaza Hotel & Casino**, *Tel. 787/253-2929*
- **Wyndham Hotel & Casino**, *Tel. 787/721-5100*
- **Diamond Palace**, *Tel. 787/721-0810*
- **Radisson Ambassador**, *Tel. 787/721-7300*
- **Embassy Suites**, *Tel. 787/791-0505*
- **San Juan Marriott,** *Tel. 787/722-7000*
- **San Juan Grand Beach Hotel,** *Tel. 787/791-6100*

Out on the island, casinos are found at:

- **Holiday Inn Tropical Casinos** in Ponce, *Tel. 800/981-2398*
- **Holiday In Mayagüez**, *Tel. 800/981-8984*
- **Hyatt Regency Cerromar Beach & Hyatt Dorado**, *Tel. 787/796-1234 or 800/981-9066*
- **Best Western Mayagüez**, *Tel. 787/831-7575 or 724-0161*
- **Palmas del Mar,** Tel. 787/852-6000.
- **Ponce Hilton**, *Tel. 787/259-7676*
- **Westin Rio Mar Beach**, *Tel. 787/888-6000*

PUERTO RICO'S FOLKLORE & FLAMENCO

LeLoLai is a program that gives visitors a week-long choice of cultural shows, music and dancing, museum and dining discounts, and tours. For information on the $10 LeLoLei card, Tel. 787/723-3135 weekdays or Tel. 791-1014 weekends and evenings. Hotels that participate by offering folkloric music and dance programs include the ***Caribe Hilton*** *and* ***Sands Hotel****. Programs are also held at the* ***Condado Convention Center****.*

SPORTS & RECREATION

Beaches

Luquillo, off Route 3 an hour east of San Juan, is one of the most beautiful beaches in the world and has many quiet areas but, if you prefer a more festive beach, it also has vendors and food stands. It's impossible to list all the beaches of Puerto Rico and its satellite islands because they go on for mile after glorious mile. Simply drive any coast road, and drop off the highway when you see a likely spot (taking all precautions, of course, in areas where there is no lifeguard).

Balnearios, or government-run public beaches have dressing rooms, lifeguards, and parking, and are open daily except Monday. For information, *Tel. 722-1551 or 724-2500.* They include **Luquillo** listed above and **Seven Seas** in Fajardo. West of San Juan, try **Punta Salinas Beach**. Also handy to the city are **Carolina Beach** in Isla Verde and **Escambron** in Puerta de Tierra.

East of Humacao is the public beach at **Punta Santiago**. Swim on the south coast at **Punta Guilarte** east of Guayana, **Cana Gorda** west of Ponce, at **Boquerón** south of Mayagüez or at **Anasco** north of Mayagüez. Along the north coast between Arecibo and San Juan are **Cerro Gordo** and the beach at **Dorado**. **Vieques** has a public beach, **Sombé**, along its southwest shore.

TAKEN ABACK

In San Juan, it is tradition to go to the beaches at midnight on June 23 and walk three times into the sea backwards to insure good luck in the coming year. It's the feast day of San Juan Bautista, patron saint of the city.

Bicycling & Horseback Riding

Ride with **AdvenTours**, *Tel. 832-2016 or 831-4023.*

Camping

Many campsites are available in Puerto Rico's national parks, national forests, forest reserves and in El Yunque. Permits, which cost 50 cents per person per night, are required. *Tel. 787/723-1718* for El Yunque information. For others, contact the **Puerto Rico National Resources Department**, *Tel. 787/880-6557.*

Fishing

Deep sea and sport fishing trips can be booked through your hotel or through **Club Nautico de San Juan**, Miramar. *Tel. 723-2292 or 724-6265.* Club Nautico is also found in Fajardo, *Tel. 860-2400* or reserve from the U.S., *Tel. 800/628-8426.*

Caving

Explore rivers and caves with **Attabeira Educative Travel**, *Tel. 767-4023,* or **Aventuras Tierra Adentro**, *Tel. 766-0470.*

Golf

Often the scene of internationally televised golf tournaments, Puerto Rico is one of the Caribbean's best choices for a golf vacation. At the **Westin Rio Mar Beach Resort**, *Tel. 888-8811,* Greg Norman designed the River Course, which is surrounded by wetlands filled with bird lifc, and George Fazio designed the Ocean Course. Both are between the ocean and El Yunque rainforest. The twin **Hyatts** at Dorado have four golf courses designed by Robert Trent Jones, Sr., *Tel. 796-8961 or 796-8916.* **El Conquistador Resort and Country Club**, *Tel. 863-6784,* has a par-72, 6,700-yard course designed by Arthur Hills. It's in Fajardo, 31 miles east of San Juan. Gary Player designed the par-72, 6,690-yard course at **Palmas Del Mar** in Humacao, *Tel. 852-6000.* The resort's second course opened in December 1997.

The closest public golf course to San Juan hotels is **Bahia Beach Plantation**, *Tel. 256-5600,* which covers 75 acres of beach and lakes. **Berwind Country Club** in Rio Grande, *Tel. 876-3056,* is a private club that is open to the public four days a week. At **Aguirre**, *Tel. 853-4052*, the nine-hole golf course is set in an old sugar plantation. The nine-hole **Club Deportivo De Oeste** course runs up and down hills near Mayagüez, *Tel. 851-8880*. In western Puerto Rico near Ramey, the **Punta Borinquen Golf Club**, *Tel. 890-2987*, is a par-72, 18-hole course known for its windy fairways.

At Ceiba on the east coast, play two courses at **Roosevelt Roads Club**, *Tel. 865-4851*. Military personnel and their guests can play the **Fort Buchanan Golf Club** in San Juan, *Tel. 273-3852*. New courses without telephone numbers at press time are the **Dorado Del Mar** northwest of San Juan, and an 18-hole course at **Coamo**. The first tee time is usually 7am. Greens fees with a cart start at $20.

Kayaking

Ismael Ortego, *Tel. 720-7711 or 759-1255,* offers night kayaking excursions that begin at 6:30pm at the Condado lagoon and caravan to Cabezas de San Juan near the Fajardo lighthouse. You'll paddle the bay for three hours at a cost of $30 per person, minimum six people. Shorter explorations of the Condado lagoon are also offered for singles or couples.

Scuba

Dive with:

- **Black Beard West Indies Charters**, *Tel. 887-4818*
- **Caribe Aquatic Adventures**, *Tel. 729-2929*
- **Caribbean Divers**, *Tel. 722-7393*
- **Caribbean School of Aquatics**, *Tel. 72806606*
- **Castillo Watersports**, *Tel. 791-6195 or 728-1068*
- **Coral Head Divers** *in Palmas del May Resort, Tel. 850-7208*
- **Dive Copmarina** *in Guanica, Tel. 821-6009*
- **Dorado Marine Center**, *Tel. 796-4645*

Tennis

The best bet is to stay at a hotel that has tennis courts. Public play can be found at the **Isla Verde Tennis Club**, which has four lighted courts in Villamar, *Tel. 727-6490*. **San Juan Central Park** at the Cerra Street exit on Route 2, Santurce, has 17 courts with lights, *Tel. 722-1646.*

Whale Watching

January through April, whale watch with **Vikings of Puerto Rico**, *Tel. 823-7010*.

SHOPPING

Puerto Rico has a special program that arranges your visits to the shops and studios of local artisans. You'll follow a network of roads called the Rutas Artesanales to meet crafters in person and see their works in progress. For information on the **Fomento Arts Program**, *Tel. 787/758-4747, extension 2291;* the **Puerto Rico Tourism Company artisan office**, *Tel. 787/721-2400*, or the **Institute of Puerto Rican Culture Popular Arts Center**, *Tel. 787/722-0621.*

Of special interest to shoppers in search of local crafts are:

- **Aguadilla de San Juan**, *205 Old San Juan, Tel. 722-0578*
- **Artesanias**, *Castor Ayala, Rote 187, Kilometer 6.6, Loiza, Tel. 876-1130*
- **Artesanos La Casita** *at the La Casita Information Center, Old San Juan. Tel. 722-1709*
- **Centro de Artes Populares**, *253 Cristo, Old San Juan, Tel. 722-0621*
- **Hacienda Juanita**, *Route 105, Kilometer 23.5, Maricao, Tel. 838-2550*
- **Kiosko Cultural**, *El Area de la Feria, Plaza Las Americas, Hato Rey, Tel. 396-5230*
- **Mercado de Artesanias**, *Plaza de Hostas, Recinto Sur, Old San Juan* (no telephone; it's open Friday evenings and weekends)
- **Plaza las Delicias**, *Ponce* (no telephone, open weekends only)
- **Puerto Rican Arts and Crafts**, *204 Fortaleza, Old San Juan, Tel. 725-5596.* It's open daily 9am to 6pm, 5pm on Sunday.

The first Tuesday of the month is **Gallery Night** (Noches de Galerías) in Old San Juan, where more than 30 art galleries stay open from 7 to 10pm. Browse from shop to shop.

If you're looking for native crafts, *santos* (hand-carved religious figures) are a popular collectable. Puerto Ricans also do basketry, leather work, papier-maché sculpture, and fine arts. Shop for antiques in buildings that are as old or older than the treasures themselves along Calle del Cristo. **Butterfly People**, Calle Fortaleza 152 in Old San Juan, is a wonderland of butterflies from all over the world, framed and frozen in time to display in your home in every size from miniature to mural. Purchases will be packed and shipped to your home if you like.

Barrachina Center at 104 Fortaleza Street, Old San Juan, claims to be the largest jewelry shop in the Caribbean and offers free samples of pina colada, which they say was invented here. Shop for custom jewelry, liquor, leather goods and sunglasses. It's open Monday through Saturday 9am to 6pm

Casa Papyrus, upstairs at 357 Tetuan Street in Old San Juan, sells music and books and is also a coffee shop hangout for artists and writers. It is open daily 10:30am to 8pm. For handmade leather goods from a famous maker, shop **Dooney & Bourke's Factory Store** at 200 Cristo Street. **La Gran Discoteca** at 203 San Justo Street, is the largest record store in the Caribbean. At **Malula**, at 152 Fortaleza Street, shop for antiques and treasures from around the world. **Joseph Machini**, whose custom jewelry is also sold in Ketchikan, Alaska, has a shop at 101 Fortaleza Street. In the patio here is the **Frank Meisler Gallery** featuring whimsical sculptures and Judaica.

Puerto Rico's divinely aromatic coffee makes a meaningful souvenir and it is seen in gift shops and supermarkets throughout the island. One brand, Alto Grande, has been produced at the same hacienda since 1939. It's available in a variety of attractive gift packages. Locally-distilled rum is an excellent buy except at the airport where it is priced higher than in supermarkets.

EXCURSIONS & DAY TRIPS

A hydrofoil makes a 2 1/2-hour trip from Old San Juan to **St. Thomas** on Saturday, returning on Sunday. Relax in an airplane-style seat and watch the movie in air conditioned comfort, *Tel. 787/776-7417*. Round trip fare is $100.

For adventure and nature tours, **Copladet Nature and Adventure Travel**, *Tel. 765-8595*, will plan your trip on foot, horseback or vehicle to the rainforest, Luquillo Beach, the caves, Caja de Muertos Island, or San Cristobal Canyon. Sign up with **Colonial Adventure** for walking tours of Old San Juan, *Tel. 729-0114*.

Book an outdoor adventure with **Encanto Ecotours**, *Tel. 272-0005*. They'll take you to one of the islands or find a hiking, kayaking, or rafting adventure to your liking. Relaxation and wellness tours to the island's best nature spots are arranged by **Tropix Wellness Tours**, *Tel. 268-2173*. Nightlife and dining tours are offered by **Rico Suntours**, *Tel. 722-2080 or 800/844-2080*.

Fun Cat, *Tel. 728-6606*, is a 49-passenger sailing catamaran sailing out of Fajardo on two-and three-hour sunset cruises that include snacks and rum drinks for $55 per person. The same skipper also has a six-passenger sailboat that sails the bay for three or four hours for $495, including a sailing lesson if you like.

Anticipation III Harbor Cruises make two-hour voyages to El Morro on Wednesday from 6pm to 8pm and Friday, Saturday, and Sundays 7pm to 9pm. The $29.95 fare includes unlimited soft drinks or wine, hot and cold appetizers, disco and dancing. A cash bar serves other drinks.

Plan an entire day for **Rio Camuy Cave National Park**, *Tel. 898-3100*, a 300-acre network of sink holes, caves, and gullies formed by the Camuy River. Trams take visitors deep into the underground, visiting a couple of sinkholes including one so large it could hold El Morro. You can easily find the park on your own, 1 1/2-hours west of San Juan on Route 129, Kilometer 18.9, but most hotels also offer day trips by bus. The visitor center has a cafeteria and theater.

El Yunque National Forest deserves at least one entire day, and longer if you're a serious hiker or wildlife buff. If you drive in, it's difficult to find parking spaces but if you come on a group tour, there won't be enough time for anything more than brief hikes. The park is threaded with rest stops and kiosks where you can get souvenirs, drinks, and souvenirs. Find it 45 minutes east of San Juan on Route 3, then Route 191. Tours are offered by most hotels, or call *Tel. 888-1880.*

Leaving from La Parduera docks in Lajas are boats that sail **Phosphorescent Bay** by night, *Tel. 899-5891 or 899-2972.*

PRACTICAL INFORMATION

Area code: 787

ATM: more than 250 ATMs around the island accept MasterCard/ Cirrus cards. They're found in settlements from Aguada to Yauco.

Crime: Keep your wits about you and always lock your room and car. Put values in your room safe or the hotel safe. Ask your hotel host about the best places to walk, drive, or park after dark. Security has been greatly reinforced in recent years, especially in tourist areas and in parking lots used by tourists.

Customs & Immigration: an agricultural inspection looks for plants and products that are prohibited entry to the United States. Many fruits are allowed to be taken to the States including basketball-size pineapple that are packed and sold at the airport to take home in season. If you're unsure about agricultural products you want to take home, call the United States Department of Agriculture, *Tel. 787/153-4505 or 253-4506.* Entry for citizens of other countries is the same as entering the United States.

Driving: holds few mysteries for the North American driver. Your driver's license is good here and most cars, equipment, and highway signs are familiar. An exception is the stop sign, which is red and six-sided but contains the word PARE. Also new to many Americans is use of kilometers in road markers. Speed limits are, however, posted in miles. Car theft is a problem; lock up and, if the rental agency provides a security device, use it.

Emergencies: much of Puerto Rico is on the 911 system, but check the telephone book in your hotel room so you will know for sure. For medical emergencies in San Juan, *Tel. 754-2222;* on the island, *Tel. 754-2550.* Travelers Aid at the airport is open weekdays 8am to 4pm, Tel. *791-1034 or 791-1054.*

Government: Puerto Rico is a commonwealth of the United States.

Holidays: bank holidays include January 1, January 6, Eugenio Maria de Hostos Day (mid-January), Martin Luther King Day on January 20, George Washington's Birthday (February), Palm Sunday, Good Friday, Easter, Emancipation Day late March, Jose De Diego Day mid-April, Memorial Day (around May 26), July 4, Luis Muños Rivera Day mid-July, Constitution Day late July, Jose Celso Barbosa's Birthday late July, Labor Day (early September), Columbus Day (mid-October), November 11, Thanksgiving day (third Thursday of November), December 25, December 31.

Tourist information: Puerto Rico Tourism Company, *575 Fifth Avenue, 23rd Floor, New York NY 10017, Tel. 212/599-6262 or 800/223-6530.* In Miami, *901 Ponce de Leon Boulevard, Suite 604, Coral Gables FL 33134. Tel. 305/445-9112 or 800/815-7391.* In Los Angeles, *3575 W. Cahuenga Boulevard, Suite 560, Los Angeles CA 90068. Tel. 213/874-5991 or 800/874-1230.* In Canada, *Tel. 416/368-2680.* On the island, information centers are maintained at the Luis Muñoz Marin Airport, *Tel. 791-1014*; near Pier One in Old San Juan, *Tel. 722-1709*; at the airport in Aguadilla, *Tel. 890-3315;* on Route 100, Kilometer 13.7 in Cabo Rojo. *Tel. 851-7070;* and in the Fox Delicias Mall in Ponce, *Tel. 840-5695.*

Towns that have their own tourism offices, usually open weekdays only, are Adjuntas, *Tel. 829-2590*; Anasco, *Tel. 826-3100, extension 272;* Bayamón, *Tel. 798-8191;* Cabo Rojo, *Tel. 851-1025;* Camuy, *Tel. 898-2240* (this one, at Kilometer 4.8 on Route 119 is open daily); Culébra, *Tel. 742-3291;* Dorado, *Tel. 7965-5740;* Fajardo, *Tel. 863-4013;* Guanica, *Tel. 821-2777;* Jayuya, *Tel. 828-5010;* Luquillo, *Tel. 889-2851;* Naguabo, *Tel. 874-0389;* Rincón, *Tel. 823-5024;* San Juan, *Tel. 724-7171;* and Vieques, *Tel. 741-5000.*

Weddings: at least ten days before you're going to be married, have a VDRL blood test from a federally certified laboratory, either in the U.S. or Puerto Rico. Have a doctor sign and certify the marriage certificate and blood test; take them to a Registro Demografico for a marriage license. A passport or other photo ID, plus copies of applicable divorce papers must be presented. Officials keep limited hours and only on weekdays, so plan well in advance. The marriage license is prepared by the minister who performs the ceremony.

FESTIVALS & SPECIAL EVENTS

Dates are subject to change, so check with tourism information (see Practical Information) for the latest news on these annual events. Participating in local festivals is an insider thing to do but, even if you're not interested in such events it's wise to know when and where they are because it may mean that banks are closed, hotels are overbooked, and roads clogged.

All Year

The **LeLoLai Program** is held Monday through Wednesday at San Juan tourist hotels, where song and dance demonstrate traditional Puerto Rican culture. Included in the $10 LeLoLai card are discounted sightseeing at the island's best historic and nature sites.

Every Saturday, prominent local dancers, musicians and artists display their talents at the **Festival La Casita** in the Tourist Information Center adjacent to Pier 1, Old San Juan.

Every Wednesday, Friday and Sunday and on holidays, **thoroughbred horses** race at El Nuena Comandante Race Track in Canóvanas on the east coast. Four major competitions for **paso fino horses** are held through the year. Other equestrian events and rodeos are also held regularly. **Auto racing** goes on through the year at Salinas International Speedway on the south coast, Caribbean Raceway Park in Carolina in the northeast, and at Puerto Rico International Speedway in Caguas, in the east-central interior of the island.

For news of athletic events including tennis and golf tournaments and soccer meets, contact the **Puerto Rico Olympic Committee**, *Tel. 787/723-3890 or 787/723-3210.*

January

January 6 is **Three Kings Day**, a day for exchanging Christmas gifts and partying. Children's events are held at La Fortaleza and the Paseo de la Princesa.

Mid-January: A three-day **San Sebastiàn Street Festival** takes to the cobblestone streets of Old San Juan.

Patron Saint Festivals lasting 10 days each January include Añaso on the northwest coast, Las Piedras in east-central Puerto Rico, Manatí on the north coast, Mayagüez on the west coast, Lajas in the southwest, Coamo in south-central Puerto Rico and Dorado in the northeast.

February

Early February: Runners from around the world compete in the **San Blas de Illescas Marathon**.

Mid-February: The **National Coffee Festival** is held in Yauco in the southwest, Puerto Rico's coffee growing region.

Carnivals: the Vega Alta Carnival on the north coast, Cristóbal L. Sánchez Carnival in Arroyo in the southeast, Ponce Carnival on the south coast, Quebradillas Carnival in the northwest, and the Ponce de León Carnival in Old San Juan.

March

Early March: Five Days With Our Land is an **agricultural and industrial fair** held at Mayagüez.

Late March: An international Triathlon is held at Cabo Rojo.

April

Early April is a season of concerts by the **Puerto Rico Symphony Orchestra**.

Months and dates vary with the church year, but **Palm Sunday, Good Friday, and Easter** are days for church going.

Mid-April: A **Carnival** is held at Salinas on the south coast.

Mavi Carnival held late April in the southern coastal town of Juana Diaz celebrates a fermented drink made from the bark on the ironwood tree. Also this month will be the Guyama Carnival, a 1940s Festival in Cabo Rojo, and a Sugar Harvest Festival in San Germán.

Patron Saint Days, each lasting about 10 days are held this month in Arecibo and Bayamón.

May

Early May: A **Bobbin Lace Festival** honors traditional *mundillo* as well as other types of weaving, lace making and handiwork in Isabela on the northwest coast. Also in early May is *Danza Week*, celebrating a popular, turn-of-the-century ballroom dance. Competitions and demonstrations are held in Ponce.

Sometime each May the **Puerto Rican Country Fair** is held in the northwestern coastal town of Hatillo. On Memorial Day, the island recognizes the many Puerto Ricans who served with the United States armed services.

Late May: The **Puerto Rico Heineken JazzFest** features international stars, who perform at the Sixto Escobar Stadium in San Juan.

Patron Saint Festivals lasting about 10 days in May are at Toa Alta on the north Coast, Carolina east of San Juan and Camuy on the northwest coast.

Mid May: Sábana Grande's Patron Saint Festival is held in this southwestern community.

June

First three weeks: The internationally famous **Casals Festival** honors the late cellist by bringing in some of the finest classical musicians in the world. It is mostly in San Juan but performances are also held in Ponce and Mayagüez.

Late June: **San Juan Bautista Day** is celebrated in the sea and swimming pools by walking backwards into the water at midnight.

Patron Saint Festivals lasting about 10 days are held in early June in Ceiba and Dorado, mid-June in Isabela, Maricao, Marranquitas, and Guyama, and late June (some extending into early July) in Orocovis, Toa Baja and Maunabo.

July

4th of July is celebrated in Old San Juan, where throughout the entire month a Tourism Artisans' Fair sells crafts, arts and foods.

Mid-July: Barranquitas Artisans' Fair features carvings, baskets, musical instruments, pottery, leather, folk music, and .traditional foods.

July 15 is **Luis Muñoz Rivera's Birthday**. The Puerto Rican hero, born 1829 and died 1916 was a poet, resident commissioner, statesman and journalist.

Mid-July: **Vieques' Patron Saint Festival** is held on the largest island off Puerto Rico's coast.

Late July: **Puerto Rico Constitution Day** is celebrated with a parade in San Juan.

Patron Saint Festivals lasting about 10 days in July include Cidra, Barceloneta, Hatillo, Villaba, Arroyo, Cataño, Morovis, Fajardo, Santa Isabel, San Germán, and Adjuntas.

August

Patron Saint Festivals, each lasting about 10 days in August are held at Comerio, Patillas, Cayey, Juana Diaz, Rincón, Hormiqueros, Moca, Salinas, and Jayuya.

September

Labor Day is celebrated just as it is on the mainland.

Sometime in September, a three-week **Inter-American Festival of the Arts** is held in San Juan featuring music, dance, and musical theater.

Patron Saint Festivals this month are held at Aguas Buenas, Peñuelas, Trujillo Alto, San Lorenzo, Florida, Aguada, Cabo Rojo, Naranjito, Utuado, and Yabucoa.

October

October 12 is **Columbus Day**. Also sometime this month, the **Puerto Rico International Film** Festival features 100 films from around the world.

Late October: The **National Plantain Festival** is held at Corozal.

Late October: Baseball season begins and lasts through mid-January.

Patron Saint Days this month are held at Canóvanas, Naguabo, Vega Baja, Yauco, Caguas, Quebradillas, and Aguadilla.

November

Mid-month: **Festival of Puerto Rican Music** features the cuatro, a 10-stringed instrument favored by local musicians.

Veteran's Day, November 11, honors Puerto Rican veterans who served with the U.S. armed forces.

Mid-month: **Cetí Festival** in Arecibo honors the cetí, a tiny, sardine-like fish found only in Puerto Rico's northern waters.

November 19 is **Puerto Rico Discovery Day**, commemorating the arrival on the island of Christopher Columbus in 1493.

Mid-month: **National Day of Bomba and Plena** honors the bomba and plena, two locally popular rhythms.

Late November: **Thanksgiving** (celebrated as it is on the mainland). Also late in the month the **Festival of Typical Dishes** is held at Luquillo where authentic native fare is served in the town square. The **Jayuya Indian Festival** held late each November honors the Taino Indians.

Patron Saint Festivals this month are held at Juncos, Las Marías, Lares, and Corozal.

December

Early December: The biggest and best event of its kind on the island is the Barcardí Corporation Artisans' Fair held on the rum factory's grounds at Cataño. The **Ballets de San Juan** perform this month in San Juan and the National Folkloric Ballet performs its annual Criollisimi Show in Old San Juan. Christmas displays fill the island and the Nutcracker Suite Ballet is performed.

Mid-month: **Petate Festival** in Sábana Grande features 50 artisans demonstrating time-honored ways of making things with palm leaves.

Mid-December: A giant Christmas tree is lit at Paso La Princesa in Old San Juan. Also mid-month is **Las Mañanitas**, a religious procession that starts at 5 a.m. in Ponce, ending at the Catholic church where Mass is said at 6 a.m. Participants play and sing songs honoring Our Lady of Guadalupe. Concerts of the Puerto Rico Symphony Orchestra continue throughout the year.

December 24 and 25: Christmas Even and Christmas Day are holy days in Puerto Rico, with feasting and family gatherings.

Late December: Hatillo hosts two festivals, one the Güiro and Typical Music Festival featuring the güiro, a hollow gourd used as a rhythm instrument. The other is the **Masks Festival**, a traditional founded by the Spanish in 1823 in which men in masks re-enact the biblical story of King Herod's order to kill all infant boys. Food, music and crafts take over the town square.

Patron Saint Days in December are held in Humacao, Guyanilla, Vega Alta, and Ponce.

15. THE U.S. VIRGIN ISLANDS

On his second voyage to the New World, Christopher Columbus dropped anchor off the Salt River in **St. Croix** on November 14, 1493, and sent a boat ashore in search of fresh water. He named the island Santa Cruz before being driven off by hostile Caribs. Sailing on to **St. Thomas**, **St. John**, and Tortola, he named the group *Las Virgenes* in honor of the 11,000 virgins of St. Ursula who died at the hands of marauding Huns.

The first settlers on St. Croix were a motley group of Dutch, English, and French who could never quite get along and soon sailed on. By 1649, the English had a settlement near what is now Frederiksted, but they were driven out by Spaniards based at Puerto Rico. Finally, the island became St. Croix in 1639 when the governor of the French islands took it over as his private game park. When he died, he left it to the Knights of Malta, a group of French aristocrats who took possession of the island and planted sugar. Their debt-ridden effort ended in 1695 and France abandoned the island.

The Danish West India and Guinea Company surveyed St. Croix in 1733, sold plantations, and soared into a golden age of sugar riches. Planned on a grand scale equal to the city that is now Oslo, Christiansted emerged at a time when neo-classical architecture, with its graceful arches, was in vogue. Spurred by strict building codes and inspections, and built by exacting artisans, the city became a showplace.

Fearing German expansion during World War I, the United States bought the Danish West Indies in 1917, giving them territorial status and granting U.S. citizenship to their inhabitants. They were administered by the U.S. Navy, then by the Department of Interior until 1952 when a governor was appointed. Islanders vote on their own government as well as their member of congress.

The Islands

St. Croix is 28 miles long and seven miles wide, the boyhood home of Alexander Hamilton and once dotted with more than 100 sugar plantations. Its terrain ranges from rainforest to dry desert.

St. Thomas, 13 miles long and three miles wide, is the capital of the U.S. Virgin Islands. Today known to cruisers as a Disneyland of duty-free and to yachties as a happy haven, St. Thomas has alluring beaches, resorts in all price ranges, a few historic sites, some notable dining, and lots of hidden pockets where the savvy visitor can find a quiet getaway only two hours from Miami.

Most of **St. John**, which is nine miles long and five miles wide, is a national park. Its settlement, **Cruz Bay**, looks like the setting for a South Seas movie. Its hills are threaded with hiking paths; its shining beaches and windex waters are unbeatable for unspoiled beauty. As leases expire on resorts, even more of the island will revert to national park status.

In 1996, the three U.S. Virgin Islands were joined by a fourth, **Water Island**, which was turned over to the territorial government by the U.S. Department of the Interior. Included are two docks, a beach, and public roads. A resort is being discussed but at press time has not been announced. Meanwhile, $3.3 million in government money is being spent to spruce up public areas. Take the five-minute ferry from St. Thomas to Water Island's Honeymoon Beach, which is open to visitors. As developments occur, they'll be announced in future editions of this guidebook.

Climate

The occasional "Alberta Clipper" cold front can come this far south to bring flag-fraying winds and temperatures in the 70s, but that's about the extent of the weather story here. Most days are 80-ish and sunny all year. During hurricane season, June through October, rain is more frequent and heavier and humidity can be cloying.

ARRIVALS & DEPARTURES

American Airlines flies into St. Thomas from JFK, San Juan, and Miami, *Tel. 800/433-7300*. **US Airways**, *Tel. 800/428*-4322 flies to St. Thomas from Philadelphia and continues to St. Croix. **Delta Airlines**, *Tel. 800/221-1212* flies from Atlanta to St. Thomas and on to St. Croix. Service is also available via other air lines through San Juan.

Local airlines serving the U.S. Virgin Islands and other Caribbean points include:

- **Aero Virgin Islands**, *Tel. 340/776-8366*
- **Air Anguilla**, *Tel. 264/497-2643* or *888-773-5987*
- **Air St. Thomas**, *Tel. 590/277-7176, 340/776-2722* or *800/522-3084*
- **Air Sunshine**, *Tel. 888/879-8900 or 800/327-8900*

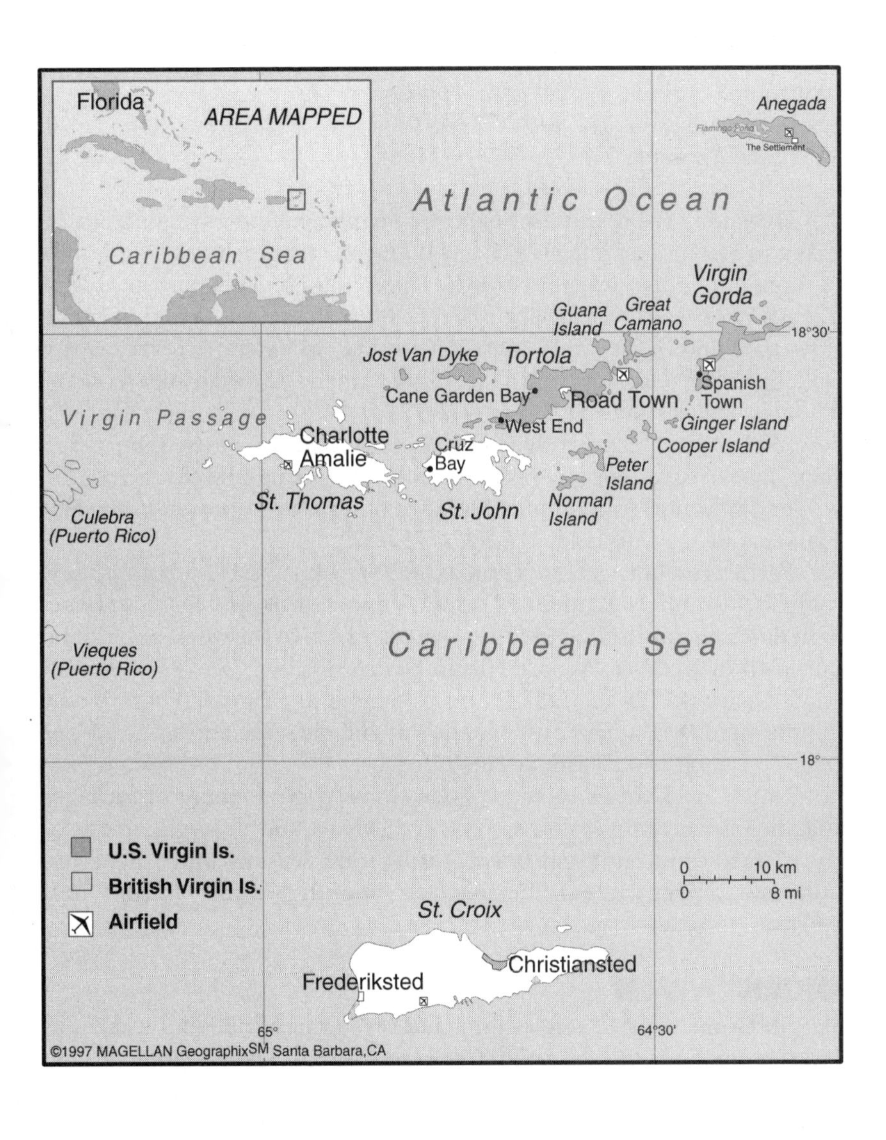
Florida
AREA MAPPED
Caribbean Sea
Anegada
The Settlement
Atlantic Ocean
Virgin Gorda
Guana Island
Great Camano
18°30'
Jost Van Dyke
Tortola
Spanish Town
Cane Garden Bay
Road Town
Virgin Passage
West End
Ginger Island
Charlotte Amalie
Cruz Bay
Cooper Island
Peter Island
St. Thomas
St. John
Norman Island
Culebra (Puerto Rico)
Vieques (Puerto Rico)
Caribbean Sea
18°
U.S. Virgin Is.
British Virgin Is.
Airfield
0 10 km
0 8 mi
St. Croix
Christiansted
Frederiksted
65°
64°30'
©1997 MAGELLAN GeographixSM Santa Barbara,CA

- **American Eagle**, *Tel. 800/433-7300* or *800/474-4884*
- **Bohlke International Airways**, *Tel. 340/778-9177*
- **Continental Airlines**, *Tel. 800/231-0856*
- **Isla Nena Air Service**, *Tel. 787/791-5110*
- **LIAT**, *Tel. 246/495-1187.* In St. Croix, *Tel. 340/778-9903;* in St,. Thomas, *Tel. 340/774-2313*
- **St. John Seaplane**, *Tel. 340/693-7000*
- **Seaborn Aviation**, *Tel. 340/777-4491*
- **Vieques Air Link**, *Tel. 340/778-9858*

Fly among the islands by **Seaborne Seaplane**. One-way fare from St. Croix to St. Thomas is $50. A 1 1/2-hour tour that includes 35 minutes of flight time is also available from St. Thomas for $55 per person, *toll-free Tel. 888/FLY-TOUR* or locally, *Tel. 777-4491.* Planes are found near the Edward Wilmoth Blyden IV Marine Terminal on Veteran's Drive, within walking distance of downtown Charlotte. Amalie. **Caribair** flies from St. Thomas or Fajardo to St. Croix, *Tel. 778-5044.*

A ferry operates every two weeks from St. Thomas and St. John to San Juan, Puerto Rico. The trip takes about two hours and the cost is $60 one way or $80 round trip, both including ground transportation to the San Juan Airport or Condado, T*el. 340/776-6282*.

Ferries run between St. Thomas and St. John and from both islands to the British Virgin Islands of Tortola, Virgin Gorda, and Jost Van Dyke. Schedules vary according to time of year and day of the week, and can be curtailed by weather. Aboard Virgin Hydro foil, T*el. 776-7417*, you can leave Charlotte Amalie at 7:15am, returning at 6:30pm. Tours by air conditioned van, safari bus, bicycle or sailboat cost $95 to $140 per person. Lunch and a swim are included.

Note: Check your local newspaper's travel pages for news of packages that include accommodations, some or all meals, and air service to one of the islands from your home town. During some seasons, more flights are added so, if your dates are flexible, ask about flights times for different weeks.

ORIENTATION

St. Croix is only 28 miles long and seven miles wide, but it takes as long as an hour to get from **Christiansted** to **Frederiksted**. It's an impractical distance just for dinner, but a lovely drive for a day-long excursion with stops for shopping, swimming, and lunch. For such a small island it offers great diversity, from dry and cactus-rich landscape of the east to the craggy rainforest with its supersize ferns and the dramatically cliffy north coast.

St. Thomas is anchored by **Charlotte Amalie**, where ferries depart and cruise ships dock. **Red Hook** is at the east extreme of the island, and **Cyril E. King Airport** is just west of Charlotte Amalie. The island is 13 by three miles.

St. John is nine by five miles, with most activity centering around **Cruz Bay**, where ferries arrive from St. Thomas. Centerline Road goes from one end of the island to the other, allowing you to get from Cruz Bay to **Coral Bay** in about half an hour. Locals refer to the stretch of Centerline after Coral Bay as East End Road. Most of the best beaches and ruins are on North Shore Road; South Shore Road leads to Gift Hill Road, which connects to Centerline. The road is inland, but plenty of roads lead down to such beaches as **Great Cruz Bay**, **Chocolate Hole**, and **Hart Bay**.

GETTING AROUND THE ISLANDS

Scheduled ferries make frequent trips among the U.S. and British Virgin Islands. A lengthy list of their schedules, which vary seasonally, is published in St. Thomas This Week (including St. John) and St. Croix This Week. Pick up free copies at any hotel. Routes go between Red Hook or Charlotte Amalie and Cruz Bay, St. John, St. Thomas to St. Croix, Charlotte Amalie and Tortola, Red Hook or Cruz Bay to Tortola, St. Thomas and St. John to Jost Van Dyke, St. Thomas to Virgin Gorda, and St. Thomas and St. John to Puerto Rico.

St. Thomas

Taxi fares are published by the Virgin Islands Taxi Association, and range from $4.50 for one person traveling from the airport into Charlotte Amalie to as high as $10 for transport from the airport to the Red Hook area. The rate for each additional passenger is about 50 cents less than the primary fare. Additional charges are 50 cents per suitcase or box, $1.50 for trips between midnight and 6am and a 33 per cent surcharge for radio dispatch. A two-hour tour for two costs $30 with $12 each for additional passengers. Waiting time after ten minutes is 15 cents per minute. In town, there's a $2 minimum. Look for taxis that have a done light and the

RIGHT WAY, WRONG WAY

For reasons we can't fathom, the U.S. Virgin Islands continue to drive on the left, English style, even though almost all vehicles have their steering wheels on the left, American style. It can be immensely confusing to visitors, especially in traffic circles. Be especially cautious, not just when driving, but when crossing the street.

letters TP on their license plates, indicating an officially licensed taxi. Others may not observe the official rates.

Taxi companies include:

- **East End Taxi Service**, *Tel. 775-6974*
- **Independent Taxi**, *Tel. 775-1006*
- **Islander Taxi**, *Tel. 774-4077*
- **Sunshine Taxi**, *Tel. 775-1145*
- **V.I. Taxi Association**, *Tel. 774-4550*
- **24 Hr. Radio Dispatch**, *Tel. 774-7457*
- **Wheatley Taxi Service**, *Tel. 775-1959*

If you have a problem or complaint, take it to the V.I. Taxi Commission, *Tel. 776-8294*. Note the driver's name and license number, which should begin with the letters TP.

Arrange an **Avis** rental car from the U.S. at *Tel. 800/331-1084,* or in St. Thomas at *Tel. 774-1468*. **ABC Auto Rentals** have cars and jeeps; *Tel. 776-1222 or 800/524-2080*. **Budget Rent-a-Car** has seven locations around St. Thomas, *Tel. 776-5774 or 800/626-4516.*

Local car rental companies include:

- **ABC Auto & Jeep Rentals**, *Tel. 340/776-1222*
- **Chariots Car Rental**, *Tel. 340/777-8400*
- **Courtesy Car Rental**, *Tel. 340/776-6650*
- **Dependable Car Rental**, *Tel. 774-2253*
- **Discount Car Rental**, *Tel. 776-4858*
- **E-Z Car Rental**, *Tel. 340/775-6255*
- **Sea Breeze Car Rental**, *Tel. 774-7200*
- **Sun Island Car Rental**, *Tel. 340/774-3333*
- **Tri-Island Car Rental**, *Tel. 340/776-2879 or 775-1200*
- **VI Auto Rental and Leasing**, *Tel. 340/776-3616*

Buses on St. Thomas are roomy and air conditioned, but are not the fastest way to get around the island. Fares are 75 cents in town and $1 for other points on the island. Not all communities can be reached by bus. Catch a bus at Emancipation Garden or at bus stops around the island. Starting at 5:30am, buses travel about once every hour between Charlotte Amalie and Red Hook. Airport buses operate 6am-9:30pm. For bus information, *Tel. 774-5678*. Parking in Charlotte Amalie is a challenge but try the municipal parking lot east of the fort. Fees are 50 cents an hour or $4 daily; free on weekends and holidays. The lot is open 6am-6pm.

St. Croix

The airport is on the southeast shore of the island, about halfway between Frederiksted, which is on the west coast and Christiansted, the island's main city located mid-island on the north coast. Routes are numbered and are easy to follow if you keep track of your location on the map that comes with your rental car.

Thrifty rental cars are available at the airport on St. Croix, or can be delivered to a hotel or home. *Tel. 800/367-2277 U.S. and Canada.* When making reservations at a hotel, ask if rental cars are available on site, or if they have a package that includes a car. Prices in high season range from about $200 to $320 weekly, plus $8 daily Collision Damage Waiver. For an **Avis** car, *Tel. 800/331-1084* from the U.S. Locally *Tel. 778-9355.* For **Budget Rent-a-Car**, *Tel. 340-776-5774 or 778-0637;* **Hertz**, *Tel. 340/778-1402.*

Other rental car companies include:

- **Caribbean Jeep & Car Rentals of St. Croix**, *Tel. 340/773-4399*
- **Centerline Car Rentals**, *Tel. 340/778-0450*
- **Go Around Rent-a-Car**, *Tel. 340/778-8881 or 778-8552*
- **Green Cay Jeep Car Rental**, *Tel. 340/773-7227*
- **Midwest Auto Rental**, *Tel. 340/772-0438*
- **Olympic Rent-a-Car**, *Tel. 773-8000 or 772-2000*
- **Tourism Industries, Inc.**, *Tel. 340/778-7720*

Taxi companies include:

- **St. Croix Taxi Association** *at the airport, Tel. 778-1088*
- **Antilles Tax Service**, *Christiansted, Tel. 773-5020*
- **Caribbean Taxi & Tours**, *Christiansted, Tel. 773-9799*
- **Cruzan Taxi Association**, *Christiansted, Tel. 773-6388*
- **Territorial Taxi Umbrella**, *Tel. 692-9744*
- **Combine Taxi & Tours**, *Frederiksted, Tel. 772-2828*

Taxi fares are posted and should be confirmed in advance. Round trip fare is double the one-way charge plus a charge for waiting time of more than 10 minutes. Between midnight and 6am, there is a $1.50 surcharge for rides out of town and $1 in town. Bags are 50 cents each; trunks are more. Minimum fare is $2. Lone passengers pay four times the rate charged per-person for two, e.g. the posted charged from the airport to Christiansted is $10 per person for two plus $5 each additional person. One person would pay $20; three people $25; four people $30.

Buses, *Tel. 773-7746,* go between Christiansted and Frederiksted every 40 minutes between 5:30am and 9:30pm every day. The route starts at Tide Village east of Christiansted and ends at Fort Frederik. By transferring at La Reine terminal, you can also get to and from the airport. Look for VITRAN bus stops. Fare is $1 for adults, 55 cents for seniors aged 55 and older. Transfers are 25 cents. Exact change is required.

St. John

If you are on a day trip and just want a tour of St. John, hop aboard one of the open air jitneys that meets every ferry. A tour is recommended, even if you're going to explore later on your own, because drivers have their own patter and style. Vitran buses run between Cruz Bay and Coral Bay. Fares are $1 adults; children under age 5 ride free.

Avis cars on St. John can be reserved at *Tel. 340/776-6374* or *800/331-1084*. **St. John Car Rental**, *Tel. 776-6103*, offers Vitaras, Sidekicks, Cherokees, Wranglers, and vans that hold up to eight people. Rental cars are available from **Conrad Sutton Car Rental**, *Tel. 776-6479*; **Courtesy Car Jeep Rental**, *Tel. 776-6650*. Jeep rentals are available from **Lionel Jeep Rental**, *Tel. 340/693-8764;* **Spencer's Jeep Rentals**, *Tel. . 340/ 693-8784* or *888/776-6628;* or **Varlac Car Rentals**, which offers Jeeps, Sidekicks, Blazers, and jitneys, *Tel. 340/776-6412.*

Water taxis are available from **Inter-Island Services**, *Tel. 776-6282.*

WHERE TO STAY

Add eight per cent government tax to all hotel tariffs in the U.S. Virgin Islands. In addition, a service charge is sometimes, but not always, applied in lieu of tipping. Rates quoted are for a double room in high season. Summer rates are lower.

Private villas can be booked through **WIMCO**, *Tel. 800/932-3222 or 401/849-8012*. Maid service and staff are available. Private pool villas and condos can be booked by the week through **Calypso Realty**, *Box 12178, St. Thomas 00801, Tel. 340/774-1620, Fax 340/774-1634; toll-free 800/747-4858.* On St. John book through **Vacation Homes**, *Box 272 Cruz Bay, St. John VI 00831, Tel. 340/776-6094, Fax 340/693-8455.*

Virgin Islands packages that include airfare, accommodations, and other features are offered by **American Airlines**, *Tel. 800/433-7300,* in four categories: moderate, superior, deluxe, and all- inclusive at savings of about 25 percent over piecemeal rates.

ST. JOHN

Expensive

CANEEL BAY, *P.O. Box 720, Cruz Bay, St. John, U.S.V.I. 00831. Tel. 340/776-6111, U.S. and Canada, 800/928-8889. Rates at this 167-room resort start at $350 double in high season. Full American Plan is an additional $95; breakfast and lunch plan, $75. Children pay $47.50 and $37.50.*

This is a resort that you'll either love or hate. Those who love it are so loyal that some rooms are booked years in advance; to stay in some areas, you have to wait for someone to die. Guests are met at the ferry dock in St. Thomas and brought to this legendary Rosewood resort and former Rockefeller hideaway. It was restored and reopened in the fall of 1996 without, by demand of its loyal clientele, the addition of air conditioning, television, room phones, and other intrusions.

On arrival you're welcomed with a chilled face cloth, then are taken by tram to your room, which will have its own patio, a mini-bar with refrigerator, coffee makings, and a wall safe. Two color schemes, one in coral and teal and another in sunny yellows and raspberry, set off handsome, handmade furniture from the Pacific Rim.

Trams make the rounds every 20 minutes and are the only way, except for more walking than is practical, around the far-flung grounds. For people whose workaday lives involve waiting for buses and trains, it can be less than amusing, especially in a tropical downpour. Picture yourself padding out to find the nearest phone to order room service or call home, and having no air conditioning in August, and you see why some people are puzzled at this resort's mystique.

Cuisine here ranks with the best in the region. Eat at the Beach Terrace overlooking St. Thomas, Turtle Bay Estate House serving gourmet cuisine and fine wines, or in the Equator in the former Sugar Mill restaurant, where the brilliant menu is based on foods found around the equator from Brazil to Indonesia. The Caneel Bay Bar has live music nightly, and drinks are also served at the popular Breezeway/Starlight Terrace. After dinner at Turtle Bay, dance to live music.

For sloths, Caneel Bay offers sunning, seven grand beaches, shaded reading nooks under rustling palms, and sunset sails aboard a private yacht. Hikers can explore the 170-acre resort's own nature trails or seek

APPLES TO APPLES – COMPARING ROOM AMENITIES

When booking a hotel or motel room, it's safe to assume that you're getting daily maid service with fresh linens, soap, shampoo, and the like. If your room has a coffee maker, it probably is provided with coffee and makings. The mini-bar is stocked with drinks and snacks.

However, in self-catering accommodations such as cottages, villas, apartments, townhouses, bareboats, and homes, services and facilities vary widely. Probably not a crumb of food, soap, tissues, shampoo or other hotel-type amenities will be provided. Know before you go. Do you get fresh linens daily? Once a week? Do you do all the cleaning, cooking, dishwashing and bed making? Must you bring your own bedding and towels? What about beach towels? Is there a cleanup fee when you leave? How far is the nearest market where you can provision? Beach? Golf course? Tennis court? Restaurant? Must you have a rental car?

Only by comparing apples to apples can you find the best value.

out advanced trails in the Virgin Islands National Park, which surrounds the resort, to see more than 500 species of plant life. Take an excursion to St. Thomas or to a sister resort, Little Dix Bay, on Virgin Gorda in the British Virgin Islands. Explore sugar mill ruins, snorkel the underwater trail, windsail, dive, or kayak. The Tennis Park has 11 all-weather courts, complimentary tennis clinics, private lessons, weekly tournaments, and an outstanding Pro Shop.

Children, once barred, are now welcome to Caneel Bay with an optional children's activities program for $50 daily including lunch. Half days are $35. Caneel Bay isn't for everyone. While loyalists love its open-air environment, we found that the open windows let in surf sounds and breezes but also admit howling Christmas winds and the conversations of other guests as they pass by. We could hear neighbors chatting on the adjoining patio and yelling at each other to be heard in the shower. Louvered windows and doors cannot be closed. So privacy, which is one of the resort's proudest features, can also be elusive. We can live without television but, for these prices, we want air conditioning that can be turned on if need be and a telephone by the bedside.

THE WESTIN ST. JOHN, *Great Cruz Bay. Rates at this 285-room resort start at $425, tel 340/693-8000 or 800/WESTINS. When you make reservations, arrange to be met at the ferry dock.*

Covering 34 acres of magnificently landscaped grounds, this resort has an enormous 1/4-acre swimming pool, restaurants, bars, entertainments, and plenty of bells and whistles. Rooms and suites are spread among ten low-rise buildings connected by gardens lined with flowers and palms and threaded with red brick walks. Play tennis on floodlit courts, dine in the restaurants, the deli or the pool bar and grill, shop the boutique for smart resort wear, and enroll the children in the Westin Kids Club. Work out in the fitness center or arrange fishing, kayaking, snorkeling, windsurfing, diving, sailing, or a golf game on St. Thomas' Mahogany Run course.

Moderate

GALLOWS POINT SUITE RESORT, *P.O. Box 58, St. John 00831. Tel. 340/776-6434 or toll-free 800/323-7229. Rates at this 60-unit resort start at $190 for a one-bedroom, one-bath unit with full kitchen, living room, and balcony. Don't bring children under age 5. You'll be met at the ferry dock and transported to the resort, which is a five-minute walk from "downtown."*

A cluster of two-story, plantation style buildings surround a cliffy coast and short strength of sandy beach on the outskirts of Cruz Bay. Units are privately owned and all different, but you can count on comfortable surroundings with everything you need to cook some or all of your meals. Sleep two in the bedroom, two more on the sofabed. Loft units, which sleep one or two more, have an additional half bath. The suites are air conditioned and have ceiling fans; some have cable television, and telephone. The resort has a pool and gift/gourmet food shop and is the home of Ellington's, one of the best restaurants on St. John.

ESTATE CONCORDIA, *mail address 17 East 73rd Street, New York NY 10021. Tel. 800/392-9004 or 212/472-9453, Fax 212/861-6210; locally, Tel. 340/693-5855, Fax 776-6504. Rates start at $135 double, plus $25 each additional person. A rental car is needed to get here from Cruz Bay, 40 minutes away.*

The views of Ram Head and the Salt Pond are breathtaking as you rough it easy in a hillside aerie with 20-foot ceilings, ceiling fan, and a full kitchen with dishwasher and microwave. Furnishings are spare but comfortable, with efficiencies and studios accommodating up to three and the duplex sleeping up to six in two twin beds, a queen-size sofabed, and roll-aways. This is the most remote corner of St. John, with superb shelling, snorkeling, and hiking. The nearest restaurants and shopping are in Coral Bay.

Budget

CINNAMON BAY CAMPGROUND, *P.O. Box 720, Cruz Bay 00831. Tel. 340/30 or 539-9998. The park's 126 tent sites and cottages are $15 to $95 depending on how much equipment is provided. Ride the campground shuttle from the ferry for about $5.*

One of the most popular campgrounds in the world, this one is booked months in advance. Choose a plain campsite for your own tent and gear, a platform with tents, cots, cooker, ice chest and tableware, or a spartan cottage furnished camping style. This is roughing it in paradise, with the sea at your doorstep. There's a restaurant and a camp store where basic supplies can be purchased. The bathroom is communal, campground style.

CONCORDIA ECO-TENTS, *mailing address 17 East 73rd Street, New York NY 10021. Tel. 800/392-9004 or 212/472-9453, Fax 861-6210; locally, Tel. 340/693-5855. Doubles are $95; additional persons are $25. Rent a car at the ferry dock for the 40-minute drive to Coral Bay.*

Perched high in isolated hills just outside the national park boundary on the southeast corner of the island near Coral Bay, Estate Concordia is one of the Maho Bay Camps but is 25 minutes by car from the other camps and 40 minutes from Cruz Bay. A rental car is a must. Permanent tents are made of fabric supported by a wood frame, with such high-tech features as solar and wind energy and composting toilet. This is living next to nature overlooking the sea and intruding as little as possible on the hills. Furnished are a refrigerator, cooking equipment, linens, and an ice chest you can supply from the office's ice machine. Guests can use the coin-op laundry. While the tents are built to catch the breezes, they can be warm when winds die. There's a big pool, or hike to the beach. Massage therapy is available for adults, infants, and youths. The registration office, where you can stop for information or to make a phone call, is only 8am-noon and 3-7pm.

CRUZ INN, *Box 797, Cruz Bay, St. John 00830. Tel. 340/693-8688 or 800/666-7688. Studios are priced from $75 plus a $5 surcharge for a one-night stay.*

Just a short walk from the dock, tennis courts, shopping, restaurants and the bus stop is a modestly furnished crash pad that gives you the bare essentials for about the lowest price on the island. Units have private bath, refrigerator and air conditioning. Apartments, which require a stay of three nights or more, sleep three to six people on beds, sofabeds and futons. All have a bathroom and kitchenette.

HARMONY RESORT *at Maho Bay, mailing address 17 East 73rd Street, New York NY 10021. Tel. 800/392-9004 or 212/472-9453, Fax 861-6210. Doubles are $95-$150 nightly plus $15 each additional person. A shuttle from the ferry costs about $5 per person.*

A step up from the same management's Maho Bay Campground, these tent-cottages are made from recycled materials and are sparsely but adequately furnished. Solar panels provide energy to heat bath water and operate the microwave. The design scoops in any trade winds, but on a calm day we wished for some high-voltage air conditioning. Furnished are kitchen gear and all linens. Your camp will have its own bathroom and deck. Use the same transportation, restaurant, cultural events and water sports as Maho Bay Campground.

THE INN AT TAMARIND COURT, *Box 350 Cruz Bay, St. John 00831. Tel. (430) 776-6378 or 800/221-1637. Single rooms with shared bath are $48; doubles with private bath start at $88. Continental breakfast is included. The Inn is in town within walking distance of the ferry dock.*

The flagstone courtyard of this unpretentious inn is one of Cruz Bay's most popular hangouts, with big shade trees, lively music, cheap food, and good booze. The location in the center of things makes it popular with business travelers and a good headquarters for island explorations. It's not on the beach and doesn't have a pool, but room rates were the best we could find on St. John for amply furnished, air conditioned accommodations with daily maid service. Walk to tennis, beach shuttles, shopping, and a bunch of restaurants.

MAHO BAY CAMPS, *Tel. 340/776-6240, 340/776-6226, or 800/392-9004. Rates are $60 nightly for two plus $10 additional per child and $12 more per adult. In summer children ages 16 and under sleep free in a parent's room.*

Visa and MasterCard are accepted. A shuttle from the ferry costs about $5 per person.

Permanently pitched tents on wood platforms are surrounded by thick, glossy, tropical foliage. They sleep up to four people in three rooms furnished with two twin beds and a sleep sofa. Bed linens, a propane stove, cooler, towels, and cooking and eating utensils are supplied. Each area shares a barbecue and water faucet. Toilets and pull-chain showers are communal.

Eat breakfast and dinner in the outdoor restaurant if you like, or shop in the camp store for frozen foods, produce, canned goods, bread, milk, juices, beer, wine, and basic paper products. Leave your leftovers in the "help yourself" center for arriving guests to use. Take an art or education workshop, snorkel and swim, hike, and enjoy the sunsets from your own deck. Pe*rstare*, a 34-foot Morgan, offers sunset, snorkel, and day sails to groups of up to six.

RAINTREE INN, *downtown Cruz Bay. Tel. 340/693-8590 or 800/666-7449. Rates at this 11-room inn are from $75; weekly rates are available.*

Efficiencies at this non-smoking property have everything you need for cooking plus private bath, air conditioning, telephone, and proximity to the socko Fish Trap restaurant. A three-night minimum stay is required. A popular choice for business travelers, the inn is your basic, budget beige, but it offers laundry service and is in a good Cruz Bay location. Children under age 3 stay free.

ST. THOMAS

Expensive

BOLONGO BAY BEACH CLUB AND VILLAS, *7150 Bolongo, St. Thomas VI 00802. Tel. 800/524-4746 or 340/775-1800. Rates at this 75-room resort start at $270 per day single occupancy or $440 per couple including room, food, drink, activities, tax, gratuities, watersports, scuba, and airport transfers. Singles take note of the attractions singles plan.*

The all-inclusive concept has immense appeal to travelers who weary of being charged every time they pick up a beach towel or book a tour. Everything here is exceptionally good quality from food and drink to

A REMINDER ABOUT RATES

Rates quoted in this book are for a double room in high season. In shoulder and low seasons you will be able to get lower rates, more features, or both except during Carnival or other special events. Rates do not include room tax, which applies to all rooms, or service charges, which are charged by some hotels.

snorkel cruises, tennis, fitness and aerobics, sauna, volleyball, basketball courts, an all-day sail, and nightly entertainment. It's a total vacation without having to open your wallet.

A semi-inclusive rate without meals and drinks is available for those who want to spend more time out on the island. All of the large, air conditioned bedrooms overlook the sea. They have television, ceiling fan, safe, private balcony with a view of the blue and telephone. Some have a kitchenette. Babysitters and cribs are available. Children under age 12 stay free with parents who are on the Continental (semi-inclusive) Plan.

MARRIOTT'S FRENCHMAN'S REEF RESORT, *Flamboyant Point, mailing address P.O. Box 7100, St. Thomas 00801. Tel. 340/776-8500 or 800/524-2000 for Frenchman's Reef, 800/232-2425 for Morning Star. Rates at this 501-unit resort start at $325; suites are priced to $1200. A meal plan is available and, in summer and fall, an all-inclusive plan. The resort is three miles east of Charlotte Amalie.*

Fully operational now after a stunning, $50 million re-do, this classic resort faces both the harbor and the Caribbean. Choose Frenchman's Reef for a hilltop high-rise with a view or Morningstar for upscale accommodations on the beach. Top of the Reef suites have a loft bedroom and fabulous views of the harbor and the Caribbean beyond. Royal Suites have a spiral staircase, balcony, cathedral ceiling, and Jacuzzi. Rooms have voice mail and data line, individual climate control, cable television with pay-per-view, hair dryer, coffee maker, safe, ice maker, and mini-bar. Together the hotels have shops, many restaurants and bars, a convenience store, a coffee bar, room service, in-room ironing boards and mini-bars, tennis courts, and a full range of watersports. The main swimming pool with its waterfalls and swim-up bar is a humdinger. Be sure to tell your driver where you're staying; the resorts' check-in desks are separate.

RENAISSANCE GRAND BEACH RESORT, *Smith Bay Road, mailing address P.O. Box 8267, St. Thomas VI 00801. Tel. 340/775-1519 or 800/322-2976. Rates at the 297-unit resort start at $285. A cab ride from the airport is $15 per person.*

This AAA Four Diamond resort on St. Thomas just keeps getting better, consistently boasting one of the highest Guest Satisfaction Index scores in the Renaissance chain. The 34 acres of grounds are groomed and gardened, providing restful views of sea and landscape. Units are spread over hill and dale but call a shuttle if you don't feel like walking. And if you can't walk at all, the resort's six wheelchair accessible units are a rare find in the Caribbean.

The beach is just off a huge pool area, so you can float the day away in the ocean, pool, sailboat or raft. The resort's Smuggler's Restaurant, where you can mix your own Bloody Mary on Sunday mornings, is an island favorite. The children's program is free, providing up to 12 hours a day of supervised fun and care.

One-bedroom suites have a balcony, coffee machine, refrigerator, wet bar, and a queen-size sofabed. High-tech equipment is furnished in the fitness center, which also has men's and women's steam, sauna, and extensive spa services. A plus is a comfortable lounge with rest rooms where travelers can hang out between checkout and a late departure.

If you prefer to stay in self-catering accommodations on the resort property, book with **Pineapple Village Villas**, *Tel. 340/777-3985, Fax 775-5516; toll-free 800/992-9232*; privately-owned villas start at $150 nightly.

RITZ-CARLTON, *699 Great Bay, St. Thomas 00802. Tel. 340/241-3333, Fax 775-4444; toll-free 800/241-3333. U.S. and Canada 800/241-3333. High season rates start at $400 per room. Ask about packages. The 148-room, four-suite hotel is 30 minutes from the airport or about $10 per person by taxi. Airport transfer by limousine can be arranged by the hotel, which is found on the island's eastern tip.*

Surely the *ne plus ultra* of St. Thomas resorts and the first Ritz-Carlton in the Caribbean, this one has all the five-star features of other Ritz-Carltons around the globe. From the moment you're welcomed at the portico and ushered across gleaming marble floors to the check-in desk, the coddling from perkily-uniformed staff is complete.

Built in the fashion of a grand palazzo, the property rims a fine beach and overlooks a brimming pool with an "infinity" edge that makes you think you're swimming on the horizon. From the main building, which houses some guest rooms, the lobby, meeting rooms, and The Cafe for fine dining, buildings cluster around a salt pond nature preserve filled with waterfowl. The rooms are spacious and come with all amenities. Specify sun or shade when you book; there's a choice of open or shaded balconies. Plan your days around swimming, the beach, sailing excursions aboard the resort's own catamaran, tennis, the fitness center,, diving, snorkeling, golf and more. The hotel has its own beauty salon, and shops selling designer clothing and accessories. Jackets are not required at dinner, but this resort calls for your very best resort wear.

Selected as one of my Best Places to Stay; see Chapter 13 for more details.

SAPPHIRE BEACH RESORT & MARINA, *P.O. Box 08088, St. Thomas 00801. Tel. 340/775-6100 or 800/524-2090. Rates at the 171-unit resort start at $310 for a suite with full kitchen. Suites sleep four; villas sleep up to six. The optional meal plan is $70. Children under age 13 stay, eat, and play free with their parents. The resort is 35 minutes from the airport, 25 minutes from Charlotte Amalie and five minutes from the Red Hook ferry.*

Check into a spacious suite decorated in cool whites and pastels. Each has a private balcony with ocean view, air conditioning, microwave, coffee maker, full-size refrigerator, satellite television, telephone, ceiling fans, air conditioning, and a living-dining area where a bottle of rum welcomes you. Maid service includes fresh flowers daily. The beach is a picture postcard of white sand and turquoise water.

Children can play all day, 8:30am to 5:30pm with other children in a supervised program filled with learning and fun. For an additional charge of $15, parents can put children in the Nite Klub until 10pm.

The resort is 15 minutes from the famous Mahogany Run golf course but, unless you're an ardent golfer, you won't want to leave the resort. It has its own marina and dive center including scuba lessons, sea kayaking, and deep sea fishing; free use of non-motorized watercraft, tennis, volleyball, a gift shop. Shuttle service into Charlotte Amalie is $7 round trip or $4 each way; into Red Hook, it's $2 each way.

Have a drink in the Seagrape Beach Bar, then dine in the Sailfish Cafe with its Mexican favorites, the Seagrape Restaurant on the beach or the Steak House at The Point. Then have an after-dinner drink at the bar, which is open until 2am. Live entertainers play five nights a week, with Calypso and steel drums three nights a week. On Sunday afternoons, the reggae beach party is not to be missed.

SECRET HARBOUR BEACH RESORT, *Nazareth Bay, St. Thomas 00802. Tel. 800/524-2250 or 340/775-6550. Studios start at $275. The resort also offers one-and two-bedroom suites and villas. It's near Red Hook, a $10 taxi ride from the airport.*

The resort and the adjacent villas were merged in 1998 to form a grand complex. Units, which are air conditioned, have a full kitchen and private balcony or patio overlooking the sea. Two-bedroom suites have two baths, but even the studios are spacious with their own patio or balcony, bed-sitting room, and a bath with dressing room. Dine in the Blue Moon seaside café, work out in the fitness center, play tennis, sail the resort's catamaran, dive with the resort's five-star PADI center, browse the gift shop, and swim in the freshwater pool. All units get daily maid service. Babysitting can be arranged.

Moderate

BEST WESTERN CARIB BEACH, *70 Lindberg Bay, St. Thomas 00802. Tel. 340/774-2525, Fax 777-4131; toll-free 800/792-2742. Rates at this 69-room hotel start at $109 plus 13 per cent tax.*

The perfect place for an affordable, weekend getaway in the sunshine, this hillside inn isn't fancy but it overlooks a flawless beach, serves modestly priced buffets nightly, and brings in entertainers often. Typical of this price-appeal chain, the hotel has television and telephones in the rooms, a swimming pool, air conditioning, tennis, and watersports

VIRGIN ISLANDS HOTEL WEDDINGS

If you want to get married in paradise, a number of companies provide complete wedding planning including accommodations for the couple and their families, the ceremony, flowers, reception, photographer, and a honeymoon hideaway. Contact:

ELOPE TO PARADISE, *Buccaneer Hotel, Box 25200, St. Croix CI 00824. Tel. 340/773-2100 or 800/255-3881.*

FANTASIA WEDDINGS AND HONEYMOONS, *Suite 310, 168 Crown Bay, St. Thomas VI 00802, Tel. 340/777-6588, Fax 776-0020; toll-free 800/326-8272*

ISLAND BRIDE, *Box 24436, St. Croix VI 00824. Tel. 340/773-3897.*

RENAISSANCE WEDDINGS, *Box 8267, St. Thomas VI 00801, Tel. 800/322-2976*

WEDDINGS BY IPS, *9719 Estate Thomas, Suite 1, St. Thomas VI 00801, Tel. 340/774-4598, Fax 776-3433; toll-free 800/937-1346*

WEDDINGS ISLAND WAY, *10-1-29 Peterborg, mailing address Box 11694, St. Thomas VI 00801, Tel. 340/775-6505, Fax 777-6550; toll-free 800/582-4784 or 800/755-5004*

WEDDINGS IN PARADISE *is the wedding planning service for the Marriott Beach Resorts (Frenchman's Reef and Morning Star). Tel. 800/367-5683.*

SAPPHIRE PRECIOUS WEDDINGS, *Box 8088, St. Thomas VI 00801, Tel. 340/775-6100, extension 8117; toll-free 800/524-2090.*

rentals. A sister **Best Western** nearby has 90 rooms and is right on the beach, so rates are higher, starting at $189; *Tel. 340/777-8800.*

L'HOTEL BOYNES, *Blackbeard's Hill, Charlotte Amalie. Tel. 340/774-5511 or 800/377-2905. Rates at this eight-room inn start at $115, single or double occupancy, including continental breakfast. Taxi fare from the airport is about $5 per person.*

Sam Boynes, owner and host of this hillside retreat is part of the hospitality magic. A great-great grandson of the French secretary of the navy under Louis XV, he named the hotel after the Paris original of the same name where Napoleon was married. Old island hands may remember the inn as The Mark St. Thomas, a dinner restaurant long revered for its fabulous city views and cozy setting in a mansion built in 1785.

Boynes has refurbished the house, adding a wealth of antiques and collectibles from his travels. He's a black innkeeper who speaks Japanese, regales his guests with island history and his genealogy, and hosts one of the most interesting inns in the Caribbean. Rooms are all different, each with private bath, ceilings that seem 20 feet high, and original, two-century-old stonework, woodwork and floors. They have cable television and direct dial telephone. Most have air conditioning.

The grounds are steep and small, but landscaped with such artistry that guests will be happy here reading and looking out over the island's best view of Charlotte Amalie. There's a tiny pool and a hot tub. Walks are steep but it's not far to the shopping and dining district downhill or Blackbeard's tower up the hill.

COLONY POINT PLEASANT RESORT, *Estate Smith Bay, St. Thomas, VI 00802. Tel. toll-free 800/777-1700 or locally 340/775-7200. Rates at the 134 suites, which range in size from studios to two-bedroom units, start at $255 nightly. Cab fare from the airport is $15.*

Spread atop a steep, cone-shaped hill like color on a snow cone, this all-suites resort has it all for the vacationing couple or family: three swimming pools, two restaurants including the renowned Agavé, a marina with motorized and non-motorized watersports, nature trails, and a tennis court. If you don't care to navigate the resort on foot, use the free shuttle service. In an unusual program, the resort allows each villa four hours use of a car daily at no cost except for a mandatory $12.50 fee for insurance and fuel.

The villas are individually owned so each is furnished differently but those we saw were fresh and attractive, with a hilltop overlook from the balcony, tile floors with jute area rugs, a welcome bottle of rum on the table, and a fully equipped tile kitchen. Suites are air conditioned and have ceiling fans.

WYNDHAM SUGAR BAY BEACH CLUB, *on Route 30, East End, mailing address 6500 Estate Smith Bay, St. Thomas VI 00802. Tel. 800/WYNDHAM. Doubles at the resort start at $270 per couple all inclusive. Ask about packages and, in summer, the kids-free program. The resort is a $10 cab ride from the airport.*

Once part of a sugar plantation, this 32-acre site has alternating strips of sugar beach and rocky headland, with views from your balcony of tireless surf. Every room has a television and refrigerator; furnishings have a mellow, colonial look accented with floral motifs. Dine outdoors and waterside at the Mangrove Cafe. Snorkel, play tennis, golf the Mahogany Run Golf Course, take a Jeep adventure, scuba dive, and swim in the interconnecting, freshwater pools where you can swim your way to from whirlpool to waterfall. Every evening, take in a boisterous revue in a cruise ship-like lounge, then dance afterwards until 1am. The hospitality is total from the moment you step off the airplane until you're taken back to the airport. Everything from food to drinks and non-motorized watersports is included in one fee.

Budget

DANISH CHALET, *Charlotte Amalie. Mailing address Box 4319, St. Thomas 00803. Tel. 340/774-5764, Fax 777-4886; toll-free 800/635-1531. Rates at this ten-room inn start at $75. It's ten minutes from the airport.*

It's like going home to the folks when you stay with Frank and Mary Davis, former yachties who settled down here and opened an inn where drinks at the honor bar are only $1. Rooms are homey, with air conditioning or ceiling fan and telephone. The restaurants and shops of town are a five-minute walk away and it's 15 minutes to some of the island's best beaches. A continental breakfast is included and it is served in a pleasant setting where you'll meet other guests. You can also share the Jacuzzi and library with a nice mix of other guests.

HOTEL 1829, *Box 1576, St. Thomas 00801. Tel. 340/777-7100, Fax 776-1829; toll-free 800/524-2002. Rates at this 15-room inn start at $75; larger rooms are priced to $170.*

This charming inn was built as a home by a French sea captain for his bride. It took ten years and was completed in 1829, hence the name. Now a National Historic Site, the house has air conditioning, private baths with each room, cable television, and balconies in some rooms. A continental breakfast is included. The restaurant here is popular and the dark little bar is straight out of the 1950s. There is a tiny swimming pool, just large enough for a cooling splash. There's no elevator, so this isn't a good choice if you have a problem with stairs.

ISLAND VIEW GUEST HOUSE, *Box 1903, St. Thomas. Tel. 340/774-4270, Fax 774-6167; toll-free 800/524-2023. Rates at this 15-room guesthouse start at $60.*

Located halfway between town and the airport, this is a good base for island exploring if you have a car. Parking is provided. Rooms are air conditioned and have television and telephone. The relaxed little inn has an arresting view of the sea far below from its own pleasant pool and breezy deck. In the foreground are acres of bright shrubs.

MAFOLIE, *Box 1506, St. Thomas 00804. Tel. 340/774-2790, Fax 774-4091; toll-free 800/524-2023. Rates at this 23-room inn start at $81 including continental breakfast; weekly and month rates are available. It's 10 minutes from the airport.*

The view of the harbor 800 feet below is one of the great pleasures of this delightful small hotel. A free shuttle takes guests to famous Magen's Bay beach, or you can spend your days in the freshwater pool with its big, sunny deck. Drink service is available at the pool all day. Rooms and suites (some with kitchenette) have air conditioning, ceiling fan, cable television, and all the comforts of a small, homey bedroom. The same nice family have been in charge for 25 years and they keep things running smoothly.

ST. CROIX

During peak seasons when bookings are hard to get, the **Small Inns Association of St. Croix** will help you find a room in a member inn. Call toll-free: *Tel. 888/INN-USVI.* Villas and condos are available through **Vacation St. Croix**, *Tel. 340/778-0361* or *800/533-6863.*

Expensive

BUCCANEER HOTEL, *Gallows Bay, mailing address P.O. Box 25200, Christiansted 00824. Tel. 340/773-2100 or 800/255-3881. Rates in this 150-unit resort start at $210 for a double room in season. Take East End Road east out of Christiansted for two miles. The resort is a $12 taxi ride from the airport.*

A historic treasure founded in 1653 by a French settler, this charming property is on ground that was once planted to sugar. Its lobby is in the remains of an old mill. The resort has been in the same family since 1947. Our deluxe beachfront room was as big as a ballroom, with cavernous closets, a big bathroom with double sinks, refrigerator and ceiling fans as well as air conditioning and remote control cable television. Butter yellow and Danish blue fabrics complement the blue and white tiles, vaulted pine ceiling, mellow rattan furniture, and mahogany woodwork. The window seat overlooking the beach is a bookworm's delight.

Swim in the pool, which has its own bar, or choose one of three surrounding beaches. Play the 18-hole golf course or eight tennis courts, choose from four restaurants, use the fitness center, or make an appointment in the spa. In addition to the beachfront units, other rooms, suites and a guesthouse are high on the hill with soaring views. Take a hike, or call for the shuttles that are always available.

CARAMBOLA BEACH RESORT & GOLF CLUB, *Estate Davis Bay, Kingshill, P.O. Box 3031, St. Croix 00851. Tel. 800/228-3000 or 340/778-3800. Rates at this 151-unit resort start at $245. Take Route 69 north from the airport and turn left when it ends at Route 80. Cab fare from the airport is $12 for one or two persons. This resort is no longer a Westin but is a time share under new management. We are told that accommodations, restaurants and other resort features will still be available to non-owners.*

Looking down from Parasol Hill, a killer hill used in the annual St. Croix International Triathlon, the hotel complex looks like a bouquet of red hibiscus, each building roofed in crimson. Rooms are as spacious as suites, most of them with a private screened porch and a dim, wood interior that provides respite from the brilliant sunshine. Luxury features abound: air conditioning, a fitness center and spa, hair dryers and coffee makers in rooms, television, telephone, and room service. The Davis Bay Suite has two bedrooms and a private veranda that the Rockefellers once used to entertain groups of up to 100.

Robert Trent Jones, Sr. designed the golf course that is only a five-minute shuttle ride away. Tennis courts are lit for night play. The restaurants provide tony dining by candlelight or a lighter, deli experience. The beach was restored after the last hurricane and looks sandy and inviting despite a few rocky areas; just off shore, the 3000-foot wall is one of the island's best dive spots. Ask about the children's program, popcorn and movies, and activities for all ages. The site, aloof and scenic, is a popular one for weddings and the hotel has its own wedding planner who can make arrangements for everything from the cake and flowers to accommodations for the entire wedding party.

Moderate

CHENAY BEACH RESORT, *P.O. Box 24600, St. Croix 00824. Tel. 800/548-4457 or 340/773-2918. Rates start at $185 for a cottage with full-size refrigerator, cooktop, and microwave oven. On the northeast end of the island three miles east of Christiansted, it's a $13 taxi fare from the airport. Add $65 per person per day for a meal plan that includes breakfast, lunch, dinner, and drinks.*

This lively, 50-unit resort has a big lap pool, a rim of beach, a locally popular restaurant with theme nights and parties, tennis, and good snorkeling just off the beach. Rooms are done in sunny colors, with air conditioning, ceiling fan, radio, television, microwave, coffee maker, dial telephone, small dining area, and mini-bar. For families traveling together, connecting cottages are available at family rates. Children are catered to with their own games and menu.

HOTEL CARAVELLE, *44a Queen Cross Street, Christiansted, 00820. Tel. 340/773-0687 or toll-free 800/223-6510; in Canada 800/424-5500. Website www.hotelcaravellestcroix.com. Rates at this 43-room, AAA Three-Diamond Hotel are from $112. It's in the heart of downtown on the water, a $10 ride from the airport for one or two persons.*

A European-style boutique hotel has been transplanted in the tropics, blending the sunny airiness of a Cruzan resort with modern amenities. It has been generations since the Virgin Islands were Danish, but Danes continue to come to this user-friendly hotel. Rooms, many of them overlooking the harbor, are air conditioned and have mini-refrigerator and cable television. There's a freshwater pool, gift shop, and free parking– a plus if you want to spend a lot of time in parking-deprived Christiansted. The staff love innkeeping, and it shows. This hotel has the highest rate of repeat guests in the islands. The restaurant, Wahoo Willy's, is a St. Croix favorite for locals and visitors alike. Golf is nearby; beaches and tennis courts are within walking distance. Ask about dive packages. In summer, a Family Degree package includes an environmental study program.

SEAVIEW FARM INN, *180 Two Brothers, Frederiksted, 00840. Tel. 340/ 772-5367 or 800/792-3060. Rates at this eight-suite inn start at $130 including Happy Hour in the bar and a basket of breakfast makings delivered to your suite each morning. Cab fare from the airport is $10.*

The look from the road is that of a Virginia farm with its white farm fence, but the tropical nature of this sprawling mini-resort emerges when you check into a breezy cottage, take a dip in the pool, and hang out at the open air grill and bar complete with model sailboats you can race. Suites have four-poster beds, kitchenette, screened porch, and plenty of cross ventilation as well as air conditioning and ceiling fan. No TV or phones in the rooms, but there is a big screen TV at the bar, and telephones at the pool bar. The view is of a salt pond filled with waterfowl, a plus for birders who like to use the inn's telescope. Massage is available by appointment. For modem hookup, ask Dulcy and Roland Kushmore, your hosts.

TAMARIND REEF HOTEL, *5001 Tamarind Reef, three miles east of Christiansted and 25 minutes, or $13 for two by taxi, from the airport. Doubles are priced $160-$180 nightly including continental breakfast poolside; children under age six sleep free.*

Every room overlooks the sea in this neat-as-a-pin resort. All rooms have air conditioning, ceiling fan, color television, clock radio, telephone, coffee maker, refrigerator, robes, hair dryer, ironing board and iron, and mini-bar service. The safe works on your own credit card, so there is no key to worry about. (Some hotels charge a key deposit for $50 or more). Spacious, airy rooms are done in sherbet pastels, with original art from a Florida artist and tiles from a Cruzan crafter. Kitchenette suites have two-burner stove, microwave oven, dishes and other galley gear. Junior suites and two queen-size beds and dining space for four. There's one suite, which connects to a deluxe-category room, so it's ideal for a family. Its roll-in shower is one of a handful on the island, making the entire suite wheelchair accessible. Dine casually in the Deep End, or elegantly in The Galleon. The beach is picturesque but rocky, so bring reef shoes. Diving, sailing, and watersports of all kinds can be arranged. The resort has tennis courts, six-wicket croquet, a marina and a big swimming pool surrounded by a sun deck. Ask about golf or dive packages.

THE WAVES AT CANE BAY, *P.O. Box 1749, Kingshill, 00851. Tel. 340/778-1805 or 800/545-0603. Rates start at $140 for a studio apartment with screened balcony and full kitchen. Cab fare from the airport is $13 for two.*

This 12-unit hideaway is a find for divers because hosts Kevin and Suzanne Ryan have their own dive shop here plus a natural pool where beginners can take their first scuba or snorkel lessons. The beach is small and very attractive. Balconies hang right over the waves. There's a restaurant, which is an inexpensive hangout popular with passers-by.

USVI VILLA RENTALS

This guide does not list privately-owned villas that are available on a one-to-one basis because we can't vouch for the condition of units that are under absentee management. However, professionally managed private homes and villas can be booked through the following places below:

ST. JOHN

***Caribbean Villas & Resorts**, Wharfside Village, St. John 00830, Tel. 800/338-0987, Fax 207/871-1673*

***Caribe Havens**, P.O. Box 455, St. John 00830, Tel. 340/776-6518*

***Destination St. John**, Box 8306, St. John 00830, Tel. 800/776-6969 or 800/562-1901*

***Holiday Homes of St. John, Inc.**, Mongoose Junction, Cruz Bay, St. John, 00831, Tel. 340/776-6776 or 800/424-6641*

***Island Getaways Vacation Villas**, Kathy McLaughlin, P.O. Box 1504, St. John 00831, toll-free Tel. 888/693-7676*

***Katherine DeMar Vacation Homes**, P.O. Box 272, Cruz Bay, St. John 00831, Tel. 340/776-6094*

***Marlene M. Carney, Star Villa Rentals**, P.O. Box 599, Cruz Bay, St. John USVI 00831, Tel. 340/776-6704*

***Mary-Phyllis Moguieira, Mameyu Peak**, St. John 00830, Tel. 340/776-6876*

***Park Isle Villas**, P.O. Box 1263, St. John 00831, Tel. 800/416-1205 or 693-8261*

***Sea View Homes**, P.O. Box 644, Cruz Bay, St. John USVI 08831, Tel. 340/776-6805*

***Serendip Vacation Apartments**, P.O. Box 273, Cruz Bay, St. John USVI 00831, Tel. 340/776-6646*

***Villa Portfolio**, P.O. Box 618, Cruz Bay, St. John USVI 00831, Tel. 800/858-7989 or 340/693-9100*

***Windspree Vacation Home Rentals**, 6-2-1A Estate Carolina, St. John 00830,Tel. 693-5423.*

ST. THOMAS

***All About Condos & Properties**, 6600 Estate Nazareth #2, St. Thomas VI 00802. Tel. 340/775-7740, Fax 775-9631.*

***Calypso Realty**, P.O. Box 12178, St. Thomas 00801, Tel. 340/774-1620, Fax 774-1634. Website www.st-thomas.com/calypso. In addition to a selection of other villas, this company has one that meets A.D.A. standards for the physically challenged. **McLaughlin Anderson Vacations Inc.**, 100 Blackbeard's Hill, St. Thomas 00802, Tel. 340/776-0635, Fax 777-4737, toll-free 800/537-6246 or 800/666-6246.*

ST. CROIX

***Islands Villas Property Management & Vacation Rentals**, 6 Company Street, Christiansted, St. Croix VI 00820. Tel. 340/773-8821, Fax 773-8823; toll-free 800/626-4512.*

***CPMI Vacation Rentals**, Tel. 340/778-8782, Fax 773-2150.*

SPRAT HALL PLANTATION, *Route 63, Frederiksted, 00841. Tel. 340/772-4305 or 800/843-3584. Rates start at $100. Cab fare from the airport is $10 for two.*

Mr. and Mrs. Jim Hurd can't seem to keep up with the maintenance of this old pile, but the scruffy charm and the Hurd's priceless fund of island lore more than make up for the lack of spit and polish. Mrs. Hurd was born here, in a greathouse that goes back to the 1650s. In the main house are two big bedrooms. Nearby are a couple of two-bedroom cottages and a one-bedroom honeymoon cottage. Hike or ride the grounds on horseback. They go on for acres of winding paths and pillowy hills planted with 700 fruit trees Eat in the dining room or in the Hurd's rustic Beach Club restaurant just a short walk away.

Budget

BEST WESTERN HOLGER DANSKE, *1 King Cross Street, Christiansted, St. Croix 00840. Tel. 340/773-3600 or 800/528-1234. Rates at this 44-room hotel start at $89 single. Cab fare from the airport is $10 for one or two persons.*

Stay in the heart of downtown with its pace and pizzazz, handy to restaurants and shopping. The hotel has a pool and sundeck; each room has a balcony or patio overlooking the harbor, telephone, and cable television. Some kitchenettes are available.

CLUB COMANCHE, *1 Strand Street, Christiansted 00820. Tel. 800/524-2066 or 340/773-0210. Rates at this 24-room hotel start at $49.50. A cab from the airport costs $10 for one or two persons.*

Convenience, a great city location, full-featured suites with air conditioning and cable television, a superb South Seas-look restaurant, a harbor view from your balcony and low cost make up for the somewhat cheesy furnishings of this 250-year-old club. Diving instruction is available in the big, saltwater pool. Rooms have air conditioning, television and telephone.

DANISH MANOR HOTEL, *2 Company Street, Christiansted. Tel. 340/773-1377 or 800/773-1377. Rates at this 34-room inn start at $85 including continental breakfast.*

A busy, buzzy downtown location is ideal for shopping and dining Christiansted, but don't expect an ocean view unless you specify a room on the third floor. Courtyard views are of a swimming pool and plenty of greenery. It's a popular gathering spot for guests. Rooms have air conditioning and cable television. The beach is a five-minute ferry ride away.

FREDERIKSTED HOTEL, *442 Strand Street, Frederiksted, St. Croix 00840. Tel. 340/773-9150 or 800/524-2025. Rates at this 40-room hotel start* *at $85. Take a cab from the airport, which is about 10 minutes away, for $8 per couple.*

The charm of a small, European hotel and the convenience of a downtown location add up to a fine value within walking distance of beaches, shopping, , and restaurants. The hotel has its own restaurant and sun deck; each room has a small refrigerator and a microwave oven.

HILTY HOUSE INN, *Questa Verde Road, Gallows Bay, mailing address P.O. Box 26077, St. Croix, 00824. Tel. and fax 340/773-2594. Rates at this five-room inn start at $85 including continental breakfast. A one-bedroom cottage is also available. Credit cards aren't accepted. Cab fare from the airport is $10.*

Hugh and Jacquie Haore found this converted 1732 rum factory and have turned it into an enchanted inn. In a region where fireplaces are almost unknown, here is a huge one that is lit on Christmas Eve. Jacquie makes her own jams for breakfast from local fruits such as tamarind and mango. After a day of diving or exploring, relax in the old library with books and television. Or sign up for one of Jacquie's famous ethnic dinners held Monday nights, with authentic mood, music, and food. Rooms are all different, and all beguiling, with wonderful angles and crannies created by old walls that were built with another use in mind. There's no air conditioning, but ceiling fans augment the hilltop breezes.

PINK FANCY, *27 Prince Street, Christiansted, 00820. Tel. 340/773-8460 or 800/524-2045. Doubles start at $75 including continental breakfast and Happy Hour drinks. Cab fare from the airport is $10 for two.*

George and Cindy Tyler are part of the magical mix of this sprawling old relic. Dating to 1780, the buildings have been refurbished with comfy wicker, shiny mahogany floors, air conditioning and ceiling fans. An old hangout for show business folks, it is decorated with old showbiz posters and memorabilia. It's still popular with business travelers who, if they want only to crash and burn, take one of the small, inexpensive rooms. The heart of the 13-room inn is the cobblestone courtyard around the pool, where breakfast and cocktails are served. There's a gazebo for small weddings, and learn-to-cook weekends are offered in summer. Parking is on the street, but you won't need a rental car if you want only to hang out around the pool and enjoy Christiansted's shopping and dining.

SANDCASTLE ON THE BEACH RESORT, *P.O. Box 1908, Frederiksted, 00820. Tel. 340/772-1205 or 800/524-2018. Rates start at $85 per person including continental breakfast. Cab fare from the airport is $8.50 for two. The resort is a half mile south of town.*

Although this inn bills itself as "proudly serving the homosexual and Lesbian community," all lifestyles are welcomed and our impression was one of a happy, homogeneous group of people having the time of their lives. Suites and villas overlook a seagrape-shaded sand beach, a warm cove with good snorkeling, and a seaside courtyard where breakfast is free and lunch and dinner are a delight. On the beach side, units have bedroom, living room, screened porch with pass-through to the kitchen, and an ocean view. Seafoam green fabrics are accented with iridescent amethyst; floors are Italian tile. A second unit across the narrow street has its own pool and two-bedroom suites.

PRINCE STREET INN, *402 Prince Street, Frederiksted, 00840. Tel. 340/772-9550 or 800/771-9550. Rates at this four-room inn start at $42. No credit cards are accepted.*

Once a Lutheran parsonage, this inn finds privacy in the heart of town thanks to its attractive gates and courtyard. Wooden cottages have living room, bedroom, bath and kitchen, adding up to a whale of a deal for the price. Walk to beaches, shopping, and restaurants.

HURRICANE UPDATE

In all the years we have been traveling the tropics, one hurricane theme is repeated time and again. "Please tell them that we are open and operating," plead hoteliers whose guests have been scared away by over-dramatic press reports. Innkeepers are partly to blame because, when damage occurs, they invariably underestimate how long it will take to get things back in order. They don't re-open on time, or they claim to be running normally, and guests find themselves staying at Fawlty Towers. Even in the worst storms, some hotels don't close at all and others have only minor disruptions such as a brief or partial power failure. There's only one way to get the straight scoop and that's to call the airlines to see if you can get in and out. Then phone the hotel itself and ask, "Are you open and operating normally?" and then pin them down, "What services are unavailable or curtailed?" If the answer to #1 is "next week", call again and keep calling until you can be assured that the hotel is (not will be) operating fully. Better still, talk to someone who has just returned from the same hotel.

WHERE TO EAT

Dinner hours in the Virgin Islands seem awfully early when compared to French and Spanish islands but, even though kitchens close at 9 or 10pm, the drinking, dancing, music, and good times might go on for hours depending on the restaurant.

ST. THOMAS

Expensive

CRAIG AND SALLY'S, *22 Honduras Estate, Frenchtown. Tel. 777-9949. It's open daily except Monday for lunch and dinner. Reservations are urged.*

Their ad promises a refreshing, convivial evening and it all comes true when you're greeted jovially by Craig while Sally creates cuisine magic backstage. Take time with the wine list, which is as daunting as it is tempting, and let a server suggest a choice. Choose from an inspired menu that tonight might feature lobster-stuffed potatoes, a butter-tender filet under a light sauce, roasted lamb drifted with fresh herbs, grilled fish, or a pasta invention.

ENTRE NOUS, *Bluebeard's Castle, Bluebeard's Hill, Charlotte Amalie. Tel. 776-4050. Main dishes are $10 to $40. It's open for dinner daily except Sunday and the month of September. Reservations are suggested. The hotel's chic, informal Banana Tree Grille is open for lunch Tuesday-Saturday and for dinner Tuesday-Sunday.*

The view of the town and harbor twinkling far below is worth the price of the evening. Hilltop breezes cool the open, airy room while servers bring on the bounty: snapper in garlic butter, Caribbean lobster, chicken, roasted duckling, perhaps even venison. Guests love the showy, tableside presentations, which include Caesar salad, cherries jubilee, or bananas foster. Ask to see the wine list, which is lengthy and varied.

HERVÉ RESTAURANT & WINE BAR, *Kongens Gade. Tel. 777-9703. Hours are Monday through Saturday for lunch and dinner and Sunday for dinner only. Find the restaurant between Zorba's and Hotel 1829. Plan to spend $30-$40 for a three course dinner; $25 for a two-course lunch.*

It's the buzz of St. Thomas. Hervé and Paulette put together a welcoming ambience and great food in a relaxed, bistro setting on Government Hill, the perfect place to take a break from downtown shopping. For a hearty meal, take the lamb shank braised with vegetables with fresh herbs and red wine. Or dine more delicately on chilled shrimp with papaya cocktail sauce, spinach and vegetables en croute, or a poached artichoke stuffed with crab and served with cold ravigotte sauce.

HOTEL 1829, *Box 1576, St. Thomas 00801,. Tel. 340/777-7100. Hours are Monday through Saturday 11am to 2pm and 5:30-10:30pm. but they vary seasonally, so check ahead. It may not be open for lunch in summer. Reservations are recommended. Plan to spend $30-$40 for dinner.*

Dine in this prestige location on Government Hill in a local landmark known for its gracious service and West Indian ambience. Try the pan-fried snapper with mango compote, or lunch on a freshly grilled mahi-mahi sandwich served with roasted red pepper mayonnaise.

THE RITZ CARLTON DINING ROOM, *in the Ritz-Carlton Hotel, Great Bay, Tel. 775-3333. Open for dinner daily; reservations are urged. Plan to spend $100 for a three-course dinner for two.*

Dining at the Ritz can be expensive but the food is so splendid and the choices so many, even the most discerning diner will be dazzled. We started with the crisp, buttery foie gras Napoleon, served with mango chutney and faintly scented with balsamic vinegar. Then we had the

Caesar salad for two, presented tableside, and went right on to dessert: the Spanish Hot Chocolate Soufflé. Only the hungriest trencherman will be able to tackle four courses but it's hard to resist trying one of the appetizers, a soup such as the velvety tomato bisque topped with a corn fritter, fresh fish or lobster, then the chocolate hazel parfait with candied cherries, or the trio of creme brulée featuring three custards, one vanilla, one lavender, and one lemon grass.

ROMANO'S, *97 Smith Bay Road on the north coast. Tel. 775-0045. Main dishes are priced $16 to $30. Dinner is served nightly except Sunday and during Carnival, when the restaurant closes for a week. Reservations are recommended.*

The pastas are not only the least expensive main dishes, they are invitingly different. Choose a simple pesto sauce, one of the seafood sauces, or the lasagna baked to creamy perfection with four cheeses. Carnivores will enjoy the veal marsala, osso bucco or a steak with a side of pasta. Fresh salmon is often on the board. Grilled to succulent perfection, it makes a toothsome meal with nothing more than a salad and a crusty bread. The desserts are homemade, and vary daily.

SEAGRAPE, *in the Sapphire Beach Resort. Tel. 775-9750. Reservations are suggested. Lunch and dinner are served Monday-Saturday; Sunday brunch is served 11am-3pm. Main dishes are priced $17-$26. Children have their own menu.*

Overlook a finest-kind beach while you dine on continental and American favorites such as grilled steak or chicken with mushroom relish, teriyaki, fresh fish, or roast lamb with a side dish of garlic mashed potatoes. The Sunday brunch is a feast featuring specialty waffles, salads, fresh fruit galore, and a galaxy of hot and cold dishes.

VICTOR'S NEW HIDEOUT, *103 Submarine Base. Tel. 776-9379. Reservations are urged, especially since you need to call for directions if you are driving (Victor's used to be at 32 Submarine Base). It's open for lunch and dinner Monday-Saturday and Sunday 5:30-10pm. Main dishes are priced $10-$50.*

Victor himself is from Montserrat, so his lobster is sauced with the style of his home island. Or, order it grilled in the shell without the cream sauce, and dip each luscious morsel into melted butter. Keep an eye peeled for celebrities of the television, movie, and music world who seek out this spot when they are on the island. Native Caribbean dishes here are done with flash and elan; the pies are like Mother used to make.

Moderate

AGAVÉ TERRACE, *in the Point Pleasant Resort. Tel. 775-4142. The resort is found on the east end of the island between the Renaissance Grand Beach Resort and Red Hook. Plan to spend $10-$15 for breakfast and $20-$40 for lunch or dinner. Reservations are recommended. Dinner is served nightly from 6pm; brunch is served on Saturday and Sunday.*

The views from this all-villa resort overlooking Pillsbury Sound are awesome. Brunch starts with a morning Happy Hour drink and Eggs Florentine or a tropical fruit plate ringed with fresh, fragrant muffins. At dinner, appetizers in the $5-$9 range include a five-pepper dip with chips, conch chowder, or iced gazpacho. Choose a pasta specialty such as linguine with tenderloin medallions and Gorgonzola-walnut cream sauce, or one of the steaks. They come in two sizes.

Ask about the catch of the day, then fine-tune your order according to cooking method and sauce. If you've had fisherman's luck today, bring your own fish and let the chef serve it to you. Dinners came with a special salad tossed table side, fresh bread, and the house pasta. It takes an entire menu page to describe the desserts, after dinner drinks, coffees and teas; the wine list won an Award of Excellence from Wine Spectator magazine. Dress is resort-casual and kids are welcomed with their own menu. Full Moon Jazz, concerts on the night of the full moon, went into eclipse for a couple of years after the hurricanes, but at press time are making a comeback. Ask about them.

CAFE WAHOO, *next to the ferry dock in Red Hook. Tel. 775-6350. The restaurant is open daily for dinner. Plan to spend about $30 for a meal.*

New owners of the old Blue Marlin have expanded the seafood menu to include French, Italian and Spanish touches but have retained the former owners' talents for creating chicken and beef dishes with subtle seasonings and a light, contemporary touch. The ambience is nautical, with a nice mix of tourists and locals mingling in the seaside air.

THE CAFE IN THE RITZ-CARLTON, *Great Bay. Tel. 775-3333. Reservations are recommended. Dinner Main dishes are $24-$29; pizzas are $11.50-$17.50. The restaurant is open daily for breakfast, lunch and dinner.*

Even if you're not staying here, come for a dining experience that includes a walk through the palatial marble lobby, down the grand staircase, and into the pleasant, open-air Cafe. The pizzas are extravagantly topped with traditional pepperoni and trimmings, or try the guava barbecue chicken with shredded jack cheese. Have carmelized onion pizza or one topped with Thai shrimp, shiitake mushrooms, asparagus and cilantro. Choose from a menu that includes grilled basil shrimp in a banana leaf or Caribbean lobster and sweet potato stew. There's also a macrobiotic selection, and, for meat-and-potatoes eaters, a superb grilled sirloin with chunky whipped potatoes.

EUNICE'S TERRACE, *66-7 Smith Bay, Route 38. Tel. 775-3975. Lunch and dinner are served Monday-Saturday 11am-10pm. Dinner only is served Sunday 5-10pm. Main dishes are priced $6 to $20. The restaurant is a half hour east of the airport.*

Locals come here for the West Indian food and entertainment, so here is your chance to discover the real thing: conch fritters, conch chowder, fried or broiled mahi-mahi, fish burgers, stewed mutton, fungi, beans and rice, fried plantains, and homemade sweet potato or Key lime pie. Try the doved (rhymes with roved) roasts, which are cooked to juicy tenderness then slathered with condiments and herbs as they are sliced. Live shows play Thursday at 9:30pm.

JOHNNY PALMS, *in Palm Passage, downtown Charlotte Amalie. Tel. 777-1059. Plan to spend $20 per person for lunch. It's open for breakfast and lunch Monday-Saturday and dinner Tuesday-Saturday 5:30-10pm.*

A cool oasis in crowded, picturesque Palm Passage, this place offers indoor seating with air conditioning or a breezy outdoor table where you can watch shoppers stream past. Have shrimp Creole, grilled mahi-mahi, a salad, or a New York strip steak, or a pasta specialty. Live jazz plans Friday evenings.

L'ESCARGOT, *12 Submarine Base. Tel. 774-6565. It's open for lunch and dinner every day. Main dishes are priced $15-$32. Reservations are suggested.*

The name suggests French cuisine, which has been a St. Thomas staple here for as long as we can remember. Gaze out over a marina filled with bobbing yachts while you dine on snails, shrimp, lamb herb-roasted with rosemary, grilled fish or lobster, or a pasta dish. For dessert, have a pillowy mousse.

POLLI'S, *in Tillet Gardens. Tel. 775-4550. Open daily except Sunday 11:30am-10pm. Dine for $10-$20. A children's menu lists $1 specials on Friday nights, but no more than two children may be brought with each adult.*

The look and tastes are Mexican, from the sizzling fajitas and bursting burritos to the homemade tamales. If you prefer a yanqui meal, have a burger, chicken, ribs, or a steak. The cooks will gladly cater to vegetarian tastes too. Live music, often a guitar and vocalist, plays Friday and Tuesday nights.

SMUGGLER'S *in the Renaissance Grand Beach Resort, Smith Bay Road. Tel. 775-1519. Call for hours and reservations, which are essential. The room is best known for its Sunday brunch and for its open-air dining with live entertainers. Dine for $25-$30; brunch for under $20.*

Sunday morning is a gala time to brunch here. Make your own drink at the Bloody Mary bar, then feast from a groaning buffet board of meats, salads, cheese, breads, casseroles, and desserts to die for. After eating, take a leisurely stroll around this rambling resort and a beach that looks like it was created for a travel brochure.

VIRGILIO'S, *18 Dronningensgade, downtown Charlotte Amalie. Tel. 776-4920. Main dishes are priced $10-$20. Reservations are suggested. Hours are Monday-Saturday 11:30am-10:30pm.*

When you have a yen for northern Italian classics, you can't go wrong here. The setting is made for old-world Italian dining under a beamed ceiling echoing faintly with strains of favorite operas and other Italian classics. A specialty of the house is a five-fish stew chunky with mussels, lobster, scallops, clams, and oysters in an intoxicating saffron broth. Order fresh fish, dolma, lobster ravioli, or grilled or roast duckling, or lamb. For light diners there are individual pizzas made to order.

Budget

BORICUA'S TERRACE, *14B Altona Street, between the ScotiaBank and the Medical Art complex. Tel. 714-1590. Dine for under $10. It's open daily for breakfast, lunch, and dinner.*

You'll think you're in Puerto Rico, thanks to a menu that features alcapurrias, mofongo and pasteles. Start your meal with a Boricuaso drink. The roast pork plate is a lot of good eating.

CHICKEN FRY, *behind Windward Passage at Kronprindsens Gade. Tel. 774-6784. Dine for under $10. Hours are Monday-Wednesday 10am-,; other days 10am-midnight. No credit cards.*

Call ahead for takeout, or chow down in unadorned surroundings in a busy, downtown spot. In addition to the crusty fried chicken and French fries, there are beans and rice or barbecued pork, chicken or ribs.

FRIGATE RESTAURANT, *Red Hook. Tel. 775-6124. Reservations are recommended. Complete dinners start at $14.50. The bar opens at 5:30 and dinner is served nightly from 6 to 10pm.*

Arrive before sunset to have a drink while drinking in the sensational view of water, sky, and islands. Add a salad bar, a slab of steak or seafood, and a fluffy baked potato or a bed of rice to make a substantial meal at a reasonable price.

RICKY'S DINER, *3B Kongens Gade, across from the elementary school. Hours are 11:30am4pm, daily except Sunday. Eat for under $10.*

Locals know this as a place to fill up on home-cooked stalwarts such as stew fish, johnnycake, beans and rice, fried fish, chicken, pork, sandwiches, and thick, fragrant soups.

ST. CROIX

Expensive

BACCHUS, *upstairs on Queen Cross between Strand and King, Christiansted. Tel. 692-9922. Plan to spend $50 per person for dinner. It's open night for dinner; reservations are essential.*

One of the best restaurants in the Virgins, Bacchus offers dining indoors with air conditioning or outdoors in the sweet, dark sparkle of a tropic night. Steaks are prime and are hand carved to your order. The wine list is lengthy, with many vintages available by the glass and champagnes by the split. After dinner, have cognac and a cigar while you repair to the club room for billiards. The setting is sophisticated and homey, an old townhouse from Danish colonial times. Dinner is serenaded by jazz and blues. In addition to the steaks, which are a house specialty, there's always lobster and other seafood and a vegetarian choice. For starters, don't miss the Napoleon, made with roasted eggplant, peppers and fresh mozzarella layered with airy puff pastry and served on tomato coulis. Homemade desserts are offered nightly, so ask about them.

DUGGAN'S REEF, *on Route 82, Teague Bay. Tel. 773-9800. The restaurant is open for dinner every day, lunch Monday through Saturday, and Sunday brunch 11am to 3pm. Main dishes start at $14.50; appetizers at $6. Reservations are suggested.*

This outdoor eatery overlooks the water and Buck Island. The house specialty is Irish whiskey lobster at $27, which can be served with a five-ounce filet mignon for $4 more. Priced by weight are baked or stuffed lobster. There's a choice of pastas, soups, and salads, with new temptations daily. The catch of the day can be served baked, grilled, island style (in vegetables and tomato sauce) or blackened, or choose the prime rib, sesame chicken, veal Parmesan, or chicken stir-fry. Desserts are homemade, or finish your meal with a fancy coffee.

THE GALLEON, *Green Cay Marina, Estate Southgate. Tel. 773-9949. The bar opens at 5pm and dinner is served nightly 6-10pm. Main dishes start at $17.50; pastas at $15; chateaubriand for two is $50. Reservations are recommended. Five minutes east of Christiansted, the restaurant is a $12 cab ride for one or two.*

Start with gravlox or the baked brie crusted with almond crumbs, then the tossed salad with the house herb dressing and a large or small pasta such as Beef Fedora – the house fettuccine tossed with wild mushroom cream sauce and skirted with thin strips of grilled sirloin in a bleu cheese demi glace. Salmon is served with dill butter; rack of lamb can be carved at your table. A house specialty is grilled filet mignon topped with lobster meat and bearnaise sauce. Everything is served with freshly baked bread, rice and vegetables. Check out the cognacs and after-dinner drinks too. Dress is resorty but elegant.

THE GREATHOUSE AT VILLA MADELEINE, *19 A-4 Teague Bay. Tel. 778-7377. A meal featuring appetizer, salad and entree will cost $35-$45 without wine. Open nightly for dinner, the villa is a $11 cab ride from Christiansted and $24 from Frederiksted. It closes in summer.*

Feel right at home in the main house of this cozy resort where a library and billiard room welcome dinner guests to make an evening of it. Start with chilled shrimp on cous cous or a lobster Napoleon followed by a romaine salad with raspberry vinaigrette and an entree such as the pork tenderloin filled with chèvre, sage, and prosciutto or the roast duck leg served with mango puree and fruited Armagnac. Salmon, lobster and catch of the day are the seafood selections, but there's also chicken, steaks and veal. On weekends, there's piano entertainment. After dinner, stargaze on the balcony with a premium cigar, a martini menu that includes the famous Choco'tini, or a creamy dessert drink.

INDIES, *55-56 Company Street, Christiansted. Tel. 692-9440. Plan to spend $30-$40 for dinner. Dinner is served nightly. Lunch is served Monday through Friday; sushi is served Wednesday and Friday 5pm-8pm only. Reservations are essential. Park free on Company Street.*

A cozy crowding of tables on the old stones of an ancient courtyard adds up to an intimate setting surrounded by greenery and cooled by ceiling fans. The effect is magical, whether you're with a group of friends or it is just the two of you with eyes only for each other. Owner-chef Catherine Plav-Driggers hand-writes her menus daily, so they vary wildly according to what looks best at the market. Start with a lobster corn quesadilla or the grilled vegetable antipasto. Follow with a soup or salad such as the mixed lettuces with citrus, then one of the brilliantly inspired main courses: cumin-lime grilled dolphin with mango chutney, mixed grill of lamb and chicken with roast shallots and tamarind glaze, penne with grilled vegetables, or a West Indian seafood curry bursting with mussels, shrimp and fresh mahi-mahi.

KENDRICK'S, *Quin House, King Cross Street, Christiansted. Tel. 773-9199. Main dishes cost $21-25; pastas $18-$22; appetizers $7 to $8.50. It's open daily in season for lunch and dinner. Reservations are advised. The restaurant is at Chandlers Wharf in Gallows Bay Marketplace just east of Christiansted. Hours are 6-9:30p.m. Monday-Saturday.*

Dine upstairs with the fine dining menu in a yacht club setting or downstairs at the clubby bar where salads and burgers are in the $8-$10 range. Chef David and Jane Kendrick are enthusiastic hosts in this big, two-story restaurant with a fine view of the harbor and lights of the city. Start with homemade eggplant ravioli in tomato-basil butter, proceed to chilled champagne gazpacho, then try a Roquefort Caesar or spinach salad. Chef David offers four pastas including homemade pappardelle with sauteed shrimp. Or order rack of lamp, filet mignon, pecan crusted roast pork, breast of duck, or a seafood specialty. The menu is inspired and extensive. Dine more formally upstairs or enjoy the pubby ambience downstairs.

SEA TOP RESTAURANT, *in the St. C. Condos, Estate St. John, 15 minutes west of Christiansted overlooking the north coast. Tel. 773-3836. Main dishes are priced $14.75 to $25. It's open daily for lunch and dinner. Reservations are suggested.*

Come here for the spectacular view. Lunch specials are a good value, featuring sandwiches, plain or chicken Caesar, or a spinach salad with toasted pine nuts. At dinner, start with escargot, hearts of palm vinaigrette or sesame chicken strips, then dine on coq au vin, duckling in orange sauce, Crucian-style conch, or a big filet mignon. Stir-fries are a budget choice, and they come in a variety of styles including vegetarian.

Moderate

ANTOINE'S, *on the boardwalk, downtown Christiansted at the Anchor Inn. Tel. 773-0263. It's open daily for breakfast, lunch, and dinner. Dinner dishes are $14 to $18; breakfast from $2.50; lunch dishes are $4 to $14. Reservations are recommended.*

A favorite with cruising sailors who anchor just off the shore and dinghy ashore here, this laidback, happy place has a sweeping view of the harbor. Make it your headquarters starting with breakfast, kalaloo soup and Cruzan crab cakes for lunch, then an afternoon of shopping before dinner. Lobster dominates the menu. It's served steamed, thermidor, Newburg, or curried. Or have duck in Grand Marnier sauce, sauerbraten, wienerschnitzel, or the very special pasta *fruits de mer*. Every day the chef offers a vegetarian special, and there's also a special kids' menu.

BANDANA'S, *in the Sea View Farm Inn, 180 Two Brothers, a mile south of downtown Frederiksted. Tel. 772-2950. Open for lunch and dinner daily, the restaurant features main dishes averaging $20.*

Watch the sunset over the salt pond from this open-air restaurant with its nautical theme, then order another round while you sail the miniature sailboats in the canals that surround the bar. The grill is hot, ready to cook your steak, chicken, or salmon to order. The menu is an uncomplicated one for meat-and-potatoes diners who enjoy a convivial atmosphere and casual eating.

BOMBAY CLUB, *5A King Street, Christiansted. Tel. 773-1838. Main dishes start at $13 after 5pm, but appetizers, salads, and fajitas at $6-$10 are good value. Open Monday through Friday for lunch and dinner, the restaurant is open for dinner only on Saturday and Sunday.*

A great place to escape from the bustle of Christiansted shops is this courtyard where you can hang out in the bar to see major sports events on television or take a table far from the bar and linger over a meal. Order a two-fisted burger, sandwich or salad, or end your day with a 10-ounce filet mignon with a salad. The BBQ spare ribs are basted with garlic and honey; the signature King Street Seafood Pasta is a triumph of pasta tossed with shrimp, scallops, fish, roasted garlic, and Brandy Alfredo. For a lighter dinner focus on appetizers such as conch cocktail, peel-and-eat shrimp, roasted garlic with brie, or cheese nachos.

CAFE DU SOLEIL, *Prince Passage, 615 Strand Street, Frederiksted. Tel. 772-5400. Reservations are suggested. Dinner is served Wednesday through Sunday; Sunday brunch is 10am to 2pm Dine for $20-$40.*

Locally caught fish is prepared with a deft touch, or try the lamb kabobs, shrimp, or Caribbean lobster. Brunch centers around fluffy omelets or feathery pancakes. Because this open-air eatery overlooks Frederiksted Harbor from the second story, it's a popular spot for cocktails and watching for the green flash. Downstairs, **Turtles Deli** offers quick sandwiches and take-out picnics, *Tel. 772-3676.*

CHENAY BAY BEACH RESORT, *East End Road, Route 82. Tel. 773-2918. Lunch for $10-$15; dine for $20-$30. Open daily 8am-9pm. Dinner reservations are recommended.*

Everyone ends up here at least once during a stay on St. Croix because of the special events such as a sunset lobster fest, Sunday brunch, the pig roast, the pasta pigout, a belly dancer, West Indies Night, Jump Up every Saturday, kick-back Sunday limin', and more. Live entertainers are on hand five nights a week to serenade diners on this pleasant outdoor terrace. Call to find out what's going on while you're here. Kids get their own menu.

COLUMBUS COVE, *at Salt River Marina, Salt River National Park. Tel. 778-5771. Open daily 8am to 11pm, the restaurant takes only American Express credit cards. Plan to spend about $15 for dinner; but luncheon fare is available all day in the $6-$10 range.*

The only restaurant within the national park, this wildly natural site is not far from the spot where Columbus first set foot on St. Croix. From the restaurant, catch a boat tour of the river and sea then stay on for a meal. For weekend brunch there are eggs Florentine or fresh fruit waffles. Lunch might be a chicken platter, fish plate, sandwich or burger. Dinners start at 6pm and feature steaks, pastas, shrimp, and fish. Homemade desserts are tempting: key lime pie, chocolate walnut pie, or raspberry Bailey's cheese cake. On Wednesdays there's a Caribbean barbecue of chicken or ribs with all the trimmings including corn on the cob.

CAMILLE'S, *Queen Cross Street near the corner of Company Street, Christiansted. Tel. 773-2985 is open for breakfast and lunch from 7:30am and all day Saturday. It reopens at 5pm daily except Sunday as a Mediterranean bistro. The kitchen closes at 10pm. Dinner will cost $15-$20.*

This air conditioned restaurant is a popular gathering spot for breakfast and lunches featuring New York-style deli sandwiches, fresh salads, and inventive soups. In the evening, locals gather in this cozy converted greathouse for a nice glass of wine to accompany hearty roasts, seafood, fish stew, lamb ragout, hot sandwiches, or light salads.

COLUMBUS COVE, *at Salt River Marina west of Christiansted off North Shore Road. Tel. 778-5771. It's open daily 8am-11pm. Dine for about $20; lunch or breakfast for under $10. Ask about the $2 drink special.*

It's a great location for a meal while you're exploring Salt River National Park or the picturebook beaches along the north shore. Brunch specials on Saturday and Sunday tend to celebration dishes like Eggs

Florentine or waffles with fresh fruit. On Tuesday night look for homemade pasta specials. Choose from fish and chicken platters, sandwiches, burgers, and steaks. Save room for one of the homemade desserts such as chocolate walnut pie or the Bailey's cheesecake with raspberries.

COMANCHE CLUB, *Strand Street, Christiansted. Tel. 773-2665. Main dishes are $12.50 to $19; daily specials are $12.50 to $15.50. Reservations are accepted. The restaurant is open for lunch and dinner Monday through Saturday. Lunch guests may use the pool for a small fee.*

An ancient war canoe hanging from the ceiling sets the scene in this locally popular, second story restaurant overlooking the waterfront. Portions are brobdignagian, so show up with a huge appetite and tear into the unforgettable Beef Curry Vindaloo with 10 Boys (a cart brings the "boys", which are accompaniments). The mixed grill brings together lamb, filet of beef and calves liver. The lobster, says the menu, is "Always scarce; always expensive." Chicken is served with oyster stuffing and, if you're in a splurge mode, have the caviar with blinis at $50. Save room for the Rum Raisin Bread Pudding with your choice of caramel or fudge sauce.

DINO'S *at the Buccaneer Hotel. Tel. 773-2100. Call for reservations and for hours, which vary seasonally. Plan to spend $25 for dinner. Dino's is open daily for dinner. The hotel's* ***Terrace Restaurant*** *is open for breakfast and dinner overlooking Christiansted; its* ***Little Mermaid****, which is at the beach, is an insider place to have lunch 11:30am-5:30pm. On Wednesdays have the West Indian buffet here. The hotel's* ***Grotto*** *serves lunch with salad bar 11am-3:30pm.*

Overlook the lights of Christiansted from this hilltop perch while dining on fresh pastas that are made right here daily. Sit in the wine bar cafe or the dressy, elegant main dining room with its stargazer view of the green terraces of a fine, family owned resort.

HARVEY'S, *Company Street at King Cross Street, Christiansted. Tel. 773-3433. Open daily except Sunday from 11:30am to 9:30pm, Harvey's takes no credit cards. Eat for under $15.*

Goat stew, stewed fish, whelks, ribs and chicken, rice and beans, fungi, sweet potato and other West Indian specialties are dependable at this crowded, family style spot. The tropical drinks are dynamite, especially the Whammy. Homemade pies made with tropical fruits such as pineapple or coconut are complimentary with your meal.

THE HIDEAWAY, HIBISCUS BEACH HOTEL, *4131 La Grande Princesse, on the beach west of Christiansted. Tel. 773-4042. It's open daily 7:30am; closing hours vary with special events. Main dishes are priced $13.50-$22.50 (or more depending on the market price for seafood). Reservations are suggested.*

Even though the official name is the Hideaway, your cab driver and other locals think of it only as the Hibiscus Beach, so ask for that. The setting, with a view of one of the island's best beaches, is too good to miss, so come here for breakfast or lunch, or come early enough before dinner that you can enjoy the sunset with cocktails and appetizers. The Hibiscus Hot Rocks are notorious for their gooey, fiery, crispy contrasts. Big shrimp are stuffed with cheese, wrapped in jalapeno, dipped in beer batter, and fried to a crusty brown. We loved the Hibiscus Chicken, a boneless breast floured with ground walnuts, sautéed, and baked in puff pastry with a brie sauce. Or, have fish or lobster, one of the pastas, baby back ribs, rack of lamb, or a steak. For lighter dining, try the grilled shrimp salad or chicken Caesar, or feast on a big burger with curly fries.

HILTY HOUSE, *Questa Verde Road, Gallows Bay. Tel. 773-2594. Fixed price dinners are $30 plus gratuity and drinks. Taxi fare from Christiansted is $5. Dinners are held weekly on Monday by reservation only. Call several days in advance. Only local and travelers' checks and cash are accepted; credit cards are not.*

Although gourmet cook Jacquie Hoard offers her international gourmet dinners only on Mondays, they are worth the wait. You'll be welcomed into a private home in an 18th century rum factory and served a theme meal – Middle Eastern, Caribbean, French, and so on, with all the right music, tableware, and accessories.

LE ST. TROPEZ, *Limetree Court 67 King Street, , Frederiksted. Tel. 772-3000. Reservations are suggested. The restaurant is open for lunch and dinner daily except Sunday. Main dishes start at $14.50. Lunches are $6.50 to $14.50.*

Daniele and Andre Ducrot are usually on hand with a personal welcome as guests are ushered into this crowded, fragrant bistro. At lunch, start with a glass of wine and then have the velvety lobster bisque or a California Salad, a toothsome blend of lettuces topped with tomatoes, hard-boiled egg, and freshly grilled chicken breast. On oilcloth-covered tables, blackboards announce tonight's soups, salads, seafood and specialties, all of them with a French accent starting with the escargot or homemade paté de compagne. The wine list is extensive and cigars are available. Ask them to put Edith Piaf on the sound system and imagine yourself in a torchlit Parisian courtyard on a moist June evening. End your meal with a selection from their imported cigars. Before leaving, visit the gift shop with its European imports.

NO BONES CAFE, *Gallows Bay. Tel. 773-2128. Take a cab from Christiansted for $4. Dinners are in the $12-$15 range. Hours are Monday through Friday 11am to 9pm and Saturday 5-9pm.*

Wild and crazy guy Chef Tamas makes his chowder with 31 ingredients, serves his catfish Cajun style, and plays 1930s and '40s jazz while serving stingers and sidecars for Happy Hour. Try fish and chips English style, double dipped shrimp, po' boy sandwiches, marinated mussels with linguine, or tonight's stir-fry special. Tamas hopes you'll order Just Feed

Me, which is each night's surprise. Don't forget to compliment Chile, the watch parrot. Takeouts are available.

ON THE BEACH, *a mile south of Frederiksted on the shoreline. Tel. 772-4242 or 772-1205. Lunch and dinner Main dishes are in the $10-$15 range. Take a cab from Frederiksted for $3.50 or from Christiansted for $20.*

Part of a small resort that fronts on a beach fringed with palms and sea grapes, this open-air favorite has a magical friendliness kindled by loyal repeat guests. Order a huge mahi-mahi sandwich with remoulade sauce, roast vegetable pizza, or a vegetarian sandwich made with sun-dried tomatoes and basil bread. Don't miss the tiny, but imaginatively stocked, gift shop.

PICNIC IN PARADISE *at the Carambola Beach Club on the north coast west of Christiansted. Tel. 778-1212. Sunday Brunch is $10-$25; lunch under $10; dinner Main dishes start at $16.50. Hours are 5:30pm to 10pm Tuesday through Saturday. Sunday brunch 10am-3pm; dinner 5-9pm.*

In a setting where the rainforest meets the sea, use one of the changing rooms after an afternoon of snorkeling the North Star Wall, then have a sundowner overlooking the Ham's Bluff lighthouse. On cool nights take refuge indoors where there's a fireplace. Luncheons star imaginative salads and classic sandwiches plus omelettes and a couple of hearty main dishes. At dinner, the chef offers a terrific terrine of roast potatoes and goat cheese salad served on a bed of greens. Try the filet mignon topped with artichoke fritters, or a Caribbean pot pie crammed with lobster, shrimp, and conch. The Vegetable and Goat Cheese Napoleon could make a vegetarian out of the most ardent carnivore.

SOUTH SHORE CAFÈ, *on the southern shore southeast of Christiansted on Route 62 at Route 624. Tel. 773-9311. Dinner costs about $20. Reservations are suggested. It's open for dinner Wednesday through Sunday; the bar opens at 5pm. Only VISA cards are accepted.*

Overlook the Great Pond and the shoreline while you dine on vegetarian specialties or owner-chef Diane Scheuber's homemade pastas, bread and desserts, seafood, prime rib, or lamb. For dessert, try the black pepper ice cream.

SPRAT HALL PLANTATION, *one mile north of Frederiksted off Route 63. Tel. 772-0305. Fixed price meals are in the $25 range not including wines. Cab fare from Frederiksted is $6 each for two. Reservations are essential and should be made between 10am and noon. Seating is 7:30-8pm.*

When you phone for reservations, you'll be given a choice of two or three main dishes and the chef takes it from there, leading you through a West Indian culinary adventure of tannia soup, pork loin with wild orange sauce, local lobster, parrotfish cutlets, freshly baked bread, conch in wine and butter, and the like. The ambience is that of a 1650 greathouse that has seen better days but has not lost its warm hospitality.

ST. CROIX CHOP HOUSE & BREW PUB, *in King's Alley on the waterfront, Christiansted, Tel. 713-9820. Plan to spend $25-$35 per person for dinner. Reservations are suggested. It opens at 11am for lunch daily except Sunday and for dinner every day 6-10pm.*

Dine upstairs for the water view or nosh downstairs on lighter fare in the island's first microbrewery. Steaks, chops and seafood are served by candlelight in the heart of town. Stop in for a savory, slow-brewed ale or come for cocktails and dinner. Live music is usually on the menu.

STIXX, *in the Pan Am Pavilion between Strand Street and the harbor, Christiansted. Tel. 773-5157. Plan to spend $15-20 for dinner; under $10 for lunch. Open daily, Stixx serves breakfast from 7am and dinner to 10pm. Reservations are recommended for deck seating.*

Combine a memorable view *of* Christiansted Harbor with a jolly mix of divers, sightseers, vacationers, and local working folks in a place that's as perfect for a quick, early breakfast as it is for a leisurely dinner. The shrimp scampi pizza is a favorite or have a buffalo burger, steak, or fresh seafood. The champagne brunch on Sundays is served 10am to 2pm.

THE TERRACE, *in the Buccaneer Resort just east of Christiansted. Tel. 773-2100. Main dishes are priced at $10 to $25. Cab fare from Christiansted is $6 for two.*

The view is sublime, whether you're looking out to sea by day, watching the sunset, or looking out over the twinkling lights of the resort. Start with rock lobster cakes with Creole mayonnaise and grainy mustard, then rum-planked salmon or a simple, tomato-eggplant turnover in puff pastry.

THE WAVES AT CANE BAY, *on Route 80 near Cane Bay Beach. Tel. 778-1805. Reservations are suggested. Hours are Monday through Saturday, 5pm to 9pm. Dinners are $17 to $25. Cab fare from Christiansted is $16; from Frederiksted, $20.*

Family-run by Kevin and Suzanne Ryan and as friendly as a hometown pub, this open-air spot on the edge of the water offers frozen cocktails, fresh fish, steak, pasta, and vegetarian choices all served in generous portions suited to hungry scuba divers. Start with the Smokin' Shrimp, jumbo shrimp stuffed with cheese, wrapped with jalapeno and dipped in beer batter. The stuffed veal chop is filled with apple tarragon dressing, or try the roasted Cornish game hem with plum sauce. The catch of the day can be served blackened or with lemon dill butter sauce, creole sauce, or a tropical fruit chutney. Kids get their own, special menu.

TIVOLI GARDENS, *Strand Street in the Pan Am Pavilion, , Christiansted. Tel. 773-6782. Main dishes are $10.50-$19.50. It's open for lunch Monday through Friday and dinner nightly until 9:30pm Reservations are suggested.*

The twinkling lights remind you of the other Tivoli overseas; the cool breezes are provided by its second floor porch location. At lunch have a sandwich or coquille St. Jacques. For dinner there are mushroom caps stuffed with lobster, broiled lobster tail, fresh fish and pastas. Lately, the menu has added some winsome oriental dishes including a Thai seafood curry and butterflied shrimp in soy-ginger sauce. End the meal with homemade coffee crunch ice cream or their popular chocolate velvet dessert. The Guava Cream Pie is a luscious twist on the key lime theme. The wine list offers more than 100 choices.

TOP HAT, *52 Company Street, Christiansted. Tel. 773-2346. Dine for $20-$25. It's open Monday through Saturday, 6-10pm. Reservations are requested.*

Owner-chef Bent Rasmussen has operated his restaurant in this charming old townhouse since the 1970s. Come here for the touch of Scandinavia and reminders of the days when Denmark owned the Virgin Islands. The menu features Black Angus steaks, fresh seafood with a Scandinavian touch, a lengthy wine list, fresh-baked breads, and hearty desserts. A salad bar, which includes hors d'oeuvres, goes with each meal.

TUTTO BENE, *2 Company Street, Christiansted. Tel. 773-5229. Dinner costs in the $20-$25 range. Hours are Monday through Friday 11:30am to 2:30pm and daily 6pm to 10pm, with dessert, drinks and coffees available until closing. Reservations are taken only for parties or five or more.*

Oh, the pastas! When Italians vacation on St. Croix, this is where they eat. The name means "all good" and you can't go wrong with hearty, peasant pastas accompanied with good bread and good olive oil. The bistro offers cozy booths big enough to seat half a dozen. There's a small bar in the corner.

WAHOO WILLY'S, *on the waterfront in the Hotel Caravelle, Christiansted. Tel. 773-6585. Open every day for breakfast, lunch and dinner. Lunch dishes are under $10; dinner main dishes average $20 but lighter, less expensive choices are also available at dinner.*

On our last visit to St. Croix, we ate here three or four times. After dark, it's magic to eat on the waterfront with a view of twinkling yachts just offshore and the chuckle of wavelets at your back. By day, choose sun or shade and a view of turquoise waters. This is the kind of tropical hangout where locals gather and travelers feel instantly at home, especially because there's a nice international mix that includes North Americans and a faithful following of Danes. The only Bloomin' Onion on the island is served here, so it's a good spot for groups to gather for drinks and appetizers that also include Willy's hot wings, Cruzan fritters and a boffo seviche. Have a salad, quesadilla, salad for two served family style, or a pizza piled to your order. It's called the Do It Yo-Own-Bad-Sef. At dinner, ask about specials, which might be Steak Diane or freshly caught lobster. There's always a nice choice of pastas, seafood, chicken dishes, and a vegetarian dish. Island ice creams such as coffee or rum raisin are dessert favorites, but there's also a nice choice of cakes or pies plus creamy drinks. On Mondays, the West Indian buffet is one of the island's best deals. Don't miss the art work by Willy Warhol, Willy Monet, Willy Picasso and other "famous" artists. Willy merchandise is sold in gift shop.

Budget

ALLEY GALLEY, *1100 Strand Street, Christiansted, under the Club Comanche bridge. Tel. 773-5353, or the* **EAST END DELI** *across from the Ball Park in Gallows Bay. Tel. 773-3232. Lunches are under $10. Both locales are open seven days a week from 8am with early closing on Sundays.*

These Caribbean versions of a classic New York deli have piña coladas on tap, duty-free spirits, supersize sandwiches made with Boar's Head lunch meats, and realms of gourmet cheeses, wines, breads, sweets, and salads. Call ahead to ask the specialties of the day, then order a picnic to take away.

BAGGY'S, *on the waterfront at Gallows Bay in St. Croix Marina. Tel. 713-9636. Eat for $10-$15. No credit cards. Hours are Monday through Saturday 6am to about 9pm. Sunday brunch is served 7am-2pm.*

Locals come here for limin' in the breezes, especially evenings at sunset and on Tuesday nights for Trivial Pursuit. Try the cheese steak or the French melt with a frozen rum drink. A pot of homemade soup simmers on the stove, burgers are grilled to order, and chicken is served with sweet and sour sauce. Live entertainers are on hand most Friday and Saturday nights. Ask about daily specials at supersaver prices.

BREEZEZ, *in the Club St. Croix west of Christiansted. Tel. 773-7077. Hours are 11:30am-4pm daily except Sunday, 4-9pm daily, and Sunday brunch 10am-2pm. Sandwich prices average $6; dinner main dishes are $12.25-$19.50.*

Splurge on the Flaming Rum Lobster or blackened prime rib. The Zydeco salad is mixed greens with bleu cheese, and there's also a nice choice of sandwiches (try the shrimp po'boy) and melts. A specialty is the luscious Linguine Rickie, tossed with garlic butter, chicken, tomatoes, olives, and bacon. Ask for daily specials.

CHEESEBURGERS IN PARADISE, *on East End Road, Route 82, 3.5 miles east of Christiansted. Tel. 773-1119. Lunch for under $10; dinners are under $20. It's open every day 11am until the crowd thins.*

This is a good-times, air conditioned place where cheerful pirates bring on the grilled chicken, nachos, chili dogs, hummus burritos, and margaritas to wash them down. The two-fisted burgers are a favorite on the island. Live music plays from 7pm Thursday through Sunday.

DEEP END BAR, *in the Tamarind Beach Hotel on East End Road at the Green Cay Marina turnoff. Tel. 773-4455. Light lunches and dinners are $10 or less. It's open daily from 11am. No credit cards.*

A popular, outdoorsy, grass-shack sort of hangout, it's very informal.

Have a drink from the blender and a sandwich, salad, hot dog, or soup special such as conch chowder or black bean. For dinner, order a burger platter or a simple main dish such as meatloaf or fish and chips. On Fridays, local artists come to the Tamarind Beach to sketch, so it's a good time to stroll around and look over their shoulders.

DOWIES, *Market Street, Frederiksted. Tel. 772-0845. Eat for $10 or less. Breakfast and lunch are served Tuesday through Friday 7am-2pm. On Saturdays, a traditional Cruzan breakfast is served. No credit cards.*

Eat in or call ahead for takeout. This is about the most authentic Cruzan restaurant on the island, with a menu featuring bull foot soup, stewed kingfish with fungi, souse with dumplings, fish pudding, and the like, washed down with maubi or passion fruit juice. For breakfast on Saturdays have johnnycake, fry fish or salt fish, and bush tea. A house specialty is the egg sandwich. For traditional appetites there's French toast, omelets and pancakes, salads and burgers.

INTERNET CAFÈ, *in the Holger Danske Best Western Hotel, Christiansted. Tel. 773-3600.*

The hotel is a price-appeal inn in the center of town on the water, popular with travelers from all over the world. You can eat and drink here but on Sunday, Monday, Thursday and Friday you can also use a computer or access the Internet for $5 per half hour. Buy diskettes for $2, and have color printing done for 25 cents. If you have on-line business to do, stop in for a byte.

LUNCHERIA, *in the Apothecary Hall Courtyard off Company Street behind Government House. Tel. 773-4247. Hours are Monday through Friday 11am to 9pm and Saturday noon to 9pm. Eat for less than $10.*

This longtime local favorite is a cluster of picnic tables in a courtyard where you can't always find full shade. Place an order at the bar and pick it up yourself. Mexican favorites prevail. We especially like the nachos with "the works". They're loaded with melty cheese, shredded lettuce, diced tomatoes, olives, and onions. Have a quesadilla, a choice or burritos or a burrito plate that includes rice and a salad, a choice of enchiladas, or chicken fajitas. There's a children's menu, and a full bar serving custom-built margaritas. Call ahead and your take-out order will be ready when you get here. .

MONTPELLIER HUT DOMINO CLUB, *in the rainforest at 48 Montpelier, Route 76. No telephone nor credit cards. It's open daily for lunch and cocktails; evening hours vary. Eat for under $10.*

Every visitor comes here for the first time to feed one of the famous, beer-drinking pigs: Miss Piggy, Tony, Toni, or J.J. They go through four cases of non-alcoholic beer a day plus grains, providing a hilarious exhibition that they seem to enjoy even more than tourists do. It's all in good fun. You buy a beer, present it to the pig, and it is able to open and drink it and spit out the can in a few seconds. The Club is also a favorite stop for rainforest visitors who sit here under the palm frond roof for a cooling drink and a light meal of ribs or chicken with johnny cake, chicken or fish, or the rotis that are served on Fridays.

PARROT'S PERCH, *43 BC Queen Street, upstairs over Columbia Emeralds. Tel. 773-7992. Lunch for less than $12; dine for about $20. It's open daily except Sunday for lunch, dinner, and late listening. The bar menu is served 10pm-1am. No credit cards.*

Overlook the harbor and bask in the faithful breezes of this upstairs favorite where live music and dancing occupy romantic, after-dinner hours. Dine lightly on soup or salad, or splurge on steak or lobster. If you don't dine here, stop in anyway for a great music–steel pan and calypso on Tuesday, live bands Thursday-Saturday, and disco on Wednesday.

THE SALOON, *on Market Street between Strand and King, Fredericksted, Tel. 772-BEER. It's a block back from the waterfront, open daily at 11am until midnight; later on Friday and Saturday, when food is served until 3am. Sandwich baskets are in the $6-$8 range.*

This tiny, pubby hangout is popular with any sailors who happen to be in port–the U.S. Coast Guard was here during our last visit–as well as with locals who like the air conditioning. There's also outdoor seating. The selection of beers is among the best on the island, and the menu of creamy drinks sounds like a candy store. Try the Peppermint Patty. The grill fires up daily at 11am, turning out chicken and burgers to be served with something simple like chips, slaw, or potato salad. Play darts, pool, or video games. Live entertainers are on hand some nights; other times there's the juke box, which sometimes plays free. There are always special events or Happy Hour specials.

SPRAT HALL BEACH RESTAURANT, *a mile north of Frederiksted on Route 63. Tel. 772-5855. Open daily from 9am to 4pm with lunch served 11:30am to 2:30pm, it accepts no credit cards.*

It's nothing fancy, but its location on one of the island's best beaches makes it a regular stop for locals and visitors like. For $2 you can use the changing rooms and showers, then have pumpkin fritters, conch chowder, tannia soup, fish salad, or some other old island specialty from the kitchen of island-born Joyce Hurd. Heartier fare includes ginger curried chicken, fresh fish steak, or a cooked vegetarian plate.

TOMMY T'S PARADISE CAFE, *on Queen Cross Street just off Company Street, Christiansted. It's open every day 7:30am-10pm. Sandwiches are $4-$7.50. Dinner main dishes are $13-$16.*

Order one of the big breakfast platters and you can skip lunch. Or, skimp on breakfast and have lunch here from one of the longest lists of sandwiches on the island. There's also soup or chili, half a dozen salads, or grilled burgers and always a daily lunch special. At dinner, choose from filet with mashed potatoes, chicken with rice, or grilled fish with rice. Prime rib or lobster are available on weekends, but at prices above the Budget category. Yes, there's a full bar.

ST. JOHN

Expensive

ASOLARE, *Cruz Bay. Tel. 779-4747. Closed Tuesdays, the restaurant is open daily 5:30pm to 9:30pm. Reservations are recommended.*

Chef Carlos Beccar Varela presides over a kitchen where the specialties are from the Pacific Rim and Asia. Closed for most of 1997 for renovations, it is once again one of the island's premier dining spots.

ELLINGTON'S, *Gallows Point. Tel. 693-8490. Reservations are recommended. Dine for about $40. Open daily, the restaurant serves breakfast, lunch and dinner until 10pm.*

Get here before sunset to enjoy the views of Pillsbury Sound. Linger over cocktails, then pace yourself for an elegant evening featuring one of the best wine cellars on the island. Choose lobster, steak, the catch of the day, or a pasta specialty. Try Beef Ellington, which is prepared for two, or the chicken with honey mustard sauce. Ask about the restaurant's name (it has nothing to do with Duke Ellington) and the Richard Ellington who was an island character in the 1950s.

DINNER WITH ANDRE, *Tel. 693-8708. Seatings are at 6pm and 8pm Monday through Saturday. Reservations are essential. Plan to spend $40-$50 per person.*

After dark, a simple sandwich shop is transformed into a delightfully intimate, 24-chair French bistro, with Chef André Rosin at the stove cooking classic continental dishes.

EQUATOR, *in the Caneel Bay resort. Tel. 776-6111. Reservations are essential for dinner, which is served 7pm to 9pm. Cars aren't permitted past the outer parking lot. Plan to spend $40-$60 for dinner.*

Dressy, elegant, and the picture of attentive service, this restaurant is in the grand, round, stone building that once housed Caneel Bay's Sugar Mill restaurant. The design, with a roof that rises several stories, is a marvel of 18th century engineering. Every dish is a still life painting: plump shrimp in miso, handmade tortillas wrapping tender cabrito, salmon under a drift of fresh herbs, and chocolate mousse garnished with candied Anaheim pepper and composed on a palette of sauces. Choose from a well-stocked cellar of good American and European vintages.

ORDER IN ON ST. JOHN

When you don't feel like dining out in St. John, call Seamus Mulcare, who operates ***Room Service****, Tel. 693-7362. A talented cook and caring caterer, he'll deliver a memorable meal with all the trimmings.*

Moderate

FISH TRAP, *in the Raintree Inn, Cruz Bay. Tel. 693-9994. Have lunch for $10-$15 and dinner for $20-$25. It's open daily except Monday for lunch and dinner. Find it across from the Catholic Church.*

Outdoorsy and informal, this is a popular limin' spot for locals. It's an easy walk from the ferry dock, but just far enough that day-trippers miss it. Chef Aaron chops and steams away in his little galley, shoving out one fine chicken, fish, and pasta dish after another. Try the stir-fry shrimp and vegetables, the black bean tostada with three cheeses or the seafood sampler salad. Save room for one of the dessert specialties made by owner Laura Willis. Her Coconut Cake with Caramel-Rum sauce was featured in Bon Appetit magazine.

LIME INN, *Cruz Bay. Tel. 776-6425 or 779-4199. Two streets up from the ferry, turn right on the one-way street just past the Lutheran Church, walking against traffic. It's open Monday through Friday for lunch, daily except Sunday for dinner 5:30 to 10pm Dine for under $25.*

A latticed garden sets the scene for fish, steak or burgers grilled over an outdoor charcoal grill. Lobster is always a favorite when it's available, and the Wednesday night, all-you-can-eat shrimp is a bonanza for shrimp lovers. Try one of the homemade soups or choose from a long list of salads.

MONGOOSE RESTAURANT, *in Mongoose Junction. Tel. 693-8677. Dine for under $20. Open seven days a week, the restaurant serves breakfast, lunch, and dinner. Reservations are accepted.*

A short walk from the ferry dock is this touristy but convenient bistro. Have a fruity drink then a deli sandwich or a Mediterranean main dish.

PANINI BEACH, *Wharfside Village, Cruz Bay. Tel. 693-9119. It's open daily for dinner only, 5:30-10pm. Plan to spend $20 per person. Reservations are suggested.*

Feast on northern Italian favorites indoors or out at this upscale restaurant at the water's edge. Special favorites are the seafood dishes but there's also veal, steaks, and some saucy chicken dishes.

PARADISO, *Mongoose Junction, Cruz Bay is open daily for lunch 11am-3pm and dinner 5:30-9:30pm. After 10pm, it turns into a night club. Tel. 693-8899. Reservations are accepted. Lunch for under $10; dine for under $20.*

Pizza, piled with the goodies of your choice, is a specialty here but at lunch there are also soups, salads, and juicy cheeseburgers. At dinner, steak, fresh fish or chicken are served with fluffy stuffed or smashed potatoes. Bring the kids, and ask to see the children's menu.

SHIPWRECK LANDING, *34 Freeman's Ground, Route 107, Coral Bay. Tel. 693-5640. Main dishes are priced $12 to $16. Hours are 11am to 10pm daily; the bar stays open later. The restaurant is eight miles from Cruz Bay.*

Come here not just for the legendary kitchen overseen by Pat and Dennis Rizzo but for the ride to the east end of beautiful St. John. Start with a rum with lime and coconut milk and a bowl of conch fritters. Then try something Cajun such as blackened grouper or snapper, a burger or a taco salad, chicken tangy with ginger, fish and chips, or a juicy steak. Live entertainment plans several nights a week, with jazz on Sunday.

ST. JOHN'S GLOBAL VILLAGE ON LATITUDE 18, *Mongoose Junction, Cruz Bay, is open every day for breakfast, lunch and dinner. Tel. 693-8677. Plan to spend $15 for dinner, less for breakfast and lunch.*

This is the best place on the island to stop in mid-afternoon, 3:30-5pm, for a nosh from the "sandy feet menu" featuring salads, sandwiches and icy drinks. Breakfast dishes are traditional fare; seafood and chicken reign supreme at dinner.

SEEING THE SIGHTS

ST. THOMAS

The **Paradise Point Tramway** is not just the island's most spectacular view, its hilltop destination is a favorite hangout for photographing the harbor and watching the sunset. In seven smooth, pleasant minutes you're 700 feet above sea level with a panoramic view of the harbor. Board the tram off Long Bay Road just above Wendy's, *Tel. 774-9809*. Fare for adults is $10, children $5. Once at the top you can shop for souvenirs, order a drink, or nosh on hot dogs, burgers or ribs. Sunset dinner specials are $13.95. *Tel. 777-1182.*

Seven Arches Museum is up Government Hill at Freeway Alley and King Street, *Tel. 774-9295*. Once the home of a Danish craftsman, it's furnished in antiques that offer a glimpse of colonial times. The $5 donation includes a guided tour and a drink in the walled, flower-filled garden. Hours are daily except Sunday and Monday 10am to 3pm.

Dive 90 feet deep to see the fish and coral off St. Thomas aboard the **Atlantis submarine**. During the two-hour tour you'll leave from Havensight Mall next to Yacht Haven Marine, then board an air conditioned submarine for a one-hour voyage that covers more than 1 1/2-miles of sea bottom. The dive can also be combined with a flightseeing seaplane tour, *Tel. 777-4491 or 776-5650* or, from the U.S., *800/253-0493*. **Coral World**, an outstanding water attraction that was destroyed by Hurricane Marilyn, is being restored. While you're on the island, *call 774-2955* for an update.

Allow at least half a day at **Mountain Top**, *Tel. 774-2400,* elevation 1,500 feet, for a look at tropical birds, an aquarium filled with tropical fish, a Caribbean village, and a museum of artifacts from pre-Columbian days through the swashbuckling pirate era. From Charlotte Amalie, take Route 30 (Veteran's Drive), to Mafolie Road (30 North) and turn left onto Route 33. Bear left at the "Y" in front of Sib's and follow the road to Mountain Top, which is said to be the home of the original banana daiquiri.

Take a self-guided tour of **Estate St. Peter Greathouse** in the volcanic hills of St. Thomas, *Tel. 774-4999.* From the 1000-foot-high observation deck on a clear day you can see 20 other islands. Sip punch while exploring the lush botanical gardens. It's open daily 9am to 5pm. From Charlotte Amalie, take Route 40 (Solberg Road).

ST. CROIX

To take a walking tour of Christiansted start at the **Old Scalehouse**, built in 1856 and cross to **Fort Christiansvaern**, 1738, which has dungeons and cannons. It's open every day, 8am to 5pm Look across the water to Protestant Cay, called that because Protestants, barred from the Catholic cemetery, were buried here. Cross Hospital Street and look at the **Steeple Building**, built as a Lutheran Church in 1735 and now a must-see **museum** of local history, *Tel. 773-1460.* It's open Monday through Friday, 9:30am to 3pm, with a one-hour closing from noon to 1pm.

Across the way, note the West Indian & Guinea Company Warehouse, built 1749. It was the site of slave auctions. It's now a post office and has rest rooms if you need some by now.

Walk up Company Street to the 18th century **Apothecary Hall**, then onto the Market Square and to Prince Street where Holy Cross Catholic Church dates to 1828. Heading down Prince Street to King, turn right to see the **Pentheny Building**, built as a private mansion in the 18th century. Walking east on King Street you'll see the library and a Lutheran Church dating to 1740. Across the street, **Government House** is a superb example of Danish colonial style dating to 1747.

To take a walking tour of **Frederiksted**, start at **Fort Frederik**, *Tel. 772-2021,* which dates to 1750. Its museum is good but it overemphasizes hurricane history when most visitors, we'd guess, are more interested in swashbuckling, battles, and pirates. Across the street see the **Old Customs House**, built in the 1700s and added to in the 1800s. It was here that local sugar was weighed for shipment. Continuing east on Strand Street, enjoy a pretty promenade of neo-classical and Victorian buildings. Turn back to King Cross Street and go two blocks inland to Old Apothecary Hall, another in the time-warp buildings that the visitor can ponder while imagining this as a swirling center of 17th century trade.

HARBOR NIGHT

Every other Wednesday is Harbor Night at the pier in Frederiksted when the docking of a major cruise ship is celebrated with a street party attended by cruisers, locals, and land-based tourists galore. Stroll the blocked-off streets to sample homemade foods and buy local crafts. Explore the old fort, which is open and well lighted. Then dance to live music until midnight. Tel. 340/772-1350. If you want o know what ships will call in the U.S. Virgin Islands and when, visit www.ships.vi on the Web or, on St. Thomas. Tel. 340/774-8784. On St. Croix, Tel. 340/772-0357.

Asking as you go if necessary, move on to the Benjamin House on Queen Street. It's an elegant townhouse with a wrought iron balcony. Staying on King Cross to **St. Paul's Anglican Church**, built in 1812, you'll pass the old cemetery. Going west now to Market Street, you'll see **St. Patrick's Catholic Church** and rectory, with a cemetery dating to the 18th century.

Turn back towards the sea on Market Street, passing the old Market Square, once the heart of the city. On King Street you'll see more historic buildings. Note the **Flemming Building** on the corner of King and **Custom House**. It was built from dismantled sugar factory chimneys.

St. George Village Botanical Garden is not only a brilliant garden stuffed with greenery and good smells, it is a National Historic District. Built on the site of an Arawak village that became a Danish community, it once contained a rum factory, greathouse, lime kiln, cemetery, and aqueduct. Stroll through orchids, ferns, an orchard of tropical trees, a cactus garden, galleries, stony ruins, and a gift shop. It's just off Route 70, east of West Airport Road, Route 64; *Tel. 692-2874* for hours, which vary seasonally. Admission is $5.

Whim Plantation Museum on Route 70 near Frederiksted is a complete plantation with a superbly restored greathouse that offers tours led by elderly docents, some of whom actually worked here years ago. Thelma Clarke, now in her 70s, showed us the grand piano dating to 1866, the chairs donated by island resident Victor Borge, 18th century furnishings, and the famous planter's chair that served as a combination chair and boot jack. Have a sugary piece of Johnny Cake, browse the gift shop, and allow an hour or two for roaming the grounds to get the true, tropical flavor of this ancient place. For information, *Tel. 772-0598*. Admission is $5 adults and $1 for children. In summer, Whim is closed on Sundays. In winter, monthly candlelight concerts feature world class, overseas musicians. Unamplified music, played by candlelight in these ancient walls, makes for a magical evening. Tickets are in short supply, but try for admission if you're on the island at the right time.

A mile north of Frederiksted, the **Carl and Marie Lawaetz Museum** at Little La Grange can be found on Mahogany Road, Route 76. Explore the house and gardens of one of the Danish founding families. Guided tours are offered Tuesday-Saturday 10am-4pm. *Tel. 772-1539.* Admission is adults $5 and children $.

Tours of the **Cruzan Rum Distillery** can be boring for little ones, but grownups like the samples and the gift shop. Admission is charged. Tours are offered Monday through Friday 9-11:30am and 1-4:15pm. For information, call the tourist bureau at *Tel. 772-0357.* Tour **Santa Cruz Breweries**, Estate La Grange, Frederiksted, to see where Santa Cruz beer is made. There's also a restaurant, gardens, theater, and museum, *Tel. 772-3663 or 772-2779.*

See the **St. Croix Aquarium** on the waterfront in Christiansted, *Tel. 773-8995,* and try to link up with one of the educational snorkel trips offered. The aquarium is open Wednesday through Sunday, 11am to 4pm.

One of the island's best nature preserves is in **Salt River Bay National Historic Park and Ecological Preserve**, which you can find on Route 751 off Route 75. Once the site of Amerindian ceremonies and the spot where Christopher Columbus is said to have first landed, it is the home of one of the largest mangrove forests in the Virgins. The bird life is abundant and varied but otherwise there are no facilities at present.

While you're out on the island, you may also want to try running up **The Beast**, also known as Mount Eagle. It's the island's highest point, at 1,650 feet, found on Route 69. When you see the words "The Beast" in the pavement you know you have arrived. Each year it's the scene of the grueling American Paradise Triathlon.

The sightseeing buzz on the island, literally, is aboard a Waco biplane with pilot Bob Wesley, who will show you the island from the open cockpit of this 1993 reproduction of a 1930s-era airplane. Two passengers sit side by side in the forward cockpit, where the view of hillsides and rainforest, beaches and waters is a thrill that brings them back for seconds. The ride is $65 for two, $110 for one, for about half an hour. Wesley can also give you an aerobatics ride for an additional $36 per 10 minutes but most folks prefer the tamer, sightseeing version. Classic Biplane Rides, Inc., is at the airport, *Tel. 690-7433.*

Hour-long guided tours of Christiansted and Frederiksted are available through **St. Croix Heritage Tours**, *Tel. 340/778-6997.* The tours accent historic buildings, courtyards and market places connected with the island's Danish background.

A BLUE RIBBON DAY

Everything you love about an old-time county fair, done with a tropical twist, can be seen at the annual Agrifest held on St. Croix in mid-February. Always the virgin Islands' bread basket, St. Croix is a major farming center and the home of Senapol cattle, which were bred for the island. Sample foods, see a roast pig demonstration, enjoy rides and games, and see local agricultural exhibits.

ST. JOHN

Since much of St. John is national park land, explorations should begin at the National Park Service Visitors Center on North Shore Road in Cruz Bay, *Tel. 776-6201 or 775-6238*. Get maps and instructions for the many hiking trails and snorkeling sites including ranger-led hikes and swims. It's a real plus to go with guides or guidance not just because of the expert narration but because rangers often provide the necessary equipment or pick-up/drop-off at a remote site. The national park user fee is $4 per person, which covers access to Trunk Bay and the Annaberg Ruins.

The whole island is peppered with ancient ruins, some barely identifiable and others as exciting as **Reef Bay Great House**, which was inhabited as late as the 1950s when the lady of the house was murdered. Various stabs have been made at restoring the house, so we don't know what condition it will be in when you get there, but the park service tends to it as funds are available.

Also administered by the park service is **Annaberg Plantation**, an 18th century sugar mill complex that has been partially restored. The views are spectacular, the ruins extensive, the nature watching excellent. Sometimes local artisans set up their shops in the plantation to enrich the scene. It's on Leinster Bay off the North Shore Road. For serious explorations, rent a four-wheel-drive and snoop into every road you see. Most will lead you either to a great beach or a great view.

NIGHTLIFE & ENTERTAINMENT

ST. CROIX

HIBISCUS BEACH HOTEL, *Tel. 773-4042.*

Friday nights feature live entertainers; Saturday evenings feature jazz. Arrive early enough for a sundowner overlooking the beach, then dinner from an inspired menu.

BLUE MOON, *on the waterfront at Frederiksted, Tel. 775-7084.*

The place for jazz, coffee, nursing a rum drink or noshing on bistro food. Open Tuesday through Friday for lunch, Tuesday through Saturday for lunch and dinner until 10pm and Sunday for dinner until 9:30.

THE SALOON, *just off Strand Street on Market.*

A block south of the pier in Frederiksted is not only air conditioned but nearly smokeless thanks to special smoke extractors. Or, sit outdoors. Live entertainment starts at 9pm. Darts start at 7:30 on Tuesday and Wednesday. There's plenty of food, free popcorn, a big beer menu, and the usual margaritas and coladas. Food is served until 3am on Friday and Saturday nights.

LOST DOG PUB, *14 King Street, Frederiksted, Tel. 772-3526.*

This pub features rock 'n roll on the jukebox, lots of brands and beer, and the most popular pizza on this end of the island. The fun goes on until 1am. Credit cards aren't accepted.

At the **BUCCANEER HOTEL**, *Tel. 773-2100*, listen to a steel band on Sunday, calypso/reggae on Friday nights, and jazz on Saturday. **CHENAY BAY**, *Tel. 773-2918*, has a steel band from 7pm on Saturday; **HOTEL ON THE CAY** features a steel band Thursday through Monday 5pm to 9pm. Guitar and song start Thursday through Sunday at 7pm at **CHEESEBURGERS IN PARADISE** and nightly at **TIVOLI GARDENS**.

For crab races, an old wagering favorite since the days of the buccaneers, be at **KING'S LANDING YACHT CLUB** Monday at 5:30pm or **STIXX** on Fridays at 5:30pm. For darts, try **KING'S LANDING** or **THE SALOON**.

Check the events schedule in *St. Croix This Week*, which is available free at any hotel for a listing of where and when to find steel bands, jazz, guitar and sing, Caribbean entertainment, calypso, reggae, or piano.

Hotspots include **YACHT CLUB** on Sunday evenings or **THE SALOON** on Tuesdays and Wednesdays from 7:30.

In 1997, laws were enacted that will result in the development of casinos on St. Croix. St. Croix also passed a special law that allows cruise ships to open their casinos while in port. Aboard most cruises you'll find shops and casinos closed in port.

SUPPORT YOUR LOCAL BEER

St. Croix' own beer, ***Santa Cruz****, is brewed near Frederiksted and offered in draft or long necks. Other brews on the Virgin Islands include:* ***Blackbeard's Ale*** *and* ***Captain Kidd's Golden Ale****; in the East End of St. Thomas, Paddy O'Furniture's Irish Brew Pub features four homebrews, including Pitbull Irish Stout made with four different malts.*

ST. THOMAS

One of the best amphitheaters in the Caribbean for the presentation of concerts and Broadway shows is the **REICHHOLD CENTER FOR THE ARTS** in St. Thomas. Check local newspapers while you're here to see if anything is playing. It could be a star or show of international importance. Also check your hotel's Dining/Nightlife Channel 4 for the latest buzz.

Other places include:

ATHENA'S, *32 Raadets Gade, downtown Charlotte Amalie. Tel. 714-1909.*

Celebrate Hump Night every Wednesday, which is also Singles Night. Ladies drink at a big discount. Happy Hour prices are in effect 5:30-8:30pm. The atmosphere is Greek; the music jazz, R&B, merengue, salsa, or disco. Dress is formal or semi-formal.

CAFÈ LULU, *in Blackbeard's Castle Hotel. Tel. 714-1641.*

Groups play evenings and on Sunday afternoon for listening and dancing.

CLUB ZINC, *Frenchtown. Tel. 513-9169.*

Pay a $5 cover charge and drink, dance, and party with the locals until 4am. It opens at 10pm.

HARD ROCK CAFE, *on the waterfront at International Plaza in Charlotte Amalie, Tel. 777-5555.*

Open all day and half the night for noshing and listening among a fortune in rock memorabilia. Come for a blimp-size burgers, a good salad, or to add to your collection of Hard Rock tee shirts. Live music plays Friday and Saturday nights.

JOHNNY PALMS ISLAND RESTAURANT & TROPICAL BAR, *Palm Passage, Tel. 777-1059.*

Friday night is jazz night in this lively restaurant, where you can eat indoors with the AC or outside under the stars. Dinner is available until 10pm and the spot is cigar-friendly.

SHIPWRECK TAVERN, *Al Cohen's Mall. Tel. 777-1293. Open until midnight, later on Saturday.*

This sports bar serves good food and drink while guests play pool, darts, pinball, air hockey, and Foosball. On Game Nights, winners (except for pool) get a free drink.

TURTLE ROCK BAR, *in the Wyndham Sugar Bay Resort, Smith Bay, Tel. 777-7100.*

Not far from Red Hook, this resort bar has a different drawing card every night. It could be live performances, karaoke, dancing, or reggae, If you want to eat here, find a good selection of dishes in the resort's Mangrove Restaurant. There's no cover charge in the bar. The fun starts

MOCKO JUMBIES

*A Virgin Islands traditional folk entertainment is **Mocko Jumbies**, stilt dancers in bright costumes who perform at every Carnival and parade. Mocko Jumbie dolls are catching on as collectible crafts.*

with Happy Hour 4 to 6pm and continues to closing, which could be any time depending on the crowd.

For an offbeat night adventure, sign up for a Thursday night snorkeling excursion with Chris Sawyer. *Tel. 777-7804*. The outing, held 5:30-10pm, includes dinner and costs $65.

ST. JOHN

The best bet for dining and nightlife on St. John is to go to downtown Cruz Bay and follow the sound of music. Hotspots include **The Back Yard**, *Tel. 693-8886* with music until midnight Wednesday through Saturday; **Global Village**, *Tel. 693-8677* for live music with dinner Friday until 9pm; **Olive R. Twist**, *Tel. 693-9200* for easy listening with dinner and later most nights; **La Tapa**, *Tel. 693-7755* for soca and jazz, and **Tamarind Court Café**, also *Tel. 693-7755* for blues and country. **Pusser's Beach Bar**, *Tel. 693-8489* is one of the most popular spots in town for drinking, listening, crab races, and limin' into the wee hours.

At Coral Bay, try **Shipwreck Landing**, *Tel. 693-5640* for guitar, vocals, and light rock, **Skinny Legs**, *Tel. 779-4982* for jazz nightly except Sunday, or **Sea Breeze**, *Tel. 693-5824* for bands and light rock Fridays until 1am.

SPORTS & RECREATION

ALL VIRGIN ISLANDS

Yacht brokers who can find the right boat and crew for your sailing vacation include:

- **Admiralty Yacht Vacations**, *Tel. 800/544-0493*
- **Bajor Yacht Charters**, *Tel. 800/524-8292*
- **Easy Adventures**, *Tel. 800/524-2027*
- **Island Yachts**, *Tel. 800/524-2019*
- **Proper Yachts St. John**, *Tel. 776-6256*
- **Regency Yacht Vacations**, *Tel. 800/524-7676, local 776-5950.*
- **Stewart Yacht Charters**, *Tel. 800/432-6118*
- **Virgin Islands Charter Yacht League**, *Tel. 800/524-2061*
- **Virgin Islands Power Yacht Charters**, *Tel. 800/524-2015*

Book anything from a brief sunset or snorkeling sail to a week-long charter on which you'll share the storybook life of a crew, usually husband and wife, who live aboard the boat. The variety of boats and their comforts is enormous, so allow plenty of time for choosing and booking. Power and sailboats accommodating two to 20 people charter for$1,200 to $1,500 per person for seven nights, including food, drinks, sightseeing, and watersports. Some of the larger boats offered by Regency Yacht Vacations even come with a helicopter and masseur! You can also book a package that combines yachting and hotel stays; for more information, *Tel. 776-5950* locally or, in the U.S., *Tel. 800/524-7676 or 401/848-5599.*

Through **American Wilderness Experience**, book a sea kayaking and camping trip in the Virgin Islands for five or seven days or sail a tall ship on an eight-day Virgins voyage. *Tel. 800/444-0099.*

ST. THOMAS

Beaches

Sailboarders and snorkelers who have their own equipment like **Bluebeard's Beach** at the end of Bluebeard's Road, Route 322, which branches off Route 30 near Red Hook. Bring your own gear; no rentals are available here. **Coki Beach** is favored for its view of Thatch Key and the Leeward Passage. The beach has bathrooms, a food stand, and snorkel gear for rent. It's on the northeast Coast. Also on the north shore, just west of Magens Bay, is **Hull Bay**, a popular anchorage for local fishermen. Waters along the western tip can be frisky, which makes it popular with surfers when the surf's up, but usually the waters are calm and clear. The bay has a restaurant.

East of downtown, next to Morningstar Beach, is **Limetree Beach**, a picture-perfect beach on a natural cove. Come to walk the sands and photograph iguanas. **Magens Bay**, which is a public park owned by the island, has been named in top-ten lists of beautiful beaches. Admission of $1 per car, $1 per adult, and 50 cents per child gains access to covered picnic tables, showers, dressing rooms, boutique, snack bar, sailboat rentals, and snorkel rental. It's on the north shore at the end of Route 35.

Morningstar Beach is a busy, commercial place with gear and lounge chair rentals, bars, boardsailer instruction, and a good view of boats sailing past the east point of the harbor. It's near town at Marriott's Frenchman's Reef Beach Resort. **Sapphire Beach** on the east end of the island is enjoyed by snorkelers and boardsailers. It has a marina, restaurants, and a dive shop that rents equipment.

Boating

Powerboat Rentals are available from **Nauti Nymph**, *Tel. 775-5066.*

Power, sail, and sportfishing charters are available from **The Charterboat Center** at Piccola Marina in Red Hook, *Tel. 775-7990 or 800/866-5714*. Speedy Mako and Scarab powerboats for exploring or skiing are rented through **See and Ski** at American Yacht Harbor, Red Hook, *Tel. 775-6265*.

Ocean Runner Powerboat Rentals at Cruz Bay, *Tel. 693-8809*, offers Hydrasports boats from 22 to 25 feet.

Diving

The **St. Thomas Diving Club** on Bolongo Bay is your key to scuba diving St. Thomas. It's a five- star PADI facility, *Tel. 776-2381, Fax 777-3232; toll-free 800/LETS DIVE.*

Golf

Mahogany Run, *Tel. 777-6006 or 800/253-7103* is a fabulous Fazio-designed course overlooking the Atlantic. It's an 18-hole, championship, 6,033-yard, par-70 course feared and famous for its "devil's triangle" of devious holes. On the north side of the island, 20 minutes from Charlotte Amalie. A new irrigation network promises year-round play on pool table greens even during dry seasons. Greens fees are in the $55-$85 range.

Horseback Riding

Kerry's Northshore Horseback Riding offers tours of the trails and beaches for $20 per hour, minimum two hours. All-day packages include lunch. Lessons are also available. Reserve at least one day ahead. *Tel. 340/779-3578.* Rides can also be booked with **Paul and Jill's Equestrian Stables**, *Tel. 340/772-2627.* **Half Moon Stables**, *Tel. 340/777-6088*, offers horse and pony tours of the east end of the island for $45 per hour. Riding lessons and clinics are also available.

Sea Kayaking

Paddle through unspoiled wetlands and mangrove swamps with **Virgin Island Ecotours**, *Tel. 340/779-2155 or 777-6200.*

Submarine Exploration

Atlantis Submarine operates out of Building VI, bay 1, in the Havensight Mall, *Tel. 776-5650 or 800/253-0493*. One-hour voyages explore the underwater mysteries of St. Thomas to a depth of 90 feet. Reservations are essential. The trip costs about $70.

ST. JOHN

Beaches

Caneel Bay can be reached through the plush resort of the same name, but it's also popular with boaters who anchor off its famous shores.

If you arrive by land, stop at the front desk for a day visitor guide. If you arrive by boat, don't set so much as a toe above the high tide line or you are intruding on private, and very exclusive, property. The bay is on the north shore, close to Cruz Bay.

Hawksnest Bay on the north shore of the island near Cruz Bay is smaller and more quiet than Trunk Bay, so it's popular with locals. Changing facilities are available. The west side of the beach is part of Caneel Bay Resort. Again, don't trespass.

Trunk Bay is famed for its underwater snorkeling trail. The beach is picture-perfect with its talcum sands and luxuriant fringe of trees and shrubs. There's a place to change, and a small shop. If you'd like more advanced snorkeling, ask at the national park about a snorkel tour to Flanagan's Cay off the southeast coast.

Cinnamon Bay at the campground in the national park offers great snorkeling in clear waters, a store, restaurant, watersport rentals, and a fine sand beach. The island's great beaches also include **Maho Bay**, **Francis Bay**, and **Leinster Bay.**

Fishing

To find a fishing guide, charter boat rental, tackle, or other connections, call the island information center at *Tel. 776-6922.*

Diving

Call **Coral Bay Waterports**, *Tel. 776-6850,* for scuba dives. **Low Key**, *Tel. 800/835-8999 or Tel. 693-8999,* is located at Wharfside Village offering equipment, dives, parasailing, kayaking, and underwater photo services.

Hiking

Thunderhawk Trail Guides offers guided trail tours for up to 50 people. Lasting about two hours, the hikes accent the history and culture of the Taino Indians. Rates are $20 to $40 including pick-up/drop-off at hotels. *Tel. 340/776-6412* or 340/774-1030.

Virgin Islands National Park is crisscrossed with miles of hiking trails, historic ruins, hills and dales, forests and flowers. When leaving the ferry dock, keep walking left and you'll come to a National Park Service information office.

Since most of St. John is part of the Park, its hiking trails are abundant and well mapped. You can go it alone or join one of the guided walks with an environmentalist who can point out natural features you might miss on your own. Notices of upcoming hikes are posted at the interpretive center of the National Park.

Horseback Riding

Ride a horse or donkey through the **Virgin Islands National Park**, which covers most of St. John, *Tel. 340/693-5778.*

Rock Climbing

Virgin Rock Sports, *Tel. 340/693-5763*, offers beginner and advanced rock climbing and rapelling courses for $80 for one or $50 each for groups or two-four. A maximum of four people can be accommodated at once. Ask about tours that can be tailored to your special interests including kayaking or sail trips to nearby islands for climbing expeditions.

Underwater Exploration

Atlantis Submarine, based in St. Thomas, operates out of Cruz Bay one day a week, *Tel. 776-5650.*

ST. CROIX

Beaches

Let your hotel host suggest a new beach every day according to winds and sea conditions, keeping in mind that you're on your own without lifeguards. West of Christiansted, **Salt River Bay**, where Columbus first landed, offers a beach with frisky winds and waves, and no facilities. Continue along the North Shore Road to **Cane Bay Beach** and **Davis Bay Beach**, which offer excellent snorkeling about 100 feet off out. From Christiansted, take the ferry to the **Hotel on the Cay**, which has a beach, restaurant, and bar.

West of town, **Estate Golden Rock** has a beach a fifth of a mile long; **The Buccaneer** on Route 82 charges admission and rents beach chairs on its beach, which has food and drinks. The beach at **Green Cay** is remote and lovely, reached by rental boat from Green Cay Marina. Also east of town watch for Reef Condominiums and the **Reef Beach** opposite them, which is popular with board sailors. Off Route 60, find **Grapetree Beach** where seagrapes offer shade and a concession offers snorkel and sailboard rentals, drinks, food, and rest rooms.

Boating & Snorkeling

A trip to **Buck Island Reef National Monument**, which lies six miles from Christiansted, is a must. Skippers provide snorkel gear so you can explore the underwater trail.. Call **Llewellyn's Charter**, *Tel. 773-9027* or **Terero II**, *Tel. 773-3161 or 773-4041.* Personal watercraft and kayaks can be rented at **St. Croix Water Sports Center**, *Tel. 773-7060.* Sails, trips to Buck Island, big game fishing, diving, windsurfing, parasailing and non-motorized watersports are available at Cutlass Cove Beach behind The

Mermaid restaurant. It's open daily 9am to 5pm. *Call extension 741 at the Buccaneer, Tel. 773-2100.* Jolly Mon, a 60-foot catamaran offers snorkeling, sailing, party sails, and weddings through **Mile Mark Watersports**, *Tel. 773-3434, 773-2638* or *800/523-DIVE.*

Bicycling

Ride mountain bikes over the rolling hills with **St. Croix Bike & Tours**, *Pier 69 Courtyard, Frederiksted. Tel. 340/773-5004 or 773-2343.* You'll climb Creque (pronounced Creaky) Dam Road if you're up to it, and explore the rainforest. Less hardy bikers can stay on flatter lands on a seashore tour to Hams Bluff.

Golf

All three golf courses offer instruction and equipment rental. The 18-hole course at **Carambola Golf Club**, *Tel. 778-5638*, was designed by Robert Trent Jones and has a Gold Medal Award from Golf Magazine. The par-72 course rolls past shining lakes surrounded by bougainvillea and palm trees. **Buccaneer Golf Course**, *Tel. 773-2100,* is a scenic 18-hole course on the seaside, said to be the prettiest course in the islands. The par-70 course has 5,810 yards of sloping fairways, water hazards, and challenging bunkers. It's designed by Bob Joyce. A nine-hole course is on the east end of the island at **The Reef Golf Course**, Teague Bay, *Tel. 773-8844*. Greens fees start at $10; riding and pull carts are available for a fee.

Hiking

Link up with the **St. Croix Environmental Association**, *Tel. 773-1989*, for serious hiking or **Take-a-Hike**, *Tel. 778-6997,* for guided walks of historic areas. Hikers will enjoy Salt River National Park, Caledonia Valley, and Estates Mount Washington and Butler Bay. Both groups require reservations. It's always a plus to go with a guide who can point out unique plants or tell you local names for familiar tropicals.

Identify catch-and-keep, monkey-don't-climb, nothing-nut, clashie melashie, cock-a-locka, and other shrubs and flowers. If you have a chance, try wild fruits such as genip (also spelled gneep), soursop, and the milky, sweet sugar apple.

Horseback Riding

Ride horseback across strands of white sand through the surf with **Paul and Jill's Equestrian Stables**, *Tel. 340/772-2880.*

Parasailing

Fly over the water by parasail, towed by a speedboat at **Hotel on the Cay**, *Tel. 773-7060.*

Scuba Diving

Hang around the **Aqua-Lounge Club** to learn about the underwater scene. Even the bartenders are divers, so everyone decompresses here from 5-7pm. Every night something new is sparking, such as bring-your-catch barbecue night, rap sessions, signups for dive buddies, and night dives. Located in an old Danish warehouse with easy access from King Street or the boardwalk, the air conditioned club offers free parking in the Anchor Inn lot. It's at 58A King Street, *Tel. 773-0263.*

Dive operators offering scuba trips, instruction, refills and gear include:

- **Cap' Dick's Scubawest**, *Tel. 772-3701 or 800/352-0107.*
- **Dive Experience**, *Tel. 773-3307 or 800/235-9047*
- **Cane Bay Dive Shop**, *Tel. 773-9913, Cane Bay, or 772-0715, Frederiksted. toll-free Tel. 800/338-3843*
- **Cruzan Divers**, *Tel. 772-3701 or toll-free 800/352-0107*
- **Anchor Dive Center**, *Tel. 778-1522 or 800/532-DIVE*
- **Mile Mark Watersports**, *Tel. 800/523-DIVE or 340/773-3434.*
- **V.I. Divers**, *Tel. 773-6045 or 800/544-5911.* We can recommend Ed and Molly Buckley as congenial hosts ashore and afloat.

Sky Diving

Float through the skies over St. Croix with the **V.I. Skydiving Center**, *Tel. 778-6670.*

Snorkeling

Guided snorkel trips are offered by the **St. Croix Aquarium and Marine Education Center**, *Tel. 772-1345.*

Tennis

In addition to the many courts at resorts, St. Croix has public courts at **D.C. Canegata Park** in Christiansted and **Fort Frederik Park** in Frederiksted.

SHOPPING

Even though Americans are still on American territory, customs limits must be observed and luggage is subject to search, either before leaving the islands or when changing planes in San Juan. Any purchases that total more than $1200 are subject to a five per cent tax and amounts over $2200 are subject to regular duty charges, even if you bought "duty free" in the islands. Island-made products in any amount are duty free, but be sure to get a receipt for any purchase of more than $25. In addition, you can ship home gifts of up to $100 per day.

Each U.S. resident over age 21 can bring back six bottles of liquor duty free as long as one of them is made in the U.S. Virgin Islands. Remember that plants and farm products can't be brought to the mainland, nor can protected products such as turtle shell and black coral. Customs questions? Locally, call *Tel. 773-5650.*

ST. THOMAS

A popular cruise ship stop, St. Thomas is famed for stores packed with crystal, china, watches, jewels, cameras, perfumes, and liquors sold tax free. Cruise passengers come ashore clutching the maps and discount coupons given to them on board and swarm into shops whose hours are determined by when ships are in port. When they are, you can shop on Sunday mornings. Otherwise, plan to shop the other six days of the week.

An open-air market along the waterfront sells mostly tee shirts, sleazy rayon sarongs, and claptrap. Some booths are piled high with brand name leather goods, which may or may not be authentic, but nothing bears a price tag so you're on your own to make a deal. Even in the best shops we saw very few price tags, so St. Thomas is a place for shoppers who know exactly what model watch or camera, what carat jewel, or what brand perfume they want, and will recognize a good buy when they see it. If you're just browsing, you'll have to ask about prices one piece at a time.

Our favorite spot downtown is the **Native Arts and Crafts Cooperative** next to the Tourism Hospitality Lounge. Local artists pitch in to run the place as well as to display their wares. *Tel. 777-1153.*

In downtown Charlotte Amalie, most shops are along **Main Street** (Dronnigens Gade) and the waterfront, and on the narrow alleys that run between them. East of downtown nearer the cruise ships docks, **Havensight Mall** also has prestige shops such as Gucci, Little Switzerland, A.H. Riise, and Columbia Emeralds International as well as a pharmacy, beauty salon, and bank. **Ritalini Shoe Boutique** there, *Tel. 776-3313,* has thousands of pairs of Italian shoes in women's sizes 4 to 12, as well as Bruno Magli shoes for men. After you get home, they'll ship additional pairs at duty-free prices.

Look for such shopping meccas as:

Hibiscus Alley along Main Street has a **Coach**, **Cardow's Diamond Center**, **Local Color** for accessories, and the **West Indies Coffee Company** as well as a store selling memorabilia connected with the Virgin Island's America's Cup Challenge, which will be sailed in the year 2000. **Lover's Lane** carries everything from exotic erotica to bridal and bath boutique items. It's on the waterfront at the corner of Raadets Gade, upstairs. **Palm Passage** is, between Main Street and the waterfront. Its stores include **Fendi**, **Nicole Miller**, **Diesel Jeans**, and **Versace**. **Scandina-**

vian Center in the Havensight Mall has handmade products from Scandinavia including a complete line of Royal Copenhagen, Georg Jensen silver and precious gems. The center also has an art gallery filled with Caribbean and Danish scenes.

Cosmopolitan on the waterfront has Bally, Sperry Topsider, Sebago and other famous name shoes plus international sportswear brands. **Drake's Passage Mall** in the historic district is the only air conditioned mall downtown. Shops sell leather foods, clothing souvenirs, sweets, and clothing. If you're been inspired by the colonial mahogany furniture of the islands, you can buy greathouse furnishings at **Mahogany Island Style** in Al Cohen's Plaza on Route 38. Poster beds, armoires and planter's chairs are shown; international art works and accessories are also sold. On Raphune Hill, Route 38, look for **Mango Tango Art Gallery** for originals, limited edition prints, and gifts. It's open daily 9am to 5:30pm, Sundays 10am to 1pm.

Located downtown and around the island are such standout jewelry stores as **Amsterdam Sauer**, **Cardow**, **Little Switzerland**, **Diamonds in Paradise**, **Diamonds International**, and **Columbian Emeralds International**. For loose diamonds and jewelry at rock bottom prices, check out the **Diamonds International Liquidation Center** at the waterfront. At Red Hook, **Doucet Stanton Jewelers** is a family-owned business featuring handmade Scandinavian silver pieces as well as local art. It's in American Yacht Harbor Building C2-1.

If you need ordinary supplies at ordinary prices, St. Thomas has a **K-mart** in Tutu Park Mall, a ten-minute cab ride from the docks. Our favorite shopping haunt is a 25-stall arts and crafts mall opposite the **Renaissance Grand Beach Resort** in Smith Bay. Local vendors display their homemade wares.

Since every American over age 21 can take back five fifths of liquor or six fifths if the liquor is produced in the U.S.V.I., it's best to get island brews such as Cruzan Rum, Havensight Liqueur, Chococo, Clipper Spiced Rum, Old St. Croix, Estate Diamond, and Southern Comfort. Exemptions apply only on purchases made in the U.S.V.I. and not to the same brands bought aboard ship.

ST. CROIX

King's Alley, the brightest diamond in **Christiansted's** shopping tiara, re-opened in 1996 more brilliant than ever before. In one spot downtown, find twelve luxury hotel suites furnished in Danish West Indian style, *Tel. 340/773-0103*, plus restaurants including a Thai and a chop house, and 20 upscale shops. Its smaller sister in Frederiksted runs from Strand Street to King Street, handy to the pier. The hotel here, by the way, is right next to the seaplane pier so it's the perfect place to stay if you're just making a quick overnight trip to St. Croix.

The shopping game in St. Croix is to choose a **Crucian bracelet**. The unique designs rely on a hook or button latch. Each jeweler has its own designs in gold or sterling and some people make a collection of as many different models as they can find. One of the most popular is from Sonya at One Company Street, across from the Steeple Building and the post office, *Tel. 778-8605.*

Also featured here is the Caribbean gemstone *larimar*, a blue stone found only in the islands. **Baci** on Company Street in Christiansted, specializes in jewelry made from ancient coins.

Also in Christiansted is **Charisma Imports** in the Pan Am Pavilion, specializing in local sarong designs known as the Cruzan Wrap. For conventional clothing in cool, tropical linens and cottons, try **Strand Street Clothing** on Strand Street, Christiansted. Also in the pavilion is Many Hands, with arts and collectibles created by local talent. For local artwork, visit an **artists' cooperative** in the Pentheny Building (ask directions from King's Alley.) It's closed Sunday and Wednesday. Because the work is shown and sold by the artists themselves, prices are lower than those in galleries.

For books try **Trader Bob's Bookshop and Gallery** at 5030 Anchor Way. It's a serious book store, with a good choice of fiction and nonfiction titles. Let Bob Elman suggest good beach reading for the Caribbean. It's also a good place to buy inexpensive trinkets for the kids and quality stationery or souvenirs, so come on a rainy afternoon for serious browsing. .

ST. JOHN

It's fun to shop in little St. John because few here try to compete with the glitzy stores of St. Thomas. Stores feature folk arts, resort wear, crafts, seashells, custom jewelry, unusual gifts, and locally made foods and spice blends. Look for books published by the **American Paradise Publishing Company**, which was founded by local mariner "Cap'n Fatty" Goodlander. His guides, cookbooks, and humor books are authentic and readable. Ask for them in local book and gift shops. Another St. John specialty is pottery featuring petroglyph motifs inspired by Arawak drawings.

It's worth a day trip to St. John on the ferry to shop **Wharfside Village**, **Mongoose Junction**, **Pink Papaya Gallery** in the Lemon Tree Mall behind the Chase Bank, and other shops, all of them a stone's throw from the ferry dock.

Columbian Emeralds, *Tel. 776-6007,* has a shop in Mongoose Junction and so does **Island Galleria**, *Tel. 779-4644,* with its crystals, perfumes, and collectibles.

EXCURSIONS & DAY TRIPS

ST. CROIX

Sweeny Toussaint, manager of **St. Croix Safari Tours**, *Tel. 773-9561 or 800/524-2026,* is a knowledgeable, attentive, and personable guide. He can arrange everything from airport transfer to sightseeing, car rental, and watersports. For a mystery trip out of St. Croix complete with lunch and champagne, let **Bohlke International Airways** set the pace, *Tel. 778-9177.* The line flies to St. Thomas, St. John, the British Virgins, St. Barts, or Puerto Rico. **Big Beard's Adventure Tours**, Christiansted, *Tel. 773-4482,* does sunset sails, private charters, and half- and full-day excursions.

Buck Island National Monument is St. Croix' most meaningful day trip. Sail, hike, snorkel, have a beach barbecue, or scuba dive. The uninhabited island is 6,000 feet long and half a mile wide, rising to 340 feel above sea level. It lies only one and a half miles off the northeast coast of St. Croix. Endangered species nesting here include the hawksbill turtle and brown pelican as well as leatherback and green sea turtles. On land, walk marked trails across the island through giant tamarind trees, hillsides covered with guinea grass, and lowland beaches. In the water, snorkel over a marine wonderland of elkhorn coral, brilliant sea gardens, and schools of darting fish. A marked underwater trail describes the sights.

Mile Mark Watersports offers dive expeditions, *Tel. 773-2628 or 773-3434*. Boats can be rented in Christiansted and half a dozen outfitters also offer half-and full-day excursions with time allowed in and out of the water. Snorkel gear is provided, *Tel. 773-1460.*

To take a self-guided driving tour, take Hospital Street out of Christiansted to East End road, Route 82 and note Gallows Bay on your left. Until recent years it was a busy port, now a good place for shopping and dining. Continuing on Route 82, pass the family-owned B**uccaneer** with its restaurants and 18-hole golf course and Green Cay Marina. Bear left, staying on Route 82 and keep a sharp eye for nesting blue heron. You'll pass **Chenay Bay**, **Coakley Bay**, the famous **Duggan's Reef Restaurant** and come to the **St. Croix Yacht Club**. Look up to your right to see a castle, which is privately owned. Ask locals about its story.

Point Udall is the easternmost point under the United States flag, but don't try to drive to the beach. Roads wash out regularly and, at press time, are impassable. From here, take Route 82 back to Christiansted or go south on Route 60 along the coast. Stay along the water and you won't get lost as you pass **Great Salt Pond** with its waterfowl. Turning left at the Airport market, Route 624 and left on Route 62, you'll continue along the south shore past farm fields filled with big Senepol cattle. The breed was developed on St. Croix. To return to Christiansted, turn right on Route 70, locally called Centerline Road, where most of the shopping centers, banks and other everyday commercial centers are found.

To take a tour of the north and west of St. Croix through the radically different terrain of the rainforest, start early in the day because there are many stops you'll want to make along the way. Take Route 75 out of Christiansted and turn right on Route 80. At the Salt River Marina sign turn right to the **Salt River National Park and Ecological Preserve**. See the place where Columbus is said to landed in 1493. Take time to look for birds, then return ro Route 80 and head west on the scenic North Shore Road with its views of the other islands in the hazy distance. At LaValle village, turn right to **Cane Bay Beach** for a swim, then stay on Route 80 to Route 69. Turn left and climb a steep hill leading to a view of Carambola. Route 76, Mahogany Road, leads to a stone quarry. On your left, watch for **LEAP**, an environmental project where items made from local woods are sold.

At Route 63, turn right and follow the shore road to **Sprat Hall Plantation**, an ancient greathouse that is now a hotel. Call ahead if you want to arrange a hike, meal, or horseback ride. Continuing along Butler Bay you'll pass the Coast Guard station and continue to Frederiksted with its shopping and dining. Leave town on Route 70, stopping **at Whim Plantation**, the **botanical gardens**, and the **rum distillery** on Route 64. Return to Christiansted via Route 66.

ST. THOMAS

Sail the *Lady Lynsey* out of the Ritz-Carlton on half day, all day, and sunset sails, *Tel. 775-3333*. Aboard the all-day sail and snorkeling expedition, you'll visit St. John or Jost Van Dyke and will be served a continental breakfast and gourmet buffet luncheon for $135-$145. A half day sail including continental breakfast (on the morning sail) and lunch costs $85 per person. The Sunset Sail is out for two hours and includes fruit, fresh vegetables, and finger sandwiches for $45.

Excursions from St. Thomas to the British Virgin Islands including the famous **The Baths** on Virgin Gorda and the hiking trails of Jost Van Dyke are available through:

- **Dohm's Water Taxi**, *Tel. 775-6501*
- **Inter-Island Boat Services**, *Tel. 776-6597 or 776-6282* Jost Van Dyke trips sail Friday, Saturday and Sunday.
- **Limnos Charters**, *Tel. 775-3203*
- **Stormy Petrel and Pirate's Penny**, *Tel. 775-7990 or 800/866-5714*
- **High Performance Charters**, *Tel. 777-7545*
- **Transportation Services**, *Tel. 776-6282 or 776-6597* Virgin Gorda trips sail Sunday and Thursday.

Take the ferry from Red Hook to St. John at 9am Tuesday, Thursday, or Saturday and catch the bus ($4.50) from Cruz Bay to the National Park

Visitor Center for a three-mile downhill trail hike led by a park ranger. Wear walking shoes and a sun hat, and bring your own food and water. You'll be back in Cruz Bay by 3:30pm. Make reservations between 8:30am and 2:30pm. *Tel. 776-6330.* For bird watching hikes in the National Park, take the 6:30am ferry from Red Hook, and a taxi from Cruz Bay and the National Park Visitor Center. A taxi takes you to Francis Bay Trailhead where you're joined by a ranger. Reservations are essential. *Tel. 776-6201.*

ST. JOHN

When you arrive at the ferry dock in **Cruz Bay** you'll be met by nattering crowds of drivers, all vying for your sightseeing business. Even if you plan later to take off on your own scooter or rental car, take at least a short tour with one of these guides if only for the theater alone. Each driver has his own "shtick," each jitney its own decorations.

One "must-see" is **Annaberg Sugar Mill**, administered by the National Park Service, *Tel. 776-6201*. More than 140 windmill ruins dot St. Croix, but St. John had only five, all of them built between 1740 and 1840. The site is a knockout, with views far out to sea. Although it was farmed well into the 20th century, its use as a sugar plantation died with the freeing of Danish West Indies slaves in 1848. Take a half-hour, self-guided walking tour of the slave quarters, village, windmill, and gardens. To reach the site, take the North Shore Road, about five miles east from Cruz Bay. Through the National Park Visitor Center you can also make reservations for ranger-guided hikes, snorkels, and bird watching.

If possible, be on St. John the last Saturday of the month when "St. John Saturdays" feature kite flying, arts and crafts, local musicians, and booths selling island foods.

PRACTICAL INFORMATION

Area Code: 340

American Express: *Tel. 774-1855*

ATM: on St. Croix, an ATM is found in the Banco Popular in the Sunny Isles Shopping Center. At St. Thomas find an ATM at the airport and at banks downtown and in shopping centers. Banks on the island include Banco Popular, Chase Manhattan, Citibank, First Federal Savings, First Virgin Islands Federal Savings, and ScotiaBank. A Chase Manhattan branch is at Cruz Bay, St. John.

Crime: when you're going to the beach, leave valuables in the hotel safe and not in the car, not even in a locked trunk. Take the same precautions you would at home.

Current: electrical service is the same as on the United States mainland.

Currency is the United States dollar.

Customs: No duties nor sales tax are charged on tourist purchases. U.S. citizens may bring up to $1,200 in merchandise (twice the allowance from non-U.S. islands) back to the mainland

Emergencies: dial 911 for police, fire, and ambulance. .

Holidays: banks and government offices are closed on most of the same holidays celebrated on the mainland including New Year's Day and Christmas plus, Boxing Day, Friendship Day on October 13, and the local Thanksgiving, which is in late October. Transfer Day is celebrated on March 31.

Immigration: Americans and Canadians need proof of citizenship such as a passport, green card, certificate of naturalization, or birth certificate plus a government-issued photo ID such as a driver's license. A driver's license alone won't do. Voter registration is no longer accepted. Britons need a passport and, to return to the United States or Puerto Rico, a passport plus green form, white form, crewmember form, or documentation of the Immigration Service indicating legal status in the United States. A pre-clearance inspection occurs in the U.S. Virgin Islands prior to a flight to Puerto Rico or the mainland. No further formalities occur after you return to the mainland.

Locals: are called Cruzans if from St. Croix.

Pharmacies: in St. Thomas include the Sunrise Pharmacy, Red Hook, *Tel. 775-6600*; K-Mart in the Tutu Park Mall, *Tel. 777-3854*. On St. Croix, People's Drug Store in Christiansted, *Tel. 778-7355* and the pharmacy in the Sunny Isles Shopping Center, *Tel. 778-5537*. In Frederiksted, D&D *Apothecary, Tel. 776-6353*. The Drug Store has branches at 69 King Street, Frederiksted, *Tel. 772-2656* and at 184C Ruby, *Tel. 4775*. It's open Monday through Saturday 8am-7pm and Sunday 8am-1pm. In Cruz Bay, St. John, St. John Drug Center, *Tel. 776-6353*. The hospital in St. Croix is in Christiansted, *Tel. 778-6311*. The hospital in St. Thomas is in Sugar Estate, *Tel. 776-8311* and it has a 24-hour emergency room. In St. John, an emergency medical technician is on call at *Tel. 776-6222*. For fastest help, ask at the hotel's front desk for the names of nearby doctors, clinics, and drug stores.

Postage: the familiar American eagle delivers the mail in the U.S. Virgin Islands and U.S. postage stamps are used. No additional postage is required to send letters and post cards to the mainland.

Taxes: there's a departure tax but it's added to your airplane ticket, so you don't have to stand in line and pay it separately as is common on other islands. Hotel bills are plus eight per cent tax. There is no sales tax.

Tourist information: *Tel. 800/372-8784 or 340/774-8784*. In Canada, *Tel. 416/233-1414*. Or write the U.S. Virgin Islands Department of Tourism, *Box 6400, St. Thomas VI 00804*. Visitor information offices are at the airports and in downtown Charlotte Amalie across from Emancipation Garden.

Weddings: to get married on St. Thomas or St. John, request a marriage license application from the Clerk of the Territorial Court, *P.O. Box 70, St. Thomas USVI 00804; Tel. 774-6680.* For a St. Croix wedding, contact the Family Division, Territorial Court of the Virgin Islands, *P.O. Box 929, Christiansted, St. Croix USVI 00821, Tel. 778-9750.* Allow plenty of time because you must both appear in person at the court to retrieve the paper work. After the application is received, filled out and notarized, it is sent back to the islands and an eight-day waiting period begins. Fees are $25 each for the application and license and $200 for a ceremony performed by a judge. (Courts are open Monday through Friday on St. Thomas and Monday through Thursday on St. Croix; if you want to get married on a weekend, arrive early enough to do the paperwork. Note holidays). Personal checks are not accepted. A number of professional wedding consultants plan weddings in the U.S. Virgin Islands. For a brochure listing them and the services they offer, *Tel. 800/372-USVI.* Also see our sidebar listing of wedding planners under *Where to Stay*.

Western Union: found at Pueblo Supermarkets on St. Thomas and St. Croix. For telegrams and money transfers on St. John, try Connections, *Tel. 776-4200.* Western Union is also available at St. Thomas Islander Services, *Tel. 774-8128.*

CASINO GAMBLING COMES TO ST. CROIX

The first hotel and casino in the U.S. Virgin Islands opened in Winter 1999 at the former Divi St. Croix Resort. The resort has been completely renovated and a 10,000-square-foot casino added, with 300 slot machines, 12 table games, a buffet, snack bar, and gift shop. It's operated by Treasure Bay Casino in Biloxi, Tel. 228/385-6052.

16. BRITISH VIRGIN ISLANDS

So closely tangled with the U.S. Virgin Islands that we couldn't resist including them in this book are the British Virgin Islands, a tiny, 35-mile-long sprinkling of cays including **Tortola**, **Virgin Gorda**, **Anegada**, and **Jost Van Dyke**. All proudly fly the Union Jack but otherwise they're much the same as their neighboring U.S. Virgin Islands – small and easy to get around, rimmed with remarkable beaches probing into hidden coves, and blessed with day-long sunshine.

Ports of entry are at Virgin Gorda, Jost Van Dyke, Anegada, Road Town, Beef Island, and at the west end of Tortola. Communities are found at **Great Harbour** on Jost Van Dyke; on Tortola at **Carrot Bay**, **Cane Garden Bay**, **Road Town**, **Sea Cow Bay**, and **Long Swamp**; on Virgin Gorda at **Spanish Town** and **North Sound**.

Most of the smaller islands are uninhabited but aloof, pricey resorts are found on **Peter Island** and **Guana Island**, on six-acre **Marina Cay**, and on **Necker Island** where a private mansion accommodates up to 24 guests.

Columbus first noted the islands in 1493 and it wasn't long before they, like the other islands of the Caribbean, were pawns in European battles that pitted Dutch against Spanish and English against French. The Dutch settled here at Soper's Hole in the 17th century, but the islands were claimed by the British in 1672 and remain today a British colony with its own, locally elected, government.

Among the famous swashbucklers who sailed through here was Sir Francis Drake, whose name lives on in the channel that separates the islands. Of all the legends, histories and half truths that have captured the public imagination, however, it is Robert Louis Stevenson's *Treasure Island* that travelers love most. The book's setting is believed to be Norman Island with its mysterious caves.

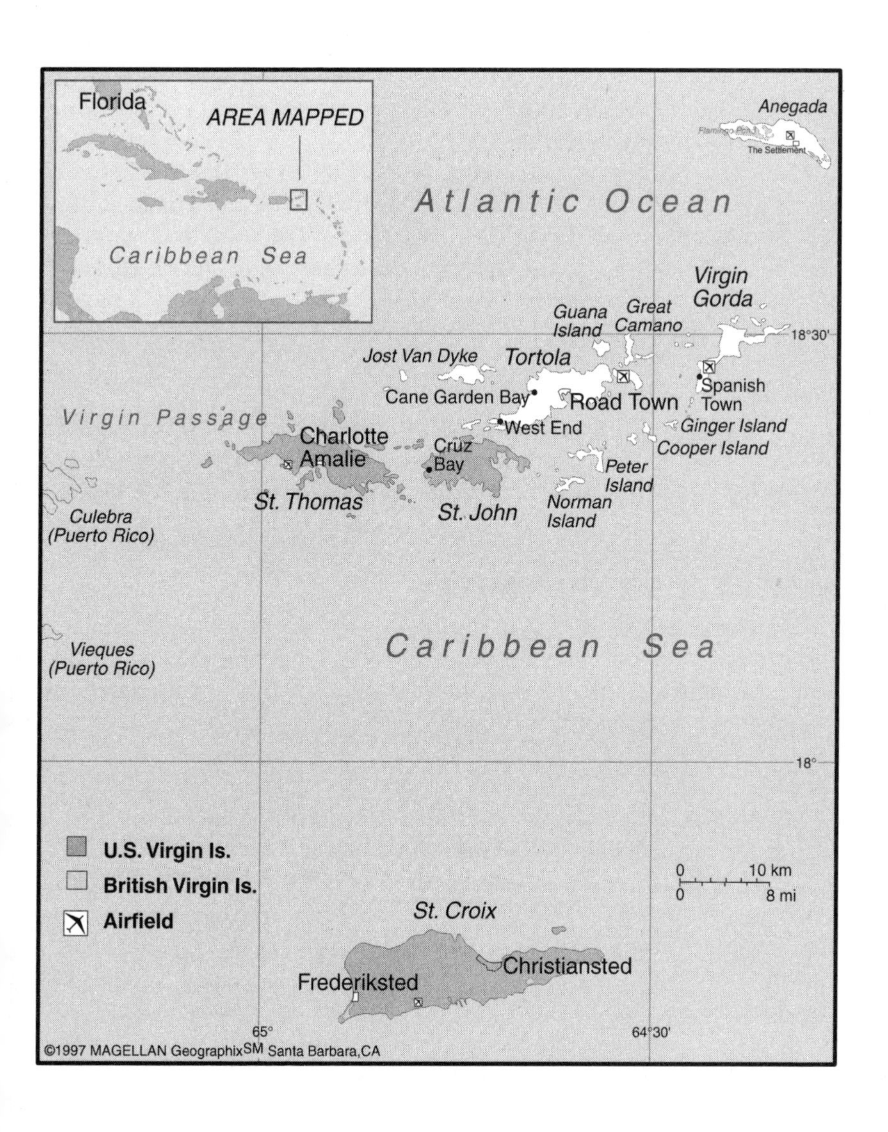
Florida
AREA MAPPED
Caribbean Sea
Anegada
The Settlement
Atlantic Ocean
Virgin Gorda
Guana Island
Great Camano
18°30'
Jost Van Dyke
Tortola
Cane Garden Bay
Road Town
Spanish Town
Virgin Passage
West End
Ginger Island
Charlotte Amalie
Cruz Bay
Cooper Island
Peter Island
St. Thomas
St. John
Norman Island
Culebra (Puerto Rico)
Caribbean Sea
Vieques (Puerto Rico)
18°
U.S. Virgin Is.
British Virgin Is.
Airfield
0 10 km
0 8 mi
St. Croix
Christiansted
Frederiksted
65°
64°30'
©1997 MAGELLAN Geographix SM Santa Barbara,CA

Do you remember the song about "Fifteen men on dead men's chest; Yo ho ho and a bottle of rum?" The story goes that the dreaded Blackbeard anchored in Deadman's Bay after a raid and got into a fight with his men while splitting the booty. He stranded 15 men on Dead Chest Island with a bottle of rum, their sea chests, and a sword. The rest is delicious speculation, conjuring up images of men fighting over the last of the supplies as they connived, killed each other or starved to death, taking to their graves the secret of where the treasure was buried. Some people are still looking for it.

Modern history began in the mid-1960s when the Rockefellers developed the resort at Little Dix Bay, Virgin Gorda, and The Moorings followed by opening a charter yacht operation. The result is a booming, blooming island group fit for a queen. During her reign, Queen Elizabeth 11 has been twice to the tiny British Virgin Islands. They're a natural addition to any trip to the U.S. Caribbean.

Climate

The strongest North American cold fronts may push this far south, bringing stinging winds, but the climate in the BVI is a non-story except during hurricane season when storms may occasionally spin up. Plan on warm and sunny days and cool nights in the 60s.

ARRIVALS & DEPARTURES

Plan your arrival as early in the day as possible, especially if your trip will involve road and ferry travel after you've landed at the airport and gone through the customs and immigration gristmill. Sometimes the post-flight part of the trip is the most arduous.

By Air

Beef Island/Tortola, the main airport for Tortola and all the BVI, is served daily from San Juan by **American Eagle**, *Tel. 800/433-7300,* **LIAT**, *Tel. 246/495-1187,* **Virgin Islands Airways**, *Tel. 284/495-1972.* **Air St. Thomas**, *Tel. 246/776-2722* flies to **Virgin Gorda** from San Juan, a route also served by **Virgin Islands Airways**, and **Carib Air**, *Tel. 284/495-5965.* Air St. Thomas and Carib Air fly between Virgin Gorda and St. Thomas. **Gorda Aero Services**, *Tel. 284/ 495-2271,* flies three days a week from Beef Island/Tortola to Anegada and Virgin Island Airways flies daily between Virgin Gorda and Beef Island/Tortola.

Inter-island service is available via **LIAT** daily from Beef Island to Antigua, St. Kitts, and Dominica. Virgin Islands Airways flies daily from Beef Island to St. Kitts. **LIAT** and **Winair** fly one or two days a week between Beef Island and St. Maarten. Charter flights are available through **Fly BVI**, *Tel. 800/1-FLY BVI (U.S.); 800/469-5955 (Canada) or 284/495-1747* elsewhere. Gorda Air Services and Air St. Thomas also offer planes for charter.

By Ferry

Ferries are an important mode of inter-island transportation, always cheaper than flying and sometimes quicker if you want to go downtown-to-downtown. Schedules vary according to the day of the week and can be affected by sea conditions, so it's crucial to verify your time of departure by telephone.

Ferry companies include:

- **Inter-Island Boat Services**, *Tel. 284/495-4166*, operates between West End and Cruz Bay.
- **Jost Van Dyke Ferry Service**, *Tel. 284/494-2997*, operates between West End and Jost Van Dyke on schedule or on charter.
- **Native Son, Inc.**, *Tel. 284/495-461*, runs between Road Town, West End, and downtown St. Thomas. There's also daily service from West End to St. John and Red Hook, St. Thomas.
- **North Sound Express**, *Tel. 284/495-2271*, operates between Beef Island and North Sound, Virgin Gorda, with a stop at The Valley with four-hour notice.
- **Peter Island Ferry**, *Tel. 284/494-2561*, links Road Town at the Peter Island Ferry dock to Peter Island Resort & Yacht Harbour.
- **Smith's Ferry Service**, *Tel. 284/495-4495 or 494-2355*, runs between Virgin Gorda and Road Town. Also from Road Town and West End to downtown St. Thomas.
- **Speedy's Fantasy/Speedy's Delight**, *Tel. 284/495-5240 or 5235*, operates between Virgin Gorda and Road Town.

ORIENTATION

It's easy to get your bearings on any island if you can just remember where you are in relation to the ferry dock (except for Anegada, where the airport is the center of interest). If you're not being met by your hotel host, you'll find plenty of friendly, eager drivers at the airports and docks. If you choose a rental car or mo-ped, a good map will be provided. A Tourist Board office is on the waterfront at Wickham's Cay, conveniently located between the ferry dock and the cruise ship dock.

GETTING AROUND THE ISLANDS

Taxis meet all flights, and you can get a cab from the **Beef Island Airport** to Road Town for $5. The town itself can be walked from one end to the other in half an hour. A leisurely tour, hitting all the high points, takes two hours or less. Waterfront Drive, home of **Pusser's Company Store and Pub**, follows the east side of the bay, with a British Virgin Islands Tourist Office at its north end. Main Street and the settlement's shopping district plus the extravagant cruise ship shops are all packed into the **Wickham's Cay** area.

Don't assume automatically that you can't manage without a rental car. Rental and fuel costs are high; roads are not good; and you can probably find better uses for the $10 that they nick you for a driver's license. You can see a lot of these small islands on foot and by boat, then take a taxi or tour if you want to explore an island or try restaurants different from those at your resort.

The most popular rentals in the British Virgins are four-wheel-drive Jeeps ($35-$60 daily), with discounts for weekly rentals. Scooters, which rent for $30 a day or $170 a week are available on most islands. Insurance of $7-$10 may be additional. Collision damage waiver is optional, although a deposit of $500 or so may be required. Bicycles are available through rental agencies and many resorts. Most rental agencies pick up free at resorts or airports, but ask in advance to be sure about pick-up and drop-off requirements, which can be complicated if they involve meeting a ferry or private launch.

Auto and scooter rental agencies include:

Anegada

- **Anegada Reef Hotel**, *Tel. 284/495-8002*
- **D.W. Jeep Rentals**, *Tel. 284/495-8018*

Tortola

- **Airways Car Rentals**, *Tel. 284/495-2161*
- **Alphonso Car Rentals**, *Tel. 284/494-3137*
- **Avis Rent-A-Car**, *Tel. 284/494-3322 or 494-2193*
- **Budget Rent-A-Car**, *Tel. 284/494-2639 or 494-2531*
- **Caribbean Car Rental**, *Tel. 284/494-2595*
- **Del's Jeep & Car Rental**, *Tel. 284/495-8018*
- **Denzil Clyne Car Rentals**, *Tel. 284/495-4900*
- **Hertz Car Rental**, *Tel. 284/495-5803*
- **International Car Rentals**, *Tel. 284/494-2516, Fax 494-4715*
- **National Car Rental**, *Tel. 284/494-3197*
- **Rencal Rent-A-Car**, *Tel. 284/495-4330, Fax 494-5085*

Virgin Gorda

- **Hertz Car Rental**, *Tel. 284/495-4405*
- **Honda Scooter Rentals**, *Tel. 284/495-5212*
- **L&S Jeep Rental**, *Tel. 284/495-5297, Fax 495-5342*

- **Mahogany Rentals**, *Tel. 284/495-5469, Fax 495-5072*
- **Speedy's Car Rental**, *Tel. 284/495-5235 or 495-5240*

WHERE TO STAY

Rates listed here do not include a seven per cent room tax and service charges, which are 10 to 15 per cent. Summer rates are usually 30-40 percent less than winter rates quoted here but some resorts add features and upgrades rather than lowering rates in the off season.

Private villas in the islands can be booked through **WIMCO**, *Tel. 800/932-3222 or 401/849-8012.* Maid service and staff are available. Guest houses, vacation houses and apartments are also available on arrangement with private owners. For a list call **BVI Tourism** in New York at *Tel. 800/835-8530.* All area codes are **284**.

Mail sent here should be posted to the address, island, then British Virgin Islands, fully spelled out. Many of the British islands hotels have mail drops in St. Thomas, where mail arrives quickly and at U.S. rates, in which case the address would end in VI, followed by the zip code. Ask.

ANEGADA

Moderate

ANEGADA REEF HOTEL, *Anegada. Tel. 284/495-8002, Fax 495-9362. Rates at this 12-room hotel, which is three miles west of the airport at Setting Point, start at $165 including three meals daily.*

So remote is the island that you're glad to find any place to lay your head, let alone a pleasant little hotel with its own restaurant and bar. In fact, the hotel is also where you can rent a car, find a taxi or bicycle, buy bait, tackle and ice, and have your air tanks refilled. Rooms are spacious and each has its own porch opening onto the beach. Be as private as you care to be, or let your host find you a deep sea fishing trip or a guide to take you out on the flats to hunt the elusive bonefish. There are just enough local characters, passing visitors, and yachties to justify the occasional barbecue or a festive evening with live music. Some rooms have telephones; all are air conditioned. Babysitting can be arranged.

Budget

OCEAN RANGE HOTEL, *in the settlement near the air strip, c/o General Delivery, Anegada. Tel. 284/485-8017 or radio VHF Channel 16. Rates start at $65 nightly.*

Ocean view rooms are plain vanilla, but you'll have a kitchenette and your own patio. Play Robinson Crusoe at bargain prices. Traveler's checks are accepted, but not credit cards.

GUANA ISLAND

GUANA ISLAND, *booking address 10 Timber Trail, Rye NY 10580, Tel. 914/967-6050. The island's number is 284/494-2334. Rates start at $675 for two including three meals daily, afternoon tea, wine with lunch and dinner, and use of tennis courts and watersports equipment. Groups can rent the entire island, which has 15 double rooms and a one-bedroom cottage. For $25 per person round trip you'll be met at Beef Island Airport and taken by taxi to the dock for the ten-minute cruise to the island. Cash and checks are accepted, but not credit cards.*

They call this the only Virgin island that still is, an 850-acre piece of paradise plunked down in the dazzling sea north of Tortola. "You guessed it, teams of decorators were not flown in from New York," say the caretakers in explaining the furniture, which isn't Chippendale but looks just fine in an island setting. Wicker and woods complement white walls with accents of fresh flowers. Louvered doors admit the tradewinds.

The island's White Bay Beach is a stunner but if you want another beach all to yourself, take a boat and a picnic to one of the other six beaches on the island. You can tramp the outback looking for wildlife and sea birds, or try to find the rock outcropping shaped like an iguana, giving the island its name. Meals make use of fresh tropical fruits, vegetables and seafood; dinner is all crystal and candlelight, catered to your whim.

If you rent the cottage, ($925 to $1290 nightly depending on the season), take your meals in the dining terrace or have them brought in. It's a three-room hillside overlook with living room, kitchen, and bath, surrounded by decks and reached by walking a secluded trail past an ancient stone wall built by the Quakers who originally peopled the island.

JOST VAN DYKE

Moderate

SANDCASTLE HOTEL, *White Bay, Jost Van Dyke. Mail address: Suite 201, 6501 Red Hook Plaza, VI 00802. Tel. 284/495-9888, Fax 284/495-9999. E-mail sandcastle@caribsurf.com. Website sandcastle-bvi. Rates at this four-cottage, two-room resort start at $170 without meals. A seven-night package that includes meals, transportation from Tortola, tax and tips are from $1350 for two. The resort is a 20-minute ferry ride from Tortola.*

Beachfront cottages garlanded with greenery and bright blooms form the ultimate beach getaway (or stay in one of the air-conditioned rooms). Candlelight dinners, beachfront honor bar. Snorkel or windsurf, shop the boutique, and take walks on the beach.

Budget

RUDY'S MARINER INN, *Great Harbour, Jost Van Dyke. Tel. 284/495-9282. In the USVI, Tel. 340/775-3558. Rates start at $85 single, with all meals. The island is 20 minutes by boat from Tortola. No credit cards are accepted.*

Living is easy at this three-room inn with its own beach bar and a locally popular restaurant revered for its fish and conch specialties served with generous helpings of side dishes. Your room has kitchen and dining areas, so you can shop local markets and try Caribbean cookery on your own if you choose not to take the meal plan.

NECKER ISLAND

NECKER ISLAND, *mail address Box 1109, Virgin Gorda. U.S. and Canada Tel. 800/557-4255. Rates for the entire island start at $11,000 per day for up to seven guests; $16,000 daily for 20-24 guests. During some periods, you don't have to book the entire island. Rooms and suites are rented separately at $9,000 per couple per week.*

The rate doesn't seem so startling when you realize that you're renting an entire, private, 74-acre island owned by Virgin Group chairman Richard Branson. With it come a ten-bedroom villa and two private Balinese cottages. All meals and drinks, helicopter transfer from St. Thomas or Beef Island, and everything else needed to pursue a grandly hedonist, out-island lifestyle are included. Use the boats, wind surfers, jet skis, books, music, a video library, games, an exercise room, swimming pool and tennis court, and let the staff of 22 cater to your every whim.

A tiny island rises out of a turquoise sea. It's rimmed with beige beaches and is topped by a mansion that looks out to sea from every direction. When you move in, you're lord and lady of the manor. There are no menus because you tell the cooks what and when you care to eat; no schedules unless you make them; no other guests unless you invite them. The island, in short, is yours to throw a house party, a reunion, a wedding, or just a vacation in paradise.

Interiors are airily raftered, rising to high ceilings that draw hot air from below, bringing fresh sea breezes through the windows. A 22-foot Brazilian table in the dining room seats everyone in elegance. The Bali influence turns up time and again in the hand-carved furniture, teak and stone surfaces, expanses of iron-hard Brazilian Ipé wood and Yorkstone floors, gauzy canopies over a four- poster bedstead, straw matting covering the rafters in some rooms, and wood balconies suspended over a view of the sea far below. When doors are flung open, it's easy to forget where indoors ends and outdoors begins. A waterfall spills into the swimming pool, fed by a desalinization plant that is run by diesel generators. Relax in the Jacuzzis, barbecue around the pool or at the beach, use the floodlit tennis courts, play snooker, or use the workout equipment.

PETER ISLAND

PETER ISLAND RESORT & YACHT HARBOR, *Box 211, Tortola, or 220 Lyon Street NW, Grand Rapids MI 49503. Tel. 800/346-4451; locally 284/495-2500. Rates at this 50-room, three-villa resort start at $415 nightly; a four-bedroom villa is $3950. The island is reached from Road Town by a 20-minute ride aboard the island's private boats, which make the trip nine times a day. Transfers are $25 per person. Guests are discouraged from bringing children under age eight.*

An AAA Four-Diamond resort, Peter Island is so exclusive that, as bareboaters anchored in its harbor, we were warned not to dry our tea towels on deck. The tony resort, which reopened for the 1998 season after closing for major revitalization, shares this island only with some wild goats, skittering lizards, and a concert of wild birds. Owned by Amway Corporation, whose soaps and shampoos are subtly provided as bath amenities, it can accommodate up to 50 guests. Snorkel, sail a 19-foot Squibb, swim off one of the five secluded beaches, or float in the freshwater pool surrounded by forests of brilliant hibiscus. Ride a bike into the hills or hike the nature trails to watch royal terns swoop among the trees. Then have a massage or work out in the fitness center. Dining is in your choice of two restaurants. The resort is dressy in season, so take jacket and tie for dinner.

Rooms have the little luxury touches expected in a four-diamond resort: built-in hair dryer, air conditioning plus ceiling fans and cross ventilation, clock radio, bathrobes, and mini-bar. Cool tile floors complement wicker and walnut furnishings; indoor gardens screen sunken bathtubs. Each room has its own lanai or balcony. Ask about packages, which include a scuba vacation and an ashore-afloat deal that combines a land stay with two nights on a crewed yacht. The resort has massage and spa services, tennis courts and lessons, nightly movies, a library, and a basketball hoop with half a court. Each week the manager throws a cocktail party and in season wine tastings are held weekly.

TORTOLA

Expensive

FORT RECOVERY ESTATES VILLAS, *Towers, West End, Tortola, mailing address Box 11156, St. Thomas VI 00801. Tel. 284/495-4036 or 800/367-8455. Drive east from the West End ferry dock, then follow the coast road to Fort Recovery. Rates start at $185 in season, with breakfast for a one-bedroom villa.*

Bring your family and settle into a villa with one, two, three, or four bedrooms. There's a manager on duty around the clock, a bar, restaurant, yoga and massages, and spectacular views of a half dozen islands across a crystal verdigris sea from your own private beach. The fort was built in the 17th century by the Dutch. Now it forms the core of this homey, British-style seaside community. Units are air conditioned and have fully-equipped kitchens, cable television, and daily maid service.

FRENCHMAN'S CAY, *Box 1054, West End, Tortola. Tel. 284/495-4844, Fax 495-4056, 800/235-4077. Winter rates start at $200. The resort is on Frenchman's Cay, a separate island across from the ferry docks at West End.*

Each of the nine villas in this breeze-cooled beach resort has a full kitchen, dining and sitting areas, and terrace. When you're not eating "in," try the resort's bar and The Clubhouse Restaurant, featuring Caribbean flavors with a continental flair. Swim in the pool, play tennis, or just roam the 12 secluded acres to bask in the tradewinds. To get out on the water, rent one of the hotel's kayaks, Sunfish, boogie boards, or board sailers, or just borrow snorkel gear and go exploring. Horseback riding, scuba lessons, tours, and day sails are cheerfully arranged.

LONG BAY BEACH RESORT & VILLAS, *mailing address: Island Destinations, 1890 Palmer Avenue, Suite 20l, Larchmont NY 10538. Tel. 284/495-4252; in the U.S. and Canada, Tel. 800/729-9599; United Kingdom, Tel. 0800-898-379. Rates start at $185. From Road Town, go south and west on Waterfront Drive, then north on Zion Hill Road and west to Long Bay. If you arrive by ferry at West End, it's a ten-minute taxi ride. Meal plans are available. Children under age 12 can sleep free in a parent's room and pay a modest daily fee for a children's meal plan. Ask about packages.*

Hillside suites look out towards Jost Van Dyke over a strand of white sand that will be your private playground while you're here. Take a day sail on an 80-foot schooner, swim, and dine in the resort's highly-rated restaurant. Air conditioned rooms suites have high ceilings and a balcony that floats out over the tropical splendor, your own seascape. Designer prints are a dramatic black and white design, which is an effective foil for the sandy walls, tile, floors, and woody ceilings. Other rooms are done in sea greens and blues while still others are sunny ochres with accents of blue. Dine outdoors on linen-covered tables under the sun or stars, or indoors in the stony dining room with a greathouse look. The resort plays intensive tennis, and offers an attractive package for tennis players, but there's also plenty here for families, divers, beachcombers, and those who want to do nothing but veg out.

SUGAR MILL HOTEL, *Box 425, Road Town. Tel. 284/495-4355, Fax 495-4696; U.S. 800/462-8834; Canada 800/209-6874. Winter rates at this 21-unit hotel start at $175 single and $190 double. A two-bedroom villa is $585 nightly. Take the MAP meal plan at $50 per person. Children under age 10 are not accepted during high season. The hotel closes August and September. It is eight minutes from the West End ferry dock.*

Visitors flock to the famous restaurant here, so consider staying here among the ruins of a 17th century sugar plantation, eating all your meals at the acclaimed restaurant hosted by Jeff and Jinx Morgan. Breezy rooms with private terraces admit tropic breezes and look out over blue seas afloat with hazy mountains. Cool tile floors and filmy draperies are complemented by candy pastels or, in the deluxe villa, mellow golds and beiges. Some of the deluxe units have a bed or beds plus a queen-size sofabed, accommodating three or four. Standard rooms are poolside and have twin beds, refrigerator, and coffee maker. Deluxe units have kitchens. All are air conditioned.

Moderate

FORT BURT HOTEL, *Box 3380, Road Town. Tel. 284/494-2587, Fax 494-2002. Winter rates start at $110 double. Take Waterfront Drive south from Road Town to Fisher Estate.*

A 300-year-old fort in the hills outside Road Town has been restored to provide seven rooms and a suite overlooking Sir Francis Drake Channel. Swim in the fresh water pool or walk to the marina for sailing, fishing, and other watersports. Each room has an ocean view, air conditioning, and television. The hotel's bar is a good place to meet locals; the restaurant features continental and West Indian favorites. Child care can be arranged.

MOORINGS MARINER INN, *Box 139, Road Town. Tel. 284/494-2332, Fax 4949-2226; U.S. and Canada 800/535-7289. Winter doubles start at $165. On Wickham's Cay 2. Take Waterfront Drive northwest from Road Town.*

The Moorings charter yacht fleet is one of the most impressive in the world, and the inn was probably planned originally as a place for visiting yachtsmen to overnight before and after their cruises. Even if you're not a sailor, however, the yachtiness is part of the charm of the place. Every room has a galley, and provisioning is available in a well-stocked general store, so you can make your own meals when you don't feel like going out. The resort's dockside restaurant and bar are abuzz with sailing yarns shared by local liveaboards as well as fly-in charterers who are here for only a week or two.

NANNY CAY RESORT & MARINA, *Box 281, Road Town. Tel. 284/494-4895, Fax 494-0555, U.S. and Canada Tel. 800/74-CHARMS. Rates start at $150. Just three miles south of Road Town, the resort is 10 miles from the airport. Taxis are available, but ask about packages that include transfers. At press time, the hotel is in receivership and is being operated by fill-in staff, so get recent references before booking. The location is good and the resort is an evergreen, so we expect it to attract a buyer.*

Twenty five acres surrounded by sea are home to a 42-unit resort and a 200-slip marina. The combination is a winning one in the BVI where liveaboards and charter sailors come ashore for evening grog with locals and guests. Your studio suite will be furnished in fading Caribbean colors and textures, with cable TV, direct-dial phone, kitchenette, and your own patio or balcony. There are two restaurants, Pegleg Landing and a poolside cafe, and two swimming pools. Tennis courts are lit for night play, and use of the volleyball court is free. The hotel can arrange a car rental, snorkeling equipment, dive trips, and anything else in watersports including board sailing lessons. It has its own, full-service marina.

PROSPECT REEF RESORT, *Box 104, Road Town. Tel. 284/494-3311, Fax 494-5595, U.S. 800/356-8937; Canada, 800/463-3608. Winter rates start at $147. Take Waterfront Drive south from Road Town through Fisher Estate.*

Spreading across a patch of waterfront overlooking Sir Francis Drake Channel and split by a tidal lagoon, this 131-unit resort has its own marina with sailing and diving trips, fresh and salt water swimming pools, tennis courts, an upscale restaurant, bars, shops, fitness center, and a pitch-and-putt golf course. All you need for a Caribbean getaway is right here just west of town. Take a studio or villa if you plan to do some of your own cooking; you can buy provisions at the resort. A courtesy bus runs to the beach and to town. In family seasons, there's a supervised program for children ages 5-12.

PUSSER'S MARINA CAY, *Box 626, Road Town. Tel. 284/494-2174, Fax 494-4775. Rates start at $150 with breakfast. This is a small, private island north of Beef Island and reached only by boat.*

Bring friends and have the whole island resort to yourself. It has four rooms and two villas, a beach, a marina, a restaurant, and a bar that attracts a lot of passing boaters.

SEBASTIAN'S ON THE BEACH, *Box 441 Tortola. Tel. 284/495-4212, Fax 495-4466; 800/336-4870. Rates at this 26-room hotel start at $110. From Road Town, go south and west on Waterfront Drive, pass Fort Recovery, and turn north (right) on Zion Hill Road, then left on Long Bay Road where the resort will be on ocean side.*

Choose a beachfront or garden room in a secluded hotel shaded by forests of palm trees. Some units are air conditioned. All have ceiling fans and refrigerator, and there's a commissary where you can stock up on snacks and cold drinks. The beach is a sugary strand, overlooked by the Seaside Grille where you can get lobster, fresh seafood, homemade soup or steak. It's open for three meals, but you're also close to other resorts and restaurants.

TAMARIND COUNTRY CLUB HOTEL, *Box 509, East End, Tortola., Tel. 284/495-2477 or 800/313-5662. Rooms start at $115. Drive west from East End for just over a mile, then right on Josiah's Bay Road. From Road Town, it's 15 minutes via Belle Vue Road to Ridge Road, then left on Josiah's Bay Road.*

High above yet another of Tortola's legendary beaches, (it's a 15-minute walk to the beach) the hotel offers ten poolside rooms and ten, two-bedroom villas. Television and air conditioning are available on request. Locals once voted the hotel's restaurant tops on Tortola; there's also a poolside bar and lounge.

Budget

BVI AQUATIC HOTEL, *Box 605, Tortola. Tel. 284/495-4541 or 494-2114. Found just east of the West End ferry docks, this 14-room hotel has rooms with bath from $25 and one-bedroom flats from $350 a week. No credit cards.*

If you want a plain vanilla place to stay close to the watersports, this is a utilitarian *pied-a-terre* with its own bar. At press time, the hotel is closed for renovation, so call ahead for current rates and availability.

CANE GARDEN BAY BEACH HOTEL, *284/495-4639, Fax 495-4820. Doubles start at $80 in winter, $45 in summer. From Road Town, take Joes Hill Road to Cane Garden Road. It's a 15-minute drive to the hotel.*

There's nothing fancy about this 24-room hotel but rooms do have telephones, air conditioning, and television, and the wind-sheltered beach is as wide and handsome as any found at pricier resorts. Available are snorkel gear, sail boards, fishing, and glass-bottom paddle boats. Meals at the hotel's restaurant feature lobster, conch fritters, and other seafood; Rhymer's Beach Bar is a favorite hangout. Once you've arrived here you can manage without a car. If you choose to leave the hotel, several restaurants and bars with entertainment are within walking distance.

HOTEL CASTLE MARIA, *Box 206, Road Town. Tel. 284/494-2553 or 2515; Fax 494-2111. Winter rates at this 30-room hotel start at $90 double. Take Waterfront Drive south from the ferry dock and turn right on MacNamara Road.*

Stay snug in the heart of things (this is one of the closest hotels to Road Town) in a mansion-like setting surrounded by flowers and foliage. Private balconies overlook the sea; the hotel has its own swimming pool. Some kitchenettes are available; rooms have television, telephone, air conditioning or room fan, and refrigerator. Local art is used throughout. The hotel's restaurant and bar are locally popular, but you can also walk to town or the ferry dock. Babysitting can be arranged.

JOLLY ROGER INN, *Box 437, Road Town. Tel. 284/495-4559, Fax 495-4184. Rooms at this 6-room inn, which is a few minutes walk west of the ferry dock in West End, start at $50.*

You're in the heart of a community with a dockside restaurant, bar, and shops. This modest hotel does have maid service and television, and watersports can be arranged, but don't count on using credit cards. It's a good budget choice if you have a rental car to get you to beaches and other adventures.

OLE WORKS INN, *Box 560, Tortola, located on Cane Garden Bay. Tel. 284/495-4837, Fax 495-9618. Doubles at this 18-room inn start at $80 in* *winter. From Road Town, take Joes Hill Road east to Cane Garden Bay Road, then south along the sea to the resort.*

Stay in a charming, 300-year-old sugar factory overlooking Cane Garden Bay. Your host, "Quito" Rhymer, offers air conditioned accommodations, each with refrigerator and oceanview balcony. Island music is played several nights a week in Beachfront Quito's Gazebo, which serves meals and exotic drinks, and Quito also has his own art gallery and gift shop.

VIRGIN GORDA

Expensive

BIRAS CREEK RESORT, *Box 54, Virgin Gorda, Tel. 284/494-3555, Fax 494-3557; U.S. and Canada 800/223-1108; United Kingdom 0800/894-057. Arrange with the hotel for airport transfer. You'll be met at the Virgin Gorda airport and taken to the launch that will deliver you to the resort. If you arrive at Beef Island, take the scheduled ferry or Biras' private launch. Rates start at $495 per couple per day including breakfast, lunch, and dinner. For single occupancy, deduct $100.*

A small thimble of land is surrounded on all sides by the blue waters of the Atlantic, Caribbean, and Sir Francis Drake Channel. It's a secluded, 140-acre setting for nature trails for hiking and jogging, two lighted tennis courts, a private beach, and a beachside, freshwater pool. Bicycles are parked outside each of the 32 suites.

Unpack in a spacious suite done in happy Caribbean colors. Your room overlooks the real thing: a neon-hued sea, an incredibly white sand beach, and blue skies that are streaked with pink morning and evening. Each room has a sitting area, separate bedroom, ceiling fans, air conditioning, direct-dial telephone, and a secluded, open-air shower. Private patios are tiled in terra cotta. In addition, Grand Suites have oversize terraces and sunken bathtubs. The meeting room is also the home of a little museum. Ask to see it. Watersports and instruction are all included, so you can snorkel, sail, spurt around in a motorboat, or board sail. Ask about the land-sea package that includes five nights in the resort and two romantic nights in a fully-provisioned, captained yacht.

BITTER END YACHT CLUB & RESORT, *Box 46, Virgin Gorda. Tel. 284/494-2746, U.S. 312/944-5855 or 800/872-2392. Rates start at $450 including all meals. Airport transfers, which are included, involve a taxi ride then a 10-min*ute boat ride.

Many of the resorts in the Caribbean are as yachty as they are landlubberly, but this one is especially salty because you can sleep on a boat or in one of the rooms for about the same price. You'll still get maid service, meals in the Yacht Club and, if you want to anchor off for a night, provisions to tide you over. Sea and sails are part of the scene everywhere, whether you're overlooking them from your hilltop villa, trading tall tales with sailors in the bar, or actually sailing one of the big fleet of Sunfish, Lasers, JY15s, Rhodes 19s and J-24s. Introduction to Sailing is a popular course for resort guests.

Zone out on your private veranda overlooking the verdant grounds, or plug into a carnival of good times: island excursions to The Baths and Anegada, snorkeling in reef-sheltered coves, swimming at the pool or one of the resort's three beaches, or joining a group to study marine science. Killbrides Underwater Tours is based at the Club and can do a complete dive package from beginner to advanced, Ginger Island to the wreck of the *Rhone.* Dine in the Clubhouse Steak and Seafood Grille or the English Carvery, then dance under the stars at Almond Walk. Not all units here are air conditioned, so specify AC if it's important to you. Provision at The Emporium, which has staples as well as baked goods and takeout dishes.

LITTLE DIX BAY, *P.O. Box 70, Virgin Gorda, British Virgin Islands. U.S. mailing address, P.O. Box 720, Cruz Bay, St. John, VI 00831. Tel. 284/495-5555, Fax 495-5661, U.S. and Canada 800/928-3000. Rates in the 102 units start at $450 double in season. For $95 daily you can add three meals daily; add $75 for breakfast and lunch. Children's meal plans for ages five to twelve are $47.50 and $37.50. Children aged four and under eat free. Escorted transfers from Tortola International Airport are $50 adults, $25 children.*

Lying serenely behind a barrier reef, Little Dix Bay has a half-mile crescent of beach surrounded by 500 acres of forest, seagrape, tamarind, and palms. Founded in 1964 by Laurance Rockefeller, it is now a grand Rosewood resort far different from the somewhat shabby resort that met us on our first visit 20 years ago. With three employees for every guest, it assures a level of pampering that's impressive even in the service-savvy Caribbean.

From the moment you are met at the airport or ferry dock, you're in a world of seabreeze, sun, and luxury. Airy, spacious rooms are furnished with wicker and bamboo, soft pastels and brightly contrasting tropic bouquets. Most rooms are air conditioned but not all are, so specify air if you want it. All have telephones, balconies or terraces. Hike nearby Gorda National Park or the resort's own nature trails. Walking sticks are provided in each room, and they come in handy on Cow Hill, the Savannah Trail, or the Pond Bay Trail.

Sightsee by boat or Jeep, play tennis, or enjoy a full menu of watersports. The resort has its own 120-slip marina where boats are waiting to take you sailing, deep sea fishing, or sunset cruising. Ferries run regularly to a sister resort, Caneel Bay on St. John, where you can eat if you're on the Little Dix meal plan. Dining here is in the Pavilion overseen by Executive Chef Benoit Pepin, in the Sugar Mill with its tropical bistro look and wood oven-baked pizzas, or the nautically themed Beach Grill featuring seafood and sandwiches. After dinner, dance to live music on the Pavilion Terrace and walk home along paths lit by tiki torches and scented with frangipani. There's a children's program in season.

Moderate

DIAMOND BEACH CLUB, *Box 69, Virgin Gorda. Tel. 284/495-5452, Fax 495-5875; U.S. 800/871-3551; Canada 800/487-1839. Rates at this 14-room inn start at $170. Villas with up to four bedrooms are available. Located on the island's west shore, the resort is two miles north of the Virgin Gorda airport and also about two miles north of the dock where ferries arrive from Road Town.*

All patios in this clubby little resort view the ocean, where you can swim or snorkel over colorful reefs. Looming over its shoulder is Virgin Gorda Peak, surrounded by a national park where you can hike and birdwatch. Units have maid service and fully-equipped kitchens where you can cook supplies bought in the commissary. Ask about packages that include a Jeep.

DRAKE'S ANCHORAGE RESORT INN, *Box 2510, North Sound, Virgin Gorda. Tel. 284/894-2254 or 800/624-6651. The resort can accommodate up to 28 guests at rates starting at $350 including all meals. The resort is on Mosquito Island, a five-minute boat ride from the dock.*

Each of the comfortable units, which include rooms, suites, or a posh villa, has its own veranda overlooking the sea. There's nothing to do and nowhere to go on this idyllic hideaway. Swim off the beach, water ski, snorkel, board sail, fish, or ride a bicycle to explore the island's four beaches. Scuba diving here is so good that the Cousteau Society visits regularly. Dining in the breezy, tropics-inspired restaurant is to die for, especially if you like flopping-fresh seafood and succulent lobster served overlooking the water. Your fellow diners will include boaters who sail over and dock here to sample the fine fare. If you prefer a native dish or something continental with a French accent, you'll find them on the *carte du jour* as well. Dining late, you'll be served by candlelight.

GUAVABERRY SPRING BAY, *Box 20, Virgin Gorda. Tel. 284/495-7227, Fax 495-5283. Only a few minutes south of the airport and five minutes from The Valley, this 21-room resort offers rooms from $135 but no credit cards are accepted.*

Available by the day or week, this homey resort is fun to say. It's named for a local, cranberry-size fruit used in the making of liqueurs. Houses on stilts soar airily over a sea of boulders and bougainvillaea, catching sea breezes. Each unit has one or two bedrooms, kitchenette, and dining area. You can buy provisions at Yacht Harbour or in the little commissary that is operated here for guests. Horseback riding, diving, fishing, or island tours can be arranged by your hosts, or swim from the beach at nearby Spring Bay. These are the handiest lodgings to The Baths and the Copper Mine, close to Little Fort National Park, the airport, and the settlements of The Valley.

LEVERICK BAY RESORT, *Box 63, The Valley, Virgin Gorda. Tel. 284/ 495-7421, Fax 495-7367; U.S. 800/848-7081; Canada 800/463-9396. Rooms start at $119.*

Stay in an air conditioned hotel room (there are 16) or rent the two-bedroom condo at this popular spot on Leverick Bay, a jump-off spot for out islands and for those Virgin Gorda resorts that can't be reached by road. The hotel looks out over Blunder Bay and North Sound toward Mosquito and Prickly Pear islands. Pass your days diving, playing tennis, water skiing, swimming or snorkeling off the beach, shopping the resort's own boutiques, or getting a massage or facial. Buck's Food Market at the marina sells everything you need to provision a villa or boat for a day or a week, including wines and liquors.

Pubby and popular, Pusser's Beach Bar here is a hangout for transient yachties, locals, and resort guests alike. For dinner, have steak or a meat pie at Pusser's or try the dining room. After dinner, dance to local bands.

OLDE YARD INN, *Box 26, Virgin Gorda. Tel 284/495-5544, Fax 495-5986, U.S. 800/633-7411. Rates at this 14-room resort start at $130. A few minutes from the airport, the Inn is on the island's southeastern thumb just outside The Valley. Included in rates are transfers from the airport or ferry dock.*

What a find! Although there are only 14 rooms, the hotel has its own locally-popular bar and restaurant, health club, a gift shop, and entertainers three times a week. You're welcomed at check-in with a rum punch, and your vacation officially begins. Choose a book from the hotel's library and stake out a patch of shade on meticulously gardened grounds. Stroll into town, relax in the pool or whirlpool, rent a Jeep or a boat, go snorkeling or day sailing, then be at the library by 9pm for the nightly movie. In the gourmet restaurant, you'll dine to classical music; the Sip and Dip poolside is the place for a snack in your swim suit. Rooms are air conditioned and each has its own patio overlooking gardens alight with hibiscus, bushy palms, and bougainvillaea.

MANGO BAY RESORT, *Box 26, Virgin Gorda. Tel. 284/495-5672, Fax 495-5674; U.S. 800/223-6510; Canada 800/424-5500. Rooms start at $129; villas are priced to $338. From the airport go north on North Sound Road, then left on Plum Tree Bay Road for less than a mile.*

Book a room or one of the eight deluxe villas, each with spacious living area, fully- equipped kitchen and large porch, all just a seashell's throw from the sandy beach. If you like, the hotel will find you a cook. The hotel has its own bar and Italian restaurant. Wind surfing and snorkel equipment are available.

Budget

OCEAN VIEW HOTEL, *Box 66, Virgin Gorda. Tel. 284/495-5230; U.S. 800/621-1270. Rooms start at $70 with a discount for stays of 14 days or more. Credit cards and personal checks aren't accepted.*

In the heart of bustling West End and less than a mile from the airport, this modest hotel has 12 rooms with cable television, telephone, and air conditioning. Meals are available in the hotels' restaurant, the Wheel House, which is well liked locally for its hearty West Indian fare.

WHERE TO EAT

The international gourmet has nothing to fear when dining in the BVI's sophisticated restaurants. Here you can find the finest French, Italian, and Asian cuisine as well as Continental-Caribbean foods that blend the best of old and new worlds. However, you'll miss a lot if you don't try such local specialties as roti (curry-filled bread), boil fish (fish in tomato sauce with garlic and onions), peas and rice (beans and rice) or patties (pastry filled with spicy beef, salt fish, or lobster).

Except for local fish and lobster, just about every mouthful has to be imported, but hosts do a good job at providing fresh vegetables and preparing dishes with a West Indian flavor. Unless stated otherwise, these restaurants accept major credit cards. It's not unusual in small islands to ask you to make reservations early in the day and to order at that time.

TORTOLA

Expensive

THE APPLE, *Little Apple Bay. Tel. 495-4437. Open only for dinner Tuesdays through Sundays in season. Main dishes average $20. Reservations are recommended.*

Just over the hill from Long Bay, Apple Bay is the surfer's beach, incredibly creamy and clear as waves boil ashore and keep the sands scrubbed clean. For a special dinner, seek out this quaint West Indian homestead framed in banyan trees. The food features local ingredients: whelk, soursop, conch, and fresh fish, all deftly seasoned and generously served by Liston Molyneaux, a Tortola native.

BRANDYWINE BAY RESTAURANT, *Brandywine Estate, three miles east of Road Town off the south shore road, Blackburn Highway. Tel. 495-2301. Reservations are requested. Main dishes start at $15.*

Revered for its Italian food, especially Florentine specialties, this country inn serves guests on a romantic garden patio surrounded by birdsong and greenery. Lobster ravioli is a specialty. You're hosted by Cele and David Pugliese, whose restaurant was voted "our favorite in the Caribbean" by *Bon Appetit* magazine.

FORT BURT RESTAURANT, *in the Fort Burt Hotel, Fisher Estate, just south of Road Town. Tel. 494-2587. Dinner will cost about $50 with appetizer and dessert but without wine. An English breakfast is available in the morning, and luncheon is served in the pub from noon to 2:30pm For dinner, reservations are essential.*

The ruins of an ancient Dutch fort are part of the scene at this hotel and restaurant overlooking Careening Cove, Road Reef, and Burt Point. Dine in a seabreeze-cooled outdoor dining area with a million dollar view. Seafood with a Caribbean overtone is the rule, resulting in great sauced filets or seafood curries but the Brits being the Brits, there's also great roast beef. Desserts are made here so they're always worth a try.

SKY WORLD, *Ridge Road. Tel. 494-3567. Dinner with wine costs $50 or more for a six-course feast; lunch is in the $20 range. Reservations are essential.*

The best game plan for a celebration evening is to arrive here an hour before sundown to watch the sky streak with color and the sun sink into the sea. From this hilltop perch you're looking down on what seems like all of Tortola and across to all the other islands. When it's time to get serious about dining, pace yourself for a parade of courses that starts with an inventive salad and ends with a selection of meltingly flaky pastries. Dinner is dressy; lunch is resort-casual.

SUGAR MILL, *in the Little Dix Bay resort. Tel. 945-5555. Take the private ferry from the Beef Island airport to the resort. Plan to spend $60 for dinner. Reservations are essential.*

Dine in one of the Caribbean's most posh resorts, long a Rockefeller holding and completely refurbished under new management by the Rosewood chain of luxury hotels. Lunch is a buffet under the high-roofed pavilion. Dinner by candlelight in the Sugar Mill features simply grilled lobster, fresh fish, and steaks with dashing presentations and garnishes. Have a drink in the lounge, where live music plays just about every night. The restaurant is not air conditioned.

SUGAR MILL RESTAURANT, *Apple Bay. Tel. 495-4355; U.S. 800/462-8834. Fixed-price lunches start at $25; dinners at $40. Daily specials offer appetizers in the $7-$8 range and main dishes at $18-$25. Reservations are a must. Drive west from Road Town on Waterfront Drive, pass Fort Recovery, then turn right over Zion Hill and, watching for signs, turn right at the T.*

Celebrities Tex and Jinx Morgan, columnists for *Bon Appetit* magazine and authors of several cookbooks, have owned this 300-year-old sugar mill since the 1980s, and their touch shows in the superb cuisine. The dining room is surrounded by original stone walls, now hung with Haitian art. The *Washington Post* called it "the island's best restaurant," but they were topped by *Business Week*, which called it "the best restaurant in the Caribbean." You might start, for example, with New Zealand Mussels in Dilled Cream or a terrine of smoked conch, followed by Tropical Game Hen in orange-curry butter or Fish with West Indian Creole Sauce.

Their signature dish is curry-banana soup, but everything here is freshly made according to whim, inspiration, and the best of what's available from the marketplace and the Morgans' own herb garden.

Moderate

CAPRICCIO DI MARE, *Waterfront Road, Road Town. Tel. 494-5369. It's open daily except Sunday. No credit cards or reservations are accepted. Plan to spend $6 for breakfast, $10 to $12 for lunch, and $20 to $30 for dinner.*

Settle into a pleasant Italian bistro setting and start with a Mango Bellini, a mixture of mango juice and sparkling asti spumante. Then have one of the pastas with a choice of tomato, seafood, cream, or vegetarian sauces. Choose one of the pizzas, a hot or cold sandwich, or just snack on cappuccino with a sweet.

MRS. SCATLIFFE'S RESTAURANT, *North Coast Road, between Cane Garden Bay and Apple Bay. Tel. 495-4556. Reservations are essential for dinner and are recommended for lunch. Prix fixe meals are in the $25 range. No credit cards are accepted.*

Mrs. Scatliffe and her family welcome you to their West Indies-style home where she cooks with locally raised goat and vegetables from her own garden. Dinner starts with a rum punch and proceeds through soup and salad followed by a meat such as curried goat, chicken, or a fish (for example, West Indian boil fish). The meal ends with dessert, usually featuring an exotic tropical fruit, like coconut or guava, followed by a lively musicale performed by Mom and the kids.

Budget

THE AMPLE HAMPER, *at Inner Harbour Marina next to the Captain's Table on Wickham's Cay. Pick up picnic makings at prices that start under $10. Hours vary seasonally.*

A popular gourmet provisioning spot for yachts, the Hamper is not an eat-in place but it has a full-service deli, imported English specialties, and delectable sandwiches made to order. It's the place to put together an elegant picnic to take to the beach or boat.

HAPPY LION, *next to the Botanic Gardens, Road Town. Tel. 494-2574. The restaurant serves breakfast, lunch, and dinner in the $10-$15 price range.*

Part of a little apartment hotel, this simple eatery is the place to get the real thing – johnnycake, goat mutton, and boil fish, as well as steaks, burgers, and sandwiches.

FORT WINE GOURMET, *Main Street, Road Town. Tel. 494-3036. Eat for $10 to $12. Reservations aren't accepted. Call for hours.*

This popular spot is a combination deli and eatery where you can linger over an espresso or grab a bag of sandwiches and cold salads for a beach picnic. The pastries are flaky and good, and the deli salads and sandwiches get high marks.

MR. FRITZ'S ORIENTAL RESTAURANT & TAKE AWAY, *on Wickham's Cay. Tel. 494-5592. Dine for under $10.*

Barbara and Fritz keep the woks sizzling with Lobster Love Boat, Singapore chicken, and fiery Szechwan pork and beef. Try the Cantonese-style shrimp.

VIRGIN GORDA

Expensive

BATH AND TURTLE, *in the yacht harbor at Spanish Town. Tel. 495-5239. Reservations are important. Main dishes are priced $15 to $28. It's open every day 7am to midnight.*

The breakfast crowd comes in early and the drinking begins with elevenses when the blender starts whirring with fruity margaritas or coladas. For lunch, have a chili dog, pizza, burger, Reuben, salad or a bowl of the four-alarm chili. Dine indoors or in the courtyard on fish fingers, coconut shrimp, lobster, grilled filet mignon, or chicken. Live music plays at least twice a week, never with a cover charge.

BIRAS CREEK ESTATE, *North Sound. Tel. 494-3555. Plan to spend $50 for dinner and more if you order a vintage wine. The dining rooms are open daily for breakfast, lunch, and dinner. Call for early for reservations. You may be asked to make your dinner selection when you phone.*

A longtime guest liked the resort so much, he bought it and the well-liked restaurant that goes with it. The view is worth the trip. Ask for a table that looks down from the hilltop to the seas below. Fresh seafood and lobster are the top draw here, but the chef is also happy to sizzle a steak any way you want it. At lunch there's a nice choice of salads, burgers, sandwiches and light dishes, and sometimes there's a beach barbecue during the day. At dinner, start with a cocktail in the elegant lounge. The menu offers plenty of variety in meats and seafood, and the wine list is comprehensive.

BITTER END YACHT CLUB, *North Sound. Tel. 494-2746. Reservations are essential for dinner, so call early. Plan to spend $50 for dinner. It's open breakfast through dinner.*

The bareboat crowd comes ashore here for drinks and dinner but the breakfast buffet is also worth the trip. Everything from fresh fruit and yogurt to cooked-to-order pancakes and omelets is on the groaning board. At lunch, choose from a big buffet of cold meats, cheese, breads, and salads, or order a hamburger or grilled fish. Grilled lobster is the dinner specialty, served plain or with a Creole sauce. There's also a choice of chicken, steak, or chops.

RESTAURANTS FOR MARINERS

Some of these restaurants can be reached only by private boat; others have docks where you can tie up free for dining or overnight for a fee; others can be reached by launch or ferry. The voyage is part of the fun, and many visitors make a day-long project out of it. Most can be reached on VHF ***Channel 16****. Always call ahead to see if they're open. Dinner reservations must be made early in the day.*

Pirate's Pub*, Saba Rock is a swim-in grill serving specialty drinks and international cuisine.* ***The William Thornton*** *is afloat off Norman's Cay;* ***The Last Resort*** *is on Bellamy Cay off Beef Island. On Anegada, which makes a good day trip, try the* ***Anegada Reef Hotel, Del's,*** *or* ***Pomato Point.***

Cooper Island Beach Club *is a restaurant and bar, and also offers beachfront cottages. Each has a kitchen, balcony, bathroom with open-air shower, and outdoor hammock, Tel. 800/542-4624.*

On Jost Van Dyke look for ***Harris' Place, Sidney's Peace*** *and* ***Love, Abe's Little Harbor, Club Paradise, Ali Baba's*** *and* ***Foxy's.***

DRAKE'S ANCHORAGE, *on the North Sound Beach. Tel. 494-2252. Reservations are essential because you'll be brought here by boat. When you book, have an idea of what you'll want to eat because they have to know before 3:30pm. Plan to spend $50 for dinner.*

The spot seems like the end of the world but somehow the chef manages to have a good selection of roasts on hand as well as the famous banana-crusted lobster or the signature chicken crepe. The restaurant and its bar, which is built of local rock, is part of a small resort.

TOP OF THE BATHS RESTAURANT, *350 yards up the trail from The Baths. Tel. 495-5497. Lunch is less than $10.*

Restaurant patrons are offered a dip in the pool here, so it's a wonderful place to cool off after scrambling around The Baths. Food has a continental touch, always with a fresh fish dish and luscious salads.

Budget

THE BATH AND TURTLE BAR & RESTAURANT, *Virgin Gorda Yacht Harbour, The Galley. Tel. 495-5239. Breakfast, lunch or dinner dishes start at $5.*

A sort of out-island Grand Central Station, this busy dock area is a great place to shop, nosh, and people watch. Try local patties and rotis, pasta salads, burgers, fresh fish, and pizza. Happy Hour specials are sold daily 4:30 to 5:30; live entertainment is offered on Wednesday and Sunday nights.

PUSSER'S LEVERICK BAY, *Tel. 495-7369. Breakfasts and lunches are under $10; dinner is in the $25 range. Reservations are suggested.*

Picturesque Leverick Bay, with its fleets of sailboats, is the scene of yet another Pusser's, this one serving steak, seafood, and pasta until 10pm. Lunch and pizza are served in the Beach Bar from 11:30am to 6pm. On Tuesdays there's all the barbecue you can eat and on Fridays all the Cajun shrimp you can eat. Live music is often scheduled, but call ahead if you want to be sure. The notorious Pusser's Painkillers here are offered in strengths one through four. Caveat emptor.

SEEING THE SIGHTS

ANEGADA

Anegada is as remote as the end of the world, a limestone and coral atoll rimmed with talcum powder beaches where you can walk for hours without seeing another human being. At its highest point, the island is only 27 feet above sea level. It's the quintessential nature sanctuary and the government is committed to keeping it that way.

Roam to your heart's content to see wild goats, donkeys and cattle, to look for 20-pound rock iguana (they look fierce but are harmless) and a host of heron, osprey, and terns. With luck you'll see some flamingoes too.

JOST VAN DYKE

Jost (yost) **Van Dyke** is the island that time forgot. A handful of people live in West Indian wooden homes around Great Harbour. **Norman Island**, famed for its caves and a port of call for boaters, has a floating bar and restaurant off The Bight.

SALT ISLAND

This little island between Cooper Island and Peter Island has only two residents, and its only point of interest is its salt ponds. Once a thriving and even crucial industry in the Caribbean, harvesting salt from the sea goes on today as it did a century ago. The island is best known as the gravesite of the *Rhone*, which sank in 1867.

TORTOLA

Take off on your own in rental car or scooter if you want only to find a beach and spend the day there. However, if you want narrative and direction, hire a taxi by the day or take a safari tour with a knowledgeable guide. Island tours of Virgin Gorda aboard safari buses are offered by **Andy's Taxi and Jeep Rental**, *Tel. 284/495-5511* and **Mahogany Taxi Service**, *Tel. 495-5469*.

Sightseeing tours of Tortola are available from the **BVI Taxi Association**, *Tel. 494-2875*; **Nanny Cay Taxi Association**, *Tel. 494-0539*; **Scato's Bus Service**, *Tel. 494-2365;* **Style's Tour Operator**, *Tel. 494-2260;* **Travel Plan Tours**, *Tel. 494-2872;* **Turtle Dove Tax Stand**, *Tel. 494-6274;* and **Waterfront Taxi Stand**, *Tel. 494-3456.*

Nature's Secret Adventure Company, *Tel. 495-2722*, sets up nature programs, sailing or kayaking adventures, fishing, and villa rentals. Flightseeing tours are available from **Fly BVI Ltd**, *Tel. 495-1747.*

North of downtown Road Town on Station Avenue, **J.R. O'Neal Botanic Gardens** are a four-acre oasis filled with native and imported tropicals plus a lily pond, waterfall, and orchid house. Bird houses attract an array of tropical birds. The gardens are open Monday through Saturday 8am to 4 p.m., *Tel. 494- 4557.* Admission is free. Shop your way down Main Street, pausing to look at the churches, 19th century post office, and the huge, shady ficus trees in Sir Olva George's Plaza.

The **Virgin Islands Folk Museum** is housed in an authentic West Indian house on Main Street. There's no phone but it's usually open in the middle of the day except Wednesday and Sunday. Admission is free. Of special interest are artifacts from the wreck of the *Rhone,* which you'll see during your visit if you're a diver, and bits of pre-Columbian pottery. Proceeding north on Main, take a picture of Cockroach Hall, built atop a huge boulder in the 1800s to serve as a doctor's dispensary. It's now a private business. Officially its name is Britannic Hall.

Next to it are two **churches**, the Anglican dating to 1746 and rebuilt in 1819, and the Methodist Church, which was rebuilt after a hurricane in 1924. Its congregation dates to 1789. Between them is Her Majesty's Prison, dating to the 1700s, where a cruel planter was hanged for killing a slave.

Climb **Fort Hill**, which is just below the roundabout at Port Purcell to see the remains of **Fort George**. It was built by the Royal Engineers in 1794 to stand sentinel against foreign powers, especially the French, and such pirates as Edward Teach, the dreaded Blackbeard. At the west end of Tortola at **Fort Recovery Villas**, you can see the well- preserved round tower that is thought to have been built by Dutch settlers in the mid-1600s.

Touring on your own, head east from Road Town, and you'll pass the ruins of **Fort Charlotte**. Now just a few walls, a cistern, and a powder magazine, it tops Harrigan's Hill. Continuing east you'll see a ruined church, which is all that remains of Kingstown, a community that was founded for free slaves in the 1830s. Along the road that runs from Ridge Road down to Brewer's Bay on Tortola's north shore, find **Mount Healthy** and a largely intact stone windmill, once part of a sugar plantation. It's the only such windmill on Tortola.

A ride 'round the island can take only three hours, but you'll want to spend days seeking out secluded beaches, trying restaurants, and hiking the hills. Don't rush it. Stop at the North Shore Shell Museum in Carrot Bay, the Callwood Rum Distillery, and Soper's Hole for shopping and to watch boats come and go.

Among the historic ruins to look for: Fort Burt, now a hotel, was started by the Dutch in the 17th century. The ruins of **Fort George** are on Fort Hill. Fort Recovery on the west end of Tortola dates, it is thought, to the first Dutch settlers in 1648. In Pleasant Valley, the ruins of the **William Thornton Estate** remain from the home of the designer of the United States Capitol. **The Dungeon**, actually a fort that has an underground cell, is halfway between Road Town and West End. It dates to 1794. Just east of Road Town, look for the ruins of The Church at Kingstown, once the center of a community of freed slaves.

VIRGIN GORDA

Just south of the Yacht Harbour, which is a beehive of sailing and sailors, **Little Fort National Park** is on the site of a Spanish fortress. Now a wildlife sanctuary, the 36-acre park still has remnants of the original fort and its powder magazine.

Between Little Fort and The Baths, **Spring Bay** is a smooth sand beach studded with enormous boulders, thrown up 70 million years ago by a volcanic eruption. They set the scene for your arrival at **The Baths**, where city-size boulders are flung about as if by angry gods. The scene changes constantly as the sun passes over and tides roll in and out, so it's a spot you can come back to time and again to explore, photograph, swim in, and commune with one of nature's great structures.

On Virgin Gorda's remote southwestern end, look for the ruins of the **Copper Mine**, which was worked by Cornishmen between 1838 and 1867. Remains of some of the buildings and works can still be seen (from a distance; they are not safe to explore). Also on the west coast is Nail Bay, where you can roam the ruins of an 18th century sugar mill made from brick, stone, and coral rock.

Fallen Jerusalem, a separate island off the south end of Virgin Gorda, can be reached only by boat and only on calm days. Its terrain is bold and dramatic, much like The Baths, a birdwatcher's mecca because of its many nesting sites.

NIGHTLIFE & ENTERTAINMENT

It's likely that your hotel or the closest bar will have live music and it will be listed in one of the free magazines such as *Limin' Times* that you can pick up around the islands. If you want to venture off property, the hottest licks are at:

THE BATH AND TURTLE BAR, *Yacht Harbour, The Valley, Virgin Gorda. Tel. 495-5239.*

Inexpensive dinner fare is available until 9:30, so stoke up on burgers, pizza, or native dishes then stay on for live music on Sunday and Wednesday nights.

BOMBA'S SURFSIDE SHACK, *Cappoon's Bay, near Cane Garden Bay, Tortola. Tel. 495-4148 is Tortola's happenin' place, especially on Wednesdays, Fridays, and on nights when the moon is full.*

The decor is early beach bum and the sound system could wake the dead, but drinks are cheap, barbecue is plentiful, and the music is authentically Caribbean until midnight or later.

THE LAST RESORT, *Ballamy Cay, off Beef Island. Tel. 495-2520. Can be reached only by launch from Trellis Bay, which will be arranged for you when you make your (required) reservations. Dinner with wine and the show cost about $50, which you can charge to a major card.*

Tuck into an English buffet including roast beef, Yorkshire pudding, homemade soups and all the trimmings, followed by a hilarious, two-hour, one-man music and comedy show.

PUSSER'S LTD, *Marina Cay, reached by a causeway from Tortola's West End. Tel. 494-2467. It stays open until 2:30 a.m.*

This is the British Virgin Islands, which means pubs and pub grub, most notably at the yachty Pusser's where the Painkiller is not for the faint of heart (or liver). Made with the rum that was once the official grog of the Royal Navy, the drink makes great accompaniment for an evening of music listening, people watching, and good conversation until 2:30am. Pusser's serves a broad range of sandwiches, pizza, and a creditable shepherd's pie.

QUITO'S GAZEBO *at the Ole Works Inn, Cane Garden Bay, Tortola. Tel. 495-4837.*

Native-born Quito Rymer switches on his microphone at 8:30pm on Tuesday, Thursday, Friday and Sunday, sits on a stool with his guitar, and lets loose with his own ballads as well as reggae classics and popular tunes.

SPORTS & RECREATION

Beaches

- **Tortola**: **Smugglers Cove** on the western tip of Tortola has good snorkeling and children love its name. Try **Long Bay** on the north shore for white sand, **Apple Bay** for surfing and hanging out at Bomba's, **Cane Garden Bay** for picture postcard views, **Brewer's Bay** for beach bars, camping and snorkeling, **Josiah's Bay** for its scenery, and **Elizabeth Bay** for sands with a fringe of palm trees.
- **Virgin Gorda**: **The Baths** is a spectacular arrangement of boulders and grottos, always changing but best in the morning before the hordes

arrive; **Spring Bay** next to The Baths has good snorkeling and white sand; **Trunk Bay** can be reached over a path from Spring Bay or by boat; **Savannah Bay** is found just north of Yacht Harbour, and **Mahoe Bay** is a superb beach at **the Bago Bay Resort**.

- **Other Islands**: **Long Bay** on Beef Island has a quiet beach, but enter from behind the salt pond so you don't disturb nesting terms. **Loblolly Bay** on Anegada has a beach bar; **White Bay** on Jost Van Dyke and Sandy Cay just off the island are reached by boat. **Deadman's Bay** on Peter Island can be reached by boat or ferry; **Vixen Point** in North Sound has white sand and a refreshment stand.

Camping

Camping on a bare site, or on a campsite with beds provided is available at **Anegada Beach Campground**, *Tel. 284/495-9466;* **Brewers Bay Campground**, *Tel. 284/494-3473*; **Tula'site Bay Campground** on Jost Van Dyke, *Tel. 284/495-9566,* and **White Bay Campground** on Jost Van Dyke, *Tel. 284/495-9312.*

THE BVI'S BEST BEACHES

Some of these beaches can be reached by car, but others can be reached only by boat. Find them on the road map that comes with your rental car, or on the marine chart that comes with your rental boat. They include:

***Anegada**: Loblolly Bay*

***Jost Van Dyke**: White Bay*

***Sandy Cay**: The entire island, which lies just southeast of Jost Van Dyke is rimmed with a picture postcard beach.*

***Peter Island**: Deadman's Bay*

***Mosquito Island**: South Bay*

***Prickly Bear Island**: Vixen Point*

***Tortola**: Smuggler's Cove (where you'll see the Lincoln used by Queen Elizabeth when she visited the BVI in the 1950s), Long Bay, Apple Bay, Cane Garden Bay with its 1.5 miles of sifted sand shaded by towering palms, Brewer's Bay, Elizabeth Bay, and Long Bay for jogging or swimming. On Beef Island is Trellis Bay, loved for its good surfing and shelling.*

***Virgin Gorda**: The Baths, Spring Bay, Trunk Bay, Savannah Bay, and Mahoe Bay.*

Diving

Diving and snorkeling in the BVI you an be rewarding almost anywhere you fall off a boat, but the islands' most famous dive is the wreck of the *Rhone*, now crusted with corals and bright with darting fish in all colors of the rainbow. The pride of the Royal Mail Steam Packet Company, she hit Salt Island during a hurricane in 1867, broke in two, and sank in 80 feet of water. Best known as the site of filming for *The Deep,* the wreck still has a complete foremast with crow's nest and an enormous propeller.

Dive operators include **Baskin in the City**, *Tel. 284/494-2858,* **Blue Water Divers**, *Tel. 494-2847*, **Trimarine Boat Company Ltd.**, *Tel. 494-2490* or *800/648-3393,* **Underwater Safaris**, *Tel. 494-3965* or *800/537-7032,* and **Caribbean Images Tours**, *Tel. 494-1147,* all on Tortola and **Dive BVI Ltd.**, *Tel. 495-5513* or *800/848-7078* and **Kilbride's Underwater Tours**, *Tel. 495-9639* or *800/932-4286,* both based on Virgin Gorda.

Specializing in underwater photography is **Rainbow Visions** on Tortola, *Tel. 284/484-2749.* Book this service through one of the dive companies above to get a custom video of your dive or to rent an underwater camera or camcorder.

If you rent a boat to go diving on your own, you'll need a mooring permit. Anchoring in most of the best diving spots is illegal because it could damage the coral. Frankly, it's best to go with one of the outfitters listed above. They know both the rules and the best scuba and snorkel sites, such as:

Alice in Wonderland is a deep dive at South Bay on Ginger Island, where walls slope downward 100 feet to huge, mushroom-shaped coral heads.

Anegada has one of the world's most notorious fringe reefs, a graveyard for at least 300 known wrecks. While the wrecks continue to break up, they form a home for worlds of brilliant fish.

Blonde Rock, found between Dead Chest and Salt Island, rises from 60 feet down to within 15 feet of the surface. Explore it to see ledges, tunnels, caves and overhangs alive with lobster and other sea creatures as well as a wonderland of gently waving fan coral.

Brewers Bay Pinnacle is a towering sea mountain abounding in sea life. Seas you an be rough, so this is a dive to take when conditions are right.

The Caves on Norman Island are so well known that they you an be swarming with people, so try to arrive early in the day to see the place that is thought to have been Robert Louis Stevenson's inspiration for *Treasure Island*. The caves make for exciting snorkeling over dark waters; Angelfish Reef nearby is a good place to see rays and angelfish.

The *Chikuzen* is a 246-foot Japanese refrigeration ship that was sunk here in 1981 to form an artificial reef. It is in 75 feet of water six miles north of Beef Island and it's home to a huge aquarium of fish large and small.

Dead Chest Island, which is where Blackbeard is said to have marooned 15 of his men with a bottle of rum and a sword, offers good snorkeling over bands of sand and coral. Great Dog and The Chimneys lie in the "dog" islands between Virgin Gorda and Tortola. Underwater canyons, some of them shallow enough for snorkelers and rookie divers, are dazzling sea gardens.

Painted Walls is a shallow drive off the south point of Dead Chest. Four long gullies are crusted with colored coral and sponge only 20-30 feet down.

Santa Monica Rock, a mile south of Norman Island on thc outer edge of the islands, lies close enough to deep water that it's a place to see pelagic fish (fish that roam freely rather than living in one reef), spotted eagle rays, and perhaps a nurse shark. The rock rises from the sea floor 100 feet deep to within about 10 feet of the surface.

Wreck of the Rhone, now a marine park, is the BVI's most popular dive. Broken in half and quickly sunk by a storm in 1867, she lies scattered and crusted, her innards open to view while coral and fish swirl through old cargo holds, the engine, and the immense propeller.

Sailing & Boating

Sailing courses including liveaboard cruise courses are available from **Thomas Sailing**, *Tel. 284/494-0333* and **Offshore Sailing School**, *Tel. 800/221-4326 or 813/454-1700.* Board sailing rentals are available from **Boardsailing BVI**, *Tel. 495-2447 or 494-0422.*

Boating is best arranged through your hotel or condo host, who has rental boats or knows where to find them plus the best fishing guide, deep sea fishing charter, day sail, or sunset cruise. This is a crowded category that changes often as boats come and go.

Hiking

The most popular hiking trails in the British Virgin Islands are the path to Sage Mountain on Tortola and the walk to **Gorda Peak** on Virgin Gorda. Sage Mountain National Park is a vest pocket-size, 92-acre preserve that the serious hiker you an cover in half a day. From Road Town, drive up Joe's Hill Road and keep climbing (4WD rental cars are popular here and this is why), watching for the small sign to Sage Mountain. The road ends at a small parking lot.

Take off on any of the three trails, which are connected, to enjoy moderately easy walking through bowers of elephant ears, cocoplum, and butter-yellow palicourea under a canopy of mahogany and manilkara trees and white cedars. In the open, find magnificent views of Jost Van Dyke across the sea to the northwest.

The islands' other popular trail is an easy walk in **The Baths National Park** on Virgin Gorda, where you'll find yourself surrounded by cathedral-size boulders catching a swirling sea. Go early in the day. By the time land-based visitors get up and passengers stream ashore from charter boats and cruise ships, The Baths you an be too crowded. Another path from the same road leads lead off to **Devil's Bay National Park** on an easy, 15-minute walk through a cactus garden and a sand beach that is less crowded than The Baths.

The more rugged, half-hour hike to Gorda Peak, which is at 1,359 feet, is found off North Sound Road. Ask directions at the ferry dock. To stay on the right path, which leads to a small picnic area, follow the red blazes.

To climb to the 1,359-foot peak that tops **Virgin Gorda National Park**, drive the North Sound Road and look for a sign that points to stairs that climb up into the woods. You can make it to the observation tower in about 15 minutes.

Sportfishing

Offshore sportfishing or action-packed bonefishing on the flats you an be arranged through the **Anegada Reef Hotel**, *Tel. 284/495-8002*. Out of Tortola, the *Miss Robbie* is available for charter by the half day, day, or cruise for marlin fishing and other blue water sportfishing, *Tel. 494-3311.*

SHOPPING

TORTOLA

Crafts Alive in the heart of Road Town is a collection of West Indies-style booths selling dollars, straw work, crochet, pottery, and the inevitable tee-shirts. One of the shops, **BVI House of Craft**, claims that at least 75 per cent of its stock is produced locally including local bush teas, honey, and condiments. It's open daily, 9am to 5pm, but hours you an vary seasonally.

Local artists show their work at the gallery at **Ole Works Inn** on Canc Garden Bay and at **Caribbean Fine Arts Ltd.** on Upper Main Street. The shop sells original art as well as antique maps, pottery, and primitives. For out-of-town newspapers and magazines try **Esmé's Shoppe** in Sir Olva George's Plaza behind the government complex on Wickham's Cay. It's open every day including holidays.

Samarkand on Main Street in Road Town has been here for 25 years selling handcrafted tropical jewelry including their own exclusive line of Tortola green jasper. They're open daily 9am to 5pm and Saturdays 9am to 1pm.; closed Sunday. Nearby, **Caribbean Handprints** sells locally silk-screened printed fabrics by the card. Also on Main Street, **Local Stuff** sells hand-painted local pottery and art work and enough chutneys, salsas, and preserves to make up any size gift basket. Island books and maps are at **Heritage Books and Arts** on Main Street.

For a large selection of island music, try **Bolo's** on DeCastro Road, Wickham's Cay. The shop you an also repair leather and develop film, and it has a good selection of souvenirs and sundries. **The Shirt Shack** on Chalwell Street between Main and Waterfront has one of the island's best selections of tee shirts and also sells handicrafts. For handmade clothes made locally, try **Caribbean Handprints** on Main Street.

Pusser's Road Town Pub & Company Store on lower Waterfront Drive south of Wickham's Cay offers one-stop shopping for pizza, burgers, dinner pies, and all the popular Pusser's logo merchandise that captivates tourists. It's open daily, 9am to midnight, and accepts credit cards. **Sunny Caribbee Spice Company** on Main Street just below Chalwell is a company spice shop and gallery. Choose island seasonings and sauces to take home, then shop the gallery for locally crafted arts.

VIRGIN GORDA

Kaunda's Kysy Tropix, *Tel. 495-5636,* at the yacht harbor in The Valley is the place to get batteries, personal electronics, film, tapes, jewelry and perfumes. Kuanda will also pierce your ears.

Pusser's Company Store is another arm of the Pusser's empire, a holy name in British islands because Pusser's Rum is the official grog of the Royal Navy. In their store at Leverick Bay, find sports and travel clothing, famous Pusser's sports watches as well as Swiss chronographs, and smart, resorty accessories.

STAMP OF APPROVAL

You don't have to be a stamp collector to go ga-ga over the stamps of the Caribbean. Each island nation strives for the brightest and best stamps featuring brilliant reef fish, butterflies, flowers, birds, and other gifts of nature. I usually hand over a dollar or two and ask the post office clerk to make a selection for me. Since stamp prices start at a penny or two, both the clerk and customer have a wonderful time with this carte blanche approach. Try it and you'll go home with a hodgepodge of the prettiest and most flamboyant stamps to paste in your scrapbook or to give as gifts.

PRACTICAL INFORMATION

Area Code: 284

Alcoholics Anonymous meets regularly, *Tel. 494-4549 or 494-3125.*

ATM: the Chase Manhattan Bank in Road Town has a MasterCard/ Cirrus ATM.

Banking: hours are generally 9am to 2:30pm on weekdays except Fridays, when they are also open 4:30pm to 6pm. A Chase Manhattan Bank with a 24-hour ATM machine is at Wickham's Cay, *Tel. 494-2662.* Hours are Monday through Thursday 8:30am to 3pm, Friday 8:30am to 4pm.

Currency: U.S. dollars accepted. American Express, VISA, Diners Club, and Mastercard are widely accepted.

Dress: it is offensive to locals when tourists appear in residential and commercial areas in bathing suits. No bare chests or midriffs, please.

Driving: a $10 temporary driver's license is required. Driving is on the left, with a maximum speed of 30 miles per hour on the open road and 10-15 miles per hour in settlements.

Drugs: stiff fines and jail sentences will be levied for possession or use of illegal drugs.

Emergencies: dial 999 for fire, police, or ambulance.

Government: British Virgin Islands are part of the United Kingdom. U.S. consular needs are provided from the U.S. Embassy in St. John's, Antigua, *Tel. 268/462-3505.*

Holidays: public holidays generally include Christmas, Boxing Day (December 26), New Year's Day, Commonwealth Day on March 11, Good Friday, Easter Monday, Whit Monday, the Sovereign's Birthday on June 8, Territory Day on July 1, August Festival in early August, St. Ursula's Day on October 21, and the Birthday of the Heir to the Throne, November 14. When making business appointments or counting on finding a bank open, ask about upcoming holidays.

Immigration: citizens of the U.S. and Canada need only a birth certificate, citizenship certificate, or voter registration; others need passports and visitors from some nations need a visa. For information contact the Chief Immigration Officer, Government of the British Virgin Islands, Road Town. Tortola, British Virgin Islands, *Tel. 284/494-3701.* Rastafarians and "hippies" are prohibited entry.

Medical care: you an be found at the B&F Medical Complex, *Tel. 494-2196,* just off the cruise ship dock at Road Town. Open daily from 7am, it offers family doctors, specialists, x-ray, ultrasound, lab work and a pharmacy. Walk-ins are welcome. At the north end of Wickham's Cay at the traffic circle Medicure Pharmacy, *Tel. 494-6189 or 494-6468,* has prescriptions, a medical lab, x-ray and medical personnel on duty.

Permits: A Fishing Permit is required for fishing or the gathering of any marine organisms. A Conservation Permit is required for mooring in any National Parks Trust moorings. If you'll be cruising the British Virgin Islands in a boat rented here or elsewhere, there's a charge of 75 cents to $4 per person per day depending on the season.

Pets: require advance permission and planning, so write well in advance to the Chief Agricultural Officer, Road Town, Tortola, British Virgin Islands.

Taxes: you'll pay a departure tax of $8 each if leaving by air and $5 per person if departing by sea. Hotel tax is seven per cent. A small tax or fee is charged to cash each traveler's check.

Telephone: the area code for the BVI is **284**; to access AT&T on your cellular phone dial 872, then Send. For Boatphone cell service dial O and Send, and an operator will take your credit card information. Cable & Wireless offices at Virgin Gorda and Road Town handle long distance calling, faxes, telegrams and telexes and also sell prepaid phone cards, which are used throughout the islands.

Time: add one hour to Eastern Standard Time.

Tourist Information: British Virgin Islands Tourist Board, *370 Lexington Avenue, Suite 313, New York NY 10017, Tel. 212/696-0400*. Serving the west coast, British Virgin Islands Tourist Board, *1804 Union Street, Union Street, San Francisco CA 94123*; *Tel. 415/775-0344*. U.S. and Canada toll-free *800/835-8530*. In the United Kingdom, write the British Virgin Islands Tourist Board, *110 St. Martin's Lane, London WC2N 4DY, Tel. 071-240-4259, Fax 071-240-4270.* For reservations for hotels, villas, yacht charters, scuba diving and car rentals, contact Virgin Islands Vacations, *111-40 178th Street, St. Albans NY 11422, Tel. 718/523-5038, Fax 523-5032.* To book a resort, airline or car rental, contact CHR Worldwide, *235 Kensington Avenue, Norwood NJ 07648, Tel. 800/633-3284 or 201/767-9393, Fax 201/767-5510. I*n Road Town, a tourist office is found on Wickham's Cay between the ferry dock and the cruise ship dock.

Weddings: you must be in the territory for three days before applying for a marriage license, which must be done in Road Town. For all details, write well in advance to the Registrar's Office, *Post Office Box 418, Road Town, Tortola,* or *Tel. 284/494-3701, extensions 303 or 304, or Tel. 284/494-492.*

INDEX

Accommodations (general) 50; also see Hotels
Aguadilla 141, 153
Aguas Buenas 153
Airlines 41; in Puerto Rico 98
Anegada 17, 222, 244, 249, 251
Arawaks 28, 96
Arecibo 100, 154
Arroyo 138
Arts: in Puerto Rico 147, 148

Bacardi Rum Plant 138
Baggage, pointers 41, 99
Ballets de San Juan 154
Banking 55; also see Practical Information each chapter
Beaches 63; also see Sports & Recreation each chapter
Beef Island 225
Beers 85
Bicycling 64, 77; also see Sports & Recreation each chapter
Birding 64, 78; also see individual chapters
Boating; also see Sports & Recreation each chapter
Boquerón 141
British Virgin Islands 17, 90-92, 222-254; Hotels 227-239; Restaurants 239-244; Villas 227
Business Hours 55; also see Practical Information each chapter

Cabo Rojo 141, 152, 153
Caguana Indian Ceremonial Park 140
Calypso 25
Camping 77; also see Sports & Recreation each chapter
Cane Bay 222
Canóvas 153
Carrot Bay 222
Casa Paoli 139
Casa Roig 140
Cayey 153
Caribbean Tourism Organization 27
Carite Forest Reserve 138
Caribs 28
Carnival 55; also see Practical Information each chapter
Castillo Serralles 139
Checklist, travel 39
Chikuzen shipwreck 249
Children 72-76; also see individual hotel listings
Christiansted 16
Cidra 153
Cigars 142
Cigatuera 57
Coffee, festival 151
Corosol 153
Credit cards 56; also see Practical Information each chapter
Cruising 20, 45-48, 92-94
Cruzan Rum 203
Cuatro 154
Currencies, about 16, 56; also see Practical Information each chapter
Current, electrical 56

Dance, Caribbean 26
Dead Chest Island 250
Diving & Snorkeling 64; also see Sports & Recreation each chapter
Drake, Sir Francis 30, 31, 222
Drinks defined 84-85

El Yunque 100, 138, 139, 149
Entertainment Guides 36

Fajardo 100, 140
Fitness 64; also see individual chapters and hotel listings
Foods, described 79-84
Frederiksted 16

GPS, about 65
Guyanilla 154
Golf resorts 20, 65
Great Harbour 222; also see Sports & Recreation each chapter
Guana Island 222

Harbor Night 202
Hatillo 153, 154
Health concerns 56-58
Hiking 65, 77, 78; also see Sports & Recreation each chapter
History, timeline 30
Home exchange 38
Homosexual travel 37
Horseback riding 66; also see individual chapters
Hotel chains 52
Hotels:
- British Virgin Islands 227-239
- Puerto Rico 101-113
- St. Croix 174-180
- St. John 162-167
- St. Thomas 167-173

Humacao 154
Hurricanes 32, 33, 34

Insurance, travel 43
Itineraries, suggested 19

Jayuya 153,154
Jazz 152
Jews, Caribbean 27
Jost Van Dyke 17, 222, 244
Joyuda Beach 141

Kayaking 66; also see Sports & Recreation each chapter

Lake Carite 138
LeLoLai 144, 151
Little Dix Bay 224
Long Swamp 222
Luquillo 100, 139,144
Lutheran Church 20

Magellan's 57
Manchineel 57
Marina Cay 222
Masks Festival 154
Mona Island 141
Moorings, The 224
Music of Caribbean 24

Naguabo 153
Necker Island 222
Nightlife:
- Puerto Rico 142-144
- St. Croix 204-205
- St. John 207
- St. Thomas 206-207

Norman Island 222, 249
North Sound 222
Nudists, travel for 36

Paradores 21,115-118
Parque de Bombas 139
Paso fino horses 151
Passports 44
Peter Island 222
Phosphorescent Bay 139, 149
Pirates 29
Ponce 138, 139, 154
Ponce de Leon 96
Postal service 58
Puerto Rico 19, 23, 24, 75, 86-88, 95-154; Hotels 101-114; Restaurants 118-135; Inns *(Paradores)* 115-118
Puerto Rico Trench 22
Punta Morillo 140

Quebradillas 153

Rastafarianism 24
Reading, suggested 53

Reggae 25
Rental cars 45; on Puerto Rico 101
Religion, islanders' 23, 58
Restaurants:
British Virgin Islands 239-244
Puerto Rico 118-135
St. Croix 185-198
St. John 198-200
St. Thomas 180-185
Rincón 141
Rio Abajo Forest 140
Rio Camuy 100, 141, 148
Rio Piedras 138
Rum punch recipe 84

St. Croix 16, 20,22, 155-162, 201-205, 211-213, 215-216, 217-218; Hotels 174-180; Restaurants 185-198; Villas 177
St. John 16, 19, 21, 155-162, 204,206, 207, 209-211, 216, 219; Hotels 162-167; Restaurants 198-200; Villas 177
St. Thomas 16, 20,21, 148, 155-162, 200,201, 206, 208-209, 214-215, 218-219; Hotels 167-173; Restaurants 180-185; Villas 177
Sábana Grande 154
Sailing 66, 78; also see Sports & Recreation each chapter
Salt Island 244
Salt River Bay 203
San German 139, 153
San Juan, Puerto Rico 20,21,99,135-138, 154
San Juan Bautisa 145, 152
Sea Cow Bay 222
Santurce 138
Senior travel 35, 37
Service charges 59
Shopping 68-71; also see individual chapters under Shopping
Single travel 40, 49
Slavery 29, 31
Soper's Hole 222
Spanish Town 222
Spas 78; also see individual hotel listings
Star Clipper, Flyer 92

Taino Indians 96
Telephones 59, 60
Tennis 66; also see Sports & Recreation each chapter
Tibes Indian Ceremonial Center 139
Time zones 60
Tipping 59
Tortola 7, 20, 222,244-246, 247, 251-252
Tour packagers 37, 44
Tours, ecotourism 77-78; also see individual chapters under Sports & Recreation and Excursions & Day Trips
Treasure Island 222
Trouble spots 60

USTOA 38, 39
U.S. State Department 54
U.S. Virgin Islands 16, 89-90, 155-221
Utuado 153
Vega Alta 154
Vega Baja 153
Vieques 140, 153
Virgin Gorda 17, 222, 224, 246, 247, 250, 251, 252
Weddings 61; also see Practical Information each chapter
West Indies, defined 14
Whale watching 146
Wickham's Cay 225, 226
Wheelchair travel 36, 37
Whim Plantation 202
Whitewater rafting 67
Windsurfing 67; also see Sports & Recreation each chapter
Windstar Cruises 93

Yauco 153
Yachting 48-50
Yaguez Theater 141

THINGS CHANGE!

Phone numbers, prices, addresses, quality of food, etc, all change. If you come across any new information, we'd appreciate hearing from you. No item is too small! Drop us an e-mail note at: Jopenroad@aol.com, or write us at:

US Caribbean Guide

Open Road Publishing, P.O. Box 284

Cold Spring Harbor, NY 11724

TRAVEL NOTES

TRAVEL NOTES

TRAVEL NOTES

TRAVEL NOTES

THE
PHILOSOPHY
OF
BLUE

PRAIRIE SOUL PRESS

ISBN-13: 978-1-998232-00-0

Contents

Foreword 1
A Surfeit of Blue … Josephine LoRe 7
Darts … Shirlee Smith Matheson 9
Invincible … Konn Lavery 15
Amped Up … Lareina Abbott 21
Love … Jessica Blackbourn 31
Hope can't Afford to be Dumb … Laurie Zottmann 37
Moose's Book of Days … Finnian Burnett 45
A Ghost Remembers Their Last Commute from Work … Chey Rivera 47
Seeking Self … Marc Watson 57
The Blue Forest … Alex Benarzi 67
Copyrights 73
More 75

Foreword

When the fragments we have of the Philosophy of Blue were unearthed in the Syrian desert, still sealed in their mayonnaise jars, we had no idea what to make of them.

If this was some ancient, mystical way of living to achieve self-actualization and transcendence, why did they mention things like fanny packs and Rudyard Kipling? If this was a modern hoax—or publicity stunt—why go to the trouble of fragmenting the tenets and including only eight of the (purported) twenty-seven?

But the mystery was soon forgotten, unsolved, as the world turned to its next fifteen seconds of fame, and the Philosophy of Blue languished on a dusty scholar's shelves (which were also dusty) for years.

Prairie Soul Press acquired the rights to the Philosophy of Blue back in 2019, but a fragmented collection of (possibly tongue-in-cheek) eight tenets to live by would not make a

particularly hefty book, even if we included the illuminations found wrapped around them[1].

To bring the eight extant tenets to the world while also giving you, the reader, a decent read, we've brought together flash fiction from some of the best up-and-coming flash fiction writers in Canada and beyond. They've written stories that bring the Philosophy of Blue tenets to life and, through their unique voice and insightful takes on each tenet of this ancient (?) wisdom, let you see the world in a slightly different way from when you started. Because finding a new way of seeing is, in my humble opinion, what the Philosophy of Blue is all about.

I'd like to thank all the writers who leant their voice to this weird little book. I believe in your stories and your voices. Your words immerse us in what it means to be a thinking, feeling person in what can often feel like an unthinking and unfeeling universe.

Stay blue,
jim jackson
founder, editor and wisdom farmer at Prairie Soul Press

---

[1] editor's note: there is some scholarly debate about whether the images commonly referred to as the "illuminations" of the Philosophy of Blue are, indeed, intentional illuminations or merely the labels of the mayonnaise jars the tenets were found in.

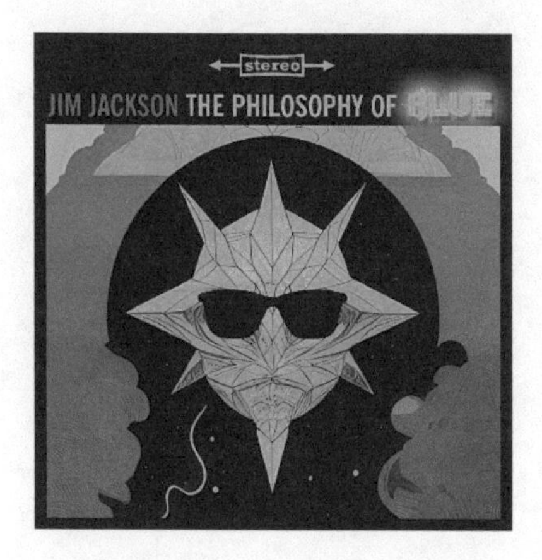

The Album

For a more immersive experience into the Philosophy of Blue, check out the accompanying album by scanning the QR code here and choosing your streaming service of choice.

PHILOSOPHY

OF

BLUE

tenet #3

The belief that "everything happens for a reason" is the fanny pack of the mind. Useful, but profoundly unattractive.

A Surfeit of Blue

… Josephine LoRe

It was the best colour, really. Boundless skies, tranquil sea. Forget-me-nots and exotic hydrangeas. A soft counterpoint to the greens that riot the earth. Why then is it the colour of sadness, Melissa wondered. When you are down, why is it not feeling grey, dun? Mucky brown or overcast? Why the blues?

Melissa had started packing for her hike the night before. Most of the accoutrements tucked into her yellow backpack … layers of clothing for hot and sunny to cool and damp, moleskin, an extra pair of dry socks. Food she had dehydrated herself. Collapsible pots, eco-friendly soap. A compass, a whistle, a map. Water tablets. Bear spray. A sleeping bag guaranteed good to twenty below. But there were some things she needed to keep close at hand. Lip gloss. One of those microfiber cloths for when her glasses

fogged up as they inevitably did when she exerted. Her puffer.

She couldn't even contemplate scaling Mount Robson without her puffer. She'd had to have it at hand since being diagnosed with asthma at the age of four. Her parents had pulled up all the carpet in the house, replaced it with hardwood, trying to keep the dust and the dander at bay. Had packed a water bottle, orange smiles, and the blue puffer from her first games of Timbits soccer. Skiing, sailing, even clubbing, her little blue friend always with her, ready to open up her bronchiole for that life-giving surge of oxygenated air.

She hadn't been planning this trip alone. But along the way, the Fearless Four had dwindled. Marcus had been invited to his new boss's cabin in the Kootenays and couldn't say no. Fiona and Charlotte had been offered a gig picking grapes down in Keremeos … the pay was good, and they could stay for free in an old logging cabin with no water or electricity. Perfect. So, after months of planning, of poring over elevation maps and picking ascents, of anticipating the five days of no cell service, no deadlines, no … no what … no nagging, no niggling, no tippytoeing around the house where she felt imprisoned. Had moved back to when she could no longer afford rent on the money she made at the second-hand bookstore. Not even with the fees and tips she collected for the private yoga classes. Maybe she should have gone on to college. Why did she think she could ride the wave, work on that novel that would go international, would be turned into a movie. Would make a name for herself.

A surfeit of hope, then. A surfeit of dreams as yet unrealized. Maybe a surfeit of anything, Melissa decided, could give you the blues.

Darts

… Shirlee Smith Matheson

The dart flies from Duke's fingers. Finds its mark. Jacko grins and steps away from the board. The crowd cheers and hoists pints. Duke steps in front of the board, Jacko aims, fires. Success. The crowd applauds, and the game begins.

The man beside me leans over. "Jacko, Duke, both top players but damn dangerous, way they play the game. See that? Crazy buggers take turns, stand with their head in front of the dart board while their partner takes aim. That's trust."

"Or insanity.

"No, shit, sheriff!" my friend snorts. "Someday one of 'ems gonna miss."

"This game is called 301. Each player has to double-in and double-out to qualify, to get into and out of the game."

"Yeah, okay." I hold up my beer glass, indicating need for a refill. "But, what was going on there?"

"Okay, you see that half-inch-wide circle just inside the perimeter of the dartboard? To get into and out of this game, each player has to land his dart inside that ring. It's called doubling-in and doubling-out." He takes a long sip from his glass. "But the way they're going at it is plumb crazy."

I learn the objective of the game is to go from 301 points to zero faster than one's opponent, but as was explained, it's crucial to place your first and final dart inside that ring.

"To increase their chances, players can aim for numbers you see written on the left or right edges on the outside areas of the board," my friend says. "A dart can drop a bit vertically and have a good chance of hitting inside the all-important ring."

I see that these numbers are about level with the players' eyes and ears in this crazy challenge game that I'm witnessing today.

"You can get pretty hot, switching back and forth, left to right," my friend adds, "and these guys are damned good. The best I've ever seen." He hesitates. "But none can be one-hundred percent good. The ambulance call-number is up there on the wall."

I want to leave. No desire to witness senseless carnage, a pierced eye or cheek. But I stay. When both players have succeeded in getting into the game, the crowd relaxes and resumes its low chatter. Bets are placed, drink rounds are ordered, washroom trips made, hotdogs or pickled eggs -- this pub's specialty -- picked up from the bar. Then, there's the wait for the finishing throws, the grand finale where each player's dart must again hit its mark inside the ring.

"Jacko's ready to double out now," my neighbour informs me. "Duke's turn to trust."

The patrons are quiet, the bartenders stand still. Duke positions himself in front of the dartboard with the vital ring encircling this head, faces Jacko, thumbs up, closes his eyes.

A bartender approaches cautiously, as if afraid a loud noise or movement might cause the dart to go wild. Then, in a low commanding tone, he says, “Step away. No more of this bullshit.”

The crowd growls in protest. We’re Coliseum spectators, preparing to bear witness to blood and carnage, privately hoping for the lion but outwardly cheering for the gladiators.

The players ignore the bartender, and he stands silent, hesitating, afraid his movement or voice will put off Jacko’s aim that cannot now be halted. Jacko lifts his dart, holds it high, warrior stance. His wrist moves back, flicks forward. The dart flies.

A perfect hit inside the ring. Duke grins, steps forward, slaps his partner’s shoulder as they change places.

It’s Duke’s turn now to double out, but the bartender, aided by the manager, demands a stop to the show. The crowd groans and boos but the house is boss. Duke will need to double out without Jacko’s head to aim around. He scores. Game over. The bartender drapes a cloth over the board, picks up the darts, shutting it down for the day. The crowd applauds the players, treats them to multiple rounds of beer.

My friend gets up to leave, while I sit back, pondering. What must it be like to cheer challenge, banish doubt? Risk serious wounds to combine peril with pastime? Demonstrate guts and glory for barroom entertainment?

I drain my glass and join the crowd to congratulate the local heroes.

PHILOSOPHY

OF

BLUE

tenet #5

Romanticism is quickly cured by experience. And that's too bad.

Invincible

... Konn Lavery

I remember being invincible. It was remarkable when love, passion, and excitement had a uniform balance. Nothing could bring me down. Love creates willingness. Passion provides motivation. Excitement generates drive. The three points of perfection let us discover new heights. Climb too high, and you'll blind your soul, slipping into darker depths with no return.

I used to see the joy in each student's eyes, like mine. There was enthusiasm in all of us. It fueled me to provide the best me I could offer. Our delight for learning was a trivial spark compared to reality's A-bomb. It seems so silly now; that lucky break in college, after a night of schmoozing with the professors, got me the opening in Flemming, Saskatchewan. My teachers saw the drive and indestructible confidence in my voice. My grades reflected it. I wonder if they sent me to Flemming to humble me.

Small towns are a great place to grow until you mature, smothered against the ceiling, or are barricaded in by death.

I stopped growing. Little did the kids know that I was a student, too, looking to thrive. The world is grey and cold, and I miss the vibrance of the day when my desire to get out of bed was never in question. Time has a way of stripping away the soul. A passive brain slows the heart. There wasn't a need to play musical pills if I had listened to my true self. I didn't, and I found a prescription that stopped me from doing something foolish with the mincing knife, which would have solved my problem long before this wretched new time.

Love ceased to be when the heart stopped pumping. During my T.A. years, I was told that studying has several curvature stages. When exploring something new, the curve has a high vertical altitude. As you gain more knowledge, the curve flattens, and you run into a bump. Getting past this growth decay takes a lot of effort before you're on a new elevation. I was up for the challenge and wouldn't stop at that middle hurdle. I don't think I will ever get past the barrier, not now. Never now.

Passion died when the sirens activated minutes before the gateway to hell opened a thousand kilometres away. People told me Edmonton was always a target for nuclear attacks. It's a significant transport city for energy and raw materials for our allies. I never believed them until I saw the behemoth fire mushroom scathe the heavens.

Excitement took on a new role of hysteria. Flemming has little to offer regarding a global conflict as warheads plummeted into Toronto, Ottawa, and Vancouver, all minor compared to the wall of fire from the south. We watched in awe and knew the aftermath of the bombs would head our way and the nuclear fallout would be worse.

The joy ended for me, not just for teaching, but for life. Experience has a peculiar way of snuffing out the flame. It isn't fair to say I failed my students. I mean, I've done what I can. In a town of seventy people, you teach all ages, and you're bound to a curriculum until post-World War III happens, and you need to improvise beyond the classic structure. The glimmer I had in educating died long before this new age. It wasn't due to my last prescription bottle, or me not getting out of bed. No. I was selfish and unaware that I wanted to keep growing, thinking I could keep pushing myself and the development would never end. Small towns weren't for me. I think my professors knew it.

There's nothing in my eyes. It's that same lack of spark in my students today.

They've experienced the most horrific event humanity has ever conceived. My misery feels foolish and minuscule compared to the springboard of experience life throws at them. Their learning has surpassed their bumps, and they excel upward not from love, passion, or excitement but for survival.

What their lives hold will be biblical.

I'll be long gone once the cancer eats my lungs.

They'll never know what it was like to be invincible.

PHILOSOPHY

OF

BLUE

tenet #8

In a world of perfect safety, unhappiness is treason. What flavor of traitor will you be?

Amped Up

... Lareina Abbott

Riley saw them piled in shivering sobbing huddles by the food delivery centre. The first to be de-amped, the first sign that things were changing. They took the weakest, those who could not fight back, and a few days later pushed them from delivery vans in disheveled groups. Riley had no feelings about this, which was the most …upset… that she could manage. She just hoped that it wouldn't happen to her. She had difficulty now in describing the feelings that used to dominate her psyche.

Back then, she thought the world was going to hell in a handbasket. Ha! What a funny term…handbasket. It felt so GOOD to laugh. It felt so right.

Whoever these change-makers were, they were wrong. Now she mattered, she belonged. She remembered the day when everything got better. 'Dictator Dan' she affectionately called him…Dictator Dan decided, (what a beautiful alliteration to that phrase), Dictator Dan decided

that the world needed some help; that everyone was just too down, down about the climate, about the virus, about the economy, seriously, everything used to be such a bummer. It's not like those 'problems' weren't there anymore, it's that she had a positive attitude now.

She got off her bus and hopped along to her job. The computers at the data control centre weren't going to plug themselves in! She LOVED what she did. She wanted to tell Owen about how much she loved her job. In the before times, they argued about what she wanted to do with her life. Where was Owen anyways? Oh right, she hadn't seen him since that day. He had, hilariously, fought back against the amp-unit team. What a goofball. Riley was a positive person and after her amp-freedom she had decided not to worry about Owen, but sometimes she forgot that he hadn't come back.

Well, she wouldn't let them de-amp her, no way, who cares that Dictator Dan was dead. Again, the alliteration, toooo hilarious! She loved her new life.

It wasn't just Owen, she didn't see any of her old friends anymore, not since the re-housing. Her and Owen used to live in a community. Oh yeah, and there was a kid…Sophia. Her step slowed and she felt a twinge, and took a breath. There was an image, of Sophia pulling Riley into a puddle with her. The pang grew into a longing, and then, thankfully, there was a rush and colour washed her memory like ink spilled over pages.

Her job existed on the eleventh floor of an industrial complex where the concrete flowed seamlessly from the parking lot to the buildings. As she approached the entrance, she noticed the sky was that beautiful ever-orange that made the sun a fierce red. Ever-orange may be her favourite colour. She followed the line of workers into the

stairwell, and up, and up and up! On the seventh floor a guard with a helmet, plastic face cover, and riot shield stepped in front of her. He gestured to the door.

"This way ma'am."

This was highly unusual; she creased her eyes.

"Okay!" She said. Might as well be positive about it.

She opened the metal door. Just like in the Calgary office buildings of her past, the whole floor was empty except for tree-like pillars that held up fluorescent light ceilings, wires fell in beautiful waterfalls into pools on the ground, and concrete floor shone like river rock. She turned.

"Owen!"

Owen stood in front of her, helmet in hand, he eyed her suspiciously. He had always been handsome and now he was even more so. Red hair over blue eyes. She loved his freckles. Even his grimace was cute.

"You're a guard, how AWESOME! You always looked so good in a uniform."

He reached for her and gave her a hard hug; she hugged him back vigorously. He pushed back and held her at arm's length and sighed. "Wow, Riley, they really got you."

"I've been gotten." She laughed.

"Listen. I love you…"

"I love you too!" Riley shouted.

"Shhh, just…don't say anything for a minute. Just…oh for crisssakes, never mind. Hey! Can you do me a favour?"

"Sure!" Riley would do anything for Owen.

"Just stand over here, and, um…look out the window for a minute."

"Sure, Owen, but you know, I have to get back to work soon."

"Of course, I would never keep you from work, I'm just finishing spot-checks. I'll need to look at your back."

She obligingly leaned on the window railing. Spot checks were routine at her work. Outside the haze rolled over the buildings like sheep on a hill. Workers happily moved from buses to jobs. Owen placed something on her back, just below her scapula on her right side. She anticipated the thump as the detection unit thumped her back, what she didn't expect was the muscle tearing pain she experienced next. She flung herself away from him and landed on the ground. Her eyes rolled wide.

Emotion rolled her like an aggressive panda, but no relief came to pull it off. "What…what…?" Her back seeped pain in sharp spurts. "What the fuck, Owen!" She grasped for her happiness, but it was not there.

"WHAT THE FUCK DID YOU DO TO ME!" She launched at him but with her weakened body he easily grabbed and bound her hands. He wrestled a gag on her that soaked immediately with saliva. She spat and coughed.

"Just shut it, Riley! I'm saving your life, but you won't know that for a few days. You're so goddamned weak that I have to feed you by IV to get you strong enough to make our escape."

She lay in a heap on the floor, trying to sob, yell, despite the gag. Owen dragged her to a walled-off space, an old office unit in an otherwise open concept hell. She grabbed a screwdriver on the way and hit herself with it to dull barrage of emotions, but Owen easily took it from her and threw it away. He tossed her into a space padded with old office moving blankets. She pleaded with him through the gag.

"Pwease, pu' it back. Pwease, if you wuv me."

"Reality is better than happiness, Riley. You'll feel better in a few days, when your adrenal glands decide to work on their own. They're a little weak right now, they've had an

eighteen-month break." He moved towards her and put something over her mouth. The sweet bliss of unknowing came over her again.

When she woke, she was on a bed, and there was an IV in her arm. She strained against the ties that held her down. Memories bombarded her like hail on a summer day.

Riley sobbed. "I can't take it Owen, I can't take it. Please, kill me or put it back. Just put it back." Darkness clung to her like tar.

"Just a few more days, and then we're out. I'm going to read to you, from the Re-knowing Manifesto. We're taking our history back."

Owen flipped open a well-thumbed hand-stitched paperback, "In the first of days we were broken…"

The next few days ached like an open wound. Her skin hung on her like melted cheese. The world through the window was ugly and spare. She could not forget Sophia. She didn't ask about Sophia, she didn't have the guts. The sharp shame she felt in losing her was like a splinter that you pushed deeper by trying to get it out.

Finally, the day came when Owen said that she was ready. After she correctly recited the first page of the Re-knowing Manifesto, he went over the plan, classic prisoner/guard situation, and donned his uniform. As they got closer to the door the never-ending drone of workers hummed like water torture. As Owen reached to open the door to the stairwell, Riley grabbed a wrench from the floor and raised it high. Her hand hovered, willing the force needed to break bone. Owen turned.

"I know where she is, Riley. I know where Sophia is."

She hesitated. Sophia. She felt something different. Puddles. Ice cream. Dad jokes. A joy that pushed itself

through her pain like a parent kissing a scraped palm. She considered.

She just wanted to smell her hair again.

She put the wrench down.

Riley straightened her uniform and held herself upright. She desperately wanted to feel okay again, but she wanted to see Sophia more, and now she realized she couldn't have both. Perhaps blanket happiness wasn't the goal. Perhaps real joy was an iceberg in a sea of shittiness. She reached out to Owen, and he hugged her in a quick grasp.

She didn't feel strong, she didn't feel ready. But at least she felt.

PHILOSOPHY

OF

BLUE

tenet #11

Fall in love with the next person you meet. Regret it, then repeat 3 times. No more. If you find wisdom doing this, please let me know.

Love

… Jessica Blackbourn

I swallowed Love at the beach. The pill's chalky residue washed down with a canned Malbec just after sunrise. That was it. Done. After all the screening and paperwork, it was easy.

I drained the slender can, tasting the shiny aluminum finish, and left the empty for someone else. A dime wine. It didn't matter. Soon there would be Love spreading like emerald algae in a stagnant pond. Love would take over, hiding all my mud.

The beach was mostly empty. Weak sun sparkled in sandy puddles. A seagull walked the tide line, away from me. Everyone always walked away. That's why I did it. Love would pull me in close, Love would make me cherish. And that's why I came here. An early morning beach drew the right kind, folk that were keen to be: dog people, cold-water swimmers, retired financial advisors who speed-walked

while the day was cool before hitting the golf course. People with lift.

I saw the child first, it carried a yellow bucket and seemed to glow, backlit with sun and sparkles. My chest spasmed, just like that. Love was quick. Faster even than its "Within sixty seconds your life will change" ad that ran a loop of side effects at the bottom of the screen. But loneliness had side effects too, and I'd never given informed consent for that.

Drawn toward the child, squatting and pointing at something by its boot, my belly fluttered with hope. It was here. Love. Then the child looked up at a woman.

Shattered. That's what I felt when I saw her face, her smile. I'd never felt a smile before, never had it land on my chest, crack it open, reach in and pull out my dusky heart. I blinked, eyes watering, and stumbled a little.

I must have made a noise. She turned, her smile glowing at me. All the sunlight swiveled too and for a dazzling moment, I couldn't see. Maybe my heart stopped, overcome.

I took a step toward her and inhaled deeply. Love's air perfumed by a rotting crab. My skin started to tingle like next-day road rash, every inch of my body alive with Love. I smiled back at her, opening my mouth a little, my tongue-tip sensitive, cayenne-ready.

Her smile faltered then, but this made it easier to see her smooth skin, her eyes. Blue like a watered sky. I was drowning, I wanted.

She stepped back, moving the child too, behind her. They didn't turn away, they were meeting my gaze, linking, leading me. They left the yellow bucket on the sand near my foot. Sharing. Love.

The salt breeze caressed my tingling palms, the sea's ripples licked sand, soft and supple under me. I was ready, lightheaded with joy. It crackled down my spine like electricity grounding me to the earth's core, to all life. A conduit, giving and receiving.

A splash. The sea spread out like silver silk, taut but for an animal sliding up and through. Sleek, shiny-wet and smooth, large round eyes locked on me from its perfect, whiskered face. It had come to me, knowing, instinctive, responding to Love's call. The seal, watching, its dark gaze recognizing everything I could be, needed to be, tethering me to its wildness. The invitation so pure, the moment divine. Tears spilled from my eyes, my throat tight.

I walked into the sea. Cold languid welcome. My feet soaked, now my knees, jeans plastered. Numb hands trembling. Love spilled over and took me into itself, enveloping, waves lapping me up. I was delicious. I tasted Love, and it swallowed me whole. The muddy thudding of my heart anchored and cherished forever, under green water.

PHILOSOPHY OF BLUE

tenet #12

Tear down the rags of winter when the light returns but keep them handy. They can be useful for mopping up excess sunshine.

Hope can't Afford to be Dumb

... Laurie Zottmann

I wake up screaming. But when you're underwater, it's only bubbles.

I gasp, and my lungs flood.

Please, not again.

Goddamn it.

I try to stop thrashing, but my body hasn't figured it out yet. So I wait.

The bubbles are silver, and as my muscles get the memo and slowly let go, my head rolls back and my eyes follow their sinewy trail, up and up. I'm dazzled by the moonlight. It's fat and full and making a whole spotlit circle shimmer prettily on the river's surface.

It's something I've grown to love down here.

With my biological processes readjusted to The After, my senses follow suit. I no longer feel the cold, just the current, and I never tire, no matter how far I swish and slither.

That last trip to the surface was rough. Not sure I've got the stomach for another. Gonna lie low a while and avoid the goddess's attention. Her sense of humour wears me out.

I head down deeper, to a silky-mud meadow that's usually quiet this time of night. I need some time to think.

But when I get there, he's waiting.

I turn to leave.

"Hang on!" he says. He tries to frogstroke toward me, but he never swam much when he was topside. He looks the way penguins do trying to hustle on land.

I roll my eyes, but my mouth betrays a quarter smile. I wait for him to struggle over.

"Thanks," he says, and he's kind of panting. He's still new here. Vestigial habits.

I brush a confused leech off the back of his bald head. It sinks, mouth gaping. No nourishment found.

"Where were you?"

"Playing dance monkey for the boss," I say.

He frowns. "Why don't you ever say no to her?"

I shrug and look away.

"Are you okay? You seem… like you haven't really come back yet," he says.

"I'm fine," I say, with a bite that means the opposite. "You're the one who's not okay."

"What do you mean?"

"How long have you been waiting here?"

"I dunno," he says slowly, and looks up toward the big Oreo filling in the sky. "A couple days?"

I roll my eyes. "You've gotta get a life," and I swim away.

He doesn't follow. I want to turn around. I want him to come. But I force myself to just keep swimming. I can't do one of our fights tonight.

I breach the surface behind a little islet and haul myself up onto a soggy log. It's got no bark left and it's snotty-slick, but I manage to dig my jagged nails into its tender flesh and get where I want to go.

I'm sitting there, swirling my legs in the eddies, when I hear a little *ahem* behind me.

I look over my shoulder, and see a big, pissed-off looking rodent. It's Critter, my best friend raccoon.

"Two days?!" she shouts, with her hands on her hips.

"What?" I ask.

"You told him you loved him, and then you disappeared for *two days* without a word?"

"It was work," I say.

"Deer shit," she spits. "You know damn well that was a voluntary assignment."

"Yeah, well…"

"You can't con a raccoon, you big, hairless brat. I know cowardice, and I know cruelty, and I'm looking at a partially bloated body full of both right now," she says, advancing on me with a little black finger wagging at my nose.

"Jesus, Critter," I say, pushing her hand out of my face. "I'm not fucking cruel. It's him! Can't you see?"

"See what?"

"I dunno," I say. "Just the way he… you know! The looks! The cringing! It's like he's scared I'm going to hit him. But then he keeps following me around. It's insane, right?"

Critter shrugs. "It's within the range of what I consider human. So, yeah. *Insane*. But why does that matter? Have you looked in the mirror lately?"

"Nope."

She rolls her eyes. "You know what I mean! Gods. If I didn't know better, I'd think you were trying to make me hate you."

I narrow my eyes at her, conjuring my best memory of my eleven-year-old, who was the Olympic champion of dirty looks. But my performance has no effect.

"I think it's even more insane to draw someone in so close they can taste your chewing gum, and then shove them away like a KFC gravy cup without even the faintest hope of a last, greasy drip."

That actually makes me feel bad. He's worth way more than a drip of the eleven herbs-n-spices.

My mind wanders toward him, the way his eyes go gooey when he's holding me, how they close when he laughs suddenly at my joke, and the way they bore into my primordial core when we're both being obliterated by our interpersonal intensity.

"He's not garbage," I mumble.

"Then stop kicking him around!" Critter says.

My eyes well up with angry tears. "I can't stop, okay? I want him so bad. But I get so mad! All. The. Fucking. Time. I just can't… Everything is so stupid! And I can see it in his face. My rage scares the squirts out of him. He says he loves me, but he can't handle me!" I turn my back to her and bawl into my hands.

Critter waddles up behind me and puts a small hand on my back.

I turn toward her and start to say, "And I just really wish…" but I hear a splash, and realize I've elbowed my best friend into the water.

"Oh shit! Critter?"

It's scary still for a moment, but then her head pops up. I laugh with relief as she dog-paddles upstream to the log. She's not amused.

I catch her under the arms and hoist her onto my lap, and we sit for a minute. She presses her head into my chest, and I stroke her back.

Then she looks up at me and says, "You've got pain, and he's got pain. Lifetimes of it. But if you could stop slapping his hand away, I think he could reach you. The real you."

"But what if we just keep reliving the same heartbreaks?" I ask. "Isn't it better to avert the tragedy before it happens?"

She puts her paw on my cheek. "The tragedies have already happened, my friend. Now, you have another chance. A different chance. If you really don't want to repeat the past, don't sabotage yourself this time. Make those phone calls. Ask for those arms. Don't go off and die."

Well, that does it. I crumple up and cry an entire estuary into Critter's fur. She just keeps her little arms around my neck.

I come up for a breath, and my sinuses are aflood. She says, "I don't mind the tears, but don't you dare blow your nose on my coat."

I laugh, give her one more hug, and put her down beside me. Then I lower myself into the water.

"Thank you, Critter. For always being there."

"Always will," she says, and she waves as I slip down into the current and ride it back to the best tub of gravy I've ever had.

PHILOSOPHY

OF

BLUE

tenet #16

There's an old Arab proverb that says "don't let a bad day make you think you have a bad life." But it doesn't hurt to keep track and run the numbers once in a while, just so you know for sure.

Moose's Book of Days

...Finnian Burnett

Moose pushes Gonzo's wheelchair over the last hill to Cabin Creek Rock where they've had more good days than bad. *A bad day doesn't equal a bad life*, Gonzo used to say when she still remembered things consistently, when the good days outweighed the bad, when the good days were, in fact, so plentiful, Moose often forgot about keeping track at all.

Where's this, Gonzo asks, her fingers curled around the arms of the chair.

Moose kisses her wife, touches her trembling lips. She rustles for the notebook, her accounting, holds it against her chest. *Moose's Book of Days*. She sets it aside and hoists a can of spray paint from her backpack, aims at the smooth rock face. *Once more*, she mutters, her fingers finding the nozzle. The swoop of her wrist creates the curved back of a G. The letter arches like Gonzo's now frail body, bends the

way she once bent over Moose, long fingers tracking paths on taut skin.

A bad day doesn't equal a bad life, Moose says, and Gonzo nods, as if she remembers. Maybe she does.

Moose's hand dances and lifts. *O. N.*

Gonzo watches and spells aloud as Moose paints and Moose thanks the universe Gonzo remembers this name, if little else. Not their love, their marriage, their children, their life. And this could be all she has, Moose thinks. All they have.

Except the book. Moose pushes it into Gonzo's hands. It's warm, pulsating, the memories lifting from the pages.

Is this a gift? Gonzo asks. It is, but Moose doesn't answer, doesn't tell Gonzo what she's giving her, what Moose had to do to give this away.

Tear out the bad days, Moose tells her wife before turning back to the rock face.

Zed, Gonzo whispers.

Gonzo's last days will make a good life, even if Moose had to give up the rest of hers to make it happen.

Moose directs the paint so the spray arcs into the soft hip-sway of Gonzo's last letter.

Oh, she breathes.

A Ghost Remembers Their Last Commute from Work

... Chey Rivera

A giant screen takes the place of everything. It turns on, and I tilt my head as I look at the image of myself on it: I'm sprawled in the back seat of my car, staring at the clouds through the window, a hand shooting to my phone to silence a timer. It's the end of my break.

The image is crystal clear. I realize it's a memory in the form of a clip. More options appear on the screen, as well as more of these clips, and I am able to control which ones I want to see.

Bored by this particular memory, I hit BACK on the screen and scroll, unable to keep myself from jumping from one to the other.

PLAY

Samantha's voice brightens a particularly dull clip and I bring the image to full screen. I always called her immediately after getting off from work. I watch myself smile as her voice fills the inside of my ten-year-old Corolla.

BACK

SCROLL

She was so smart—*is* so smart. And I mean scholarship-winning, minority-summer-internship smart. In high school we dreamed of going to college together. I used to fall asleep every night thinking about it.

My father's face looms in one of the video thumbnails.

PLAY

I can see his whole body now, squatting down to sit on a low chair in our kitchen, old wallpaper peeling behind him in a blur of dirty dijon yellow. The image lacks twenty-first century sharpness, like an old episode of *Friends*, but I can still discern his disappointment. It's right after I tell him I want a degree in cinematography. He hasn't taken off his work clothes yet. His mustard-colored boots, haloed by cement crust, have trailed fine dust from the front door to the small kitchen.

"Cinemat–cinematro–" he struggles with the word. "Where will you work? How much will you make?" he asks instead.

"I'm not really thinking about money," I say.

"*¿No estás pensando en dinero?* That doesn't make any sense." He stands up with a grunt and walks to the bathroom, turning his back to me.

BACK

SCROLL

Eventually, Samantha got into a creative writing program, and I got a job at the grocery store.

Mr. Jacobson was my boss. A tall middle-aged man with thinning hair and eyes so small you couldn't see the whites. Forty hours a week sounded like too heavy a sentence in a place like that, but it was the price of survival. Stocking the shelves, mopping the floors, bringing in the shopping carts people left in the parking lot, bagging groceries and helping people carry them to their cars.

PLAY

"You're gonna wanna give the bathroom a couple hours," a customer jokes. Deep wrinkles multiply around his mouth when he laughs, and then over his forehead and brow when he coughs. It's mortifying how the resolution is a thousand times better than in any other clip I've played so far. He hesitates on his way to my register, the only one empty.

"Good morning, did you find everything you were looking for?" I parrot the greeting I was taught.

He grimaces at my accent and doesn't reply. I wonder if he can't understand me or if he just doesn't like me. I charge his items in silence.

"Follow me," Mr. Jacobson says after the old man leaves. He takes me to the bathrooms and hands me a plunger. I pull the blue apron he makes us wear over my face. This was not what I had signed up to do. Mr. Jacobson looks at me, perhaps waiting for me to say something. I know I would have to find another job if I did. My father is always saying that I should be grateful for any opportunity to make money, but I feel a bit sick. Has my father ever felt this way, too? How many times? The thought makes my stomach hurt. Or maybe it was the smell. I feel like throwing up.

PAUSE

That was my first day, four years ago. After a month of working full time in that grocery store, I finally accepted I had to let go of everything else in my life: the towering stack of unread books sitting in a corner of my room; my short films, shot in our barrio and released to the world via YouTube; the third draft of a new script I was working on with Samantha, something longer and different and exciting.

In a thumbnail under the current paused clip, Samantha's disappointed face stares at me.

PLAY

"Tomorrow's your birthday. What do you mean you can't go?" she asks. I get lost in the way her long eyelashes flutter to fight away tears.

"Mr. Jacobson says he needs me."

"But he said you could have the day off. *Because. It's. Your. Birthday.*" She enunciates every word in her last sentence the same way my math high school teacher used to do when I asked a question twice. Samantha's American accent is so good now it hides every trace of her native language.

"Sorry." I shouldn't have promised her anything.

"I had a surprise for you," Samantha says, pressing her hands to her eyes.

BACK

I remember hoping we wouldn't go to the zoo again. Last time, people kept taking pictures of the owls, their nocturnal eyes blinded by white camera flashes, an unseen someone making money off it.

I never found out what she had planned.

REFRESH

PLAY LATEST

This is the night I died. Samantha is reciting Robert Frost with her roommates for fun.

"I have a workshop tomorrow," she tells me. "You remember that piece I was working on about Hypatia?"

Hypatia of Alexandria, a brilliant woman brutally murdered and dismembered by Christians in 415 AD. I remember. Samantha is thinking of doing a minor in history, a promising new muse, she called it. I can barely remember what it was like to have homework.

I can hear two people in the background arguing about whether the Henry David Thoreau quote from Dead Poets Society is correct.

"It's unfair how you don't have time to read anymore," Samantha says. She sounds upset, but I don't know if she's upset with me or for me.

To make up for this, she had started reading to me over the phone while I drove home from work.

Tonight, the night I died, she reads me poetry.

"The woods are lovely, dark and deep,
But I have promises to keep,
And miles to go before I sleep,
And miles to go before I sleep."

It's one in the morning now, no longer my birthday, and the roads are silky with rain and almost empty. I'm on autopilot, completely focused on the voice of the twenty-two-year-old girl I love. She moves on to The Walden, the bit her friends were just discussing, and I listen as my body aches from my twelve-hour shift.

"I went to the woods because I wished to live deliberately, to front only the essential facts of

life, and see if I could not learn what it had to teach, and not, when I came to die, discover that I had not lived."

Her voice is as bright as the winking stars above, all trace of the sadness from yesterday is gone.

White lights erase the road ahead. Someone is driving right towards me, in the same lane, against the traffic. It takes me a second to process this, to break through my highway hypnosis. I untangle my brain from Thoreau's prose and swerve too late. The clip stops in a blinding flash of headlights and smoke, and the screeching of tires against pavement—

BACK

SCROLL

Now I can't see my dad or Samantha in any of the thumbnails. Here's the grocery store from outside, stray shopping carts haunting the parking lot; a shot from above of my old converse shoes next to a dirty mop; me bending over shelves; me smiling at strangers.

I've noticed some clips are of higher resolution than others, longer-lasting, kept sharp with repetition when I lived, like the sound the cash register made when I charged an item, or me wishing people a good day again and again, until the words lost all meaning.

It takes me a while to find him, but here's my dad again.

PLAY

He's making dinner, turning his face to talk to me. I think he's smiling. His features are blurred, already eroded in pixels. This makes me panic.

BACK

SCROLL

I look for Samantha. The memories of her I had already found begin to slip away from me, scrolled out of sight.

My alarm increases, but underneath the fear there's an undertow of anger. I feel wronged, but I can't tell who wronged me. All I know is that any clip worth watching will soon bc unplayable. I will be left with the worst before I am left with nothing. Before I myself am nothing.

And I know it won't take long for Mr. Jacobson to throw away all the pictures I had stuck to my station, to pass down my apron to someone else. Someone young and faceless—and grateful for the opportunity.

PHILOSOPHY
OF
BLUE
tenet #19

There's a little yellow idol to the north of Kathmandu. But finding it will in no way help you become who you want to be.

Seeking Self

... Marc Watson

In a world full of dubious transportation methods, he had come to the conclusion that none were ricketier and more questionable than the "bus" (in reality more of a converted flat-bed truck) he'd just taken from Kathmandu to the small villages of Helambu. It was an hour, but it was also his entire life.

It was worth it, he thought. I've almost made it.

Made what? Made an idiot of himself was the most likely answer, but he was too far into the weeds now.

He disembarked and approached a local merchant, asking for directions that could change his life. He was disappointed to find that they were so simple: "Follow that path, the monastery is at the end. Bring water. Buy one of these necklaces for good luck!"

He followed the path, well-hydrated and now sporting only the finest of Hyolmo beaded neckwear (*Every little bit helps*) and started off.

He was beyond obsessed at this point. The time and money he'd invested in this journey had hurt him. However, he could see the end in sight, and beyond that were limitless possibilities. His long-time girlfriend thought he'd gone mad, but she also admitted the writing had been on the wall for some time. He had spoken of the Sum Steph Grhaatse quite a lot lately, and eventually she realized his mind couldn't rest until he'd found it. She also realized he likely wouldn't be the same when he returned and warned him their very relationship could be on the line.

He loved her dearly.

And yet, he was still hiking though the highlands of Nepal. Alone.

It wasn't quite the towering roof of the world that was the Himalayas beyond, but the hills and rolling grasslands would soon give way to the snows of the highest places the world had to offer. Hopefully he wasn't going that far.

Hopefully.

His backpack weighed heavily on him now. It was fully loaded with things to help him endure the environment, but not so full as to house anything that could keep him alive if the weather turned or he found himself out here when the sun went down. He wished his beyond-rudimentary Hyolmo language knowledge was better than it was, but he only had so long to study once he found out that the Sum Steph Grhaatse was real.

Real. Real and ready to fix things. Fix everything.

A lot of weight to place on what was essentially a trinket, but what choice did he have? The chat rooms and message boards he'd immersed himself in over the last three years

doubted him, but had also convinced him to be where he was right now, to trek where only the bravest (or most foolhardy) dared go.

He paused, taking in the view around him. It was breathtaking in every possible way, and yet the giddy little monster in the back of his head that went by the name Obsession refused to allow him a full moment to appreciate it. It gnawed at him mercilessly. It needed feeding. If it didn't get what it wanted, it would start to devour him from the inside out.

It already has, he knew. I just need to stop before it hits something vital.

As if a sign from the force that drove him, beyond the next hilltop he saw the monastery, its humble rooftop jutting beyond the grass and scrub. It looked nothing like how the forums had described it, but he knew they were armchair adventurers locked in their chairs with no idea of real-world realities. He was out here, exhausted, cold, far from home, and with his hands literally and figuratively dirty.

He approached slowly, each step feeling like a thousand.

The Sum Steph Grhaatse. It's here. I know it's here.

A young man, dressed in the traditional robes of the faith, emerged and stepped towards him, raising his hand in greeting, with a welcoming smile flashing large teeth.

This must be real, he thought. My imagination would never make anything so vivid.

The young man motioned him over, calling in a strange language over his shoulder. As they stepped to meet, more emerged from behind the low walls and shrubbery, each smiling and gesturing to the stranger to come closer.

What do I do? Who do I ask?

He decided to start with the simplest question. “English?” he asked. “English? Anyone?”

An older gentleman stepped forward, smile larger and more misshapen than all the others, a light in his eyes that was irrepressible. “Hello hello!” he said quickly. “You come! Come.” He motioned to the gate and the humble courtyard beyond.

Inside the rudimentary walls were small huts and homes, nothing like the things he’d imagined. A sudden sense of dread started to germinate in his guts.

Have I made a mistake?

No. No, he wouldn’t think that. He couldn’t. He’d risked too much. Gone too far. Hurt himself and others on this mission.

The man who had spoken to him said something unintelligible to the young man who he had seen first, and he ran off, returning a moment later with a cup of hot tea. Even the cup wasn’t what it was supposed to be. Instead of earthen and raw, it was a chipped porcelain mug with some long-faded and unintelligible corporate logo on it, no different than the billions of similar ones wasting space in kitchen cupboards and half-hearted gift bags from potential vendors the world over.

He accepted the tea, not wishing to be rude, but did not drink from it just yet. Instead, he turned to the older gentleman.

“Thank you. Thank you. But, I’m sorry…” He prayed he wasn’t about to butcher the pronunciation. “Sum Steph Grhaatse? I’m looking for the Sum Steph Grhaatse. Do you know it?”

The man stopped smiling, as did all those that now surrounded the newcomer.

Oh lord, I’m a dead man.

The man held out his hand and motioned to a small open building near the back of the compound. Silence hung in the cold mountain air like a vulture.

"There," he said at last. "Sum Steph Grhaatse there."

Well, that was surprisingly easy. He thanked him and stepped towards it, heart fluttering with no discernable pattern while his hands stayed clutched to the ubiquitous mug. No one followed him as he moved. They all simply watched, curious.

The small open hut was much deeper than it appeared when he had first seen it. It appeared to go deep within the wall beyond, and angled downwards.

Ominous. No one is going to believe this.

The roof was low, and he ducked down into the space beyond. It was foolish, and more than a little terrifying, but he continued. He had to. If this was where his goal was, then this was where he was going to go.

The space smelled of dry earth and old wood. Beyond was more darkness, but cutting though it was a faint, yellow glow.

Dear God, he thought, there it is. I've made it.

The glow grew larger, until it was just beyond his reach. He had a flashlight, but in the moment, the drama leading to the here and now, he had forgotten about it completely.

And then, he saw it.

Sum Steph Grhaatse.

A small, yellow, glowing figure, no larger than the toys he played with as a child.

He reached out and touched it, not believing it to be real. But it was. It was real. And it was…

It was…

…

Nothing.

Well, it was *something*. It was hard to tell in the dark, but it almost looked like a faded Christmas decoration.

Flustered and confused, he scrambled back out, scraping his knees as he went.

The monks had gathered around the entrance in a semi-circle, waiting for him to emerge. He came out, crawling and crying, looking in his hands for the truth.

This thing… it wasn't what he thought. It wasn't what they said it was. It was just… a thing. Not valuable or spiritual or amazing.

Had he gone this far for nothing? Risked his life and relationships for a false idol?

The older man stepped towards him, kneeling to his level. "Sum Steph Grhaatse." He repeated. "It is there," he pointed at his hand. "It not here," he pointed to his forehead. "There. It is there. You find it. You find. But it no find you."

No. This couldn't be it. There had to be more!

Why? What says there is?

Realization hit.

"*It no find you*," he'd said.

Oh… he felt faint. *Oh my*…

The man helped him to his feet and led him away, while his hands released the nothing he'd dedicated so much to and let it fall uselessly to the ground.

"It no find you."

PHILOSOPHY

OF

BLUE

tenet #26

We need to prepare for winter so much less than our ancestors. Unfortunately, that leads us to believe we don't need to prepare for winters of the spirit, either, and they catch us off guard.

The Blue Forest

... Alex Benarzi

Few enter the blue forest. Fewer leave.

The wind pelts her cheeks red and (greedy-fingered) reaches into her lungs to draw out breath.

Payment upon entry.

Two unplowed roads diverge in the blue forest. She reaches out to shoo the fog of war from each—

left

Yes—light is the answer. She strips off her gloves: instantly the wind feasts on fingers but she forces herself to maintain control.

Reaches into her bag

right

But the fog is frosted glass on the car window and as the child presses her hand to it, she can feel the potential of shattering glass. The child removes her hand and draws with her index finger—abstract shapes: a

and draws out the matchbook. First there is smoke, her breath visualizing frustration as the first match tumbles into the snow and the second snaps in half and the third is snuffed out by a staccato *fuck*. She abandons the matchbooks and stares down the left path.

portrait in condensation.

"Turn the fucking heat up, will you?" Dad leans forward, attempting to penetrate the whiteout. He could have moved his hand to twist the knob, but he chose to yell at Mom instead. Mom dutifully turns up the heat.

"Mom?" the child mouses.

A thunderclap. "What." Mom's blow. The child grabs her forest-green blanket and throws it over her head, folds down into a ball with hopes of waiting out the storm.

Deep breath. Fight through the pain. Don't think about crying: that will make it worse. Focus on the task.

Through the barrier, she sees the painted line in the snow—red text seared into white: abandon all hope…

before

She laughs in spite of the shortness of breath and remembers her and Isabel watching the older boys pee their names into the snow. They tried to imitate it with food-colouring, but it wasn't the same. There's her hope: the other end of the forest where dense trees become toboggan hills and mugs of hot

now

Yes, there is no more hope, the child thinks. She rocks back and forth, the soft fleece muffling the snow, which batters the car on all sides. She can't block out the horn blasts.

"Move," he shouts. "Cars are for driving, so fucking drive already."

"Chris," Mom mouses.

Under the blanket, the child

cocoa. And laughter: her laughter, not the wind's or the menacing blue crows invisible in their treetops.

One foot after the other. Shoulders up, head down. Find the path and mind the bears. She folds her gloved hands into her coat and balls her fists until the feeling returns to her fingers. She steps across the line.

The path narrows as the blue trees close in on each side, choking the light. She continues to light her matches, specs of life in the dead land.

A twig snaps. She drops the match and takes a defensive stance as a scared rabbit runs across her path.

jams her fingers into her ears.

But they still love each other. Abandon all hope…

Isabel came to school after Christmas break and, unlike the rest of them, she didn't talk about the gifts she had gotten, which was strange, because Isabel's dad gave her the best gifts. Instead, she didn't talk at all until the child drew from her, in razor-thin ribbons, the details of her parents' divorce.

The child listened. The child hugged Isabel, but the child was thankful she didn't have to switch houses every two weeks. Mom and Dad love each other.

No, she will not abandon all hope. She peeks out from under the blanket. Everything will be fine.

What is that sound? So far off, as though blaring from a car's speaker ahead. Or an impossible parrot that perched on a violinist's shoulder. A song of a tragic heart.

She closes her eyes and focuses solely on the song, allowing the rise and fall to guide her steps. The trees remain obstinate. Blind, she can feel their presence as the air beside her grows heavier. The music, its pain reverberating through the blue trees, grabs her wrist and gently guides her.

She's in a clearing. The music fades. The wind dies down. The sun heralds serenity.

Don't be fooled: it's only temporary.

yearning

It's true. Just as she begins to feel her toes for the first time, the sun shakes its beams in hideous laughter, a disco pattern across the snow. The returning wind blows in ominous clouds, and she is in the dark once more.

Even worse, not knowing how she came, she doesn't know where to go.

Three paths stretch back into the trees. Indistinguishable, no one more trod over than the other.

"Please," she looks up, "give me a sign."

A woodpecker in the distance. A squirrel closer by. These are not signs, but residents of the blue forest, oblivious of each other or her.

She has some yarn. She can carry it down one path and find her way back to the clearing if that path abruptly ends. She could

longing

The child was right. The windshield wipers clear away the gathered snow; the impenetrable white wall gives way to the frosty outlines of buildings rising around them as they inch down the icy hill.

"Was that a hawk?" Mom asks, her finger tracing the bird's path.

"It was an eagle," Dad says, "the beak was curved." And Mom doesn't ask how he could have possibly seen that given the snow and the bird's speed. The child wraps the blanket around her shoulders. Everything is good again.

Not far until their apartment comes into view, until she is drawing on her tablet when Mom interrupts her with a mug of hot chocolate, peering over her shoulder to compliment her drawings. The child has a knack for eyes, Dad likes to say.

What she truly loves to draw is forests. There is nothing more satisfying than seeing

then try the next, and the next until she finds her way out. She removes the tangled ball from her bag: not enough to get very far.
And the sun is descending, faster than it should. Falling into the hungry maws of treetops.
"It's all mine," the wind hisses. "Just like you."
And she knows it's true: one chance at the right path before the cold drops her to the floor and slowly shuts out the world around her. She closes her eyes, straining for her former guide, but there is only wind.

the abstract lines and curves form dense trees.
But all that lay stretched out ahead, and between now and will be is a long line of stars brought down to earth, twinkling in the dwindling light.
The return of the car horn and Dad yelling at people to drive. Mom seeking the concrete forest for something to take Dad's mind off the idling truck consuming their windshield. A new form of whiteout the wipers can't wipe away.

She thinks about why she set out in the first place. She thinks about the comforts she had and the invisible hand that drew her from them. She thinks about how it's all her fault. She thinks about how much happier her parents would be without her. She thinks about how she belongs in the blue forest. She thinks about the strange pamphlet she saw in the doctor's office: the one with the blue forest, the shadow of a small girl on a deserted path. She thinks about taking the pamphlet so she could draw it when she gets home. She thinks about Mom smacking it out of her hands. "That's not for you—that's for sad girls."

She surreptitiously grabs another pamphlet.

Copyrights

More

For more, go to ThePrairieSoul.com/press

PRAIRIE SOUL PRESS

Manufactured by Amazon.ca
Bolton, ON

36114199R00046